Fashioning Socialism

WITHDRAWN

Fashioning Socialism

Clothing, Politics, and Consumer Culture in East Germany

Judd Stitziel

BERG

Oxford • New York

First published in 2005 by
Berg
Editorial offices:
1st Floor, Angel Court, 81 St Clements Street, Oxford, OX4 1AW, UK
175 Fifth Avenue, New York, NY 10010, USA

Berg is the imprint of Oxford International Publishers Ltd.

Library of Congress Cataloguing-in-Publication Data
Stitziel, Judd.
   Fashioning socialism : clothing, politics, and consumer culture in East
Germany / Judd Stitziel.
      p. cm.
   Includes bibliographical references and index.
   ISBN-13: 978-1-84520-281-1 (cloth)
   ISBN-10: 1-84520-281-3 (cloth)
   ISBN-13: 978-1-84520-282-8 (pbk.)
   ISBN-10: 1-84520-282-1 (pbk.)
  1. Consumption (Economics)—Germany (East) 2. Consumer
behavior—Germany (East) 3. Clothing trade—Germany (East) 4.
Fashion—Germany (East) 5. Socialism—Germany (East) I. Title.

HC290.795.C6S75 2005
306.3'0943'109045—dc22   2005009257

British Library Cataloguing-in-Publication Data
A catalogue record for this book is available from the British Library.

ISBN-13 978 1 84520 281 1 (Cloth)
ISBN-10 1 84520 281 3 (Cloth)

ISBN-13 978 1 84520 282 8 (Paper)
ISBN-10 1 84520 282 1 (Paper)

Typeset by Avocet Typeset, Chilton, Aylesbury, Bucks
Printed in the United Kingdom by Biddles Ltd, King's Lynn

www.bergpublishers.com

To my parents,
Mariel and William Stitziel

Contents

Illustrations

Front cover: Two women, wearing dresses by the VEB Bekleidungswerk Zwickau and accessories by the German Fashion Institute, with coal miners. Helga Borchert, "Kumpels, Kohlen, Kapriolen," *Sibylle* 3 (1958) 4: 25. (Photo: Altendorf; photo reproduction: Friedhelm Hoffmann)

Back cover: Work clothes for female farmers designed by the Institute for Clothing Culture in 1955. Marianne Schlegel, "Praktisch und doch ansprechend. Das Arbeitskleid unserer Bäuerin. 40 Modelle des Instituts für Bekleidungskultur diskutiert und bejaht," *Die Bekleidung* 2 (1955) 1: 27.

Acknowledgments

One of the best things about finishing this book is finally being able to thank in print the people and institutions that have helped me along the way. Financial support came from The Johns Hopkins University, the Kingsley Trust Association, the Universität Bielefeld, the Humboldt-Universität zu Berlin, and the Berlin Program for Advanced German and European Studies at the Freie Universität Berlin.

It is impossible to list the ways that Günter and Jutta Groß have supported this project from start to finish. Suffice it to say that their contributions, both material and intangible, were crucial to this book's inspiration, execution, and completion. Benno and Inge Ameskamp also helped in numerous important ways, including hosting me in Bielefeld. Helge Andrä, Birgit Frotscher, Jana Schenderlein, and Mike Ulich graciously opened their homes to me during research trips. Benno Steegmans provided many rides between Berlin and Coswig.

Dorit Lücke of the Stiftung Stadtmuseum Berlin's Modearchiv provided expert archival guidance, made my research more enjoyable and informative by sharing her extensive first-hand knowledge of East German fashion during afternoon teas, and went above and beyond the call of duty in helping with the illustrations. Marianne Fischer of the Archiv des Verbands der Konsumgenossenschaften, as well as the staffs of the Bundesarchiv in Berlin-Lichterfelde, the Bundesarchiv Außenstellen in Coswig/Anhalt and Dahlwitz-Hoppegarten, the Breitestraße and Kalkreuthstraße branches of the Landesarchiv Berlin, the Sächsisches Staatsarchiv Chemnitz, the Sächsisches Staatsarchiv Leipzig, and the Bundesarchiv-Filmarchiv provided invaluable assistance with my archival research. Dagmar Klenke and Karin Goihl of the Berlin Program gave creative suggestions about resources and contacts in Berlin. Karin continued to help long after my fellowship, most recently by assisting with illustrations. Peter Dittrich, Angela Heinrich-Fieweger, the Konsumverband e.G., the Stiftung Stadtmuseum Berlin, and the Berliner Verlag kindly granted permission to reproduce images.

Scores of people who had lived in East Germany before 1990 helped to inspire and shape this book by sharing with me, both in informal conversation and formal interviews, their personal experiences of life, clothing, fashion, and market research in the GDR. In particular I would like to thank Jochen Finger, Erika Frotscher, Ruth Weichsel, and my friends and acquaintances from Dresden in 1992/1993.

Anna-Sabine Ernst gave this project a tremendous boost in its earliest stages by critiquing my initial ideas and giving me her collection of primary and secondary sources. Ellen Anderson, Anja Baumhoff, Ralph Jessen, Hartmut Kaelble, Andreas Ludwig, and Thomas Welskopp offered criticism and encouragement as my ideas began to take shape. At various stages of the project, I have benefited from conversations with Henrik Bispinck, Pipo Bui, Timothy Dowling, Greg Eghigian, Karianne Fogelberg, Sabine Haustein, Stefan Hoffmann, Annette Kaminsky, Julie Kimmel, Mark Landsman, Paul Lerner, Ina Merkel, Katherine Pence, Dylan Penningroth, Patrice Poutrus, Michael Schwartz, Sebastian Simsch, and Jennifer Tucker. I also am grateful to the following individuals and institutions for giving me the opportunity to discuss my work and receive feedback in various seminars, colloquia, and conferences: Roger Chickering, Ludolf Herbst, Christoph Kleßmann, Thomas Lindenberger, Dirk Schumann, Michael Schwartz, the Berlin Program, Emory University, the Graduiertenkolleg Sozialgeschichte at the Universität Bielefeld, the Institut für Zeitgeschichte, the Institute for European Studies at Cornell University, the Internationales Studienzentrum Berlin, and the Zentrum für Zeithistorische Forschung Potsdam. David Crew and Paul Betts gave thoughtful criticisms of two articles that became parts of Chapters 3 and 7, respectively. Berg's anonymous reader also provided helpful criticisms and suggestions. Parts of Chapter 3 appeared previously in modified form as "On the Seam between Socialism and Capitalism: East German Fashion Shows, 1945–1971," in *Consuming Germany in the Cold War*, ed. David Crew (Oxford: Berg, 2003), 51–86.

At Hopkins, my advisors, Vernon Lidtke and Judith Walkowitz, and my colleagues Christine Johnson, Bradley Naranch, Eli Nathans, and Dirk Bönker carefully read multiple outlines and drafts and gave exceptionally insightful and helpful comments. Dirk deserves special recognition for his unstintingly generous, extensive, and thoughtful critiques and assistance, which continued right up to the end. Simone Ameskamp read and commented on my entire dissertation, improved it significantly, and was instrumental to its completion. I am especially grateful to Corey Ross, who generously read an early draft of the manuscript and used his deep knowledge of the GDR to offer extremely helpful critiques, suggestions, and support.

Joe Gitchell and Elizabeth Mumford lent support in myriad ways at crucial points. Mary Glendinning provided valuable assistance during the project's final stages. Thanks to Alon Confino and Rudy Koshar for their role in getting this book published, and to Kathleen May and her colleagues at Berg for so efficiently guiding the process along.

It may be a cliché, but my deepest gratitude belongs to my family. Amber Stitziel Pareja and Nathan Stitziel have found ways to help despite the distance, while my parents, Mariel and William Stitziel, and my late grandmother, Helen

Reeves, have given me the love, material and spiritual support, and curiosity that made possible this book and many other undertakings.

Despite extensive research, it was not possible to identify and contact the copyright holder, if any, of every illustration contained in this book. If you believe that you have a possible copyright claim, please contact Berg Publishers.

Introduction

Amidst the rubble of the years immediately after World War II, Germans in all four Allied occupation zones not only coped with existential crises but also dreamed of a brighter, affluent future. The economic and political path to that future, however, remained uncertain and highly contested. Although Germany's "zero hour" was far from a totally blank slate, the chaos and disorientation caused by the National Socialist regime's collapse necessitated state regulation of consumption and prompted debates over the relative merits of a market versus a planned economy.[1] As Cold War divisions intensified, each of the two German states that were founded in 1949 sought to prove its superiority by promising to ensure social justice while fulfilling its citizens' material needs and desires. By 1956 West Germany's version of a capitalist welfare state, the social market economy, became encapsulated in the promise of Ludwig Erhard, the minister for economic affairs, to guarantee "prosperity for all."[2] In East Germany, the promises of future affluence made by the ruling Socialist Unity Party (Sozialistische Einheitspartei Deutschlands or SED) formed a central component of a vision of a much more radically transformed society, one in which class and social differences would disappear as wealth became distributed to each individual according to his or her needs. Relying on the support of the Soviet Union, party leaders sought to realize their version of Marxism–Leninism by transforming large-scale political, economic, and social structures, which included changing the ownership and means of production and opening up educational and professional opportunities to the lower classes. These structural transformations were to be complemented by internal changes within each member of society. The goal was to cultivate a "socialist personality" with new needs, habits, and values that would be in harmony with the needs of society as a whole and thus help to create a communist utopia.

The exact nature of this utopia was highly contested from the start and continued to evolve during the first two decades of the German Democratic Republic (GDR). Confronted with the often conflicting influences of their socialist neighbors to the East, their increasingly affluent German cousins to the West, and their

1

own prewar experiences, East Germans debated the contours of an ideal, "socialist" consumer culture.[3] Despite the SED's claims to control every aspect of life in the GDR, the ideals of East German consumer culture were not dictated by a monolithic and all-powerful party-state apparatus, but rather emerged slowly as the result of negotiations both within official institutions and between the regime and ordinary citizens. In contrast to developments in the sphere of production, neither Marxist–Leninist theory nor Soviet leaders offered much of a blueprint for the sphere of consumption. Armed primarily with Marxist theories of commodity fetishism and critiques of capitalists' use of mass culture to exploit and manipulate the working classes, party leaders were poorly equipped to offer a consistent and attractive alternative – even in theory – to either the consumer culture that East Germans knew before the war or the one that began to blossom in West Germany during the 1950s. The lack of a clear party line, together with the SED's inability to exercise absolute power over social practices, meant that the construction of an ideal consumer culture evolved during the four decades after World War II through implicit negotiations that involved moments of both conflict and consensus. In formulating and executing policies, party and state functionaries continually sought consumers' approval and quickly changed course at signs of significant resistance or discontent.

During this period, a distinct consumer culture did in fact evolve in the GDR, not according to these negotiated and officially propagated ideals, but rather from an often contradictory mixture of continuities and changes in mentalities, ideological premises, political promises, popular expectations, social practices, and the workings of the GDR's so-called planned economy. This problematic combination of ideological imperatives, cultural continuities, and economic realities complicated, distorted, and partially blocked the SED's goal of building a new society and cultivating a socialist personality. The regime's efforts to invent an alternative consumer culture ultimately failed because a variety of internal and external checks thwarted official attempts to shape and control a new society. Contributing to this failure were the nature of the regime itself, conflicting interests within the regime and the population, the GDR's economic system, political compromises that the SED made in response to internal and external pressure, and consumers' own agency.

This book tells the story of the genesis, development, and consequences of both the ideals and realities of the GDR's distinct consumer culture and politics by focusing on one type of consumer good, namely clothing. This concentration enables *Fashioning Socialism* to trace the changing meanings and power relationships inherent in the exchange and circulation of goods.[4] An examination of the production, distribution, and consumption of images and objects illuminates tensions within the regime, both between various ministries and between central and local authorities, as well as among the general populace.[5] Attention to a wide variety of actors and forums not only permits the analysis of multiple perspectives and interests – from party leaders and state planners to industry and trade officials, from fashion designers and members of the media to ordinary consumers – it also enables the book to draw connections among a variety of discourses and pseudo public spheres.

As something that everyone needs and uses, clothing is an ideal consumer good through which to study these exchanges and issues. Clothing's role in everyday politics and the economy made it one of the most important and complex consumer products in East Germany. One of the three "basic needs," along with food and shelter, clothing also could be a "luxury." It not only was the quintessential consumer good associated with the first industrial revolution and mass production, but also served very important economic roles in the GDR. Possessing a long tradition in middle Germany, the textile industry served as both a major source of accumulation for the state and as an employer of large numbers of workers, the vast majority of whom were women.

An investigation of clothing and fashion offers unique insights into interrelated discourses on women, gender, citizenship, and the state. The frequent personification of fashion as a fickle, impulsive woman driven by conspicuous consumption reflected the common perception of women as being susceptible to irrational desires, exaggerated sexuality, and "false" needs that threatened to undermine the state's attempts to rationalize both production and consumption. Officials sought to channel and control female desire by connecting women's rights as consumers with their roles as producers and by promoting rational "socialist consumer habits" as an important component of citizenship. With their purchases, women could cast powerful votes for or against the GDR's political and economic system. Their growing contributions to the sphere of production constituted another component of citizenship. Tensions arose, however, between the rhetoric of women's important duties and tasks on the one hand and the reality of their continued marginalization in the political economy and in the workplace on the other.

Discourses on clothing, the "second skin," also influenced constructions of femininity and the body, which were replete with class tensions. As Georg Simmel noted at the beginning of the twentieth century, clothing can serve both as a vehicle of individual identity and social distinction and as a marker of belonging to a group.[6] The balance between these two impulses proved highly contested in the GDR, as officials and consumers attempted to balance principles of egalitarianism and desires for individual and social distinction. An exploration of clothing as material culture helps to reveal these aspects of the politics of everyday life.

The difficulties involved in attempts to create and control fashion and taste are not unique to the GDR. From medieval sumptuary laws to today's seasonal fashion lines, a variety of actors – from local communities to states to multinational corporations – have tried with varying degrees of success to define and consolidate particular modes of dress and consumption.[7] The Nazi regime's failed attempts to define and impose "German fashion" offer particularly interesting points of comparison for the East German case.[8] While all types of states – socialist, capitalist, fascist, or otherwise – have encountered many of the same basic difficulties in attempting to control consumption, such efforts were arguably nowhere more central to the state's self-definition and legitimation than in the GDR.

The 1950s and 1960s witnessed the crucial moments in the development of a consumer culture in the GDR. Already in the late 1940s, areas of conflict and consensus began to emerge concerning visions of the ideal socialist consumer culture and the means to attain it. While more dogmatic functionaries pushed Stalinist policies that stressed investments in heavy and basic industries, a minority suggested that consumer demand could serve as an engine of economic growth. Although all agreed that one of socialism's primary goals was to fulfill every individual's "basic needs," the definition of that category remained highly contested. The consumption of clothing was viewed as an important vehicle for educating consumer-citizens, cultivating in them "socialist consumer habits" such as being thrifty and making rational purchasing decisions, and ultimately transforming them into "socialist personalities."

But these concepts also were subject to conflicting visions and ideas about the categories of class and gender. Whereas some functionaries advocated proletarian and rural styles as the ideal aesthetic in the self-proclaimed "first workers' and peasants' state on German soil," others used Paris as their lodestar and sought to emulate "international" haute couture. While some rejected fashion altogether as a manifestation of female folly, others argued that women's new and growing public roles in the sphere of production required them to be fashionably dressed as a sign of their own self-confidence and as a model of good taste for men and children.

During the 1950s the population's growing expectations and the increasingly seductive example of West Germany contributed toward the East German regime's halting acceptance and even promotion of more consumer-friendly goals and initiatives. But official promises and concessions to consumers' demands resulted in ambiguous and self-contradictory ideological goals. The regime's simultaneous marginalization and acknowledgment of the importance of consumer goods, fashion, and women created one of the basic tensions in the politics of consumption in the GDR. Another source of these contradictions was the fact that the SED shared with the West a vision of modernity and modernization that largely predated World War II. Despite the SED's efforts to fill old forms with new content in order to overcome the legacies of capitalist society, the regime proved incapable of inventing and marketing a new, desirable aesthetic and system of values. Instead it competed with the West on the basis of a shared set of modern symbols of affluence such as haute couture and values such as choice and individual distinction. By the end of the 1950s, officials sought to encourage the production of expensive, highly fashionable apparel and even founded special fashion boutiques for the sale of exclusive items at exorbitant prices. These goals and initiatives inevitably created tensions and contradictions in a society supposedly based on socialist, egalitarian principles.

The practices and shortcomings of the GDR's planned economy and bureaucracy exacerbated these contradictions. The actual quantity, quality, and prices of clothing items both violated the SED's self-proclaimed ideological principles and policies and failed to come close to matching officially propagated images and promises. The GDR's centrally planned economy depended on unplanned, improvised actions at the local level to compensate for the system's shortcomings. But officials and workers at the grass roots generally acted according to their own interests and perceptions of what was right, which often did not correspond to the orders that they received from above. In addition to these tensions between center and periphery, the regime was plagued with dysfunctional relations among its central branches. The ministries and institutions responsible for planning, industry, and trade often had conflicting interests and failed to communicate and coordinate their actions. This lack of coordination also applied to the media, which frequently advertised articles that were nowhere to be found in stores.

The chronic gap between production and consumption resulted in both extreme shortages and enormous surpluses, both of which caused serious economic losses and political problems. The debacles associated with official attempts to regulate the relationship between supply and demand by adjusting prices illustrate both the limits of the party leadership's control over the state apparatus and the extent to which it had backed itself into a self-constructed ideological trap that gave political control and legitimation priority over economic rationality. The development of the East German textile and garment industries during the 1950s and 1960s only made matters worse. Although the regime gradually succeeded in specializing and increasing the size of factories, eliminating small private manufacturers, and increasing the magnitude of production series, the GDR's economy proved incapable of producing differentiated assortments and sufficient quantities of both inexpensive standard garments for normal stores and high-quality, fashionable items for fashion salons. Quality stagnated, clothing became more uniform, and apparel drifted further and further from consumers' increasing and diversifying needs and desires.

The 1960s witnessed the regime's gradual abandonment of the political and cultural project of creating a uniquely socialist alternative to Western consumer culture and marked the concurrent rise of economic concerns and a push for modernization. The promotion of standardization and the development of synthetic fibers typified these modernizing impulses. By the end of the decade, the GDR's consumer culture only partially reflected the ideals that had been envisioned and negotiated during the previous two decades. The crass contrast between official promises and propagated images on the one hand and the bleak reality of everyday experiences on the other both contributed to East Germans' disillusionment with the entire system of state socialism and encouraged their enchantment with the West. In part because socialism shared with capitalism the goal of a modern consumer's paradise and mobilized the same symbols to visualize it, the SED proved incapable of creating a desirable alternative consumer culture based on distinctly socialist values.

The regime had staked a large share of its legitimacy on claims to fulfill consumers' needs. After two decades of socialism had failed to accomplish this, East Germans both within and outside the regime questioned its legitimacy with growing impatience. These expectations and pressures were one of the factors behind the formulation of the "unity of social and economic policies" announced at the SED's Eighth Party Congress in 1971. The regime abandoned its previous emphasis on the need for abstinence and moderation, for making consumption dependent on production. Instead of the promise of future rewards as the incentive for hard work in the present, Erich Honecker and other party leaders hoped to increase productivity by first increasing East Germans' consumption. This strategy precipitated mounting debt and an economic crisis, to which party leaders responded by further diluting the offerings of fashion salons and using them instead to simply make money through the sale of scarce goods.

Located at the intersection of the history of modern Germany and interdisciplinary studies of consumption, gender, and fashion, this book draws connections among realms that previously have been examined separately: ideology, gender, politics, economics, bureaucratic machinations, culture, and society. It demonstrates how East Germans themselves drew connections between discourse and practice. In addition to analyzing ideological statements and political calculations of party leaders, this book investigates the day-to-day bureaucratic, industrial, and commercial practices of the institutions and actors responsible for realizing official policies and propaganda. This approach highlights the tensions between the center and the periphery within East German party and state institutions and avoids the simplistic polar oppositions between state and society of both top-down and bottom-up interpretations of the GDR.[9] Instead, *Fashioning Socialism* joins recent studies that focus on the interactions between the state and ordinary citizens, the ways in which society was differentiated, and the ambiguity of the borders between state and society and the power relationships within them.[10]

In its attempts to shape and control every element of society, the SED and its state apparatus extended their tentacles so far that they necessarily adopted much of the logic and cultural elements of society.[11] At the grass roots, local party and state functionaries were indistinguishable in many respects from individuals who nominally were outside the state apparatus. The lines became especially blurry when it came to the regime's efforts to control attitudes and practices that were deeply ingrained in long-standing social and cultural patterns. The central institutions responsible for designing and propagating the official "fashion line of the GDR," for instance, often publicized models that directly contradicted the wishes of many party leaders. Yet the appearance of the models in the media throughout the country made them just as much an expression of official ideology – and a more concrete and visible one, at that – as the resolutions of party congresses. In addition, it often was difficult to say exactly how certain designs or ideas did or did not conform to the frequently vague and abstract policies resolved by the Politburo and the even more ambiguous tenets of Marxism–Leninism.

By examining "from the middle" how the political was produced and practiced in everyday life within party and state institutions, this study challenges the common notion of "*the* SED-ideology" or "*the* official party line." While some semblance of a party line could be constructed at the level of abstract cultural and economic policies, the ideologically marginalized sphere of consumption was relatively untouched by Marxist–Leninist theories. It also proved exceedingly difficult for the hundreds of thousands of people who worked in party and state institutions to consistently apply abstract ideological principles to their everyday decisions and practices.

These limitations manifested themselves in conflicts within the regime as well as within the GDR's own pseudo public sphere. Although the media were subject to both external and self-censorship, they encouraged the appearance of a free and open forum, which in fact was filled with criticism. Of course this criticism remained within certain boundaries and followed unwritten rules, but that did not make it completely devoid of meanings or consequences. The maintenance of a consistent party line also was made more difficult by the increasing numbers of people who nominally worked in state-owned enterprises but who continued to espouse opinions that resisted or even contradicted official policies. By examining a variety of published and unpublished sources, this study shows both how these different spheres were in direct and indirect dialogue and how they were subject to subtly different unwritten rules.

Fashioning Socialism demonstrates that one need not search for society in state socialism only in tiny niches, but instead can find it in the heart of the state, in official institutions at all levels and especially at the grass roots. Both full-time employees of official institutions and ordinary citizens exercised agency within constantly shifting boundaries of power, domination, and meaning. But here again, the borders between state and society, official and unofficial blur. The planned economy depended on local, improvised actions to mitigate the inevitable contradictions that resulted from the plethora of orders from above.[12] Although it is tempting to claim that these informal networks and unplanned actions existed outside official structures, they actually formed a mutually advantageous and contested relationship with them. Informal networks and consumers' own production of consumer goods provided a degree of individualization and differentiation that the GDR's mass-produced wares lacked. Consumers' everyday improvisations thus compensated for many of the East German economy's shortcomings while disrupting its ability to function according to plan. Consumers still depended on the formal system, but the SED also relied on individual consumers' informal, unplanned actions. This co-dependency meant that these formal and informal systems overlapped, shaping and limiting each other.[13]

This book also challenges the periodization of the history of consumption in the GDR and, by extension, of the GDR itself. Previous studies of East German consumption have tended to concentrate on periods either after or before the construction of the Berlin Wall in 1961. While I join recent works in pushing back the birth of postwar consumer culture and politics from the late 1950s or 1960s to the late 1940s and early 1950s, I draw strong lines of continuity between the 1950s and 1960s that undermine previous interpretations of the construction of the Berlin Wall as the major caesura in the history of East German consumption.[14] Studies that argue that the Wall represented the ultimate sign of the regime's failure in the realm of consumer politics fail to explain why party leaders, after stopping the drain of people and currency to the West, launched a program of market-oriented economic reforms, managed to improve consumption in many ways, and later became more willing make to economic and ideological compromises in order to appease ordinary citizens.

Fashioning Socialism helps to explain these developments by offering a broader, less deterministic, and more nuanced narrative of often subtle struggles between domination and agency that continued long after the regime's attempt to create more favorable circumstances by building the Wall. This book joins recent scholarship on the GDR in arguing that the cluster of political and economic changes around the announcement of the "unity of social and economic policies" in 1971 formed a more important and fundamental breaking point.[15] By the same token, the book demonstrates, in part by emphasizing the everyday politics of consumption, that these shifts had stronger and earlier roots in the 1950s and 1960s than scholars focused on high politics have acknowledged.[16] This broader perspective helps to demonstrate that the GDR's consumer culture and politics were crucial factors in the collapse of the regime in 1989 and in the development of a culturally and politically powerful nostalgia for the old East Germany after unification with West Germany in 1990, a sentiment that continues even today.[17]

Fashioning Socialism also contributes to our understanding of the two postwar Germanys, their relationship to each other, and the place of consumer culture in broader narratives of twentieth-century Germany and modernity.[18] It places issues of consumption and material culture at the heart of Cold War competition, both on German soil and across the globe.[19] Economic prowess as expressed through consumer goods formed a key component of both states' sources of legitimacy and claims to represent the true interests and continuation of the German nation. Both West and East Germany shared a vision of modernization and an ambivalence about the mass culture that stemmed from the growth of mass consumption earlier in the century.[20] This book conceptualizes the history of state socialism in the Soviet bloc as one particular branch of modernity and industrialism in the "long twentieth century."[21]

Such an approach can help avoid the facile use of the concepts of Americanization, Westernization, and Sovietization, whose top-down perspective often has led to one-sided models of political, economic, and cultural borrowing.[22] These concepts frequently have been used as polar opposites and equated simply with modernization in the West and Stalinization in the East. While the Soviet Union exercised a constitutive influence on the GDR's economic and political structures, East Germans filled them with their own distinct content. This book, the first full-length study of fashion behind the iron curtain, shows that everyday life and culture were even less prone to a simplistic process of Sovietization.[23] Rather than adopting Soviet models, East Germans joined their comrades from the Soviet bloc in emulating Western fashions and other cultural forms that scholars have classified as expressions of Americanization in West Germany. The contested propagation of transnational haute couture in Eastern Europe suggests new narratives of identification with and emulation of (West) European culture, narratives that can modify and complement the well-known story of anti-Americanism in Europe. Rather than the often one-dimensional, one-sided, and top-down models of Americanization and Sovietization, *Fashioning Socialism* suggests that it is more fruitful to examine the transnational nature of many cultural phenomena in the GDR.

This book's multifaceted approach shows how consumption is inextricably linked with production. It integrates the concerns of economic-oriented historians with production, technology, income, and prices on the one hand with cultural historians' attention to gender, class, and national identity on the other. This integrative approach draws attention to the political dimensions of consumption, both on the level of high politics and within everyday life, particularly as expressed in the concept of consumer citizenship. Recent scholarship has examined consumption as a highly contested sphere in which the state's efforts to discipline consumers – and women in particular – clash with consumers' insistence on certain rights and the fulfillment of certain promises.[24] By demonstrating the importance of consumption to politics and economics and by exploring women's interrelated roles as consumer-producers and consumer-citizens, *Fashioning Socialism* reinforces the centrality of women and the category of gender in broader narratives of political, economic, social, and cultural history.

The materials from which this book draws its sources mirror the subjects and disciplines that it strives to integrate. The use of a mixture of published and unpublished texts and images that were produced by a wide range of actors creates a multilayered narrative that is told from several perspectives. Published sources include trade publications intended for specific groups of professionals, from state planners to textile engineers to retail and wholesale officials; fashion magazines; magazines for women, for youth, and for general entertainment; daily newspapers, including both party organs and local, nominally independent publications; reports on fashion during the *Augenzeuge* weekly news films; and a variety of cultural products, including etiquette manuals, feature films, and musicals. Unpublished sources include the internal records and correspondence – most of which were kept secret to some degree before 1990 – of a variety of institutions in the party, state, industry, and trade from the highest levels at the center down to the grass roots in the provinces. Among these archival sources are the internal market research reports upon which published versions were based and petitions written by ordinary citizens to various official institutions. Although all these sources circulated within official institutions, a careful reading of them provides insights into unofficial practices and attitudes both within and outside this official sphere.

The structure of *Fashioning Socialism* highlights negotiations, conflicts, and points of consensus among a range of actors as well as the evolution of a distinct consumer culture and politics over time. I develop the narrative and argument through thematic chapters, which follow in rough chronological order. Chapter 1 outlines the discursive and economic frameworks of the politics of consumption that developed in the GDR during the 1950s, emphasizing the contestation and negotiation of socialism's ideological principles and utopian promises both within official institutions and between the regime and ordinary citizens. Discourse analysis is complemented by an examination of the economic and political importance of clothing and an analysis of competing proposals for realizing the party's utopian visions. Chapter 2 analyzes the basic logic and practical functioning of production, distribution, and planning, and investigates the causes of the GDR's miserable supply of cloth and apparel. In addition to demonstrating different groups' conflicting interests, the chapter explains how the regime's economic policies contributed to clothing's increasing uniformity and a brewing economic crisis.

Chapter 3 examines competing proposals for a socialist alternative to Western, capitalist consumer culture, focusing on tensions in the state's evolving attempts to regulate and rationalize the aesthetic dimensions of clothing toward political and economic ends. The focus shifts from aesthetic ideals to concrete economics in

Chapter 4, which investigates official policies and practices concerning price, value, and quality. Chapter 5 examines the regime's responses to the growth of unsold garments, which included price reductions, special "cheap stores," and season-end clearance sales. The regime's efforts to get rid of low-quality goods were complemented by initiatives to increase the prices of selected goods and to encourage the production of high-quality and more fashionable apparel. Chapter 6 analyzes the practical and political problems that the regime encountered in its attempts to produce these articles designed to satisfy certain customers' desires for social distinction. The chapter focuses on official efforts to produce and sell extravagant, expensive apparel in special fashion salons.

Building on the context created by the previous chapters, Chapter 7 explores the world of East German consumers. The first part of the chapter focuses on quotidian techniques used to compensate for the system's shortcomings and to fulfill sartorial needs and desires. The second part analyzes pseudo public spheres in which East Germans complained about not only chronic shortages but also the crass contrast between publicized images and official promises on the one hand and the bleak realities of everyday life on the other. The Epilogue explores the consequences of the consumer culture and politics that had become established in East Germany by the early 1970s. The new economic and social policies announced in 1971 contributed in the long run to the disillusionment, discontent, and economic crises that eventually led to the GDR's collapse in 1989/1990 and the subsequent birth of nostalgia for life under communism that continues to this day in the united Germany.

–1–

Ideologies and Politics of Consumption

Regardless of whether one espoused Marxist–Leninist doctrines, everyone within East German society was involved directly or indirectly in state socialism's utopian project of solving the problems and injustices of modern, industrial society. This broad base of participation meant that Marxist–Leninist theory, rather than constituting a blueprint for ideological and political unity, provided only the discursive framework for debates over the exact form and content of ideals as they evolved during the "transitional period" from capitalism to socialism. The capitalist past, both real and imagined, contributed to contradictions that arose from the persistence of cultural continuities in the new order. These discourses and ideologies did not exist simply in isolation but influenced and in turn were influenced by political and economic policies and practices. Clothing provides an ideal locus to analyze these connections and mutual influences. Party and state officials at various bureaucratic levels, functionaries responsible for fashion, managers in industry and trade, and members of the media all used a shared set of terms and discourses to discuss consumption and clothing, whether in internal correspondence or published propaganda. An analysis of this discursive framework is essential to understanding the moments of conflict and consensus that took place within it.

"To Each According to Her Needs": The Consumer in the Socialist Utopia

"Need" (*Bedürfnis*) was the most important concept in the East German discourse on socialism's goal of a sort of consumer paradise.[1] Through a radical reorganization of society, socialism promised to create enough material abundance and to distribute it in a way that allowed every individual to satisfy his/her needs. Party doctrine posited that socialism's ultimate goal of fulfilling individuals' needs differentiated it from capitalism, in which production primarily served to increase capitalists' profits. Thus the fulfillment of needs represented the measure of socialism's success as a socio-economic system, marked its superiority to capitalism, and served as a foundation of the regime's legitimacy.

At the base of orthodox Marxist–Leninist doctrines on consumption lay the notion of certain unchanging, essentially biological "basic needs" (*Grundbedürfnisse*), namely food, clothing, and shelter. Perhaps in part due to party leaders' experiences with periods of grave shortages during the previous decades, the SED stressed that socialism would first and foremost guarantee the fulfillment of these basic needs. Although this emphasis fit the existential crises of the immediate postwar years, East Germany soon moved beyond what might be termed a subsistence economy. But the materialist, essentialist, and functionalist notions of human nature inherent in the concept of basic needs continued to shape the general Marxist–Leninist discourse on needs. Like Adam Smith and other classical economists, Karl Marx had viewed consumption as the "last finish" in the process of production. Labor produced goods that possessed a "use-value," which in turn facilitated the satisfaction of needs. Ignoring the cultural and historical sources of perceived needs, orthodox Marxist–Leninists considered any dimension of goods that did not have a "use-value" as "wasteful." Jean Baudrillard and others have criticized Marx for turning utility into a fetish by failing to recognize it as a mystifying signifier of social relations.[2] But Marxist–Leninists were not alone. The distinction between "true" and "false" needs as well as a critique of "luxury" had been common themes of critics of consumerism in Europe and the US from at least the early nineteenth century.[3]

While cruder Marxists stuck to this functionalist approach to needs, a more complex model increasingly gained currency in the GDR during the 1950s. According to this view, needs evolved in a dialectical but ultimately subordinate relationship with production, the real driving force of historical change.[4] Officials from the German Fashion Institute, the central state institution responsible for overseeing the creation and propagation of fashion in the GDR, interpreted Marx to mean "that production not only contributes to the satisfaction of humans' needs, but it also actively influences, independently of humans' will, the creation of new demand-wishes [*Bedarfswünsche*]."[5] Such citations helped legitimate the regime's production-oriented policies and ideology. But party leaders acknowledged that "demand" (*Bedarf*) and "wishes" (*Wünsche*) differed from "needs" and were not necessarily related to productive capabilities. As the Council of Ministers declared in 1956, "with law-like necessity, the population's demands rush ahead of production."[6]

According to this more complex model, the advancement of production naturally led to the development of needs into ever "higher" forms, more and more removed from the base of "fundamental," biological needs. This theory created a hierarchy of needs: fundamental, primitive, physical needs – which included the use of clothing to protect one's body against the elements – preceded and took priority over "higher," more advanced cultural, social, and intellectual ones like aesthetics and fashion, which appeared with the progress of society and production during the second division of labor into mental and bodily work.[7] While most orthodox theorists allowed for its use as adornment, they still defined dress in terms of its relationship to production. Fashion belonged to the cultural superstructure built on a material and economic base.

The definition of humans' most fundamental needs shifted during the life of the GDR. Already in 1960 some state officials conflated aesthetics and use-value in their definition of basic needs: "To dress oneself beautifully, tastefully, and usefully is one of the most elementary life-needs of humans, the satisfaction of which is the goal of socialist society."[8] But this goal was a moving – and rising – target. In 1963 Walter Ulbricht proclaimed that economic functionaries should not be surprised or unhappy that consumers were "becoming increasingly more demanding, that today they no longer buy what they [previously] asked for in all the relevant stores," for "it is a law of our socialist development that the population's demands on a product, on its usefulness, its beauty of form, and its purposefulness rapidly increase."[9] The satisfaction of "ever-increasing needs" thus formed an integral but problematic component of the socialist utopia. Not the satisfaction of "basic needs," but rather that of "higher needs" became the measuring stick of a rising standard of living and the success and legitimacy of socialism. According to a resolution of the SED's Sixth Party Congress in 1963, "the goal of communist production" was "constant progress of society [and] material and cultural goods for each member of society according to his/her growing needs, individual demands, and inclinations."[10]

But not all wishes were recognized as "legitimate needs." Demands that far outstripped productive capabilities and that had no relation to any recognized "use-value" generally were labeled the result of false consciousness or capitalist decadence. "Luxury" items were those that both did not fulfill "basic needs" and could not be produced in sufficient quantity to allow their distribution to every citizen.[11] But luxury was not to be condemned automatically. In fact, official propaganda promised that "luxury" items that currently only a small proportion of the population could afford would become "standard" items available to all in the future. The trick was to prevent consumers' wishes and expectations from becoming totally detached from economic reality. Paul Fröhlich, first party secretary of the SED's regional organization in Leipzig and a candidate of the Politburo, remarked in 1962: "It is totally natural, it is a human need, that everyone wants to eat more, wants to dress himself, wants to have a nice home. He wants to claim for himself everything that he sees and that exists. That is totally natural." But Fröhlich argued that the extent to which the GDR could already satisfy such needs "depends not on the good or bad will" of the government or party, but rather on "the objective laws that work in the economy."[12]

These definitions of needs resulted in ambiguities and contradictions. Although the SED's orthodox ideologues insisted on the primacy of production, social and cultural factors formed crucial elements of the model of ever-increasing needs. While the SED claimed that socialist consumer culture was based on the fulfillment of material "needs" and "use-values," in reality party leaders, along with trade officials and the media, found themselves acknowledging the importance and legitimacy of wishes, desires, and the communicative and social dimensions of commodities. Ironically, the SED's own promises of a consumer utopia, along with the real and imagined production and technology of the capitalist West, were major driving forces behind East Germans' desires – which in turn proved inseparable from "needs" and progressed far beyond any recognizable "basic needs."

The definition of needs became even more crucial in the context of socialism's promise to one day distribute society's wealth "to each according to his needs." This promise potentially conflicted with other goals of socialism. On the one hand, the promise implied strong egalitarian principles and policies of social justice. The goal was to eventually distribute wealth based on needs rather than individual achievement.[13] On the other hand, the phrase implied that each individual has his/her own specific set of needs. Socialism explicitly strove to eliminate social differences through the eradication of class conflict, social inequality, and widespread poverty. This would lead to growing similarities among classes, and between town and country, physical and mental work, and, to a certain extent, between men and women. But in the reality of the GDR, these differences still existed and were even partly encouraged by the regime. The SED found itself both violating and struggling to uphold its principles of equal distribution and social leveling.

Questions of social distinction were a part of the larger dilemma caused by the conflict between the needs of the individual and those of society. The socialist utopia depended on the belief that individual and societal needs eventually could be harmonized and that this would resolve the classic conflict between freedom and solidarity.[14] The harmonization of needs was crucial to two related prerequisites of future abundance: the most efficient use of resources and the elimination of waste. One of the main obstacles to these objectives was the antagonism between consumers' desires and producers' goals. Although the SED claimed that socialism eliminated the opposition found in capitalism between profit-seeking manufacturers and rational consumers, who supposedly sought only to extract the maximum "use-value" from goods, party officials acknowledged the continued existence of a disparity between consumers' wishes and the exigencies of production.

To address this problem, the SED proposed techniques that bore a striking similarity to contemporary proposals in the West. Like Wilhelm Vershofen, the father of German consumer research, and other Western economists and market researchers, the East German regime sought to produce and consolidate a certain consumerist rationale and to use symbolic representation to synchronize the two otherwise antagonistic systems of production and consumption.[15] Advertising and market research were key components of this project in the GDR, as in the West. East German functionaries sought to distinguish these activities under socialism, however, by contrasting manipulative, misleading, and profit-seeking advertising (*Reklame*) and market research in the West with enlightened, educational, and beneficial advertising (*Werbung*) and "needs research" (*Bedarfsforschung*) in the GDR.[16]

Another uniquely socialist technique of harmonizing production and consumption, according to SED officials, was the education or cultivation (*Erziehung*) of "socialist consumer habits" in East Germans' everyday lives. These ideals were propagated not only in books and the media. The consumer goods themselves were to help shape individuals' environments and thus educate them through everyday contact. Advertising, market research, and *Erziehung* all contributed to the project of rationalizing, planning, and guiding societal processes, which was the necessary pendant to the organization of production in the GDR's "planned" economy. Such coordination proved elusive, for party and state leaders, factory managers, designers, wholesalers, retailers, members of the media, and market researchers all had their own opinions on the exact content of official norms. Party leaders constantly lamented the failure of the GDR's state and industrial apparatus to faithfully reproduce at the grass roots a coherent and consistent vision of a socialist utopia.

One of the most difficult party lines concerned women, who stood at the center of discourses on rational consumption. Just as in West Germany, women in the GDR were viewed as potentially dangerous and disruptive elements in the national economy.[17] Allegedly prone to shift their families' buying power in unpredictable, frivolous directions on the basis of whims or fashion, women frustrated efforts to align demand with production. Both East and West German state and economic leaders assigned to women, as the quintessential consumer experts, a key economic contribution.[18] By disciplining and rationalizing otherwise unproductive and wasteful female desires, women could contribute to the deferment and channeling of consumerist desires in ways that benefited the project of postwar reconstruction. The construction of the postwar (female) consumer thus entailed a fundamental tension between acknowledgment of growing desires and reminders of the limits of economic realities.

"As You Work, So You Will Dress Yourself in the Spring!": Consumers as Producers and Consumer-Citizenship

The link between individuals' and especially women's rights and responsibilities as consumers and their roles as producers formed another central component of discourses and politics of consumption in the GDR. The SED's constant reminders in the 1950s and 1960s that East Germans could consume only what they themselves had produced served multiple purposes. On the surface, the slogans that peppered party propaganda in the late 1940s and 1950s such as "Produce more – distribute more justly – live better!," "As we work today, so we will live tomorrow," "First work better and then live better," or "As we work, so we will be able to buy," were designed to encourage hard work and foster the moderation or deferment of consumerist desires.[19] The proposition that increases in productivity were the precondition for a growing number and variety of offerings of consumer goods formed a central component of "work morals" (*Arbeitsmoral*), which in turn was the "heart" of the "socialist morals" proclaimed at the SED's Fifth Party Congress in 1958.[20]

East Germans were to think of themselves first and foremost as workers and only secondarily as consumers. By reminding consumers of their primary role as producers, the regime shifted a significant portion of the burden of responsibility for shortcomings in the realm of consumption from the state onto the working population and particularly onto women.[21] The Politburo used a typical expression of this rhetoric in a Communiqué in 1960: "The working people in enterprises best secure their interests as buyers through the production of wares that match demand and the needed assortments, through high quality, and [through] sinking prime costs."[22] The concept of consumer-producers thus stabilized and even strengthened the regime's paternalistic claims to provide for (*versorgen*) individuals' well-being.[23]

But this discourse, combined with an increasing employment rate and socialism's promises of the satisfaction of ever-higher needs, helped to establish the notion of producers' rights to more and better consumer goods in the foreseeable future. The regime promised to fulfill "the legitimate wishes and demands of those who work."[24] Applied to clothing, by 1960 this meant that "with the progressive socialist development, the working population has the right to make ever higher demands especially on clothing. To be well dressed is not only need or necessity but also positive expression of the socialist attitude toward life."[25] The press and internal official documents constantly listed consumers' "legitimate" complaints about missing or low-quality goods, ranging from noting "the justified and severe accusations of our mothers" about a shortage of children's clothing to acknowledging that "the population justifiably demands fashionable footwear."[26]

Gender was central to the discourse on an individual's interconnected roles as producer and consumer. Although production in the politically favored basic and heavy industries remained overwhelmingly masculine, the regime needed more workers and made special efforts to draw women into the workforce.[27] But official propaganda and practices attempted to rhetorically, visually, and physically separate the masculine and the feminine in the sphere of production. During the late

1940s and 1950s this division could be seen in the contrast between the two most celebrated icons of the "Activist" campaigns to promote increased productivity. Starting in 1947, the first and ideal *Aktivist*, the coal miner Adolf Hennecke, was modeled on the Soviet Union's Aleksei Stakhanov of the 1930s; both men embodied masculinity and the drive to increase quantitative output in heavy and basic industries.[28] While hard work and increased productivity were to be rewarded by immediate material rewards, the emphasis was on quantity rather than quality, as reflected in mottoes such as "produce more – distribute more justly – live better!"[29]

On the other hand, Frieda Hockauf, the first female "Hero of Work" in the *Aktivist* campaigns, was a somewhat portly textile worker whom the media depicted not at work, but rather in a dress on a stage. The slogan that she propagated in 1954 emphasized quality, not quantity: "As we work today, so we will live tomorrow." Hockauf's message reflected both consumers' rising qualitative demands and the association of attention to quality and appearances with femininity. Fred Oelßner, one of the SED's leading ideologues until 1958, made explicit the gendered subtext of Hockauf's slogan in notes for a speech he gave in January 1957 to women workers of a state-owned women's clothing factory in Berlin: "As you work today, so you will dress yourself in the spring!"[30]

Official propaganda not only made producers responsible for consumption but also made consumers responsible for influencing production, at least during the late 1940s when such ideas were still credible and before party leaders shifted much of that responsibility onto trade officials. Although some elements of this early discourse disappeared, many remained until the end of the GDR. The most important remnant was the concept of consumer-citizens who were obligated to be selective and to use their buying power as an economic lever to force industry to improve its offerings. This discourse established itself even as textiles were still being rationed. In introducing the new point system of textile rationing that went into effect on 1 January 1949, *Frau von heute*, the organ of the women's committees associated with the SED, asserted that women had a duty to "emphatically and steadfastly assert their rights as consumers" by refusing to spend their "valuable points" on "shoddy production" and on textiles and garments that did not match their "wishes and necessities." Women thereby would make inferior wares disappear from stores and cause production to shift to manufacturers of better goods.[31]

Given the highly politicized nature of consumption in East Germany, the concept of consumer-citizens who were responsible for judging the products of socialist labor implied that with their marks they cast a powerful vote for or against the GDR's entire economic and political system. The meaninglessness of citizens' votes at the ballot box heightened the political meaning of purchases: consumers' decisions to buy or reject GDR-manufactured goods or to shop in West Berlin served as an indirect plebiscite on the GDR's economic system and the regime's promises and policies that were inextricably intertwined with it. Party leaders were acutely aware of this, especially as the existential shortages of the immediate postwar years subsided and consumers became increasingly unwilling to defer their wishes for higher-quality consumer goods. Fred Oelßner noted in 1957 that "millions of people" judged and bought or rejected textiles "not only according to the volume of the offerings, but rather to the same if not greater extent according to their coloring, fashionable design, quality, and use of raw materials." These factors shaped "consumers' judgements" not only of "the capability of our socialist textile industry" but also the GDR's entire "socialist planned economy."[32] Paul Fröhlich recognized that trade organizations functioned as "a political seismograph" – "if [provisioning] becomes tight in certain areas, then that certainly is where the most political discussions are concentrated."[33] One store manager later summed up the relationship between consumption and politics in one sentence: "We know very well that politics is conducted behind the store counter."[34]

Modernization, Measures of Affluence, and Competition with the West

By its own definition, the regime's political success or failure depended in large part on its ability to supply its citizens with consumer goods that satisfied not only "basic needs" but also a variety of ever-increasing desires. Clothing played a key role in this political project, for it satisfied one of the three "basic needs," along with food and shelter, and functioned – in the form of fashion and improved fabrics – as one of the most significant and visible yardsticks of socialism's material successes and political legitimacy.[35] In the words of a State Planning Commission official in 1956, *"no other industry is a gauge of affluence to such a degree as the textile industry"* (original emphasis).[36]

Apparel's political meaning was especially acute, not only because of its visibility but also because it literally came in direct, daily contact with East Germans' bodies. Clothing was on the front line of everyday relations between the citizens of the GDR and their state. As a fashion functionary noted, "a bottleneck, for example, in machine construction or in the iron and steel industry" did not "directly affect the mood of our population. But when the supply of clothing, textiles, shoes, and ready-to-wear in our stores is inadequate, all our population groups talk about it."[37] In 1958 Walter Kahl, assistant director of the German Fashion Institute, expressed common ideas about clothing's effect on individuals' psychological and emotional well-being: clothing could make one "feel angry or friendly," it could give "great self-confidence" or "inferiority complexes."[38]

Capitalist affluence just across the border in West Germany increased the potential for feelings of inferiority and heightened consumption's political importance in the GDR. State socialism, especially the East German version, defined itself to a large extent as an alternative to capitalism, yet shared much in common with it. Both systems contained the characteristics and problems of modern, industrial societies, and the advocates of both systems hoped that modernization would help them to achieve a common endpoint: affluence, or a sort of consumers' paradise.[39] Although Marxism-Leninism proposed broad-based solutions to problems of capitalism such as socio-economic inequality, East German party leaders shared with their Western counterparts many ideas about the ideal path of modernization. In the sphere of production, East German industry strove to attain the "world level" (*Weltniveau*) established by Western technology and production techniques. In the sphere of consumption, the SED accepted the basic outlines of capitalist modernization and set out, in the words of a highly publicized party slogan, "to overtake and to catch up" (*überholen und einholen*) with the West in both production and consumption.

Consumption also played a vital role in the political and diplomatic competition between East and West in the context of the Cold War. Due to its geographical location, the GDR was positioned better than any other Soviet-bloc country to "radiate onto the population of a capitalist state."[40] Economic strength, symbolized above all by plentiful and inexpensive consumer goods, formed the "decisive prerequisite to the peaceful reunification of Germany on a democratic basis" – that is, on the GDR's terms – according to party leaders.[41] Walter Kahl summarized the importance of fashion for the prestige of the GDR in comparison with West Germany in 1958: visitors to the GDR "measure the state of our development in large part by the impression that they receive from the offerings, the street scene, and the clothing of our people." If the clothing is poor, "one will speak disrespectfully about us, one will say 'they can't even dress themselves properly and yet want to construct socialism'." After all, "people are inclined to measure the value of the one or the other society starting out with the things of their daily lives, with the external world of appearances."[42] Soviet leaders bolstered these ideas. Soviet Premier Nikita Khrushchev's doctrine of peaceful coexistence, announced in 1956, stressed economic rather than military competition between socialism and capitalism. Recognizing that this economic battle and the direct comparison of material conditions were most intense and visible in divided Germany, the Soviets promoted the GDR as a "showcase" for the Soviet bloc.[43]

The competition between the two systems on these terms became particularly intense in the late 1950s and early 1960s. In the summer of 1958 at its Fifth Party Congress, the SED announced that the GDR would prove "the superiority of the socialist societal order over capitalist domination" by having the per-capita consumption of the East German working population in "all important foodstuffs and consumer goods" surpass the per-capita consumption of the entire West German population within a few years.[44] Walter Ulbricht later specified that the GDR would achieve this "chief economic task" by 1961. The party's commitment to this goal, which must have seemed illusionary to realistic observers, probably resulted from a mixture of optimism about the potential of socialist production and a complex calculus of domestic politics and foreign policy.[45] The impulses behind the "chief economic task," however, were not unique to the GDR: the centrality of consumption to Cold War competition was underscored in 1959 during the famous "kitchen debates" between United States Vice President Richard Nixon and Nikita Khrushchev in which domestic consumer appliances symbolized measures of modernity and progress.[46]

Such debates suggest that both sides largely agreed upon standards of affluence. But East German party leaders were ambivalent about cultural and social norms left over from capitalism – it was not always easy to definitively label something as capitalist or socialist, and socialist alternatives were often not as attractive as the Western versions. The regime's reliance on the language of individualistic mass-consumption and affluence, of (capitalist) standards and cultural norms left over from before the war, exposes the degree to which it tried to compete with capitalism on capitalists' terms.

Ideology, Politics, and Economics

Many of the basic tensions in the politics of consumption in the GDR stemmed from the relationship between discourses on modernization and material affluence on the one hand and the regime's actual political and economic policies and practices on the other. The ideological and political importance of consumer goods in the GDR stood at odds with the regime's Stalinist economic policies, which insisted on the forced rapid development of heavy and basic industries at the expense of consumer goods.[47] Not until July 1949 did party leaders begin to turn some of their attention from iron and steel to consumer goods like textiles and shoes, resolving to approach prewar production levels within two years.[48]

Party leaders' ambivalent and often contradictory policies about the relative importance of production versus consumption were at the heart of the uprising of 17 June 1953.[49] The SED's Second Party Congress in July 1952 announced the "accelerated construction of socialism" and with it a package of unpopular social and economic policies that generated an explosive political mixture. Both male and female workers resented new increased norms and decreased wages and grew increasingly impatient with the party's insistence that they defer their consumerist desires. The result was passive resistance, strikes, election boycotts, and a flood of departures to the West. The breaking point came when the SED, under pressure from the Soviet Union, announced the "New Course" on 9 June 1953, which curtailed investments in heavy industry in favor of consumer goods and softened the recently proclaimed "heightened class struggle." Although the resolution gave far-reaching concessions to the middle classes, farmers, and intelligentsia, it did not revoke the 10-percent increase in workers' norms that had been enacted in May and which effectively meant a decrease in wages. Protests and work stoppages by construction workers in Berlin on 16 June quickly spread throughout the country by the next day, resulting in the most traumatic event for the regime until its disintegration in 1990.[50]

The uprising of 17 June 1953 had long-term effects not only on the state's relations with workers in the work place, but on the sphere of consumption as well. One of the most immediate changes was a shift in official rhetoric and a growing acknowledgment of the legitimacy of workers' demands for better and not just more consumer goods. Whereas in April 1953 the Ministry for Trade and Provisioning still argued that industry's "constantly increasing production [...] makes possible a sufficient satisfaction of the demand [*Bedarf*] for textiles and footwear," by October local officials in Berlin stressed that "the population's demand for the best qualities is justified. For this reason, industry and trade have the duty to work in all earnestness to comply with the wishes of the population."[51] Although the SED essentially had rescinded the New Course's economic components and shifted investment back toward heavy industry by the end of 1954, the regime could reverse neither its promises to improve consumption nor its rhetorical shifts from quantity to quality and from the objective category of "need" or "demand" (*Bedarf*) to the subjective category of "wishes."[52]

As several scholars have argued, the party leadership compromised its bargaining position against workers and consumers in the wake of 17 June 1953 and remained so fearful of another uprising that it allowed wages to outpace productivity and consumption to run hopelessly ahead of production.[53] During the next three and a half decades, the regime was highly sensitive to the unrest and discontent caused by extreme shortages and unpopular consumer policies. The SED became trapped in its own promises and fears and fell into a dangerous pattern. In part because it refused to admit publicly that it could not fulfill its promises, the party often acquiesced to consumers' demands despite the economically disastrous consequences.

In practice, economic considerations figured just as prominently as ideological and political goals in the motivations of party leaders to fulfill consumers' wishes. Consumer goods played a crucial role in the GDR's economy. By charging high prices for most industrial goods, the state could gather the money needed to subsidize foodstuffs, "basic" consumer goods, housing, transportation, health care, and other types of social consumption. But the state could not realize this source of accumulation if consumers did not buy these more expensive industrial goods. Already by the early 1950s, functionaries warned that East German industry had to come closer to matching consumers' rising sartorial demands or be stuck with enormous surpluses.

The most common economic argument, which also had clear political implications, for making the production of fashionable apparel a priority was the fact that the GDR was losing millions of marks each year as its citizens bought clothes made in West Berlin and West Germany. The Central Committee's Department for Light Industry noted in 1955 that "the stimulus to buy textiles from West Berlin is created mostly by the appearance of a new fashionable direction in taste that eventually causes the consumer, in order to look fashionably dressed, to satisfy the desire to shop [*Einkaufsverlangen*]."[54] The East German state was painfully aware that the FRG was producing higher quality, more fashionable goods at much lower prices than the GDR, even taking into account the exchange rate of around one to four.[55] Not all of East Germans' purchases in West Germany could be blamed simply on the seductive powers of Western decadence. In fact, most functionaries viewed such purchases as the inevitable result of the GDR's miserable offerings of apparel and the regime's inability to satisfy individuals' normal, "legitimate" wishes, which included "fashionable" and "tasteful" apparel.[56] The East German clothing industry's failure to produce fashionable apparel prompted especially women and youth to "cover their needs [*Bedarf*] for fashionable clothing" in West Berlin, resulting in purchases that "naturally have political and financial-political consequences."[57]

The importance of clothing, economics, and ideology in the conflict with the West is illustrated well by the official campaign to develop Berlin as a "fashion center" (*Modezentrum*). As part of the New Course in 1953, regional party officials in Berlin resolved to restore the city to its former glory as a "center of German fashion."[58] Before the Third Reich, Berlin had been the heart of the German ready-to-wear industry, which had a reputation for producing good, affordable copies of Parisian high-fashion models.[59] In 1936, 85–90 percent of Germany's clothing exports originated in Berlin, concentrated almost exclusively in the city's old center – the predominantly Jewish quarter around the Hausvogteiplatz – and the eastern parts of the city in what later became East Berlin.[60] During the Third Reich, the industry was decimated by the dispossession, displacement, and murder of Jewish owners and workers.[61] Without mentioning these crimes and the loss of lives, traditions, and expertise, municipal officials in Berlin laid out ambitious plans in 1953 to develop the area stretching from Hausvogteiplatz to Dönhoffplatz to Spittelmarkt into a full-fledged "ready-to-wear quarter" (*Konfektionsviertel*) in which "all representative institutions of the clothing industry" would be located, including a "Fashion House Berlin," the Institute for Clothing Culture, a cultural house (*Kulturhaus*) for the workers of the clothing industry, a department store "in which the population can dress itself from head to toe," sales offices for cloth and other materials used by the apparel industry, and specialized shops for women's, men's, and children's apparel as well as for furs and knitted goods.[62] In the context of the Cold War and a divided Germany, the *Modezentrum Berlin* was to fulfill a specifically nationalistic purpose: "Exactly as Prague fashion has a name in Czechoslovakia and Europe, we must succeed in making Berliner fashion a concept for all of Germany and Europe. Berlin must set the tone for German fashion."[63]

The initiative remained little more than good intentions in the years after 1953. Whereas Berlin clothing factories accounted for 40 percent of the GDR's output in 1950, by 1955 the figure was only 25 percent.[64] Meanwhile, SED officials lamented that after 1948, West Berlin had built up virtually from scratch a formidable garment industry equipped with "the most modern technology," an industry that not only was leaving East Berlin's outdated factories behind on international markets, but also was stealing the GDR's best skilled garment workers.[65] Berlin officials noted that the ready-to-wear industry was the only industrial branch in West Berlin "that developed faster than the corresponding industrial branch" in East Berlin.[66] But hope sprang eternal in the young GDR, and the *Modezentrum Berlin* initiative received a new impulse in 1958 in connection with the GDR's "chief economic task."[67]

The textile and garment industries indeed had a very significant, concrete economic importance to both the state and consumers. The area that became the GDR had a high concentration of light industry, the source of most consumer goods, and almost no heavy or basic industries. Saxony in particular had been the cradle of the German industrial revolution, and the textile industry was one of its most important industrial branches, both symbolically and economically.[68] The textile and garment industries, "the most important branch of the consumer goods industry," accounted for over 58 percent of the gross production of light industry in 1958.[69] The textile industry's share of total gross industrial production, while starting to decrease in the early 1950s as heavy and basic industries increased, still was about 13 percent in 1959.[70] Textiles and clothing comprised roughly 38 percent of retail sales of industrial goods and between 16 and 17 percent of retail sales overall in the 1950s and early 1960s, making the branch the second largest consumer goods industrial sector after food, alcohol, and tobacco products.[71] From the state's perspective, the sector's true economic importance was even greater than these numbers suggest because of its role as "an important source of accumulation for the state."[72] In the mid-1950s the textile industry accounted for 10 percent of the gross domestic industrial product and for more than 15 percent of the profits of state-owned factories.[73] The export of textiles and clothing served as an important, short-term source of hard Western currency, which the state desperately needed in order to import crucial machines, technology, and finished products that the GDR lacked.

Industrially manufactured clothing also played critical political and economic roles in the state's policies regarding women. The textile and garment industries, which traditionally employed predominantly female workers, were crucial to the state's effort to harness women's labor, both in the workplace and at home.[74] About 17 percent of industrial workers, or one of every six, were employed in the textile industry in 1957.[75] Women comprised over 70 percent of employees in the textile industry and about 85 percent in the garment and sewing products industry in the late 1950s (compared with an average of about 60 percent in light industry and 40 percent overall).[76] The textile and garment industries offered ideal means to redirect women's labor from relatively inefficient sewing and knitting in the home to more productive work in the factory, which would also help ameliorate the GDR's chronically tight labor market.[77]

Requisite to women's abstinence from self-made or professionally tailored clothes were the increased quantity and especially quality of ready-to-wear and a corresponding decrease in cloth sold by the meter. While party officials proudly asserted that "through the realization of the principle of equal rights, the proportion of working women here is significantly higher than in West Germany," this meant that the GDR's per-capita consumption of finished clothing had to exceed that of the FRG if the lives of these working women were to be made easier. A "large selection" of "moderately priced, pretty, and well-fitting ready-to-wear" was essential to sparing working women "the time-robbing work of home tailoring for themselves and their children."[78] Increasing sales of ready-to-wear also would undercut the business of black-market (female) tailors, who damaged the state both financially by not paying taxes and politically by often basing their models exclusively on Western fashion magazines and exerting on their customers an "ideological influence that is hostile to us," officials asserted.[79] There were further economic benefits: "compared with individual custom tailoring, industrial clothing manufacturing mean[t] a significant increase in productivity" and supported the broader goals of increasing accumulation and soaking up consumers' buying power.[80] As free time received more emphasis in party propaganda during the 1960s, officials modified this productionist argument to cover women's activities outside the workplace: the ability to conveniently buy ready-to-wear was now an important way of allowing women to pursue "more meaningful" leisure activities.[81] But regardless of clothing's ideological, political, and economic importance, conflicting impulses within the regime, industry, and trade resulted in inconsistent policies that were undermined by the actual practices of manufacturers, wholesalers, and retailers, as the next chapter demonstrates.

–2–

The Logic and Contingencies of Planning, Producing, and Distributing

Within the GDR's economy, the processes of planning, producing, and distributing consumer goods each possessed their own logic which often ran counter to the party's ideological goals and political promises and had no direct connection to consumers' aesthetic and material wishes. As Arjun Appadurai has suggested, one can view commodities as having a "social life," and tracing their paths from the planning stages to the final consumer can reveal social and economic relations of the human actors involved.[1] Practical difficulties, ideological and political imperatives, and often conflicting interests shaped both everyday and long-term decisions and actions in East Germany. These structures and interests help explain the simultaneous existence of shortages and surpluses as well as changes in the characteristics of textiles and garments in the GDR over time. By shaping the quantity and quality of consumer goods in stores, the social practices of planning, production, and distribution, together with macroeconomic policies, played constitutive roles in East German consumer culture.

Production Problems

During the first decade after World War II, the textile and garment industries in the Soviet Zone faced difficulties that stemmed from the war, the dispossession and murder of Jewish businessmen and workers by the Nazis, and the deepening divisions of the Cold War.[2] Following the destruction of longstanding traditions and expertise through the "aryanization" of the industries during the Third Reich, many factories had suffered damage during the war or had been converted to wartime production and needed to be retooled.[3] Chaos and crises made shortages of labor and raw materials unavoidable during the immediate postwar years. Although the Soviet Zone contained a disproportionate share of Germany's prewar textile industry, production suffered from what East German officials called "disproportions."[4] The dissection of German industry according to political boundaries, the loss of territories in the East, and the flow of refugees westward resulted in enormous regional imbalances in population, natural resources, raw materials, and productive capabilities.[5] For instance, the Soviet Zone contained nearly all of Germany's prewar stocking manufacturers, but most of the silk industry was located in the Western zones; the Soviet Zone possessed excess capacity for building textile machines, while the Western zones had the vast majority of factories for constructing sewing machines.[6] In addition, the dismantlement and confiscation of factories as part of reparations were especially acute in the Soviet Zone.[7]

As a result of these conditions, the textile and garment industries realized only a small fraction of their production capacities during the first postwar years, and energy and material shortages forced many factories to close.[8] Relative to the population, however, the textile and garment industries in the Soviet Zone possessed excess capacity and quickly increased their output. The garment industry raised its production from 48 percent of its 1936 level in 1946 to 98 percent by 1950.[9]

Cloth and apparel are complicated industrial products that involve over 100 steps of production and refinement, from harvesting and refining raw materials, to spinning and dyeing yarn, to weaving and printing cloth, and finally to cutting and sewing the finished garment.[10] Each stage of the production process needs to be executed well and on time; a snag anywhere along the way causes problems for all later stages. The East German textile and garment industries experienced major problems at every stage of production, which naturally spelled trouble for the final product.[11]

Difficulties began with raw materials. Prewar Germany had imported its entire supply of cotton and a large proportion of its wool. Initially unable to afford these expensive materials, the Soviet Zone continued wartime trends resulting from the Nazis' goal of autarky and dramatically increased its domestic production of spun rayon, an item for which it had inherited very strong production capacities.[12] But even here, in what should have been their strong suit, East German factories spun yarn of extremely poor quality, and difficulties with the chemical preparations frequently stopped production altogether.[13] Since the development and production of other synthetic fibers were essentially non-existent, the regime dramatically increased imports of cotton and wool from the Soviet Union and the other Soviet-bloc countries to replace low-quality and undesirable rayon during the 1950s.[14] However, in addition to being expensive and costing valuable foreign currency, imports, which comprised approximately half of the GDR's raw materials until the late 1960s, proved to be in discontinuous supply and qualitatively poor.[15] Low-grade cotton and wool resulted not only in low-quality yarn and cloth but combined with inferior dyes to create dull, drab colors that bled during the first washing.[16]

Even when industry obtained good raw materials, later stages of production could ruin them. Officials complained that the textile industry's "ancient" and poorly maintained machines destroyed material and produced inferior yarn and cloth.[17] Printing works and garment factories could in turn spoil good cloth.[18] A chronic lack of space and poor storage techniques also led to dirtied, crushed, moldy, or damaged goods.[19] Transportation difficulties delayed shipments of materials and finished products. Labor issues also posed major problems: work in the poorly ventilated textile factories was uncomfortable, difficult, tedious, and low-paying, contributing to high drop-out and absentee rates.[20]

Bureaucratic, Industrial, and Commercial Structures

Before examining some of the structural causes of production problems, it is necessary to introduce the main structures and organizations of the GDR's state and party bureaucracies, industry, and trade. According to the principle of "democratic centralism," the structure of the central party and state apparatus was replicated in successively smaller and more numerous units at the regional and district levels.[21] The conflicting interests of central authorities on the one hand and regional and local officials on the other formed one of the central tensions in the everyday workings of the party, state, industry, and trade. Starting in 1952, the central government oversaw roughly fifteen regions (*Bezirke*), which were subdivided into over 200 districts (*Kreise*), each of which were subdivided into localities (*Orte*). Orders originated from the central government and were passed down through the regions and districts, while reports on performance and problems percolated upwards. The SED and the state maintained separate but parallel apparatuses, although the personnel overlapped at the highest levels and most important state functionaries were also party members. The party technically made only recommendations to state institutions, which formally held the right to make laws and conducted the government's daily business, but the SED in fact held a monopoly on executive authority. The Politburo of the Central Committee (Zentralkomitee) was at the pinnacle of the party apparatus while the presidency (*Präsidium*) of the Council of Ministers (Ministerrat) – and during the 1960s the State Council (Staatsrat) – was the highest governing body of the state.[22] The State Planning Commission (Staatliche Plankommission) was under the Council of Ministers but also reported to the Politburo as the central organization in charge of planning and overseeing the day-to-day functioning of the economy.[23]

Individual factories were classified according to ownership and the level of the state organ that planned and oversaw them. The textile and garment industries were comprised of three main types of factories: privately owned, state-owned (*Volkseigener Betrieb* or VEB), and half-state-owned (*Betrieb mit staatlicher Beteiligung* or BSB).[24] The largest state-owned factories of each industrial branch were managed by a centrally administered Association of State-Owned Factories (*Vereinigung Volkseigener Betriebe* or VVB), while regional and local VVBs monitored and planned mid-sized and small state-owned factories.[25] Regional and district state organs planned and oversaw private and half-state-owned enterprises.

The institutions responsible for distribution remained almost entirely unconnected from those of production, despite having a similar structure. East German party and state officials used the term "trade" (*Handel*) to refer to the entire system of distribution as well as the units working within it. I use the term "trade" throughout this book in roughly the same manner that East Germans used it, both in order to reflect officials' mentalities and the realities of the workings of the GDR's planned economy and because there is no exact equivalent in capitalist systems. Trade was comprised of two main components, wholesalers and retailers. The state-owned wholesalers (*Großhandel*) were organized into six Central Wares Offices (*Zentrale Warenkontore* or ZWK), which reported to the Ministry for Trade and Provisioning (Ministerium für Handel und Versorgung). Among retailers (*Kleinhandel*), which primarily were placed under the responsibility of local authorities, the state-owned HO stores (Handelsorganisation) and the consumer cooperatives' "Konsum" stores gradually replaced private stores.

The Institute for Clothing Culture (Institut für Bekleidungskultur), founded in 1952 and renamed the German Fashion Institute (Deutsches Modeinstitut) in 1957, was the central state institution responsible for designing, propagating, and facilitating the production and distribution of the official "Fashion Line of the GDR" (*Modelinie der DDR*).[26] Its tasks included writing and publishing essays on aesthetics, taste, and clothing design; designing models that were exhibited and pictured in the media as typifying ideal apparel; and educating officials from industry and trade about its fashion line. Although these tasks required the coordination of numerous branches of industry, trade, and the media, it was not placed under a central state institution like the State Planning Commission that oversaw the entire economy but rather under the VVB Konfektion, the central association of state-owned garment factories that was part of the Ministry for Light Industry.

The Logic of "*Tonnenideologie*"

One structural cause of qualitative production problems was the logic of production itself in the GDR's economy. An analysis of the framework of motivations and circumstances in textile and garment factories helps explain the systemic nature of production problems and industry's disregard for factors, such as fashion or consumers' demands, that stood outside the production process.[27] In the context of the existential crises and extreme shortages of the immediate postwar years, party and state leaders understandably focused on increasing the quantity of production and downplayed questions of quality. But this orientation remained inherent in the

logic of East Germany's economy long after industry had reached prewar production levels in the early 1950s and stockpiles began to form. By the end of the
decade, party officials began a campaign against *"Tonnenideologie"* or
"Mengenideologie" (ideology of tons or of quantity), which they defined as
industry's preoccupation with fulfilling its plans for gross production, finances,
and productivity as well as its simultaneous neglect of quality and consumers'
demands.[28] The term reflected party leaders' tendency to claim that the GDR's
most important problems had ideological causes, but the phenomena it described
were intrinsic to the logic of East Germany's planned economy itself, which
encouraged the fulfillment of quantitative goals above all others. Except for a relatively brief but hopeful period of limited experiments during the reforms of the
1960s, the basic logic of planning remained unchanged during the entire life of the
GDR.[29]

The drive to fully utilize industrial capacities was a central component of East
Germany's planned economy in both theory and practice. By planning production,
socialism theoretically could avoid the cyclical production crises of capitalism and
keep factories running at full capacity, thus achieving greater productivity and
ensuring full employment. The state also pushed factories to produce at full
capacity because it feared the political, social, and economic consequences of
reduced production and underemployment.[30] Since wages were based on the
piece-rate system, reduced production meant lower wages, which in turn meant
dissatisfaction among workers, many of whom left to work in higher-paying positions or in West Germany.[31] Especially after the trauma of the uprising of 17 June
1953, the state could not afford to encourage rumors about decreases in production that would create "mass unemployment" in regions like Saxony where the
textile and garment industries employed a very high proportion of total industrial
workers.[32] Although concerns about maintaining full employment faded after the
construction of the Berlin Wall, the state's push for full utilization of industrial
capacity remained until the end of the GDR, especially since growth in wages
chronically outpaced gains in productivity and factories were plagued by stand-
stills, shortages of supplies, and underproduction.[33] The state was caught in
another of its self-made ideological traps: in order to avoid the waste and social
consequences associated with adjusting production, as under capitalism, the logic
of production in the GDR's planned economy led factories to produce constantly
at full capacity, which resulted in another kind of waste – the characteristic shortages and surpluses.[34]

Another reason for the state's concern – some might say even paranoia – about
exhausting industrial capacities was factories' deliberate underestimation of their
productive capabilities in order to negotiate "soft" plans that they could easily
fulfill or even overfulfill. János Kornai and other students of state socialist
economies have noted the general tendencies of "suction" and "slack" in state

socialist "shortage economies": factories hoarded raw materials and labor (suction) in order to build up stockpiles of supplies (slack) that they could use for future production or trade with other enterprises for needed materials.[35] The scale and complexity of industrial production in the GDR meant that central authorities depended on local officials and individual manufacturers for information about capacities and resources. This prevented them from simply dictating plan figures. Instead, the creation of the plan entailed a multi-step process of exchanging information and negotiating production targets. In their negotiations with state planners, factory managers tried to perform a delicate balancing act. On the one hand, they strove to reduce targets for gross production in order to create "soft" plans that their factories could easily overfulfill with their extra reserves of materials and labor.[36] But this tendency was checked by the impulse to expand and increase production in order to acquire more responsibilities, resources, and money. To counteract manufacturers' push for "soft" plans, central planners tended to call for unrealistically high, overly "taut" plans. But this could be counterproductive, for managers and workers would not even try to fulfill targets that they knew from the start were unrealizable.[37] Such considerations were behind leading officials' incessant calls for uncovering and utilizing factories' "reserve capacities."

The negotiations and latent conflicts between state and industry over production targets represented just one manifestation of manufacturers' own logic of production, which often stood at odds with the plans and intentions of the central authorities and remained unconnected to the demands of trade officials, fashion experts, and consumers. The regulations that governed prices, profits, premiums, and fulfillment of the plan figured first and foremost in producers' decisions about what and how to produce. With wages and premiums based solely on quantity, workers and factory managers alike had no incentives to care about quality, let alone fashion.[38] Until the mid-1960s, industrial prices were calculated according to price regulations inherited from the wartime economy, which differentiated not according to quality or demand but rather according to the type of factory ownership and the amount and kinds of raw materials and labor used. Party leaders bemoaned the "ideological" problem of factories' ability to manipulate these regulations in "selfish" pursuit of their own interests.[39] In accordance with the logic of price regulations, factories attempted to use the least amount of cloth made out of the most expensive material in order to more easily fulfill their profit and productivity targets and thus qualify to receive cash bonuses from the state.[40] This tendency encouraged hidden inflation, as factories strove to produce the most expensive products possible and avoid less expensive ones.[41] Depending on the price calculations used, the stage of production, and the nature of their current reserves of raw materials and labor, factories could increase their profits by using more yarn than necessary, producing cloth that was much thinner than allowed, eliminating important production steps that price calculations did not recognize while adding unnecessary but profitable ones, producing cloth mainly in solid colors or monochrome designs, avoiding complicated patterns and checkers, and eliminating larger sizes because they required more material per unit.[42] Given the logic of *Tonnenideologie*, factory managers regarded fashion, aesthetics, and the demands of trade organizations and consumers as disruptive factors that could be largely ignored. Within factories, managers marginalized designers and accused them of "floating in the clouds" and being out of touch with the realities of production.[43]

The dominance of *Tonnenideologie* was not absolute. Other factors intrinsic to the GDR's economy stymied factories' ability to achieve full production capacity. The chaos of an economy of managed shortages precluded the complex coordination of hundreds of factors that modern production processes required. Many qualitative problems with cloth resulted from the fact that the right kinds of wool were not present at the same time in order to create the proper mixtures.[44] Under pressure to produce quantitatively as much as possible, factories had to improvise when faced with shortages or surpluses – for example, by using coat material for women's pants.[45] Unpredictable shortages and chaotic conditions not only resulted in poor quality but also stymied the official goal of long-term planned production in series as large and as unchanging as possible in order to maximize output and productivity, minimize costs, and simplify distribution.

Trade as "Representative of the Population's Interests"?

Like production, trade had its own logic in the GDR. Unlike industry, however, trade at least partially registered and was affected by consumer demand. Trade found itself in a very precarious position, marginalized by the production-oriented regime yet charged with fulfilling highly sensitive and visible political functions. During the postwar society of rations, trade's main function of passively distributing rationed goods was reflected in names like "Distribution Office" (*Verteilungsamt*) or "Large Distributor" (*Groß-Verteiler*).[46] In the last half of the 1940s, few questioned the practice of distributing goods based on the contents of warehouses and storage rooms rather than according to differentiated demands. But by the early 1950s, as extreme shortages faded and surplus goods piled up, party and state leaders began to cast trade in the role of mediator between industry and consumers, responsible for harmonizing supply and demand. As the "representative of the population's interests" (*Interessenvertreter der Bevölkerung*), trade was to relay consumers' wishes to production and pressure industry to fulfill them.[47] At the same time, trade was to work together with production to measure, steer, and shape demand. In reality, however, the GDR's economic and political structures as well as trade officials' own interests prevented trade from fulfilling either role.

Trade's task of measuring and reporting consumers' needs and demands illustrates both typical shortcomings of the GDR's economy and trade's marginalized position within it. Although the history of modern market research in Germany remains largely unwritten, its origins can be traced back to the years after World War I.[48] By World War II, German market researchers had developed sophisticated techniques of measuring and analyzing economic and demographic data and concentrated increasingly on psychological approaches to explaining, predicting, and manipulating consumer behavior.[49] While Wilhelm Vershofen, Georg Bergler, and other leading market researchers in West Germany continued to develop psychological approaches in postwar West Germany, East German authorities initially rejected such techniques as capitalist attempts to exploit the working class and to manipulate their needs. Instead they assigned trade the task of *"Bedarfsforschung"* (needs or demand research), which entailed registering the quantity and to some degree the quality of consumer demand. Industry officials were supposed to use these findings to adjust production accordingly.

Although it improved with time, *Bedarfsforschung* employed rather primitive and inaccurate methods.[50] If conducted at all, *Bedarfsforschung* until the early 1950s consisted of simply asking stores which articles they sold, thus equating consumers' purchases with their desires.[51] Well into the 1960s, rather than endeavoring to estimate the growth of demand if supply increased, *Bedarfsforschung* primarily registered demand that could be satisfied using existing stock.[52] Researchers also falsely assumed that all inventories would be sold and consumed and that higher revenues equaled increased per-capita consumption.[53]

Until the mid-1960s, individual stores carried most of the burden of directly measuring consumers' demands. Each HO and Konsum salesperson was supposed to keep a daily record of the goods normally in the store but temporarily sold out, wares carried by the store whose quantity was insufficient, and goods not carried by the HO but for which a demand was developing.[54] "Industry stores" (*Industrieläden*), which were supplied directly by manufacturers, also were charged with registering consumers' wishes and testing the popularity of new and future products.[55] These industry stores sent "demand analyses" (*Bedarfsanalysen*) to their affiliated factory while the regular stores sent reports to local state trade officials, who sent summaries of them to the next level of bureaucracy where they were again summarized and forwarded. The resulting reports generally were extremely impressionistic and subjective.[56] Central officials complained that trade organizations "unsystematically" employed disparate methods and nomenclatures in determining demand, making the comparison and compilation of their results all the more difficult and arbitrary.[57]

Even if planners could have translated such qualitative, incomparable, and often contradictory reports into meaningful, hard figures, other inaccuracies would have distorted predictions of demand. Consumers inquired about the same scarce items in several different stores, thus inflating the perception of demand, while many stores did not bother to register customers' wishes at all. In 1960 state trade officials at the local level did not even know the structure of the population of their districts in terms of age, gender, and number, and planners made errors like forgetting to include unsold items in the number of goods available to the public the following year.[58] Despite their best efforts to estimate the percentage of satisfied demand (*Bedarfsdeckung*) for specific product categories, officials were painfully aware of the fact that demand itself could change suddenly, dramatically, and unpredictably in response to fluctuations in production, the quality and appearance of goods, fashion, prices, and wages.[59] Rather than providing long-term predictions based on the interaction of these factors, trade based its notoriously tardy market research reports largely on perceptions of current demand as measured by sales and stores' stock.[60] Trade could measure swings in demand only very roughly and after the fact.

The combination of inaccurate predictions and shifting demand led trade to drastically change its production orders shortly before or even during a plan period. Such calls fell on the deaf ears of factory managers, who were incapable of such flexibility and simply continued to churn out the assortments long anchored in the plan.[61] Besides, changes in assortments increased costs and endangered the fulfillment of the material and financial plans, a risk that factories had absolutely no reason to take.[62]

At the end of the 1950s, party and state leaders intensified their perennial calls for improved *Bedarfsforschung*, and "primitive approaches" (*Daumen x Zeigefinger*) based on "coincidental occurrences" (*Zufallserscheinungen*) slowly gave way to "scientific" (*wissenschaftlich*) and systematic methods during the 1960s.[63] The Politburo established an Institute for Needs Research (Institut für Bedarfsforschung) within the Ministry for Trade and Provisioning in March 1961.[64] Research techniques became noticeably more sophisticated during the 1960s and increasing emphasis was placed on market research's role in helping to steer demand. The analysis of market mechanisms and irrational consumer behavior received official if ambivalent endorsement in 1967 when the regime changed the institute's name to the Institute for Market Research (Institut für Marktforschung).[65] By employing methods of social science, including representative surveys and qualitative interviews, researchers gained a more complex and detailed picture of consumers' desires, motivations, and habits.[66] However, despite official claims that this knowledge would be used to better satisfy individuals' needs, East German industrial managers and state planners all but completely ignored the Institute for Market Research's findings.

Within trade itself, wholesalers and retailers often found themselves at odds. To reduce the administrative and labor costs associated with organizing warehouses, wholesalers resisted carrying a broad assortment of styles and sizes. At the same time, they became frustrated when retailers refused to buy unwanted items that clogged factories' and wholesalers' facilities.[67] Retailers, whose direct interaction with shoppers made them more sensitive to their wishes and fears of uniformity, accused wholesalers of being unresponsive to consumers' tastes and not exerting enough pressure on manufacturers to produce desired articles.[68] Of course, retailers also acted according to their own interests, which did not necessarily match consumers' desires.

The most significant conflicts of interest and lack of coordination existed between industry and trade. From the first years after the war, these two columns of the economy acted largely independently of each other and had divergent interests.[69] In the words of one official, production and trade met only "if it somewhere, somehow is burning."[70] While manufacturers strove to produce a small number of items in large series based on long-term plans, trade functionaries wanted to be able to change their orders on short notice to adjust to demand and prevent the growth of surpluses. But trade officials remained excluded from the production planning process, which belied the incessant calls of party leaders and official propaganda starting in the early 1950s for trade to force producers to consider consumers' interests.[71]

It seems logical that producers would have the upper hand in a seller's market like the GDR, but the relationship between industry and trade was not as simple and one-sided as most scholars have portrayed it. Though they clearly were underdogs, trade officials employed often ingenious techniques in pursuit of their own interests. Most of their efforts may have been in vain, but their improvised and sometimes illegal actions unwittingly contributed to undermining the functioning of the planned economy.

Certain circumstances allowed trade to resist production's dominance and at least make known its displeasure. As surpluses began to clog storage and retail space in 1949, trade officials could afford to refuse to sign contracts with factories whose products were equivalent or inferior to those already in stock.[72] By 1953 state officials became alarmed when trade officials' purchase orders totaled only 35 percent of factories' total capacities.[73] Encouraged by entreaties from party and state leaders that trade should "very vigorously refuse wares that do not match the appropriate delivery date, season, and assortment," HO and Konsum officials defied state regulations stipulating that they accept all shipments from industry. Instead they demanded sizes and models that had not been produced.[74] Trade officials also used bureaucratic loopholes to refuse unwanted deliveries due to imperfections or contract violations.[75] The highpoint for trade came during the few years before and after the announcement in 1963 of the New Economic System, a reform program that called for bureaucratic decentralization, introduction of elements of market mechanisms, and increased responsibility of state-owned factories for the sale of their products. Although these reforms sounded impressive on paper, they proved unenforceable in practice.

Unable to obtain desired products through official channels, trade officials often turned to semi-legal and illegal means, which bore a striking resemblance to the techniques that individual consumers used to obtain or create the objects of their desires. Just as consumers ordered the same item at several different stores or through two different mail-order catalogues, trade organizations ordered more than they actually wanted because suppliers frequently reduced or delayed deliveries.[76] Trade also collaborated with industry outside the plan. Such "black market" activity involved making illegal "o P" (for "ohne Plan" or "without plan") contracts over and above the plan.[77] Without informing state authorities, trade officials asked factories to shift their production from one assortment to another or had private factories tailor cloth from store shelves into ready-to-wear apparel.[78]

Despite trade officials' resistance and the state's half-hearted attempts at reform, everyone knew that "production determines what trade has to take."[79] Factories continued to produce without purchase orders and to violate contract terms that specified material compositions, prices, and delivery dates.[80] By threatening not to sell anything to those who rejected even a few of their products, producers could force special terms on trade organizations that directly contradicted trade's interests.[81] Without the leverage of a united front or the state's full support, individual trade organizations could not prevent manufacturers from finding other buyers or simply producing without contracts. While privileged trade organizations snapped up the few desirable items that had not been exported, those that followed had to settle for the remainders from previous purchasing rounds.[82] Unable to obtain desired goods, trade officials lamented that they had to buy the next best thing with "tightly shut eyes"; otherwise they would get nothing.[83] Even if trade functionaries theoretically could change their orders during the course of a planning period, bureaucratic regulations contained significant financial disincentives to do so, such as forcing them to pay for the costs incurred and to accept the goods produced up to that point.[84] Trade's position also was weakened by the fact that manufacturers did not have to rely on domestic buyers. Throughout the 1950s and well into the 1960s, the state exported vast amounts of industry's surpluses to the Soviet Union and other socialist countries. For political reasons, the regime was reluctant to place state-owned factories in a bad light and burdened trade with much of the blame for unsold goods.

Balancing Planned Inflexibility and Improvised Damage Control

In theory, state planners arbitrated between industry and trade and helped to coordinate their actions. In reality, this task proved simply overwhelming. Far removed from their utopian vision of masterfully guiding a perfectly planned economy, party leaders and state planners found themselves primarily reacting to crises. The impossibility of collecting, analyzing, and acting on every bit of information about production, distribution, and consumption forced state planners to give individual factories and trade organizations a certain amount of leeway and to rely on them to cooperate with each other in order to improvise solutions that served the state's best interests rather than their own. As the preceding sketch of relations between industry and trade demonstrates, these expectations proved unrealistic.

Both centralized control and decentralized decision-making are necessary components of any complex economy. But in the GDR, the rigidity of the plan and the chaos of improvisation worked at cross-purposes. On the one hand, the stricter and more centralized the plan, the more difficult it was to correct its inevitable shortcomings through decentralized "operational measures." On the other hand, decentralization meant giving up the ideal of an omnipotent plan and the concentration of power that it symbolized. In practice, party leaders vacillated between demands for strict, centralized control and experiments with decentralization, particularly during the reform efforts of the 1960s.

The task of tracking and planning thousands of factories and trade organizations and tens of thousands of assortments simply overwhelmed state planners. At the end of the 1950s, the state-owned textile wholesalers alone handled up to 15,000 articles and approximately 9,200 stores sold ready-to-wear.[85] Since central state planners acknowledged the impossibility of planning the entire industry from above, they concentrated on centrally controlled, state-owned enterprises and left the remaining factories to regional and local officials. Internal reports constantly noted that the high number of small, private factories and poor communication between central and local authorities prevented state planners from achieving even an "overview" of the assortments produced: only 250 of the GDR's more than 3,000 textile and garment factories were planned centrally.[86] Planners at all bureaucratic levels were able to collect and analyze only a fraction of available information. Planners were forced to concentrate on rough, general figures and had virtually no information about the numbers and types of assortments, signed contracts, delivery dates, and back-orders – let alone materials, colors, sizes, and designs.[87]

The division of responsibilities, lack of control, and poor communication among central, regional, and local authorities caused additional chaos. During the first decade after the war, central party and state officials ordered the construction of superfluous garment factories because they did not know that the Berlin garment factories, which regional and local officials managed, already possessed the necessary capacities.[88] Communication and coordination were poor among different departments and ministries even at the central level. In 1958 the head of the State Planning Commission's Section for Textiles, Clothing, and Leather Goods first learned of a major price reduction for leather shoes from the daily newspaper *Neues Deutschland*. He had to rush off to Leipzig the same day to make arrangements to meet the resulting increased demand.[89]

Party and state leaders perennially lamented the lack of "strict control" over the execution of central authorities' orders and generally resisted calls to give local institutions more room to maneuver.[90] But general bureaucratic orders from above often made no sense or proved impossible to execute when applied to real conditions in the factories at the grass-roots level.[91] Although many vociferously complained about such situations, most industry and trade officials quietly made do with available resources and found ways to inconspicuously disregard orders from above that were infeasible or contrary to their interests. Such unpredictable and unreported divergences further distorted the plan and created one of planners' many nightmares.

The logic of *Tonnenideologie* and the cumbersomeness of the plan resulted in extremely slow and inflexible production, which stymied the state's efforts to both shape and react to changes in clothing fashions. Industry alone needed one to two and a half years between the choice of pattern and the delivery of the final garment.[92] Long production timetables resulted in ill-informed decisions and guesswork. Since materials were planned before production began, textile and garment factories had to order dyes and cloth before they even received production contracts.[93] Trade organizations in turn had to place orders more than a year before they received the final product.[94] As state planners themselves observed, such "long-term planning of the textile industry forms a fundamental contradiction to short-lived fashion and to the wishes of the population and of trade."[95] Since plans were finalized long before the demand for "individual fashionable assortments" crystallized, they were "based exclusively on experience, or let's say, 'suspicion'," as one functionary put it.[96]

Throughout the life of the GDR, and especially during the 1950s and 1960s, party and state leaders suggested and sporadically implemented a variety of new strategies and techniques to make planning and production faster and more flexible. These suggestions sometimes simplified and sometimes complicated planning procedures but always promised to make them more flexible and able to adjust to demand, often by simply shortening the duration of a plan period.[97] Another proposed antidote to the economy's chronic inflexibility was the creation of "reserves" of raw materials and productive capacities.[98] These reserves, which some suggested should be as much as 20 percent of total capacity, theoretically could be mobilized at short notice to respond to changes in demand and fashion.[99] It is ironic that industry already maintained its own unofficial reserves, as explained above, and that the proposal bore a striking resemblance to East German consumers' practices of hoarding goods. In any case, the idea had little chance of success. Critics argued that such "capitalist economic practices" worked contrary to the superior mechanisms of the socialist planned economy and led to the mistaken belief that shortages and swings in demand were "objective, law-governed" phenomena rather than the result of "subjective deficiencies in economic management."[100] Besides, both industry and state functionaries never swayed from their commitment to keep production running at full capacity at all times. Other officials claimed that direct distribution and the establishment of "standing relationships" (*Stammverbindungen*) between manufacturers and stores would simplify and rationalize distribution channels while reducing the power of trade officials, whose alleged conservatism prevented fashionable apparel from reaching consumers.[101] But direct distribution entailed its own problems and inefficiencies.[102] Not only was the shortest path between two points not necessarily the most rational form of distribution, but stores signed contracts with as many factories as possible in the hopes of increasing the chances of receiving desired wares.[103]

These proposed solutions to the mismatch between production and consumption addressed only symptoms while leaving intact systemic causes rooted in the logic of the plan and *Tonnenideologie*. Despite the inordinate amount of energy that officials invested in reforming distribution channels, in the words of one private retailer at the end of the 1960s, "in the end the product is still *allocated* (*zugeteilt*) and *divided up* (*aufgeteilt*)" (original emphasis).[104]

Stalinist Economic Policies and the Rationalization of Production

The SED's long-term political goals and Stalinist economic policies left their stamp on consumer goods, shaping the GDR's consumer culture in constitutive and quotidian ways. The regime's emphasis on basic and heavy industries meant chronically low investment in textile and garment factories, which helps to explain the poor quality of their products. The gradual elimination of private enterprises, the specialization of factories and stores, and the rationalization and standardization of production resulted in increasing uniformity of apparel and other consumer goods. But leaders themselves were often ambivalent about these goals and found their policies and initiatives blocked by various factors, including the GDR's reliance on private garment factories, the logistical shortcomings of bureaucracies and state-owned factories, and resistance from industry, trade, and consumers.

Among the underlying causes of production problems in the garment and textile industries was a lack of investment. Party leaders realized early on that they could greatly increase the textile and garment industries' production without substantial investment.[105] Although the GDR inherited a region that had been home to many of the world's leading textile machine manufacturers in the 1920s, an almost complete lack of investments since the early 1930s resulted in very old and inefficient factories and machines. In 1956 the average machine in the GDR's textile industry was thirty-three years old.[106] Official investment policies meant, as the director of the VVB Konfektion noted in 1958, "that in principle the factories of the VVB have to get along with only maintenance funds."[107] But the regime's meager investments did not even suffice to maintain the branch's physical plants.[108] The situation was particularly desperate in the textile industry, whose fixed assets were in "the worst physical condition" of any industrial branch in the mid-1960s.[109]

In addition to forcing the growth of heavy industry, the SED's Stalinist economic policies called for the nationalization of industry. Not only were the means of production to be placed in the hands of the workers, but small, inefficient factories were to be replaced by large, efficient ones. The realization of this goal, however, proved difficult in the textile and garment industries. Small private firms not only comprised an unusually large proportion of production, but their products generally were more attractive and fashionable and of significantly better quality than those produced by state-owned factories. Although private enterprises made the state-owned ones look bad and provided counter-evidence of socialism's claim of the superiority of nationalized industry, party leaders begrudgingly granted them a place in the economy because they both helped address shortages and produced high-quality products that generated significant income for the state. These tensions between ideological and practical imperatives help explain the party's fluctuating policies toward private enterprises as well as the middle classes (*Mittelstand*) in general until the early 1970s.[110]

The "accelerated construction of socialism" announced at the Second Party Congress in 1952 intensified the push to nationalize and consolidate factories. The process of "concentration" typically combined several distinct production units under one centralized management.[111] By 1953 private enterprises comprised only 29 percent of planned production in the textile industry, 46 percent in the garment industry, and 31 percent in the leather-working industry.[112] But the regime hesitated to eliminate all private enterprises, especially in the garment industry, because party and state officials admitted internally that they were more flexible and produced better goods in terms of quality, taste, and fashion.[113] Production contracts reflected this: while state-owned garment factories needed only 30 percent of their capacity in 1955 to fulfill their contracts, private enterprises had more orders than they could handle.[114] Such conditions led to official concerns about private industry's potential to overproduce, disturb the balance of the plan, and divert valuable resources from the putatively more productive, centrally controlled, and politically favored state-owned enterprises.[115] Private firms thus found themselves last in line for raw materials and finished products and bore the brunt of reductions in production ordered from above.[116] Faced with such obstacles and high taxes that eliminated their profits, many owners sold their enterprises to the state or abandoned them and fled to the West.

Starting in February 1956, the state adopted a new method of gradually eliminating all private industry by giving private firms the "opportunity" to accept "state participation" (*staatliche Beteiligung*).[117] In the garment industry, half-state-owned enterprises' share of production grew substantially over the next decade.[118] While private enterprises still comprised 44 percent of total gross production in 1955, the figure shrank to 28 percent in 1958 and to only 10 percent in 1966. In 1958 half-state-owned garment factories already produced 8 percent of the branch's total production; by 1966 the figure had risen to 33 percent. But changing the ownership status of enterprises contributed little to socialism's goal of reducing the number and increasing the size of production units. After modest growth during the early and mid-1950s, the number of state-owned garment factories remained relatively steady until the late-1960s and continued to represent a disproportionate share of total production. The twenty to twenty-five centrally managed state-owned garment factories, which averaged over 1,000 employees each, represented only 2 percent of the total number of factories but employed almost 25 percent of all workers and accounted for 25 to 30 percent of total production. While the total number of garment factories decreased from 1,628 in 1953 to 1,275 in 1958 to 978 in 1966, the overwhelming majority, representing 60 to 70 percent of total production, remained small and mid-sized, locally controlled enterprises. In 1958 almost 88 percent of the GDR's garment factories had an average of less than forty-five employees.[119] In 1966 small and mid-sized firms still represented over 90 percent of the total number of garment factories, and the average number of employees per factory for the entire branch had increased only slightly during the previous eight years from 95 to 105.[120]

The more mechanized production processes and greater percentage of large enterprises in the textile industry allowed the regime to centralize it to a greater degree.[121] Between 1950 and 1957, state-owned enterprises continued to account for about 13 percent of all textile factories, while their share of the branch's workforce increased from 64 to 73 percent and their share of gross production increased from 65 to 78 percent. During the same period, private textile enterprises represented about 86 percent of the total number of factories, while their share of the workforce slipped from 36 to 27 percent and their share of gross production from 35 to 22 percent. In 1960 there were already 158 centrally managed, state-owned factories; by 1968 the number had risen to 182. Although there were 2,287 private and half-state-owned enterprises and 117 locally managed, state-owned factories in 1968, they accounted for less than one-fourth of the industry's gross production.

Economic motives also stood behind the push for the gradual elimination of private enterprises and the growth of centralized large-scale industry. The concentration and specialization of factories and stores contributed to the goals of increasing the standardization of products, increasing serial production runs, and decreasing the number of assortments. Party and state functionaries constantly railed against the "fragmentation" (*Zersplitterung*) of the textile and garment industries into a large number of small enterprises that each inefficiently produced a wide variety of goods in very small series.[122] Despite regulations that set minimum series sizes, large factories with over 1,000 workers often produced only twenty to twenty-five dresses per model and trade organizations frequently ordered less than ten pieces of a particular ready-to-wear article.[123] At the end of the 1950s, centrally managed state-owned garment factories still were producing outerwear in series sizes starting at twenty and rarely averaging more than 1,000.[124] Nevertheless, the series sizes of state-owned factories were still two to three times larger than those of private enterprises.[125] Party leaders lamented that although wholesalers and retailers offered a large number of different articles, they completely lacked "assortment depth" – that is, stores carried a broad variety of items, each of which was available only in small quantities.[126] In 1959 an audit revealed that the HO Bekleidungshaus Karl-Marx-Stadt offered 86 sports coats in 35 different styles and 233 suits in 50 different styles, while the Modehaus Zentrum carried 132 suits in 70 different styles. Officials argued that the average store's offerings of two sports coats per style did not guarantee sufficient assortments of either sizes or colors.[127] By reducing the number of models produced and the number of stores that distributed them, manufacturers and stores could cut production and administrative costs while helping to ensure the necessary assortment of sizes.[128] To complement these efforts, officials planned to reduce the textile industry's 1,148 basic types of machines with approximately 12,000 variations in 1959 to only 350 basic types with 2,260 variations by 1965.[129]

Factory managers would have gladly produced in larger series, but the still widespread use of subcontractors in the garment industry as well as the unstable supply of raw materials and intermediate parts frustrated their efforts.[130] Manufacturers' erratic shipments of extremely small quantities in turn caused trade officials additional work and complications.[131] Labeled a "remnant of capitalist society" by party dogma, the fragmented, uncoordinated textile and garment industries and network of retail stores embodied the antithesis of the ideal socialist mode of production.[132]

Specialization was another important component of the official push for increased industrial efficiency, especially during the first two decades of the GDR. A reduced number of specialized factories and stores theoretically would increase both productivity and the depth and stability of offerings while improving coordination among the various stages of production and distribution.[133] The average garment factory was supplied by twenty weaving factories before the introduction of specialization; by 1959 the number had sunk to only seven.[134] In the short term, poor bureaucratic decisions about the assignment of specializations created chaos and shortages.[135] In the long run, specialization resulted in a few or sometimes only one manufacturer holding a monopoly over a certain product, which led to growing homogenization.

The state's initiatives to rationalize, standardize, and specialize production began to produce measurable but mixed results by the mid-1960s. In 1965 the number of factories that produced only one assortment of women's outerwear had increased by 18 percent during the previous two years, while the number that produced five assortments had decreased by 44 percent.[136] At the central buying negotiations for the first half of 1965, the average series size for ready-to-wear outerwear increased by over 225 percent compared with the previous year, while production volume increased by 18 percent and the number of models decreased by 64 percent.[137] Compared with just a few years earlier, the breadth of assortments in several important garment factories in Berlin had narrowed by two-thirds in 1965.[138] Although by 1966 the garment industry achieved an average of series size of 3,500 for dresses (traditionally the assortment with one of the lowest series sizes), party leaders pushed for significantly higher numbers.[139]

But the growth of series sizes was limited as long as small and mid-sized factories continued to dominate the textile and especially garment industries. The breakthrough came in the late 1960s and early 1970s when the regime finally realized its investment plans for the construction of large-scale textile and garment factories and the establishment of vertically integrated combines. These new factories operated on a completely different scale: in 1971 VEB Textilkombinat Cottbus produced 6.9 million square meters of cloth (*Großrundstrick*), enough for 1.5 million pieces of outerwear.[140] Officials planned for Cottbus to produce 2.2 million men's suits, 1.5 million pants, and 800,000 women's suits by 1973.[141] In the GDR's shortage economy, the accelerated growth of large factories inevitably meant shifting materials and resources away from small and mid-sized enterprises, as many officials had long advocated.[142] Industry theoretically could now achieve an ideal kind of specialization: while large factories would churn out the "basic assortment" (*Grundsortiment*), small factories would produce the "fashionable supplementary assortment" (*modische Füllsortiment*).[143] Whether or not officials could have foreseen it, the consequence was the further polarization of production into "standard" garments and "high-quality and fashionable" apparel.

The Downward Spiral of Foreign Trade

The textile industry, like most industries in the GDR, initially depended heavily on imports. As discussed above, the vast majority of natural raw materials came from other socialist countries but were of poor quality. For the higher-quality raw materials needed to make finer goods, such as fine wool and long-staple cotton, the GDR had to turn to the West.[144] It also depended on Western imports for items that were not produced domestically or that were either so scarce or so low-quality as to seriously disturb production processes; these included textile dyes and dyeing aids as well as polyester and other synthetic materials.[145] The GDR also imported Western machines rather than rely on hopelessly outdated and inefficient East German textile and garment machines and inferior domestic mechanical engineering.[146]

Starting in the late-1960s and increasing in the 1970s, the GDR even imported finished products from the West in order to fill various shortages and to at least partially satisfy consumers' wishes, regardless of the costs.[147]

To obtain the necessary hard currency to pay for imports, the regime strove to export as much as it could. In line with Stalinist economic policies, the rule of thumb was that "we can import only as much as we export," as one union official explained.[148] The GDR's textile and garment industries indeed achieved dramatic increases in exports during the 1950s. Exports of textiles doubled between 1950 and 1955 and increased by 56 percent in 1956, while exports of ready-to-wear outerwear doubled between 1958 and 1960.[149] In the early 1960s the textile and garment industry was the GDR's "largest exporter in the consumer goods industry," responsible for a significant proportion of total exports.[150] The state encouraged the export of a very large proportion of total industrial production by setting export targets in factories' plans and by making exports profitable for producers. Although the textile and garment industries exported about one-fourth of total production, the proportion of exports among high-quality and fashionable goods was much higher.[151] The best factories exported over 70 percent of their total production or sometimes 95 percent of a particular item, such as women's fine nylon stockings.[152] Most of these high-quality wares went to capitalist countries, where they could earn hard currency. Exports of high-quality items thus came at the expense of fulfilling consumer's wishes at home; only serious shortages could persuade the regime to redirect goods meant for export to the domestic market.[153]

The vast majority of exports, however, were inexpensive, low-quality goods. Throughout the 1950s the GDR used other socialist countries and especially the Soviet Union as a sort of dumping ground for surplus production, as an "outlet" (*Ventil*) for both low-quality, unmarketable goods and items that factories relentlessly produced without any consideration of demand.[154] But this began to change in the late 1950s as the Soviet market for inexpensive, low-quality textiles became saturated and as other socialist countries like Czechoslovakia, Hungary, and Yugoslavia began to produce less expensive and better products than the GDR.[155]

The increasingly competitive global textile market and the GDR's undiminished need for hard currency led the regime into an economically disastrous downward spiral. While the GDR could command fairly high prices for its best goods during the 1950s, the stagnant or worsening quality of its products in the context of heightened competition during the 1960s forced a shift in its exports from high-quality, high-profit items to mass-produced, low-quality ones with low profit margins. Party leaders hoped that industry's ever-larger series sizes would reduce costs and make East German textiles more competitive on the world market. But despite exporting its best products, the GDR had the reputation of being a "cheap wares" (*Billigewaren*) country and of supplying West Germany with low-end products.[156] By the end of the 1960s, the GDR found itself competing with the Third

World on the export markets for West Germany and other capitalist countries. The combination of high production costs and stiff competition resulted in huge economic losses for the GDR. The prices of even the best East German textiles on the world market did not cover production costs.[157] The regime nevertheless continued to increase exports, thereby exacerbating economic losses, because its constant, pressing need for Western currency outweighed any long-term economic concerns about profitability or fiscal consequences. The regime used the GDR's light industry to provide short-term liquidity in hard currency, regardless of the long-term consequences.

Already in the early 1960s, the GDR had begun a pattern in foreign trade that the new economic policies of the early 1970s exaggerated and accelerated. In order to clothe its citizens, compensate for its technological inferiority, and remain competitive on the international market, the GDR imported expensive technology, finished products, and high-quality materials from the West while losing money by exporting cheap finished goods to pay for them. In search of more profitable methods of gathering Western currency, the regime increasingly turned to a special division of the Ministry for Foreign Trade, Commercial Coordination (Kommerzielle Koordinierung, or KoKo), which engaged in shady deals with foreign firms and governments, and the Intershops, which were modeled on duty-free shops and sold imported Western goods for Western currency.[158]

Synthetics: A Case Study of East German Modernization and Foreign Trade

The story of the development of synthetics, the quintessence of the GDR's attempt to modernize its textile and garment industries, illustrates many of the problems and contradictions in the regime's investment and foreign trade policies. Already in the early 1950s, Ulbricht and others advocated the domestic production of artificial fibers as the key to accomplishing many of the SED's political and economic goals. Continuing many aspects of the Nazi's failed autarky campaign, the East German regime believed that the steady, plentiful production of high-quality synthetic threads could end the GDR's expensive reliance on imported natural raw materials, facilitate increased exports, and raise consumers' standard of living by providing low-maintenance apparel that lasted significantly longer than clothes made of natural fibers.[159] Powerful symbols of modernity across Europe in the 1950s, synthetic materials and plastics had strong cultural meanings and political importance.[160] In the GDR, this was seen in the renaming of nylon from "Perlon" to "Dederon," which was supposed to echo "DDR," the country's initials in German.[161] The development of synthetic threads, however, proceeded very slowly and matched neither the quantity nor quality that leaders had envisioned, despite the heavily publicized "Chemical Program" in 1958 that called for drastic improvements.[162] The GDR's production of synthetic fibers fell farther and farther behind the West, resulting in increased difficulties for East German exports to both capitalist and socialist countries.[163] Lacking the necessary technology and production capabilities, the GDR imported these materials from capitalist countries and used them to produce finished goods, most of which it then exported back to capitalist countries at a loss.[164]

Although East Germany's production of synthetics continued to flounder in the 1960s, party leaders became increasingly enthusiastic about the benefits of the materials and hopeful that they could not only end the GDR's dependency on the West but also increase exports. In October 1967 the Politburo passed a resolution that eventually resulted in the construction of the giant synthetic fiber processing plant VEB Textilkombinat Cottbus and the expansion of the chemical fiber combine that had been established in Guben in 1959.[165] The resolution stipulated an investment of 1.55 billion marks to build plants for the production and processing of polyester and polyurethane. The construction of these plants, which supposedly would represent the cutting edge of modern technology, was to guarantee a stable, growing, and profitable stream of exports, especially to capitalist countries. But the resolution itself was laced with contradictions: in order to quickly overcome the GDR's lag behind the West (conservatively estimated to be six years), the Politburo ordered the import of Western know-how and machines.[166] In Cottbus the first construction phase alone required the import of about 16 million West German marks worth of Western knitting and sewing machines.[167] Until Guben's synthetic production capacities were fully operational, the GDR had to import millions of marks worth of polyester fibers during its first few years of operation.[168]

These investments were a case of too much too late. The GDR did not start to catch the "chemical fiber wave" (*Chemiefaserwelle*) until after it was already subsiding in the West.[169] In search of a great leap forward after a decade and a half of stagnation, the regime invested inordinate sums of money in production technologies and capacities that soon became out-of-date. While officials proudly predicted at the beginning of the Polyester Program that the GDR would surpass West Germany's production levels of synthetic materials by the early 1970s, they witnessed the unfortunate fulfillment of their augury as Western countries began to shift their production to new, lighter synthetics and to mix synthetics with natural fibers.[170] East German industry could not hope to keep up with these changes – the heavy investments of the late 1960s and early 1970s and the regime's refusal to invest more in the branch had locked its course in place. From only 3.6 percent in 1963, the proportion of synthetic fibers in total production rose to 9.6 percent in 1967, 36 percent in 1969, and reached 90 percent by 1980.[171] When the easy-care synthetic apparel of the 1970s gave way to the cotton fashion that originated in the West in the early 1980s, the GDR was in no position to adjust its production accordingly.[172]

The logic and practices of planning, production, and distribution in the GDR, together with the SED's macroeconomic policies, produced trends that did not bode well for either East German consumers or the regime itself. Chronic mismatches between supply and demand and increasingly uniform and homogeneous apparel failed to fulfill East Germans' needs and desires, while the textile and garment industries, the SED's export policies, and international developments pulled the GDR ever deeper into a downward economic spiral. While this chapter examined the industrial, commercial, bureaucratic, and economic dimensions of clothing in the GDR, the next chapter turns to cultural and aesthetic aspects of the regime's attempt to create a distinctly socialist consumer culture.

–3–

From "New Out of Old" to "Socialist Fashion": Patching Together an Alternative Consumer Culture

"In this year we wear everything that fits and suits us and – has survived the chaos of war. When someone inquisitively looks at the new summer dress made from old curtains, then we just laugh coyly over our shoulder …and lightly say: 'That's now the latest.'"[1] When these words appeared in March 1946 in the magazine *Die Frau von heute* (Today's Woman), the organ of the women's committees (*Frauen-ausschüsse*) in the Soviet Zone, Germans had been experiencing hunger, physical hardships, and devastating shortages for several years and would continue to do so for several more. Civilian wardrobes were in dire straits: clothing rationing had begun already a few days before the outbreak of World War II and many of the few existing clothes had been destroyed or damaged in the war itself.[2] After the war, refugees from the East arrived often with little more than what they wore, while the textile and garment industries produced at only a fraction of prewar levels due to the war and the dismantlement of entire factories as reparations for the Soviets.

But already at Germany's mythical "*Stunde Null*," the supposedly empty "zero hour" after the war, debates began over the contours of the society under (re)con-struction, including its material and consumer cultures. A complex and conflicted mixture of norms from the past and visions of the future, cultural continuities and partial breaks with traditions complicated this discussion during the "transitional period" from capitalism to socialism in the Soviet Zone. Proposals for the aesthetic and material characteristics of clothes in socialism contained normative notions about the appropriateness of social distinction, processes of cultural dissemina-tion, women's "nature" and role in society, and measurements of societal progress and change – in short, the characteristics of the future "socialist personality" and "socialist consumer habits."

Much of the discourse about clothing and ideal consumer habits during the immediate postwar years focused on the necessity for women to make clothes for themselves and their families in order to compensate for industry's assumedly temporary shortcomings. The ubiquitous slogan "make new from old," an entreaty that German officials had propagated during both World War I and II, typified this attitude.[3] Women enacted this motto by ingeniously transforming everything from old clothes, rags, and tablecloths to parachutes, uniforms and military bed sheets into "new" patchwork dresses (*Flickenkleid*) or shirts, which were even featured as early as September 1945 in fashion shows that appeared primitive by prewar standards.[4] Consumer magazines supported these practices by publishing countless paper patterns to help women make their own apparel.[5] While the images that appeared in newspapers and magazines allegedly served as a source of "inspiration" for industry, trade, and consumers, cut-out patterns constituted an implicit admission that consumers themselves had to produce what the GDR's industry could not.

Both the SED and consumers understood the practices of "making new from old" and tailoring one's own clothes as making a virtue out of necessity in order to cope with a presumably temporary situation, one that would give way to the practice of buying an increasing number and wider variety of new, industrially made apparel in stores. The seemingly superfluous fantasies expressed in the media and women's efforts to make their improvised apparel as attractive and fashionable as possible even amidst the rubble and existential crises of the immediate postwar years also suggest more complex underlying desires than the mere wish to satisfy the supposedly objective, biologically based "basic needs" that were the foundation of orthodox Marxist–Leninist theories of consumption.[6] By the late 1940s, the desires and fantasies of a well-developed consumer culture were already re-emerging in the GDR, but its form was hotly contested.

Refashioning Taste, Class, and Gender

> Today we have in Germany – as a result of Hitler's war of conquest – neither raw materials nor processing industries that could be the basis for a fashion. The fashion goddess is, like so many other false gods, dethroned. Her "leadership principle [*Führerprinzip*]" is over. No, here there's no fashion in the previous sense and there won't be any for years to come. But what will take its place? ... That is a new problem.[7]

This declaration in *Die Frau von heute* in February 1946 expressed common hopes for a fresh start and for new cultural forms that could serve as the basis of transformed attitudes toward consumption and social distinction. The *Trümmerfrau*, or rubble woman, with her work clothes and a scarf over her pulled-up hair, personified for many Germany's "zero hour" – also in the world of fashion – and later became an important mythological component of West and East German identities.[8] However, she could serve neither as a personification of both states' promises of prosperity nor as a symbol of the differences between East and West.

Female figures who performed these functions emerged by the mid-1950s, as the chaos of the immediate postwar years subsided and both Germanys increasingly fought their Cold War battles on the grounds of consumption (Figure 3.1). Both East and West Germany used displays of consumer goods and discourses on consumption to prove the superiority of their respective politico-economic systems, to make claims to represent the German nation, and to establish the legitimacy of the state and encourage allegiance to it.

The visualization of official promises and the evolution of displays of apparel beyond the level of "make new from old" engendered intense controversy. In addition to criticisms that many official displays and images encouraged premature consumer fantasies, vehement attacks by dogmatic party functionaries on "fashion" made even the word itself taboo in official circles in the highly charged ideological atmosphere of the Cold War and the party purges of the late 1940s and early 1950s.[9] Anti-fashion East German Marxists claimed that capitalists deliberately stimulated the "unreasonable fickle moods of fashion," as Marx had called

Figure 3.1 Juxtaposition of "Ingrid" wearing two different dresses: one obtained through the textile card rationing system amidst the rubble in 1949, and the other produced in 1954, the GDR's fifth year of existence. Front cover, *Neue Berliner Illustrierte* 10 (1954) 41. (Courtesy Berliner Verlag/bpk/Gerhard Kiesling)

them in *Capital*, and used them to manipulate the masses, to create "false" needs for new clothes, and thus to increase corporate profits.[10] Leading capitalist designers such as Christian Dior "dictated" fashion and strove for "newness at any price" in order to render "the latest old and unmodern" and to awake "new needs."[11] Such charges formed an interesting echo to anti-Semitic tirades and scapegoating that had circulated in Germany since at least World War I and became especially virulent and pernicious during the Third Reich. According to these accusations, profit-seeking, capitalist Jews produced "indecently French," overpriced, immoral, "un-German" fashions.[12]

Those who objected to giving fashion a place in socialism elaborated a familiar narrative both inside and outside socialist and communist circles that cast women as passive, malleable objects of the capitalist market, as "slaves to fashion."[13] Until the late 1960s, most East Germans considered women the primary consumers of fashion, which itself became mystified and reified through its personification as an arbitrary, fickle, and impulsive woman.[14] In the words of one contemporary, "it can't be prevented that Mrs Fashion [*Frau Mode*] is a downright moody lady."[15] Even those who argued that fashion, by allowing women to appear always new and different, was their great "ally" and "servant" admitted that women's weaknesses and enthusiasm for the seductive powers of fashion occasionally undermined work discipline and productivity.[16] Anti-fashion functionaries posited that a combination of the advancement of production and capitalists' competition for customers artificially accelerated an otherwise natural process of gradual stylistic change.[17]

Many of those who rejected "fashion" as a capitalist, bourgeois invention instead celebrated the proletariat as representatives of the true interests of the

Figure 3.2 Work clothes for female farmers designed by the Institute for Clothing Culture in 1955. Marianne Schlegel, "Praktisch und doch ansprechend. Das Arbeitskleid unserer Bäuerin. 40 Modelle des Instituts für Bekleidungskultur diskutiert und bejaht," *Die Bekleidung* 2 (1955) 1: 26.

German nation. Encapsulated in the term *"Proletkult"* (cult of proletarianism), this broad strand of nationalist claims glorified "timeless" proletarian and rural forms, such as "good, solid" overalls, aprons, and dirndls, worn by stocky women performing manual labor or confidently standing with their hands on their hips, a typically working-class posture (back cover and Figure 3.2).[18] The embodiment of a vision of Germanness rooted in work, these women spent rare leisure time in self-made dirndls, which were based on folk costumes and could be made out of old scraps of material (Figure 3.3). Such "fashionable" work clothes were meant to encourage joyfulness at work while fulfilling "practical" purposes. A combination

Figure 3.3 A dirndl. "Das Dirndl," *Die Bekleidung* 1 (1954) 2: 13.

of the SED's emphasis on "culture" (*Kultur*), the regime's claims to represent the German nation, and the politically privileged status of rural workers in the GDR during the highly controversial efforts to collectivize farms in the early 1950s led state clothing designers to place special emphasis on the use of "motives of folk art stemming from cultural heritage for the development of so-called traditional costumes [*Trachtenkleider*]."[19] Symbolizing the "timeless" dirndl's opposition to volatile urban fashions, women wearing dirndls were portrayed either in a nondescript indoor setting or out in a country field, but not on city streets. This was a very selective interpretation of the style. East Germans simply ignored both the dirndl's striking continuity with officially propagated women's clothing under National Socialism and its adoption by haute couture designers during the late 1930s and World War II.[20] The denial of the dirndl's recent history allowed its advocates to portray it, along with overalls and aprons, as the embodiment of a socialist "clothing culture" (*Bekleidungskultur*) in the "first workers' and peasants' state on German soil."

But *Proletkult* had a limited appeal, even in most official circles. Proletarian and rural work clothes and folk costumes may have symbolized the regime's celebration of work in the present but proved inappropriate for embodying modernity and visualizing socialism's promises of future affluence. *Proletkult* gradually gave way to the fundamental social conservatism of bourgeois values by the mid-1950s, as expressed in official, gendered discourses on "culture" and "good taste." In the terms of contemporaries, the new socialist woman was to subscribe to the rules of *Herr Geschmack*, Mr Taste, in order to resist the arbitrary moods of *Frau Mode*, Mrs Fashion, which allegedly were dictated by Western, capitalist designers.[21] The new woman thereby helped to cultivate "clothing culture," which stood in opposition to ephemeral "fashions" and drew on "the great heritage of good taste that has been accumulating for centuries" that included classic figures of German culture such as Dürer, Holbein, Menzel, Goethe, Schiller, and Beethoven.[22]

The preservation and promotion of "culture" was one of the GDR's foundational myths and stood at the heart of the SED's understanding of the civilizing mission of the new socialist society – a "society of culture" (*Kulturgesellschaft*), as Dietrich Mühlberg has termed it – which combined the promotion of bourgeois "high culture" with the impulse to counteract the degenerative influences of capitalist mass consumer culture.[23] "Clothing culture" was just one of a slew of other "cultures" – including "retail culture" (*Verkaufskultur*), "housing culture" (*Wohnkultur*), and "transportation culture" (*Reisekultur*).[24] The SED certainly must have derived much of this terminology from the promotion of "culturedness" in retail trade in the Soviet Union.[25] The push for "culture" in the realm of clothing found institutional expression in the founding of the Institute for Clothing Culture (Institut für Bekleidungskultur) in Berlin in late 1952, which was charged with the task of "promoting a clothing culture connected to our national cultural heritage."[26]

The official privileging of high culture, however, created continual tensions and contradictions in an explicitly anti-bourgeois, socialist state. East German workers were to "storm the heights of culture," in the words of a ubiquitous SED slogan, but only in order to take the place of the former bourgeois occupants, not to make any changes in substance or form. The tension between proletarian and rural role models on the one hand and urban bourgeois norms on the other found expression in schizophrenic fashion shows that often started with "female farmers" (*Bäuerinnen*) in work clothes and dirndls and ended with "working women" (*berufstätige Frauen*) modeling chic suits and extravagant evening apparel.[27] Another source of tensions and contradictions was the fact that official East German notions of good taste were virtually identical to dominant norms found in West Germany at the time, as seen in the dozens of best-selling manuals on good manners (*Benimmbücher*) in both Germanys.[28]

The dominant definition of "good taste" in both Germanys stressed the "timeless" and "classic" values of moderation, simplicity, practicality, and wearing apparel appropriate to the occasion as well as one's age and body type. These aesthetic preferences and cultural biases supported the SED's economic goals and helped make a virtue out of the realities of the GDR's shortage economy. "The commandment of our time," *Die Frau von heute* proclaimed in 1946, was "few clothes – but the right ones."[29] Officials emphasized the "timelessness" of good taste in order to encourage slow, gradual change in styles, colors, and types of apparel and thus match industry's production needs and capabilities. Moderation meant "well-tempered" forms and colors and abstinence from "breath-taking extravagances and daring fashion stupidities."[30] Simplicity was the key to "elegance," which official literature touted as one of the most desirable characteristics a woman could possess.[31] Official propaganda used this emphasis on moderation and thrift to claim that in socialism good taste provided the basis for a truly democratic society by counteracting the bourgeois and capitalist proclivity for conspicuous consumption. Socialism allegedly had rendered void the old equation of good clothing with wealth and status and instead established good taste as a truly democratic standard accessible to all.[32] By the end of the 1950s, official disapproval of the proverb "clothes make the man" summarized the constructed opposition between socialist respectability and capitalist decadence and conspicuous consumption.[33]

In the context of East Germany's planned economy, one of the biggest problems surrounding the issue of mutable styles was the common assumption that "one cannot plan fashion."[34] Signifying unbridled, irrational, uncontrollable feminine desires that defied regulation and rationalization, *Frau Mode*'s whims directly undermined state socialism's drive toward planning the economy and steering societal development through well-ordered and predictable production and consumption. Paradoxically, the propagation of East German designs was itself supposed to counteract the disruptive forces of fashion. By exhibiting role models for East

Germans to emulate, the media theoretically would contribute to the cultivation (*Erziehung*) of "good taste" and "socialist consumer habits," which in turn would guide, domesticate, and channel consumers' – and especially women's – desires and thus help to harmonize production and consumption, supply and demand. Such attempts to define and control socially acceptable tastes fit into a familiar pattern – not specific to the GDR or other Soviet-type societies – of the exercise of power by politically and culturally dominant groups.[35] East German officials nevertheless claimed that, removed from their function under capitalism as instruments for the creation of "false needs," newspapers, magazines, and fashion shows under socialism served as democratic forums for the collection of feedback from educated consumers, allowing "women themselves [to] choose their fashion!"[36]

The attempt to cultivate good taste through the media and fashion shows often involved the presentation of images of "false" or "tasteless" fashions – especially Western ones – as a foil for "correct" styles. Under titles such as "Like this or like that?" (*So oder so?*), these shows sometimes were enlisted in the battle against "American cultural barbarism."[37] For instance, an article in the newspaper for youth *Junge Welt* in 1958 juxtaposed two pictures of the same young couple taken during an educational fashion show. In the first photo they are dressed "according to their own taste"; the girl, with her hair pulled up and back, wears a blouse and pleated skirt and carries a handbag while the boy is dressed in a suit and tie. In the other photo, labeled "Texas-Billy Masquerade," the girl sassily plays with her long, frizzy hair and wears a tight-fitting white T-shirt and equally tight jeans, while the boy wears pants that are rolled up well above his ankles. According to the sartorial and body idioms of the 1950s their clothes and stances suggest rebelliousness and premature sexuality. The article claimed that "small squads" dressed in similar attire stood every evening on the Petersstraße in Leipzig: "The boys in jeans with skull-and-crossbones medallions and blaring radios, the girls in skin-tight tops [*Angströhren*] with tousled hair, clumsily garishly made up." These youth allegedly inspired the local Free German Youth group to put on a fashion show featuring the "Texas-Billy" parody in order to "put a mirror in front of them [and] show [them] how dumb and silly they look." The show's "practical, comfortable, modern, and tasteful" clothing would "demonstrate to them how one can leave a better impression on one's environment" through "fashionable clothing."[38] The article typifies official attempts to use "educational fashion shows" to contrast a supposed minority of East Germans whose clothing, mentalities, and behavior were still corrupted by capitalism with the alleged majority of GDR citizens who espoused "healthy" tastes.[39]

But as the previous chapter demonstrates, the GDR's textile and garment industry and its wholesale and retail trade organizations did not, could not, and had little or no incentive to produce "tasteful" apparel in sufficient numbers. The organization and logic of the GDR's industry and trade ran counter to the party's goal of producing and selling goods worthy of socialism's consumer utopia. The appearance of apparel in stores resulted from industry and trade officials' economic concerns and tastes, not from centrally propagated images, displays, or guidelines. The often complete lack of coordination among planners, producers, wholesalers, retailers, advertisers, and the media resulted in countless advertisements for goods that were unavailable in stores. Theories, promises, diatribes, and advertisements could not provide a basis of legitimacy and a source of motivation for the construction of socialism – the SED had to offer a concrete, positive, and distinct alternative to Western goods.

Socialist Haute Couture

Continuing the shift toward modern, urban ideals and symbols of affluence, in late 1956 the Institute for Clothing Culture began to turn its focus from work clothes and daily wear to apparel "in haute couture character" (Figure 3.4). The Institute signalled this move in 1957 by changing its name to the German Fashion Institute

Figure 3.4 A dress designed by the Institute for Clothing Culture. "Sportliche Eleganz," *Sibylle* 1 (1956) 2: 37. (Photo: Kurt Kümpfel)

(Deutsches Modeinstitut).[40] Although it may seem antithetical to the egalitarian claims of Marxist–Leninist ideology, the propagation of certain haute couture designs fit perfectly into dominant ideas about cultivating the socialist personality and good taste through a process of trickle-down cultural dissemination. In the eyes of both socialists and capitalists, (Parisian) haute couture represented the peak of a fashion pyramid from which "inspirations" spread downward and outward, reaching ever broader geographical and socio-economic segments of the population as it trickled down and was replicated in simplified, mass-produced forms.[41] This scheme also was in tune with party leaders' elitist and paternalistic conceptions of education (*Erziehung*), their mistrust of mass culture and celebration of high culture, and their goal of planning mass-production well in advance. Just as in the West, the media ideally would publicize a few exclusive designs which were either hand-made or produced in small series by specialized factories. These "fashionable forerunners," "test models," and "custom ready-to-wear apparel" would be expensive but provide feedback on the models' resonance among consumers and simultaneously stimulate demand for them.[42] This would give the textile and garment industries enough time to mass-produce simpler, less expensive versions of the original models during the following year.[43] East German officials partly justified this hierarchical structure by correctly observing that the new postwar social and economic structures had forced Western haute couture to broaden its base of customers. Fashion was becoming increasingly democratized as a growing share of the profits of couture houses came from licensing agreements that put their names on thousands of mass-marketed products, from dresses to perfumes to purses.[44] By guiding and channeling tastes and serving as the basis for mass-produced models the following year, the promotion of haute couture could contribute to the regime's project of creating a relatively homogeneous, mass consumer market and facilitating the long-term planning of mass-production.

A crucial and problematic component of this project was the creation of a "new type of woman" – a "working woman" (*werktätige Frau* or *berufstätige Frau*). Many characteristics of this new type of woman formed striking similarities to the "new women" in bourgeois, social democratic, and communist circles during the interwar period in Germany and Austria. Common to all these new women was their inconsistent and ambivalent public depiction. Among the East German working woman's positive traits were self-confidence, active participation in the sphere of production and public life, financial independence, acceptance of modern technology, and adoption of moderate fashions. But just like previous new women, she had to walk a fine line and avoid the dangers of Americanization, "masculinization," cheap mass consumer culture, homogeneous superficiality, extreme fashions, and premature, exaggerated sexuality.[45]

It was vital that the socialist working woman was devoid of class differences and claimed universal appeal. Many functionaries theorized that the eventual dissolution of class and social distinctions under socialism would reinforce and increase the importance of constructions of gender and heterosexuality. As the new working woman learned to confidently represent herself and "hold her own like a man" (*ihren Mann stehen*) in the sphere of production, she threatened to destabilize gender boundaries. Most fashion functionaries therefore were quick to assure themselves and others that women's new roles and legal equality with men in society and in the sphere of production did not necessitate the loss of femininity, classical ideals of beauty, or the so-called natural order. Instead, the new working woman's apparel embodied the masculine attributes of being "practical and appropriate for daily work," but at the same time corresponded to "the woman's sense of beauty." This duality enabled the working woman to embody a universal ideal of feminine beauty: according to German Fashion Institute officials, everyone – and especially the working woman – wished "to be young and beautiful, slender and elegant."[46]

The predominant official orientation toward haute couture came under heavy fire from some functionaries and consumers who claimed that the promotion and universalistic claims of exclusive, individualistic designs were completely out of touch with the more down-to-earth tastes of the majority of East German women. Not only did such dress stand in opposition to women's new roles and rights under socialism, so the argument went, it also contradicted socialism's central egalitarian principles. In a letter to the Central Committee in 1958, the Women's Commission (Frauenkommission) of the SED's regional leadership in Frankfurt/Oder sharply criticized the German Fashion Institute for not being in tune with what it claimed were working women's true needs. It asserted that working women, young girls, and garment workers unanimously rejected the Institute's fashion line. The line was "for a few extravagant and crazy ones, but most women consider it beneath their dignity to dress like that. [...] This fashion trend does not at all correspond to our societal conditions and does not take into account that 43 percent of all women work." The Women's Commission claimed to speak for "women workers, female collective farmers, white-collar workers, [and] intellectuals" whose "life differed fundamentally from that of the past." The GDR was full of women whose main concern was work, both outside and inside the home, and who had little patience for the frivolities of high fashion, the Commission claimed. "It is not our thing to sit for hours in the afternoon over a little cup of tea in order to gossip about the most eccentric models and novelties. We would detest such a life. We pitch in and get down to business in order to fulfill our societal duties, sharing equal rights with men." A fashion institute, the Commission continued, should advise women how to dress "simply yet elegantly corresponding to a woman's dignity" in her profession, as a woman, and as a mother. In sum, the Institute's staff had "no connection" to the women of the GDR.[47]

The press resounded with calls for the Institute and the other leading producers of fashionable apparel in the GDR to "finally show something that we can really put on, what suits us, our lifestyle and habits."[48] The Institute allegedly lacked "direct contact to the people" and was "bloodless," in part because it did not have "customers"; that is, it did not produce models for paying customers but rather simply in order to abstractly "lead" and "inspire" industry and consumers' tastes.[49] Many insisted that the Institute's mission was not to show that the GDR could make "high fashion," but rather to benefit all women.[50] *Neues Deutschland*'s fashion correspondent Inge Kertzscher summed up these tensions by asking whether the Institute and the GDR's industry should produce "runway-fashion or pretty dresses for everyone."[51]

The media and popular culture encouraged the common myth of a battle of representatives of the "people's taste" against the GDR's elites in industry, trade, party, and state. In *Messeschlager Gisela*, a controversial musical that the regime banned only a few weeks after its debut in 1960, Gisela, a young, idealistic woman fresh out of school, designs an eponymous model "for every woman," which instantly gains the nearly unanimous approval of her colleagues in the textile factory VEB Berliner Schick. Robert Kuckuck, the factory's director, rejects her design, however, in favor of the ridiculously exaggerated "Melon" model, the "inspiration" for which he received during a trip to Paris.[52] At the musical's climax, Kuckuck's "Melon," modeled by his Western-oriented, uncouth secretary, flops and "Gisela" triumphs at the Leipzig Trade Fare's international fashion show, a clear victory for moderate "good taste" that suits and is affordable for "every woman" over "tasteless," Western, elitist decadence.

Fashion for "Stronger Women" as "Socialist Fashion"?

Fashion functionaries and the East German media also constructed hierarchies of women's bodies. Starting in the early 1950s, officials propagated models designed expressly for "stronger" (*stärker*), "full-figured" (*vollschlank*), or "chubby" (*mollig*) women (Figure 3.5). Pictures of the models populated special spreads in every consumer magazine that covered fashion; several magazines even published special issues devoted solely to the needs of this supposedly distinct group of consumers. Consistent with dominant conceptions of "good taste" that stressed dressing according to one's "body type," the media sought to teach all women how to accentuate their bodies' "positive" characteristics while hiding the "disadvantageous" ones.[53] Officials felt obligated to educate the "woman with a stronger figure" who unfortunately bought "a dress made of fabric with large flowers because she thought that the same dress was pretty on her well-shaped friend."[54] While "full-figured" women had to "learn to abstain from the enchanting wide skirts," they were reminded that "there is no reason for mourning," because "good taste, creativity, and some initiative of one's own let also a chubby figure appear flattering and elegant."[55]

Figure 3.5 A dress for the "stronger woman" in 1960: model number 110 "Morning" ("Vormittage"). (Courtesy Stiftung Stadtmuseum Berlin, Modearchiv; photo: DMI – Sitte; photo reproduction: Hans-Joachim Bartsch)

As calls for a distinct "socialist fashion" became louder at the end of the 1950s, fashion functionaries began to argue that special models for "stronger women" distinguished the aesthetic content and underlying role models of clothing in socialism from those in capitalism. In contrast to capitalism's objectification of women and its worship of the young and slender female body, under socialism all women supposedly enjoyed a right to clothing appropriate to their bodies.[56] However, despite the official insistence that "to be round is no misfortune," and that "the ideal of beauty of the socialist person does not allow itself to be influenced by measurements in centimeters and body weight," functionaries stressed that "of course the special attention to clothing for the stronger woman will not create an attitude that propagates or justifies an unaesthetic bodily fullness."[57] Implicitly and often explicitly, the "normal" or "ideal" body remained thin, even under socialism.[58] As suggested by mottoes like "full-figured, yet nevertheless chic," special designs for heavy-set women aimed to create optical illusions – for example, by using vertical stripes – in order to emulate the still reigning ideal of slenderness.[59] Teaching women "how one with a chubby figure can have a refined, fashionable appearance without great luxury" implied that "chubby figures" were inherently unrefined (*ungepflegt*) and needed to be disguised.[60] Institute officials and others even advocated using tight-fitting underwear to "make the figure appear firmer and skinnier."[61] Indeed, the "stronger women" that appeared in the media and advertisements often seemed to be only slightly heavier than the models with Twiggy-like figures.

Rather than contributing to the emancipation of women from the strictures of narrow ideals of beauty and desirableness, the East German media and fashion shows reinforced the social stigma attached to being overweight. The women who modeled the special designs were almost all middle-aged, despite the fact that half of the East German women with allegedly "stronger figures" were under 40.[62] When designs for overweight women appeared in fashion shows and magazine spreads, the announcer or the text usually explicitly differentiated them from the "normal" ones worn by younger, thinner women. While women with slender figures "enjoyed" wearing their clothes and were the subject of desirous male gazes, "stronger women" at best were consoled that they, too, could be "fashion-able" and "refined" (*gepflegt*) with a little extra effort. Such practices made the "stronger" female body the exception and underscored East Germans' subscription to the same modes of visual pleasure as in Western Europe.

By the end of the 1960s, most official propaganda no longer pretended that "fashion today is for all age groups and figures" and that "the only thing that matters is to choose with reflection and taste."[63] Consumer magazines increasingly reminded the "stronger woman" of the only socially acceptable solution to her dilemma: "Resolve starting tomorrow to try a little more intensively and deliber-ately to reduce your weight by a few pounds, which separate you from the general ideal of beauty."[64] Since "the fashionable ideal image remains slim," the only way to match it was to lose weight: "As long as one has a few too many pounds, one must wear what is advantageous for the figure."[65] While young, slender women were free to follow the latest, changing fashions, overweight and older women had to conform to certain stigmatized and unchanging rules – such as wearing vertical rather than horizontal stripes and avoiding broad belts.

Many women resisted official efforts at education and entreaties to conform to the "rules" of dressing according to one's "body type." An Institute official bemoaned in 1959 that "private tailors confirm that precisely the stronger women choose models from the fashion magazines that are to be worn exclusively by slim figures." These heavy-set women "do not like to let themselves be persuaded and convinced that such a model is not suitable for them."[66] Many larger women instead insisted that their body types be included among the propagated norms. "I, too, despite my somewhat stronger figure, would like to be modernly dressed (I am 19 years old, 1.65 meters tall, and weigh 73 kilograms)," wrote Renate M. to the editors of the television show *Prisma* in 1968. "One must also consider that not all girls are slender like those, for instance, that [East] German Television showed yesterday as models. Would it not also be advantageous and more correct if one occasionally also took into account the stronger women and girls? That would certainly find a great resonance among the population!"[67] Fashion-conscious women did not want to seem like middle-aged overweight women trying to look thin, but rather like the svelte, young models publicized by the media.

While dogmatic party officials insisted on the "educational" role of images of clothing, designers and organizers of fashion shows realized that such displays served more as expressions of dreams and desires than vehicles for teaching women rational consumption habits and "rules" for dressing according to one's "body type." Two cartoons in the satirical magazine *Eulenspiegel* conveyed the insincerity and ultimate failure of official efforts to make all body types acceptable and even desirable. In one drawing a heavy-set woman sits at the dinner table eating a piece of cake and gazes longingly at a fashionable dress hanging on the door that is obviously too small for her.[68] In the other, a woman attending a fashion show looks at the pant-suit being modeled by a "full-figured" woman and comments, "A delightful model. Too bad that I'm not so fat!"[69] Envy of larger women was as rare in the GDR as it was in the West – the ideal body was virtually identical on both sides of the Cold War divide. Despite the SED's conflicted attempts to establish special models for "stronger women" as a unique aspect of "socialist" fashion, here too the SED failed to create a desirable alternative to capitalist norms.

Official efforts to promote and sell special models for "stronger women" also encountered considerable obstacles on the supply side. Despite extensive efforts to facilitate the industrial production of "special" sizes, the GDR's garment industry and retail trade had significant disincentives to produce and distribute special models, as the previous chapter explains. As was the case with haute couture garments, the state propagated models for "stronger women" at significant expense, while industry refused to produce the models because they were too costly. Despite the state's promises and the plethora of propaganda for haute couture and clothes for larger women, the actual articles were very hard to find, a situation all too typical of East Germany's consumer culture in general.

Confronting and Competing with Western Europe

The failure of the promotion of fashion for "stronger women" was just one aspect of the GDR's larger and equally ambiguous confrontation with Western fashion. East German functionaries stood before a difficult conundrum. They hoped to create "socialist fashion" as a distinct, independent alternative and yet admitted that West European haute couture had long exerted a dominant, transnational influence on "international fashion" and continued to do so.[70] This dilemma was similar in many ways to the Nazi regime's failed attempts to define and propagate "German fashion" despite the continuation of Germans' love-hate relationship with French fashion and its cultural and economic influences that dated to at least the eighteenth century.[71] Just as in other Soviet-bloc countries, East German officials responsible for the GDR's official fashion line used West European fashion as their lodestar and traveled several times a year to Paris, Milan, Düsseldorf, and other capitalist fashion centers to attend haute couture shows and industrial exhibitions, justifying their trips by claiming that they could not afford to wait for months until the latest fashions and their imitations appeared in Western magazines.[72] Except for a pause from 1962 to 1965, trips to the West continued until the end of the GDR but became increasingly infrequent as Western currency became harder to obtain.[73]

The corollary of these attitudes and practices was the both official and unofficial goal, established by the mid-1950s, of "matching the rhythm of," "keeping up with," and "reacting quickly to" international fashion.[74] The East German textile and garment industries failed to achieve this goal, however, and criticism that fashion in the GDR "lagged behind international fashion" by at least one to two years littered East German newspapers and official speeches throughout the 1950s and 1960s.[75] The GDR seemed destined, in the words of two fashion functionaries, to be forever "in the tow of capitalist fashion happenings."[76]

The general acceptance of West European high fashion as the standard of a modern aesthetics of affluence presented the SED with the puzzle of how "socialist" fashion could "keep up with" and even influence "international fashion" from the position of an understudy that constantly borrowed from it. East German officials attempted a tricky and often contradictory balancing act between criticizing certain "capitalist" designs and promoting others. "Socialist fashion" essentially consisted of accepting Western Europe's fundamental leadership, producing variations of "moderate" and "tasteful" Western designs, and nominally rejecting "extremes" and "exaggerations" that allegedly resulted from capitalists' competition for profits.[77]

One of the prime venues for official East German confrontations with capitalist fashion was the annual International Clothing Contest, renamed the International Fashion Congress in 1957. Initiated by the GDR and Czechoslovakia in 1950 and held in a different Soviet-bloc country each year starting in 1955, the contests featured a fashion show during which a technical and an aesthetic jury evaluated scores of models designed by the central fashion institute of each country (Figure 3.6).[78] Through prominent coverage of the contests in the East German media, officials hoped to use the contest as a counterweight to capitalist haute couture shows. In the eyes of many East German officials the shows provided an important forum for the visual and material competition between socialism and capitalism,

Figure 3.6 Models from Czechoslovakia, Poland, the GDR, Hungary, and Romania (left to right) at the Sixth International Clothing Contest in Berlin in 1955. Katja Selbmann, "Treffpunkt Warschau," *Die Bekleidung* 3 (1956) 2: 4.

especially after the shows became integrated into the formal structures of the Council for Mutual Economic Assistance (CMEA or COMECON) in 1960.[79] East German officials even brought socialist and capitalist models together on the same runway at the biannual trade fair in Leipzig starting at the end of the 1950s.[80] The direct juxtaposition of similar models from capitalist and socialist countries, however, only reinforced the common prejudice that socialist designs could perhaps "catch up to" and "match" but never surpass or inspire West European ones.

Rather than presenting a distinct alternative to West European haute couture, these gatherings served primarily as an opportunity for the socialist countries to collectively look to the West and "critically" adopt only "the best" elements to fit each of their "national" circumstances while looking for "confirmation" that their designs had a "connection" to "international" fashion.[81] In reality, designs from Soviet-bloc countries were virtually indistinguishable from those of Western, capitalist ones. While some may have paid lip service to an alleged "Marxist–Leninist aesthetic," if it existed, it certainly did not possess any characteristics that unmistakably differentiated it from Western fashion. In fact, East German fashion functionaries themselves sometimes boasted that their models "in no way deviated from the colors and designs of the fashionable offerings of other [Western] countries."[82] Although official propaganda attempted to differentiate the "open" and "cooperative" proceedings of socialist fashion congresses from the cutthroat competition and fashion spies lurking at capitalist haute couture shows, the socialist countries continued the traditional format of such displays, including runway etiquette, orchestral accompaniment, and a male announcer.[83]

East Germany's adoption and superficial modification of modern, Western visual and cultural symbols found further expression in the official promotion of Heinz Bormann as the face of East German fashion. Originally the owner of a private garment factory in Magdeburg, Bormann accepted partial state ownership in October 1956 and quickly became a highly publicized role model for the new category of half-state-owned enterprises. By heavily promoting Bormann, the SED could flaunt, both at home and abroad, socialism's achievements and capabilities, claim that the GDR could match the West on the runways of haute couture shows, and benefit economically from the firm's exports.[84] Continuing a prewar tradition of celebrating the genius of individual designers who owned firms, the media emphasized Bormann's personality and personal leadership of his firm and explicitly compared him to top West European designers. As one radio program declared, "in the GDR, Mr Bormann is what Dior is in Paris and Schubert in Italy."[85] But such claims did not sit well with many party leaders, who periodically objected that Bormann's fashion shows were far too expensive and "did not work to steer and orient demand" toward products that corresponded to "our macro-economic possibilities" and "our socialist attitude toward life," but rather gave a "false orientation toward Western fashion trends" and "awoke demand for so-called 'Haute Couture' (Paris)."[86] To make matters worse, the East German media, having been given a green light to promote Bormann, sometimes went beyond the boundaries implicitly intended by party leaders. For instance, Central Committee functionaries severely criticized an article in the magazine *Freie Welt* entitled "Men with Millions" that dubbed Bormann "The Red Dior" and compared his lifestyle – including a large house, antique furniture, and old paintings – to that of the West German designer Günther Sachs.[87]

In July 1958 the emphasis on "keeping up" with "international fashion" seemed to find at least indirect support at the highest levels of the party and state with the SED's declaration of the ambitious goals of the "chief economic task," which stated that the GDR would surpass the FRG in per-capita consumption of all important consumer goods and foodstuffs by 1961. This orientation encouraged many East German officials and members of the media to advocate frequent changes in styles and to emphasize "new" designs and types of clothing, in direct contradiction with previously articulated ideals of socialist production.[88] This in turn led to a backlash among more conservative functionaries, who warned that many officials responsible for fashion in the GDR were making Parisian modes into a "fetish" and called for a more critical and systematic evaluation of Western fashion.[89]

By 1959 the celebration and blatant imitation of Western fashion had gone too far for the tastes of most top party leaders, who feared that the GDR was trapped in a fatal, never-ending cycle of trying to "catch up" to Western fashion. "When pointed shoes are the fashion in Italy," SED General Secretary Walter Ulbricht declared, "we make propaganda for pointed shoes one year later. Meanwhile, in Italy or France broad shoes are already the fashion. We just can't keep up with the running behind!"[90] The GDR had to figure out "how one gets away from the 'running after' of fashion."[91] As hundreds of thousands of East Germans continued to resettle in the West and the German Cold War conflict intensified in 1960/1961, many officials called for the GDR to take the offensive and actively create and shape new and distinct fashions rather than simply react to Western trends.[92] Institute officials admitted in 1961 that in the "evaluation of international fashion there exist no ground rules, no systematization, no concrete instructions where a party-line [*parteilich*] evaluation begins and where it ends."[93] In that same year, Ulbricht sarcastically asked, "When in the West someone coughs, do all our fashion designers catch a cold? When they [the West] go for the color of asphalt, we also come out with asphalt a year later [...] We must not ogle the Kurfürsten-damm [the famous shopping avenue in West Berlin] so much. That is decidedly unhealthy."[94]

The same sorts of aesthetic preferences and consumerist norms that had fallen under the cultivation of "clothing culture" now became phrased in calls for the creation of "socialist fashion."[95] However, despite East German officials' claims that the construction of the Wall offered better conditions for the establishment of the GDR's own fashion line, no new initiatives were undertaken and the situation remained essentially unchanged.[96] Officials often admitted that stores' offerings "did not reflect comprehensively enough a distinct conception and a distinct line" and that the GDR's designs at the Fashion Congress did not support claims that "sooner or later" a "divergence" between Western and East German designs would develop.[97] By the mid-1960s, calls for "a critical evaluation" of capitalist fashion according to the will of the Party (*Parteilichkeit*) had become so rehearsed that they lost credibility.[98] Officials had to perform self-contradictory verbal gymnastics in order to explain the GDR's unwanted but unavoidable connection with and dependence on Western fashion.[99] The criticism of the "extremes" of Western fashions became more pro forma and the emulation and copying of capitalist designs more blatant.[100] "Ideological ambiguities" about "Marxist aesthetics" and Western fashions continued to saturate official institutions for the rest of the GDR.[101] Reality remained, in the words of an Institute official, that Western "inspirations lead to copying."[102] Fashion functionaries pushed the goal of creating "socialist fashion" farther and farther into the future. In 1967 Institute officials themselves predicted that a socialist "clothing style will not be able to fully form" by 1980.[103] One of the SED's perennial problems in the realm of fashion, as market researchers noted in 1978, was that "fashion phenomena develop internationally, and the GDR does not belong to the fashion-determining countries."[104]

The official practice of selectively adopting and adapting fashions from the West to fit circumstances in the GDR precluded the creation of an entirely independent alternative. Unable to create independent and unique aesthetics and symbolic measures of prosperity, East German officials were left only to react to Western fashions, criticizing them and proposing more "moderate" East German variations. "Socialist" and "capitalist" fashion shared the fundamentals of a symbolic language that the West undeniably controlled.

Rationalizing and Standardizing Fashion

The push for socialist fashion had not only aesthetic but also technological and economic dimensions. The growing emphasis on the "scientific–technological revolution" (*wissenschaftlich–technische Revolution*) beginning in the late 1950s encouraged a shift in the efforts to shape fashion and consumption from "cultural–educational" approaches toward scientific and economic techniques: science was to help *Herr Geschmack* domesticate *Frau Mode*.[105]

Throughout most of the 1950s, many officials and the media had suggested that the solution to the perennial conflict between economic exigencies and fashion was primarily a matter of espousing the correct ideology and working together. Given enough will power and the right attitude, industry supposedly could find ways to produce high-quality, fashionable apparel. *Modell Bianka*, a feature-length film released in 1951 by the GDR's state-run film studio DEFA, provides a rich example of this sort of proposed solution.[106] The film tells the story of Jochen Rauhut, a clothing designer at the garment factory "VEB Saxonia" somewhere in Saxony who has designed two women's models: "Bianka" (an "elegant *Verwandlungskleid*," a dress that can take on numerous forms) and "Ursel" (a *Kostüm* or suit). But Jochen's genius initially appears to be condemned to remain in the form of sketches, for the head of the cutting division and the bookkeeper, both men, insist on reducing the required amount of material by 20 percent. Jochen objects that "exactly the few centimeters that you want to cut away here, precisely they make the line!" But the final word comes from the factory manager, who claims that Jochen's two designs are "much too expensive" and "not appropriate for large series" and insists that Saxonia sticks to its "solid, sturdy production," which is suitable for mass production and allegedly guaranteed to sell well. Unwilling to compromise his artistic vision, Jochen refuses to accept any changes to his design. In a moment of drunken despair during a trip to Berlin, Jochen gives his sketches to a man whom he just met in a bar and who says that his financee would love to make the models for herself. The stranger, however, works for the Berlin garment factory VEB Berolina and gives the sketches to his firm's director, Ursel, and head tailor, Hilde. Both women instantly fall in love with the designs and hand tailor them for themselves, since they cannot be put into production without knowing their designer. As luck would have it, Jochen and his colleagues from Saxonia meet Ursel, Hilde, and their colleagues from Berolina during a ski trip at a union vacation facility. After overcoming feelings of mistrust and a series of mishaps, Berolina manufactures and showcases Jochen's models at the fashion show of the Leipzig fall trade fair without explaining how they were suitable for industrial mass production. The female managers of Berolina, in contrast to the male managers of Saxonia, do not allow purely economic calculations to prevent the fulfillment of artistic expression and consumerist desires. At several points, various characters explicitly explain the film's morale: the socialist form of "competition with" (*Wettbewerb mit*) other firms is clearly superior to the old form of "competition against" (*Konkurrenz gegen*) other enterprises under capitalism. The film taught that socialist competition, through encouraging the collaboration of both men and women and Saxons and Berliners, could overcome the natural antagonism between male industrial mass production and female fashion.[107]

By the end of the 1950s, party leaders hoped to scientifically control fashion in order to make it change "according to plan" and facilitate the harmonization of consumption and production. But the SED encountered resistance to these initiatives both within official institutions and among consumers. Party leaders accused fashion functionaries of neglecting "the laws of technical discipline like design and technology" and isolating themselves in the ephemeral, subjective world of aesthetics away from the practical, everyday world of planning, production, and distribution.[108] At the same time, the SED had to fight against the common opinion "that fashion does not allow itself to be brought into harmony with the economy, especially with standardization."[109] At the heart of the discourse on the "scientific" analysis of fashion and its industrial realization was the perennial conflict over the question of how to harmonize production on the one hand and consumers' needs and wishes on the other.[110] Consumers' dynamic needs, wishes, and demands – as embodied in fashion – seemed to be always at odds with available raw materials, productive capacities, and the drive toward increasing productivity of the GDR's industry.

While many officials insisted that fashion follow economics, others struggled to demonstrate various ways in which fashion was compatible with the exigencies of production.[111] Grete Wittkowski, a high-ranking party and state official responsible for issues of consumption, insisted that textile production "must more quickly and flexibly adjust itself" to "the changed demand-wishes" (*Bedarfswünschen*) that shifted even during the course of a year.[112] Many criticized the widespread exclusion of fashion from the planning of production and argued that the traditional conflict between fashion and the drive for rational production did not have to be a zero-sum game.[113] Fashion functionaries instead proposed a variety of "scientific" solutions to the conflict between industry's and consumer's demands. Many used the language of social science and economics to simply recast old, unsystematic ideas and stereotypes as "laws" (*Gesetzmäßigkeiten*) of fashion and aesthetics.[114] Reviving an idea that had enjoyed some popularity in Europe and the United States in the 1930s, some officials at the Fashion Institute claimed to have identified predictable "cycles" of styles, which could be used to improve economic performance.[115]

Other officials combined elements of mass psychology and economics in proposals to exploit fashion's characteristics as a mass phenomenon.[116] State and party functionaries admitted that capitalists better understood that low prices of fashionable apparel for the masses could cause a snowball effect and serve to concentrate demand, coordinate industry and trade, and increase productivity.[117] By focusing demand and production on a relatively small number of designs within "very specific time periods," fashion as a "mass phenomenon" (*Massenerscheinung*) offered "favorable prerequisites" for long, uninterrupted production series, standardization, reduction of the number of assortments produced by individual factories, specialization of factories, and the general rationalization of production. This would contribute toward increased work productivity, lowered costs, improved technical quality, and higher profitability.[118] By the mid-1960s, most party and state officials acknowledged that fashion did not contradict "a rational model of consumption in socialism" but rather was "necessary, since it is the first prerequisite for the rational production of consumer goods (especially in the clothing sector)."[119]

Essential to the exploitation of fashion as a mass phenomenon, according to German Fashion Institute officials, was the centrally designed and propagated "Fashion Line of the GDR" (*Modelinie der DDR*), which was to shape consumers' tastes and demands and prepare them for items that would appear soon in stores.[120] Newspapers, magazines, *Augenzeuge* news reports shown before films in theaters, and, by the end of the 1950s, even television programs publicized the Institute's biannual fashion lines – one for fall/winter and another for spring/summer. Thousands of publications and scores of fashion shows each year placed images of the Institute's models before the eyes of millions of East German citizens.[121]

The fashion line also was supposed to help overcome the perceived irreconcilable conflict between inflexible production and dynamic fashion. During the 1950s, the belief in the inevitability of this opposition led officials to divide models into two categories, "standard" and "fashionable."[122] While the "basic assortment" represented "the typical, relatively unchanging variety of products," "fashionable" assortments changed each season, fulfilled "individual" needs for distinction, and thus allegedly defied any sort of standardization.[123] As fashion became an increasingly "broader field of activity for individual taste" by mid-decade, officials struggled to solve the "seeming contradiction" between "fashion" and "modern industrial mass production."[124] Proposals included varying only colors and printed patterns in order to achieve "a rational limitation" of assortments and designing one "basic cut" that could yield three or more "different" models through changing or augmenting details.[125]

Partly due to prejudices about the incompatibility of fashion and mass production and partly due to the general lack of control and scientific management of the GDR's textile and garment industries during the 1950s, standardization remained largely ignored throughout the decade.[126] That slowly began to change in 1959 when the SED launched a highly publicized campaign to promote standardization in all industrial branches and to eliminate the common view that "standardization equals homogenization."[127] Officials acknowledged that there was general consensus that "fashion in socialist society may not be a homogenization but rather must be diverse" and that for personal items like clothing, the need for variety and some degree of individualization should take precedence over the drive for economic efficiency and productivity.[128] As a member of the Central Committee's Economic Council insisted in 1958, "in the GDR we all don't want to wear the same hats, to eat with the same spoons, to have the same suits, etc. Especially articles of applied art and items of taste should not all be produced uniformly, although that of course would be much more profitable."[129] Edith Baumann, a candidate of the Politburo, assured that, "we are not posing the question of the abolition of individuality."[130]

Many officials tried to assuage consumers' fears about standardization by differentiating technical devices and purely "functional" clothing on the one hand from "fashionable" products on the other. A speaker at a press conference held in conjunction with the Conference on Standardization in 1959 had "still not found anyone who had gotten upset" that the 2.5 million Volkswagen cars on the roads were homogenized, nor could he imagine that East Germans would object to standardized refrigerators, vacuum cleaners, or the fact that the GDR produced only two standardized automobiles. On the other hand, he continued, "I don't believe that there are such fools among us who would imagine offering all women standardized hats (approving laughter [from the audience]) or men standardized ties or something similar."[131] But that was precisely what many officials had in mind.

The regime's main solution to the apparent conflict between radical standardization and fashion was the "building blocks principle" (*Baukastenprinzip*), which had originated as a technique to facilitate serial production in industrial branches like construction, mechanical engineering, and electronics but soon spread to all areas of production.[132] Instead of creating entirely new designs for each new fashionable clothing article, this enabled producers to efficiently construct new models by combining a variety of standardized cuts, silhouettes, parts (such as pockets and collars), details, colors, and fashionable accessories.[133] State industrial officials explained that season after season both foreign and domestic fashion designers used only eight "basic silhouettes" but created "the most varied variations" through changing the length and small details, such as the treatment of the shoulders and collar (Figure 3.7). The standardization of clothing parts and long production runs of "classic" models would allow "even the most fashionable

Figure 3.7 Drawings intended to illustrate that standardization is possible even for women's outerwear. Christa Kirmse and Maria Landgraf, "Standardisierung auch in der schweren DOB möglich," *Die Bekleidungsindustrie* 6 (1960): 4.

production" to be executed "in modern garment factories at an industrial level with highly specialized machines," facilitating "the often rapid change of forms and a multitude of solutions that serve the satisfaction of individual taste."[134]

The German Fashion Institute's "Fashion Line of the GDR" also was to help industry and trade to hold variation within certain bounds while avoiding the appearance of uniformity or a "fashion dictate" handed down from above, as could be inferred from the term "fashion line" with its ideological and military overtones.[135] But functionaries often complained that the regime's fashion propaganda was ineffective because it was too short, superficial, haphazard, unsystematic, and decentralized.[136] Although the Institute distributed descriptions, drawings, and photographs of exemplary models of the official fashion line, each publication or author interpreted them differently and combined them with designs from various local enterprises. Retailers and producers independently created and published their own advertisements, which only further confused the public presentation of official fashions. A much more serious challenge for the Institute, however, was its lack of resources and institutional power and the impracticality of its designs.[137] The Institute's models often required materials or production processes that were either unavailable or prohibitively expensive, and industry and trade had myriad other reasons to not exert any extra effort to comply with the fashion line, as the previous chapter explains. Trade officials' refusal to adhere to the fashion line was irrelevant in any case because wholesale and retail buyers frequently had to order a large percentage of their total stock before the fashion line for the relevant year had even been published.[138]

Industrial and organizational problems were not the only obstacles to the creation and realization of a coherent and useful fashion line. The fashion system itself was changing. Styles were becoming increasingly diversified and diffuse during the 1960s and subsequent decades. In the West, haute couture's seasonal fashion lines gave way to the more fluid and varied rhythm of the ready-to-wear industry, which catered to ever smaller market niches, substyles, and subcultures. Despite East German industry's inflexibility and the growing magnitude of its serial production runs, the GDR's media largely followed the West and propagated an increasing variety of styles for particular groups of the population. Unwilling to abandon completely the idea of steering fashion changes from above, German Fashion Institute officials continued to assert that haute couture exercised a significant, although diminishing influence on mass fashions in the West, which in turn influenced East German demand.[139] Although party leaders were unwilling to legitimate the social differences implicit in these diverse styles, they acknowledged the need to increase the differentiation of clothes according to age. This acknowledgment and political motivations led the regime to establish the Youth Fashion Program (*Jugendmode Programm*) in 1967 in an attempt to create a special, isolated system of production and distribution to cater to this distinct group of consumers.[140] Despite these efforts, the rapidly diversifying fashions during the last three decades of the GDR pushed the regime ever farther away from its goal of creating, propagating, and producing a coherent and consistent fashion line.

Behind the Curtain

East German citizens ultimately judged the achievements of socialism not by officials' theories or images of consumer goods but rather by what they could actually purchase in stores. While fashion shows and media reports may have served well as a showcase for socialism, they formed a crass contrast with the reality of stores' offerings. In general the displayed models either were one-of-a-kind, handmade garments or supposedly would be produced six to twelve months later in series sizes of only 200 to 300, of which four-fifths or more would be exported. Due to the GDR's cumbersome and disconnected apparatuses of planning, production, trade, and the media, "inspirations" from the official fashion line and models on display rarely materialized on store shelves. But that did not prevent fashion functionaries from tirelessly propagating their creations in newspapers, magazines, film, television, radio, press conferences, and fashion shows.[141] The structure of the GDR's economy not only allowed but encouraged the publication of images to proceed independently of the production and distribution of actual goods.[142]

The Berlin Fashion Week illustrates many of the tensions between the regime's displays of idealized apparel and consumers' resentment of these illusions. Starting in August 1958, the biannual event was to serve a variety of political, educational, and cultural purposes.[143] The "achievement show" was intended to demonstrate the "state of development" of the GDR's state-owned garment industry, to underline the GDR's commitment to the "chief economic task," and to contribute to the recently revitalized goal of turning Berlin into a "fashion center" that could create and control "German fashion."[144] In addition to serving as "a school of good taste," the exhibition was meant to "directly politically influence the consciousness of the visitors" by presenting them with "concrete examples" of the achievements of East German industries.[145] The event also was to "establish direct contact" between production and trade on the one hand and consumers on the other, a task which included introducing all three of these groups to the Institute's official fashion line.[146]

In keeping with these tasks, the first three Fashion Weeks, in August 1958, February 1959, and September 1959, were full of educational lectures and fashion shows. Fashion designers from the state-owned women's garment factories in Berlin, from the fashion magazine *Sibylle*, and from the German Fashion Institute staffed booths at the exhibition, informed the public "how fashion comes into being from the drawing board to production output," gave individual fashion advice, and drew sketches.[147] Fashion shows with titles like "Well Dressed – In a Good Mood," "Does Your Husband Dress in a Modern Fashion?," and "The International Fashion" mixed displays of models with educational commentary and a "cultural" framework that included a "good salon-orchestra" and dancers from opera houses.[148] Supporting the event's educational goals were lectures on such topics as "Cosmetics is a Part of Fashion," "Natural Beauty Through Healthy Nutrition," "Also the Stronger Woman Can Dress Fashionably," "Small Fashionable Transformations with Great Effect," "Sport: A Requirement of Fashion," and "To Each Type the Suitable Haircut."[149] A "Youth Forum" treating the topic of "how do some of our youth dress and how could and should they dress" included a fashion show and was supplemented by a question-and-answer session with "experts' from the garment industry, the German Fashion Institute, "a well-known athlete, and a well-known actor."[150] In addition to the large, central events, smaller fashion shows were to take place in various districts throughout East Berlin and in factories during lunch breaks.[151] A central "high-class fashion ball" with 800 guests and an entrance fee of 20 DM per person was a "societal event" intended to be the week's "high point."[152]

The entries in the guest book of the fashion exhibition of the second Berlin Fashion Week in February 1959 provide detailed insights into the public's mixed and often contradictory reception of the event.[153] Reflecting a wide spectrum of tastes and expectations, visitors' overall reactions to the exhibition ranged from ecstatically positive to sarcastically negative. Not surprisingly, many judgments directly contradicted each other. While Hanke B. declared, "never have I visited such an exhibition that was constructed with so much love," Genta P. found the exhibition "loveless" in comparison to the previous year's event. A small number of visitors gave unqualified praise, such as W. Jausch, who commented, "I am really enthusiastic. Definitely an advantage and sign for the development in fashion." M. Leischke even wanted to "personally find" those who had written "negative criticisms" in order to "ask them what they accomplish in *their* profession. My opinion: 'One can no longer overlook that the GDR has a presence and can have a say in the area of fashion!'" (original emphasis). At the other extreme, several visitors expressed nothing but criticism of the models and the exhibition itself. Genta P. wrote, "the exhibition absolutely disappointed me," and joined several other visitors who resented the admission fee of 0.50 DM. Several visitors criticized the exhibition's partially improvised decor, including "makeshift bicycle lamps as additional lights," which failed to provide sufficient illumination, according to some. Echoing the well-known official endorsement of "lively, cheerful" colors under socialism, some visitors criticized the "dismal" colors of both the exhibition's decorations and models. However, none of the visitors criticized the models for being too exclusive or for not matching the tastes of the "general public."

The vast majority of visitors mixed praise of the exhibited models with often blunt criticism of the visual contrast between the idealized images and their everyday experiences of shopping. Referring to the exhibition's title, "Berlin shows what one wears," one visitor commented, "What is the meaning and purpose of this exhibition? It says that Berlin dresses as such! Unfortunately not." Other visitors were more tactful and optimistic: "This exhibition shows us what is supposed to be worn for 1959. Hopefully these charming models will also make it into [our] homes!" wrote Helger M. from Stendel. Most visitors wanted concrete information on how to immediately obtain the exhibited articles. "Where can one buy these things? That's what is of greatest interest," wrote R. Sunfer. Another visitor lamented, "The exhibited models are very pretty, but what use is that when one doesn't get to buy them." Renate J. expressed skepticism about their availability in more sarcastic tones: "It would be desirable if the models would make it into production: and that hopefully before 1965."[154] Undertones of resentment saturated many comments that stressed the frustration of seeing the models in the exhibition but not in stores: Ilse N. entreated, "Please take care for us that all the beautiful things that are to be seen here also are really to be had in the stores for us." Closely following concerns about the availability of the displayed items were questions about their prices. Behind such questions was the common assumption, generally quite correct, that apparel on display without a price tag was expensive.

Another cluster of complaints concerned the lack of variety and differentiation of the displayed models. Sarcastically referring to the exhibition's title, F. Gross joined others in criticizing the limited number of assortments on display and the small exhibition space. A few visitors complained that the exhibition seemed exclusively oriented toward young, thin women. A certain "Kleimann" asked simply, "Does fashion exist *only* for young people?" (original emphasis). Those who described themselves as belonging to a certain demographic group, including "chubby," "elderly," and "smaller" women, expressed feelings of neglect. "Once again I'm very disappointed," wrote Gisela B. from Berlin, "where are the models for the stronger lady? I am still young and would like also to be nicely dressed. When will one think for once of us." Another visitor lamented, "One can marvel at very beautiful things here. But where again are we chubby ones? How often, almost always we get to hear: unfortunately only up to size 42." M. Gubler added, "Unfortunately in this exhibition one did not at all consider that there are also older ladies who like to dress well in the theater, in the afternoon, and also on the job." Mixing criticism of the exclusion of women who did not match the ideal young, slender figure with her frustrating everyday experiences of shopping, E. Becher wrote, "Please think of the older stronger women who would like to look nice on every occasion; the sizes 42, 44 are always there but 46, 48 are missing." But the exhibition also did not satisfy all of the young visitors. "Why wasn't more thought given to male youths?" asked L. Neumann. "They don't only wear suits."

Partially in response to the criticisms of the disparity between the exhibited models and stores' actual offerings, officials increasingly sought to ensure that displayed models were indeed available for purchase.[155] This new emphasis gradually shifted the event's focus from educational and cultural to economic purposes. Officials expanded the assortments that were for sale at the Berlin Fashion Week to include not only accessories, jewelry, and cosmetics, but also shoes, dresses, suits, and children's clothing.[156] Sales doubled from 1.2 million DM in the spring of 1960 to 2.5 million DM in the fall of the same year. By the fall of 1961 revenues totaled 3 million DM.[157] In order to ensure an impressive display of models for sale at the Fashion Week, central authorities even ordered trade officials in Berlin to hoard goods in storerooms during the preceding weeks.[158]

Increased sales, however, did not indicate success in the eyes of many officials. After the fall 1961 Fashion Week, state garment industry officials complained that these trends diluted the event's "socio-political statement," undermined the goal of propagating a distinct "fashion line," and led visitors to view the event, particularly during the first two days, as "solely a good shopping opportunity, especially for scarce assortments."[159] In October 1961 state officials planned to hold the spring 1962 Fashion Week "with a new trend" that would stress the popularization of the official fashion line and fashion colors and feature specific assortments of clothing, such as apparel for youth.[160] Increased publicity was to help reinstate some of the event's original orientation despite its increasingly commercial character. The Berlin Fashion Week ended quietly and abruptly in 1962. Although explicit orders have not been found, it seems plausible that the decision stemmed in part from the regime's sensitivity to consumers' growing impatience with industry's inability to deliver the "inspirations" on display and in part from the establishment and expansion of Exquisit stores, which offered "extravagant" apparel at extremely high prices. The next two chapters provide the context of these stores and the conflicts surrounding them by analyzing the regime's price policies and practices.

–4–

Economies of Value and Politics of Price

Official policies and practices concerning price, value, and quality were just as central to socialist consumer culture and politics as matters of taste, aesthetics, and fashion. Ambiguities and contradictions inherent in the SED's price policies were amplified by the realities of the GDR's economic system, which undermined the party's principles and promises. Under the pressures and unavoidable inconsistencies of this constellation, party leaders frequently proved willing to compromise ideological principles in pursuit of practical political and economic goals.

In setting price policies, party and state functionaries attempted an extremely difficult balancing act. Prices had to embody often contradictory aspects of socialist ideology, steer and control demand, and contribute to the economic goals of increasing accumulation and absorbing buying power. In practice, these tasks often not only proved mutually exclusive, they also were undermined by the unique economic rationale of the GDR's planned economy. The GDR's bureaucratic industrial regulations resulted in prices that were based solely on factors of production and had no direct relationship to either Marxist notions of use-value or consumers' sense of fairness. By continuing to produce relatively homogeneous products at ever-increasing prices, industry acted in direct opposition to many of the SED's central consumer policies. Party leaders backed themselves into a self-constructed ideological and political trap and proved either unwilling or unable to fundamentally reform an ideologically inconsistent and economically unsound system of prices.

The Political Economy of Price

Perhaps more than any other single economic aspect of the GDR's consumer culture, prices were linked directly to the legitimacy of the regime and of state socialism in general. Party leaders had fostered this association and were highly sensitive to the consequences of discrediting the regime's price policies. In a society that strove toward a communist utopia but still used money to a significant

78

extent to regulate the distribution of wealth, price was to embody and contribute to the realization of fundamental Marxist–Leninist principles.

Foremost among those principles was the promise to fulfill the "basic needs" of each member of society. The regime guaranteed that "normal," "standard" clothing always would be available to everyone at a low price. This principle, central to the concept of rationing, retained a strong foothold in both official propaganda and consumers' expectations and was a major point of consensus at all levels of the party, state, and society throughout the life of the GDR. The SED often claimed that this overriding commitment to fulfilling the basic needs of all its citizens distinguished socialism from capitalism, which was driven primarily by corporations' hunger for profits. One direct consequence of the promise to satisfy basic needs was extensive subsidies for goods like children's and work clothing.

The egalitarian impulses behind the principle of fulfilling everyone's basic needs stood in an uneasy relation to the SED's ambiguous endorsement of differentiation and the distribution of wealth according to "achievement." Although it rejected "individualistic" consumption, the SED agreed with East German citizens that an ideal socialist consumer culture had to address the "human need" for individuality. The value placed on choice concerning personal items like clothing constituted a major point of agreement between the regime and its citizens and contributed to the establishment of choice as a virtual right. In part due to this attitude and in part due to economic considerations, the regime encouraged the production and distribution of different "genres" of clothing in order to address the different needs and wishes of various groups of consumers. In addition to "normal" assortments at low prices, consumers were to have the option of spending more to obtain higher-quality or more fashionable apparel. Access to genres above the "standard" one thus was limited and based on the principles of achievement and choice rather than egalitarianism. The SED's price and wage policies were to facilitate "the distribution of products according to achievement" rather than needs.[1] In theory and in practice, the egalitarian principles of fulfilling everyone's "basic needs" clashed with the principle of fulfilling "higher" needs on a differentiated basis.

The SED also rhetorically linked price policies to the success of socialism by promising that prices would decrease or at least remain constant. According to one of the fundamental economic "laws" of Marxism–Leninism, socialist organization of production would result in an "uninterrupted increase in productivity and decrease in prime costs in the realm of production," which in turn made "possible and necessary a policy of the systematic decrease of prices."[2] According to the SED, sinking consumer prices gave East Germans a tangible criterion by which to measure their increasing standard of living under socialism and ensured that the GDR did not compare unfavorably with West Germany.[3] Reducing prices of industrial goods also made an important contribution toward the SED's goal of shifting consumer spending from food products to industrial goods, which party leaders viewed as a sign of modernization that had already occurred in most Western industrial nations by the 1950s.

The interrelated concepts of "use-value," "quality," and "value" comprised another ideological driving force behind the SED's price policies. But here, too, a tension appeared from the start: Marxism–Leninism could be used to justify two different theoretical methods of determining a commodity's price under socialism. The more orthodox approach defined price solely in terms of the "value" of the labor invested in the production of a commodity, while the other approach posited that prices should reflect products' "use-value" to consumers.[4] Focusing on the relationship between a good and its consumer, this second approach defined quality in terms of use-value and declared that higher quality justified a higher price. The SED expected prices to closely reflect both "value," as defined in the sphere of production, and "use-value," as defined in the sphere of consumption. But this feat proved impossible within the structures of the GDR's planned economy.[5]

The SED's insistence that a product's price and its "quality" stand in direct relation to each other meant that the definition of the latter became quite contested. Since price in the GDR's planned economy was not determined by market mechanisms but rather by bureaucratic regulations as well as ideological and political considerations, the SED realized that it needed to justify prices in part by connecting them with "objective" definitions of quality. Party leaders knew that prices could not be based solely on Marxist–Leninist theories or factors of production but instead had to appear justified in consumers' eyes. Party and state leaders nevertheless justified higher prices and price increases for goods that contained "more valuable" (*hochwertig*) materials that in turn increased the products' "use-value" (*Gebrauchswert*).[6] By the mid-1960s, the regime's long-term plans simply declared that the quality of clothing would increase and that this naturally would mean an increase in clothes' average prices.[7]

The regime's argument that better quality justified higher prices caused friction both within party and state institutions as well as between the regime and consumers. Until the mid-1960s, most consumers were willing to pay more for what they considered better quality. In the GDR's planned economy, however, quality and prices often had no perceptible relationship to each other, as defined by either the state or consumers. East Germans resented prices based on official definitions of "quality" or bureaucratic industrial calculations, neither of which matched their own perceptions of a fair price. In addition to the tensions inherent in its own ideology, the SED's price policies had to address practical economic concerns. Price decreases in state-owned factories and stores not only were expensive for the state but also resulted in increased demand that often could not be met. Lowering prices also ran counter to the regime's goals of absorbing consumers' excess buying power and using the sale of clothing as a source of accumulation for the state.

Expensive, Low-Quality Apparel

The textile and garment industries' role as a source of accumulation for the state was one of the major reasons why even the most basic articles of clothing generally were quite expensive by any standard. After peaking in the first years of the 1950s, prices for garments, textiles, and shoes in the mid-1950s were still at least three to four times their level in 1936.[8] Apparel and shoes also were expensive relative to other consumer goods. Despite steeper price decreases than other products during the first half of the 1950s, clothing in the GDR remained more expensive, compared with prewar levels, than almost all other consumer goods, which caused financial burdens especially for households with lower incomes.[9] To make matters worse, East German apparel was much more expensive than clothing in West Germany. Despite an exchange rate of at least four East German marks to one West German mark, the prices for East German clothing were roughly double those of similar West German articles during the 1950s and into the 1960s.[10] Many assortments were three or four times more expensive in the East than in the West. Central Committee officials estimated in 1960 that East German textiles and garments overall were 74 percent, men's outerwear 130 percent, and women's outerwear 162 percent more expensive than the corresponding categories in West Germany. Even children's outerwear, which the East German state heavily subsidized and which generally was made of inferior materials, was still 7 percent more expensive in the GDR than in the FRG.[11] From the SED's perspective, postwar price developments made clothing a particularly vulnerable point for comparison with West Germany, where goods like heating materials and food cost approximately the same as in the GDR but where textile prices had sunk back to prewar levels by the early 1950s.[12] During the course of the decade, prices in the GDR for textiles and clothing increased relative to most other consumer goods and especially food, while West Germans experienced the opposite trend.[13]

As East German officials themselves noted, the difference in value between East and West German goods actually was much larger than the disparity in prices because West German goods clearly surpassed their East German counterparts in terms of quality, material, and fashionableness. While West German textiles contained high-quality wool and cotton as well as new and highly desirable synthetic fibers, East German articles were made predominantly of low-quality spun rayon and inferior natural fibers imported from the Soviet Union. Despite their promise that the GDR would surpass West Germany in per-capita consumption of important consumer goods, party leaders were well aware that the GDR continued to fall further behind the FRG in both quantitative and qualitative measures of clothing consumption at the beginning of the 1960s.[14]

One of the most striking aspects of official discourses on quality is the general consensus about the poor quality of East German clothing and its inappropriately high prices. The regime acknowledged the fundamental correctness and legitimacy of consumers' dissatisfactions with the quality of apparel and their expectations that expensive articles be of high quality. Already in the early 1950s, officials noted that consumers' expectations were rising and that they were unwilling to pay high prices for low-quality items.[15] Although critical articles in the media and isolated voices within official institutions had been calling for improvements in the quality of East German apparel since the early 1950s, the cause did not gain full official endorsement until the end of the decade, as unsold goods piled ever higher and Cold War competition with West Germany heated up. Once it got rolling, the campaign to improve clothing's quality became omnipresent, assuming a variety of forms and publicizing countless examples of poor quality as part of the fight against the "ideology of tons" (*Tonnenideologie*). This included shifting industry's emphasis from quantity to quality, from being concerned solely with "economic thinking in quantities and value and the percentage of fulfillment [of the plan]" to considering "the final product as use-value for the consumer."[16] At the Textile Conference in 1959 an exhibition entitled "The Population Refuses Such Quality!" was to display items that either did not match the criteria specified in production contracts or whose quality was "so bad that one cannot dare offer them to the population."[17] *Neues Deutschland* ran a series of articles that featured "Mister Botch-Up" (*Herr Murks*) and "Miss Quality" (*Fräulein Güte*), who fought a battle of the sexes over issues of quality.[18] The media reproduced popular jokes about the poor quality of specific factories' products. The VEB Modedruck (Fashion Print) was known as the VEB Fehldruck (Misprint) and the VEB Treff-Modelle was the subject of a rhyme: "If you need a new skin, don't ever buy a Treff model."[19] An exhibition in Leipzig in December 1959, entitled "The Bottom of the Barrel of Quality" (*Schlußlichter der Qualität*), displayed examples – often with sarcastic commentary – of shoddy products or wasteful production from sixty-eight different manufacturers.[20]

These publicity campaigns as well as officials' remarks behind closed doors demonstrated that the vast majority of apparel for sale in the GDR did not fulfill even official ideals and standards of quality. The party's yardstick for quality, as for so many other aspects of the GDR's consumer culture, was in fact the "world level" (*Weltniveau*), the "modern" and "international" level of quality that the capitalist West had achieved and constantly pushed forward and further out of reach of the GDR's textile and garment industries.

Price Calculations and Creeping Inflation

Actual industrial, wholesale, and retail prices undermined the SED's policies, resulted in economic inefficiencies and losses, and created major political problems for the regime. In the GDR's planned economy of the 1950s, prices resulted from complex, confusing, and inconsistent bureaucratic regulations. Individual textile factories calculated their own industrial prices by using over 320 bureaucratic regulations, the bulk of which dated from the period between 1936 and 1944.[21] Partly due to the large number and variety of enterprises, the price regulations governing the textile industry were the most differentiated and complicated of all industrial branches and involved highly technical and often bewildering procedures.[22] Adding to the chaos was the ability of factories after 1947 to apply for exemptions in order to raise certain prices due to special individual circumstances.[23] Prices were assigned mechanically based solely on factors related to production within an individual factory, including the type and amount of materials used, the minutes of labor required, and the factory's form of property ownership.[24] The materials used were extremely important, for they comprised 75 to 85 percent of a garment's price.[25] The complexity and opaqueness of price regulations led to both honest mistakes in categorizing and labeling thousands of individual assortments and illegal manipulation by factory and store managers.[26]

Not surprisingly, actual prices frequently failed to correspond to official definitions of quality and use-value. Officials listed countless cases of "false price relations" that steered demand in economically and politically undesirable directions. Similar or seemingly identical articles with the same use-value could have widely disparate prices because they contained slightly different mixtures of materials (for example, a 50/50 versus a 30/70 mixture of wool and spun rayon), came from factories of different types of ownership, or were different sizes (for example, certain articles of men's apparel cost more than boys' apparel of the same size, and larger sizes could cost more than smaller ones of the same type).[27] Conversely, items of significantly different quality, use-value, or production costs could share the same price. For example, artificial leather cost roughly as much as natural leather, a woman's sweater made of pure wool was even slightly less expensive than one made of a mixture of wool and spun rayon, and hand-tailored garments sometimes cost the same as ready-to-wear.[28]

Party and state officials were acutely aware of "negative discussions" among ordinary citizens, who complained about prices that seemed bizarre and arbitrary. One reason for officials' sensitivity certainly must have been that consumers simply demanded that the regime live up to its own principles and promises. Officials generally shared consumers' sense of fair prices and considered the elimination of "false consumer prices" to be "urgently necessary because the currently different prices lead to many annoyances among the population."[29]

The semi-autonomous development of bureaucratically calculated prices also often resulted in economic losses even when items were sold at their original prices. This was due primarily to the fact that "in the factories there is virtually no relationship between the development of costs and price calculations."[30] In numerous cases this meant that prices did not even cover costs.[31] Prices for raw materials stood in the wrong relations to each other, encouraging factories to waste costly resources.[32] The low prices of natural fibers compared with synthetic ones, for instance, represented a major obstacle to the SED's efforts to shift both production and consumption from the former to the latter.[33] The state thus heavily subsidized imported wool and cotton only to impose high taxes on the finished products.[34] To make matters worse, the factory prices of products made of synthetic fibers generally did not cover even the prime costs.[35]

The bureaucratic regulations used to calculate industrial and consumer prices also resulted in hidden inflation, another phenomenon inherent in the GDR's planned economy that directly contradicted the fundamental tenets of the SED's price policies. Party and state leaders constantly bemoaned the ability of factories to achieve "unjustified price increases" by manipulating the amounts and types of raw materials and the array of assortments or by introducing technological "improvements" that had no practical effect.[36] This would not have been so bad by itself, but factories also managed to gradually reduce or cease production of their less expensive models. Consumer price inflation in the GDR thus resulted not from price increases for specific items but rather from the gradual displacement of less expensive articles by more expensive ones on store shelves.[37] An audit of the buying negotiations for ready-to-wear in 1959 discovered that "dresses in cheaper price ranges ... are totally lacking."[38] Other officials noted in 1962 that the average prices of apparel sold in 1961 significantly exceeded the prices specified in the plan for that year as well as the average prices of the same categories of goods the year before.[39]

Consumers did not need statistics to notice these inflationary trends. Since new items often appeared identical to old ones and new, higher prices did not necessarily correspond to improvements in quality or fashionableness from the perspective of consumers, the less expensive items sold out quickly, giving the impression of unjustified and insidious inflation.[40] Just as frustrating and outrageous to consumers, officials noted, was the fact that the scarcity of cheaper apparel "forced" consumers, including those who could least afford it, to buy more expensive clothing that was supposedly "better" but did not appear so.[41] East German consumers did not silently accept their fate. The records of central party and state authorities abound with reports of "negative discussions" among the populace about "*schleichende Preiserhöhungen*" (creeping or sneaking price increases).[42] Their complaints fell on largely sympathetic ears. The use of the term in official correspondence suggests that party and state functionaries indeed considered consumers complaints "justified criticism," as one leading state official phrased it.[43] Fred Oelßner noted already in 1957 that "among the population the complaints are multiplying that textile goods constantly are becoming more expensive" and proclaimed that "this peculiar price politics of a few enterprises discredits the politics of our government and angers the population."[44] The scarcity of assortments of "normal" quality at low, affordable prices belied the regime's promises to fulfill everyone's "basic needs" and to provide a range of goods at a variety of prices for consumers with different incomes. Party and state leaders were well aware that irrational prices and creeping inflation weakened the political effect of price reductions that the regime had introduced with great public fanfare during the first half of the 1950s.[45] They knew that price increases and the disappearance of cheaper goods "stunt the growth of real incomes foreseen by the plan and limit the [motivating] effect of the principle of material interest. That is true especially for lower income groups and families with many children."[46]

Such concerns led party and state leaders to call for guarantees of the availability of inexpensive assortments. The lack of such assortments was one of the problems to be addressed by the reforms of the New Economic System starting around 1963. The head of the Economic Council's Department for Textiles, Clothing, and Leather reiterated the three basic "principles" of the regime's price policies: "a) Ensure that bargain assortments are not discontinued or limited when the demand for them is present. b) Ensure a sufficient supply in all price classes, especially in the bargain assortments. c) Ensure that higher prices are allowed only if material prices and labor demands require it and it results in a higher use-value."[47] This was easier said than done. Despite Walter Ulbricht's demand that "in the future, bargain assortments must bring enterprises the same economic advantages as the production of expensive wares," concrete methods to accomplish this goal never materialized and seem not to have been seriously attempted.[48] Officials admitted in 1963 that previous decreases in factories' costs had not lowered consumer prices but rather benefited the state's coffers: "In essence, for poorer quality the population paid unchanged, thus exorbitant [*überhöht*] prices."[49]

In Search of Uniform, Stable Prices for a Variety of "Genres"

In order to ensure a direct correlation between price and quality and to eliminate creeping inflation, the SED strove to establish permanent, uniform, fixed prices for all assortments of textiles and garments. The elimination of price calculations ranked high among the "basic principles" for the prices of all consumer goods that the Council of Ministers outlined in a seminal policy document in February 1953.[50] Uniform fixed prices theoretically would ensure the same price for the same types of products and eliminate individual factories' ability to manipulate prices and cause creeping inflation.[51] Officials also hoped that reform of regulations governing prices and costs would enable the state to more accurately calculate and compare the productivity of factories with different types of ownership.[52]

In preparing to set fixed industrial prices in the mid-1950s, officials had to decide where to place the new price level within the range of prices that were the legacy of pre-1945 regulations. Setting prices at the highest level within the range would help ensure that they could cover costs but would also result in across-the-board price increases, a politically untenable outcome. Setting them at the lowest level certainly would be the most politically popular option but would entail huge economic losses. Thus the regime initially attempted to set new fixed prices in the middle: the losses of some factories would be offset by the profits of others while price increases would be balanced by price decreases. The state had used this principle in lifting the rationing of textiles, clothing, and shoes between 1951 and 1953. The new consumer prices for these articles had been set between the extremely high prices in the HO, where one had been able to purchase the items "freely," and the low prices guaranteed by rationing cards. While exact figures are not available, this method actually resulted in an overall price increase for consumers, since more people had been using rationing cards than shopping in the HO.[53]

The reform of industrial prices, however, presented a much more difficult problem than the elimination of rationing. While the state quickly established fixed prices in heavily nationalized industries with a small number of large factories, developments proceeded much more slowly in the textile and garment industries. Despite the theoretical and ideological importance of fixed prices, state officials did not begin to propose methods for their practical implementation in the realm of textiles and garments until 1956.[54] The delay was due in part to the more pressing problems of the early 1950s and in part to the fact that the textile and garment industry was the "most complicated" industrial branch for which to set prices.[55] Infamously incomplete and inaccurate statistical information added to the challenge, as did the fact that several different types of factories – from spinning and weaving mills to dye producers and garment manufacturers – were involved in the production of a single article of clothing.[56] Extreme variations in costs and productivity both among the different categories of ownership as well as among individual factories within each category further complicated efforts to devise uniform industrial price calculations "on the basis of costs."[57] Officials searched in vain for a golden mean that would ensure the profitability of the industry as a whole and yet not result in price increases. Although smaller private enterprises had higher costs than larger state-owned factories, the inherited pre-1945 price regulations allowed them to calculate generally higher prices for their products.[58] One set of regulations that governed the calculation of prices in factories of all types of ownership thus would inevitably lead to price increases, since private and half-state-owned enterprises initially accounted for such a large proportion of total production.

The regime encountered resistance even within its own ranks to the goal of setting fixed prices, for the task exacerbated the conflict between those hoping to centralize power and control over the economy and those pushing for decentralization in order to achieve more flexibility and economic rationality. The complexity of the textile and garment industries led some state officials to question the feasibility and wisdom of setting uniform, fixed prices and even to advocate other methods of controlling prices. For instance, Willi Behrendt, the head of the State Planning Commission's Main Department for the Planning of Light Industry, asserted in 1956 that consumers' "different types of wishes for assortments" made the establishment of fixed prices "hopeless." He instead advocated working with "arithmetical price limits" (*kalkulatorischen Höchstpreisen*) in order to give "the law of value" (*Wertgesetz*) freer reign.[59]

Textile and garment prices were also affected by more general trends in the regime's price policies. Until 1958 the regime advocated setting fixed prices at a level between the lowest and the highest previous prices.[60] However, consumers' complaints about the resulting price increases apparently were a major reason why the Council of Ministers resolved in January 1958 "that fundamentally no price increases may occur during the introduction of fixed prices."[61] Countless party and state officials argued during the late 1950s and early 1960s that the average prices of textiles and garments had to drastically decrease if the SED were to achieve its goals of competing with the West, surpassing the FRG in per-capita consumption, eliminating a major economic drain from East to West, and shifting consumers' habits from hand-tailored to store-bought apparel and from food products to industrial goods. High prices also were viewed as a major factor behind stagnating sales and growing surpluses. Due to the large disparity between prices in the GDR and FRG and the fact that clothing and shoes, along with food products, were "politically and provisioning-politically [*versorgungspolitisch*] of outstanding meaning," a special committee consisting of representatives from several ministries and central state institutions recommended to the Politburo's Economic Committee in 1958 that in the future "price-political measures" for textiles and shoes should receive priority.[62]

The SED's commandment at the end of the 1950s that the new fixed consumer prices be set at the lower end of previous price ranges placed severe restraints on state officials' efforts to achieve meaningful price reforms. In correcting "false price relations" of raw materials, officials were forbidden from raising the prices for "high-value materials."[63] Instead, the only feasible option was to decrease prices for lower quality and less desirable materials such as spun rayon. But setting fixed prices at the lowest current level ultimately proved untenable because it entailed extensive, permanent discounts that would both reduce state revenues and increase consumer demand that already could not be met. As officials at the Ministry for Light Industry asserted in 1955, although official suggestions to suddenly and dramatically reduce prices of textiles and clothing undoubtedly would meet with the approval of consumers, the regime had to "abstain" from such price reductions "because the textile industry would have largely shirked its duty as meaningful bearer of accumulation for the state budget and such a sudden burden would have damaged the construction of our state."[64]

Even if the state could afford the reduction in revenues, party and state officials realized that industry's production capacities were still insufficient to meet the increase in demand that invariably accompanied price decreases for desired goods.[65] The SED knew this from experience: price decreases of children's clothing by 35 percent in 1956 and of leather shoes by 50 percent in 1958 had triggered dramatic and extended increases in demand and sent state officials scrambling to boost supplies through a combination of increased production and imports.[66] Officials took these lessons to heart and frequently considered the potential increase in demand a sufficient reason to reject proposed price decreases for desirable goods.[67] The regime's commitment to keep prices low for certain politically important goods such as children's clothing necessitated extensive subsidies for these products, which had to be paid for with high accumulation rates for other goods, such as men's and women's regular outerwear.[68]

Such political and economic considerations contributed to extended and ultimately unsuccessful attempts to introduce fixed consumer prices for specific categories of textiles and garments in the GDR. After two years of work, state officials presented "the first useable proposal" for building fixed prices for textiles and garments in 1958.[69] But in September 1959 the Politburo admitted that the party could not achieve its goal of establishing fixed prices for all goods by mid-1959: uniform consumer prices for textiles could be "introduced only in stages and over a longer time period."[70] During the following years, officials repeatedly revisited the issue of fixed prices but attempted only partial solutions, which only made the situation more confusing and chaotic.[71] Between 1960 and 1964, the regime managed to add only quilts and bedspreads to the modest list of textiles and garments with fixed consumer prices, and the bureaucratic method used to accomplish this, retail price catalogues (*Handelspreiskataloge*), quickly proved inflexible and unwieldy because of the thousands of periodically changing articles they contained.[72] In 1962 state planners noted that the realization of fixed prices would require drafting approximately 110 price regulations in approximately ninety working groups that would include at least 500 representatives from factories and VVBs in addition to officials from the Economic Council.[73] One Economic Council official remarked that despite numerous efforts to set fixed prices "the many partial regulations have only increased the opaqueness of the situation."[74] In its most optimistic form, the New Economic System aimed to reform the GDR's planned economy from the bottom up in order to establish more direct relationships between "real costs" and prices and to introduce market elements that would help to coordinate supply and demand. The reforms were to proceed in three stages: after correcting the false prices for raw materials in basic and heavy industries, officials would reform industrial prices and finally consumer prices. But in reality, the first stage was never successfully completed. State officials were limited to relatively superficial administrative measures because more fundamental structural reforms would have called into question the system's very foundations.[75]

In November 1964 officials at the Ministry for Trade and Provisioning admitted that "for the overwhelming portion of textile products, the price regulations from the period before 1944/1952 are still valid today" and that "even for standardized textile products there exist many different prices for similar products."[76] Once again, state trade officials proposed two general approaches to setting fixed consumer prices for textiles and clothing. They rejected the first alternative, the unification of prices at the lowest current level, for the same reasons that the same proposal had failed in 1959: officials predicted that the resulting "steep price reductions" would cost the state at least 700 million marks and cause demand to increase, requiring approximately 1 billion marks worth of additional goods, a feat that the GDR's industry could not hope to accomplish before 1970, even according to the regime's own overly optimistic plan.[77] The state trade officials thus recommended the second option, fixing most of the new prices at the average level of previous prices.

Although this theoretically would neither result in economic losses for the state nor increase overall consumer demand, the officials cautioned against the disappearance of "certain low prices" that "influenced the appearance of offerings," even though they constituted only "a small portion of the market." Officials knew that customers perceived many of these low prices to be the "normal" ones. To address these concerns, functionaries recommended setting the prices for goods "on the lower border of quality" as well as "certain, selected groups of wares" (such as children's clothing) that had "a great provisioning-political meaning" near the lowest current price while the "middle and good quality" goods would be unified at the weighted average price. For groups of goods in which "similar qualities until now were sold at different prices," the state's task was "to create new qualities in low price ranges."[78] In justifying these measures to ordinary citizens, the state trade officials acknowledged that "two principles, however, must be abandoned that until now have stood very strongly in the center of publications: a) that individual prices within an assortment may not increase; b) that uniform prices are striven for in general in the [GDR] for all products." The officials instead recommended emphasizing the stability of the overall "price level" of each group of goods, price decreases for selected categories of products such as children's clothing, and the introduction of "stronger differentiation in quality."[79]

Although the regime was able to at least formally enact regulations that established uniform procedures for calculating industrial prices for the same types of articles made in different factories, the SED stopped short of reforming consumer prices. The failure of efforts to enact meaningful price reforms became unmistakable by 1966 when the Politburo and the Council of Ministers declared that all consumer prices would remain unchanged during the third stage of the price reform, which was scheduled to begin on 1 January 1967, and admitted that prices would remain the same even for similar wares that had different consumer prices.[80]

The basic structure of price calculations remained in place through the last two decades of the GDR. All factories, regardless of the type of ownership, may have been using the same price regulations by the mid-1960s, but prices continued to be based on the calculations of individual factories, which meant that creeping inflation and price disparities for similar products continued unabated. Central Committee officials warned already in 1965 that the ever-increasing production of expensive synthetic fibers would inevitably lead to constantly rising prices unless the regime undertook structural and not just operational reforms.[81] Average prices for textiles and garments indeed continued to increase throughout the 1960s with alarming speed, due in large part to the increased use of synthetic materials.[82] Between 1966 and 1970, average prices for men's outerwear increased by 30 percent, women's outerwear by 35 percent, and children's outerwear by 40 percent.[83] The introduction of a special type of synthetic material (*Großrundstrick*) in 1969 exacerbated this inflationary trend, which peaked around 1970 but continued at an only somewhat slower pace thereafter.[84] In 1970 state trade officials summarized a familiar dilemma: the determination of consumer prices according to the calculations of individual enterprises "does not allow the influencing of average prices according to plan."[85]

Attempts to establish uniform, fixed prices in order to prevent "creeping inflation" may have been stymied by political, structural, and economic obstacles, but at the same time, party and state leaders had several reasons to tolerate and even to unofficially encourage rising prices. Inflationary prices made good economic sense from the state's perspective, for they increased the state's revenues while helping absorb consumers' perennial excess buying power. They also helped ensure that produced goods would not result in decreased revenues for the state, assuming that they were sold.

Regardless of whether it was unable or unwilling to control "creeping inflation," the regime had to counteract the potentially damaging political consequences of consumers' perceptions that prices were increasing for no justifiable reason. While the regime experimented with various methods of encouraging factories to improve the quality of their products, officials placed a new emphasis on labeling and explaining quality in order to make price increases seem justified in the eyes of party and state officials as well as consumers. Officials were to educate consumers and convince them that certain goods had a higher "use-value," even if that was not immediately apparent.[86]

While most officials asserted that consumers would always be willing to pay more for higher quality, some cautioned that retailers could not legitimately demand a higher price for "improvements in quality that must be viewed as 'normal qualitative demands,' given the current general state of development."[87] Most officials, however, still claimed that the rising average prices for textiles and clothing were a natural and legitimate consequence of consumers' increasing desires. Fashion Institute officials argued that the East German garment industry increased "the proportion of easy-care [i.e., synthetic] apparel and clothing with high representative qualities" starting in 1965 in response to consumers' demands for "a substantial qualitative improvement of clothing." An increase in average prices allegedly "was the consequence of this substantial improvement" of clothing's "material structure."[88] By the mid-1960s, many functionaries began to counter the argument for raising prices based on increased "use-value" by invoking the Marxist–Leninist principle that prices should correspond to the "value" of the labor invested in production. The highly-publicized increases in the productivity of the GDR's industry, so the counter-argument went, should result instead in decreased prices, according to the "laws" and promises of socialist production.[89] Regardless of the theoretical arguments for increasing or decreasing prices, officials noted that consumers increasingly demanded both high quality *and* low prices.

The Problem of Subsidies

An analysis of aborted attempts to eliminate subsidies for children's clothes complements the story of the regime's failure to either set fixed prices or to enact even minimal price increases. Subsidies illustrate how the SED backed itself into a corner through its own price policies and promises as well as its hesitancy to disappoint ordinary citizens' expectations. Although subsidies were essential to the fulfillment of the SED's promises to satisfy the "basic needs" of all East Germans, such measures had been regarded from the beginning as "a necessary evil" that was justified "only under special conditions," in the words of party leader Heinrich Rau in 1954.[90] Nevertheless, political pressures to avoid price increases led the regime to establish direct and indirect subsidies for numerous politically important items such as children's clothing, work clothes, certain food items, culture, health care, transportation, and housing. Children's clothing, which the regime began heavily subsidizing after major price reductions in 1956, offers a telling case study.[91]

Calls for the elimination of subsidies for children's clothes began in the late 1950s and intensified in the 1960s within the context of the New Economic System. There were myriad reasons why the subsidies made neither economic nor socio-political sense. They were so extensive that consumers could buy ready-to-wear children's clothes for less than the cloth used to make them.[92] Despite the fact that 35 to 50 percent of the price of children's clothes was subsidized by the state. functionaries lamented that the extent of the tens of millions of marks in subsidies was "not generally known" among the population nor sufficiently publicized in the media.[93] Even worse was the fact that the subsidies often did not fulfill their purpose. It was well known that small adults and foreign tourists bought large children's clothing, while large children had to buy more expensive adult clothes.[94]

The solution to these problems seemed simple: eliminate subsidies for children's clothing and simultaneously increase the allowances that the state directly gave parents to defray costs associated with their children (*Kindergeld*). Although this suggestion was made as early as 1961 and revived again in 1968, the subsidies remained untouched even when the child allowance was raised marginally in 1968 and 1969.[95] Although official explanations and exact calculations from the 1960s are unavailable, one can assume that party leaders considered it politically infeasible to increase prices enough to overcome the enormous gap between the prices of subsidized children's clothing and those of adult clothing that served as a source of accumulation. Alternately, the regime could have equalized the disparate price levels at some middle ground, but this would have entailed significant financial losses due to the reduction of profits from adult clothing.

The issue gained urgency in 1970 when the plan foresaw increasing production of children's clothes at the expense of adult clothes in order to meet an alleged increase in demand.[96] In June the regime proposed to both eliminate subsidies and to use "normal" price calculations for children's clothes.[97] The average price for children's clothes would increase by 42.5 percent, but prices for certain items would increase up to 95 percent. The proposal, however, reflected the Politburo's commandment that the total amount of price increases not only be equaled but even surpassed by the total increase in child allowances. Such overcompensation would have been necessary to justify to its citizens a measure that otherwise would have undermined one of the main principles of the regime's price policies and thus undercut its legitimacy. As Central Committee functionaries commented, viewed by themselves, the price increases were "no longer economically justifiable and politically irresponsible."[98] The political necessity of increasing child allowances more than the prices of children's clothing made the entire proposal economically infeasible for a state with serious fiscal troubles. Such considerations contributed to the Politburo's decision in 1971 to not eliminate subsidies, despite the alarming growth rate for such expenditures, and instead to return to its advocacy of cutting production costs as the primary method of eliminating subsidies.[99]

At the end of the 1960s, functionaries registered numerous expressions of fundamental doubts within the regime about the SED's price policies and economic realities. As one local official in Berlin remarked, "the disbelief in the correctness of our price policies" went "far into the ranks of our party."[100] Most officials agreed with market researchers who wrote in 1969 that the GDR's mixture of subsidies and overpriced goods was a "fundamental macroeconomic problem."[101] The SED's inability to escape its self-constructed ideological and political trap contributed both to its delegitimation even in the eyes of its own members and to ultimately disastrous economic policies.

–5–

The Embarrassment of Surpluses

The regime's price policies and the unique logic of planning, production, and distribution in the GDR contributed not only to the well-known shortages of consumer goods but also to an equally important and characteristic element of the economy and everyday life in state socialist societies, namely surpluses. The concentration on shortages in popular and scholarly discussions of consumer politics and culture has tended to emphasize a perspective from above while occluding the fact that the East German market for consumer goods encompassed demand as well as supply, even if the relationship between the two seems to be rather one-sided.[1] The phenomena of shortages and surpluses were two sides of the same coin; both were socially constructed and resulted from social practices. An examination of surpluses contributes to our understanding of consumers' albeit limited, yet significant agency as well as weaknesses in the party-state apparatus and limits of the regime's power to control production and consumption. Attempts to eliminate surpluses also reveal conflicts of interest inherent in GDR's political and economic structures that resulted partially from social dynamics, cultural continuities, and ideas that were not contained in any party line.

The palpable presence of an overwhelming number of goods that remained unsold in stores for months and years exacerbated consumers' already significant anger over the lack of desired items. These unsold wares formed a highly visible indication of the dysfunctional elements of the planned economy and its failure to fulfill consumers' needs and desires. Given the highly politicized nature of consumption and the practical meaninglessness of citizen's votes at the ballot box, the purchase or refusal to purchase East German products could be considered part of an indirect plebiscite on the GDR's political and economic system. This chapter focuses on the regime's attempts to eliminate these physical manifestations of political failure in everyday life through a variety of means, including conducting seasonal and clearance sales, establishing special stores, and exporting or physically destroying unsold goods.

The Growth of Surpluses and their Economic and Political Implications

Surpluses of many types of goods, and especially textiles and clothing, were an intrinsic part of the GDR's planned economy from the start. Textiles and ready-to-wear garments worth millions of marks began piling up in stores and warehouses as early as 1949.[2] From April to August 1950 the retail trade's stock of textiles and garments rose from 117 million to 175 million points – a sum equivalent to 138 percent of average monthly sales.[3] After the elimination of rationing in 1953, unsold textiles as well as other types of wares were common enough to gain the generic moniker of "stock in excess of the plan" (*Überplanbestände*) in official correspondence.[4] This euphemism was complemented by the term "holes in the assortment" (*Sortimentslücken*), which referred to shortages. Both expressions reflected the popular official myth that shortages and surpluses resulted primarily from logistical difficulties in planning, production, trade, and the coordination of these activities rather than fundamental, systemic problems.[5]

By 1954/1955 surplus textiles and garments totaled an estimated 1.2 billion DM.[6] If the sheer quantity of clothing items in stores, factories, and warehouses had been the decisive factor, East Germans would have been well supplied by the mid-1950s. Officials estimated in 1955 that the amount of men's outerwear in storage was enough to meet demand for an entire year; the 788,878 suits in Berlin could allow each man in the city to buy two during the year.[7] Grete Wittkowski, a candidate of the Politburo and the leading party official responsible for issues of retail trade, noted in 1959 that "during the last three years we have produced half of the supply of wares for the warehouse."[8]

The actual volume of surplus wares probably exceeded official estimates due to inaccurate and sometimes falsified accounting. A chronic lack of storage space meant that warehouses were bursting at the seams and goods had to be scattered over multiple storage sites.[9] The chaos and confusion caused by the enormity and complexity of storage tasks overwhelmed local officials. Not surprisingly, this situation resulted in goods being lost, forgotten, or remaining unpacked for years in chaotic, overfilled storage facilities, which only exacerbated the growth of surpluses.[10] Although officials admittedly had no exact overview of the assortments, ages, and marketability of the stockpiles, they were well aware that stores and warehouses were full of "*Ladenhüter*," goods rejected by consumers that clogged retail and storage space for years.[11] An audit of ready-to-wear apparel in 1960 revealed that two-thirds of wholesalers' stock and almost half of retailers' inventory had been stored for at least nine months.[12] Another audit of garment factories in Berlin at the end of 1960 revealed that only 16 percent of their stock on hand had been manufactured that year. Almost 59 percent had been produced in 1959 and 25 percent in 1958.[13]

The enormous stockpiles caused serious economic losses and political problems. Improvised facilities, lack of space, and poor storage techniques often caused clothing to be crushed beyond repair, to be eaten by insects, or to become moldy.[14] The chaos and inefficiency caused by surpluses hindered the distribution of the precious few desirable, high-quality, and reasonably priced wares. Surpluses also entailed political costs. Already in February 1953, a local party official in Berlin registered the widespread disillusionment of warehouse managers and others, remarking that "reports are always demanded, but no one pays attention to them and everything remains at the status quo. The money is frozen and the things gather dust. The colleagues are justified when they say we can't build socialism like this. The colleagues lose interest in their work and trust in our government."[15] The Council of Ministers itself admitted in 1956 that "the many needs of the working population for necessary and valuable mass-consumption goods were not fully satisfied, while on the other hand wares were manufactured that quantitatively and qualitatively do not correspond to the constantly rising needs (*Überplanbestände*)."[16] Party officials were very conscious of the visual effect of surpluses and the frustrations that could stem from such deceptive apparitions of abundance. As State Planning Commission officials remarked in 1956, "the high surplus stocks in textiles arouse the appearance that abundance [*Überfluß*] is present in some assortments. In reality, these are largely textiles made of raw materials that the population no longer accepts because of their qualitative characteristics."[17]

Surpluses represented an expression of consumers' limited agency, of their refusal to buy products that did not match their wishes, expectations, and perceptions of value and a fair price. State planners constantly bemoaned the remarkable elasticity of demand for clothing and consumers' tendency to radically and unpredictably shift their buying power from one assortment to another or from clothing to food or other consumer durables.[18] Consumers often postponed a purchase and waited for better materials or lower prices.[19] For instance, since trench coats made of spun rayon were almost as expensive as those made of cotton, many men waited until the next shipment of cotton ones, leaving the others to become *Ladenhüter*.[20] Perceptions of uniformity caused by a high concentration of identical garments and cloth patterns in certain stores or towns was another reason for consumer abstinence.[21] Trade officials also noted that rumors of an upcoming price decrease in the 1950s led to decreased demand and contributed to the growth of surpluses.[22] These practices resulted in one of the biggest frustrations about surpluses from both the state's and consumers' perspectives: many of the assortments that lay in stores for months or years paradoxically were the same ones that consumers urgently demanded. Although a consumer might be looking for a coat, for instance, she/he would abstain from a purchase because of objections to the materials, quality, prices, or sizes of the coats that happened to be available in the visited stores.

Most officials acknowledged that surpluses resulted from a mismatch between consumers' expectations and goods' qualities and prices. Until the mid-1950s, there may have been some truth to the claim that surpluses consisted of older items that had been passed over in favor of better and less expensive ones during an era of improvements in quality and stable or decreasing prices. But already at the beginning of the decade, more plausible explanations for surpluses pointed to the combination of increasing volume, stagnant quality, consumers' rising expectations, and high and rising prices.[23] Functionaries noted that premature promises of improvement and false advertising for goods that were unavailable in stores often exacerbated the problem. Local officials in Berlin, for instance, argued that "the newspaper notices that made great promises about the rapid improvement in materials" led consumers to reject the millions of square meters of spun rayon still in production and in stores in 1953 in expectation of new and superior woolen clothing items promised by official propaganda.[24] Officials recognized that the "false" relationships between quality and price that were intrinsic to the GDR's planned economy also contributed to the creation of surpluses: consumers snapped up the bargains and left the low-quality, expensive wares on store shelves.[25] The mismatch between the quality, fashionableness, and price of the apparel in stores on the one hand and consumers' expectations on the other remained one of the most common explanations for surpluses until the end of the GDR.

But many officials downplayed the role of these "subjective" factors and instead viewed surpluses as a result of technical, economic, or logistical problems that plagued the spheres of planning, production, and distribution. These included the macroeconomic difficulties of planning and coordinating prices and wages; industry's erratic but relentless delivery of low-quality, unwanted goods; faulty market research; trade's modification or cancellation of production contracts; and "inadequate cooperation and coordination of the plans" between industry and trade.[26] There were as many explanations and excuses for surpluses as there were problems with the GDR's economy.

Early Attempts to Liquidate Surpluses

There were as many strategies for eliminating and preventing the reappearance of surpluses as there were explanations for them. But everyone seemed to agree with local party functionaries in Karl-Marx-Stadt who warned already in 1955 that the build-up of surplus textiles "demands immediate measures in order to prevent catastrophic consequences."[27] The most immediate concern was the disposal of surplus wares already produced. In addition to holding special and seasonal clearance sales and authorizing both temporary and permanent price reductions for specific items, party and state leaders ordered industry and trade to export, refashion, give away, and even destroy unsold goods. The execution of these orders exposed fundamental tensions and weaknesses in the SED's price policies as well as limits of the regime's control over its state and economic apparatuses.

The seemingly simplest and quickest method of eliminating stockpiles of unsold goods was to reduce their prices. But the types and quantity of items to be included as well as the discount rates proved highly contested. In addition to becoming lost in bureaucratic chaos, orders from above were often carried out by lower-level functionaries in ways far removed from the intentions of party and state leaders. The first attempts to reduce stockpiles of unsold goods began already in November 1949, as textiles and garments still were being rationed by means of "point cards," when the Ministry for Trade and Provisioning ordered local trade officials to create lists of "point incapable" (*punktunfähig*) textiles and garments. The subjective definition of such articles created confusion and reflected the regime's reluctance to allow any price reductions whatsoever: "*Punktunfähig* are only such wares that are unmarketable due to their bad quality or workmanship, not however such wares that appear to be difficult to market because of exorbitant prices or seasonal reasons." Although the Ministry explained that "substantial indications of the point incapability are revealed in the length of storage," it did not explain how local officials were supposed to decide the exact reason for a particular item's stagnation.[28]

Officials at the central level realized that price reductions required individual, subjective judgements at the grass roots. Ever distrustful of lower-level officials' execution of orders from above, central authorities ordered an audit of the process, which concluded that 10 to 50 percent of the wares judged to be *punktunfähig* were actually perfectly capable of being sold at their original prices.[29] It appears that such concerns and difficulties led the regime to reduce by half the number of points required for nearly all rationed textiles and garments in October 1950.[30] Although this across-the-board price reduction cost the state a one-time charge of 130 million DM plus an additional 80 million DM per month thereafter, the party's generosity should not be overstated. As central state trade officials noted, there would be no "rush" on the low-quality discounted wares: by late 1950 the HO offered the same goods in "better qualities at not very exorbitant prices, relatively speaking." Since point values for "the wares that are especially demanded by the population, like underwear, stockings, bed linens, and lining materials (by the meter)," remained unchanged, the trade officials admitted that the group of those interested in the reduced-point goods was limited to "the especially needy population with less buying power."[31]

Rather than contributing toward more egalitarian consumption patterns, such price reductions reinforced hierarchies and social distinctions that were created in the sphere of production. Although official propaganda emphasized the social welfare component of price reductions by boasting that they were "necessary for the easing of shopping conditions for the population," central state trade officials acknowledged that the other main purpose was economic: "as stimulus for the purchase of wares for the purpose of absorbing buying power."[32] What appeared on the surface as a measure to improve social justice was in reality far from altruistic: by reducing prices for undesirable and unsold goods, the regime attempted to soak up what it could of the buying power of its citizens with the lowest incomes.

Regardless of officials' motivations, unsold goods embodied economic failure, and price reductions appeared to many as an amelioration. Since sizable, across-the-board price reductions were unaffordable, party and state leaders hoped to hold economic losses to a minimum by continuing to introduce discounts for only the least desirable wares. After the problematic centralized attempts of 1949/1950, modest initiatives began on the local level in 1951.[33] These efforts grew into a centrally directed, nationwide undertaking not long after September 1953, when Walter Ulbricht endorsed "annual seasonal clearance sales (*Saisonausverkäufe*)" as a method of preventing "seasonal wares from being left unsold."[34] In February 1954 the Ministry for Trade and Provisioning resolved to hold two distinct kinds of regular sales. Week-long "season-end sales" (*Saisonschlußverkäufe*) at the end of February and at the end of August each year would "cleanse stocks of genuine seasonal wares" while special "inventory clearance sales" (*Inventurausverkäufe*) would rid stores of all kinds of old, unsold goods.[35] Individual stores were to suggest price reductions, which had to be approved by both the Ministry for Trade and Provisioning and the Ministry of Finances. The state would compensate stores for the resulting losses.

Several provisions of the original resolution hinted at difficulties that later developed during its implementation. Officials tended to conflate the two types of sales, which meant that true season-end sales effectively did not exist. Hesitant to admit that the prices of certain goods, especially fashionable ones, had a limited life span, state trade officials at the central level did not issue guidelines for conducting seasonal sales. At the same time, they gave extensive instructions about what the inventory sales were to include and exclude. The criteria were based not on perceptions of the goods themselves but instead on factors related to their production, including when they were produced, whether they were still being manufactured, and what materials they contained. The rules also contained many exceptions. In general, the special sales were to include shoes and ready-to-wear garments that had been made before 1953 and were no longer produced in 1954. Items from 1953 whose workmanship was "not better" than those from 1952 as well as all women's ready-to-wear were also eligible for price reductions. In addition to being old, the planned sale items were of low quality and made of inferior materials.[36]

Central state trade officials ordered stores to collect these items and place them on "bargain tables" (*Wühltische*) in department stores and larger retail stores until 15 March 1954, at which point any unsold goods were to be transferred to "special stores" (*Sonderverkaufsstellen*) that would be built expressly for selling such wares on a permanent basis.[37] The state clearly did not intend for these sales to offer consumers the "bargains" associated with "season-end sales" but rather to rid stores of dregs by selling old, low-quality goods to people with low incomes who could not afford anything better.

The sales contained the potential for conflicts between officials at the local level with those at the central level. A minority of functionaries acknowledged that the textile and garment industry's "fashionable and seasonal wares" would "never – even with the best workmanship – totally sell out" and argued that individual stores could determine "a thrifty valuation" more accurately than a committee of functionaries at the central level.[38] But most party and state leaders balked at the idea of reducing an article's price solely for seasonal reasons, viewed price reductions as justified in only the most desperate situations, and insisted on maintaining centralized control over the entire process of adjusting prices. Time and again during the next nine years, central authorities would see their hopes dashed, their intentions distorted and undermined, and their attempts at centralized control thwarted.

The sales started off slowly in 1954, but intensified activities the following year crystallized many of the conflicts and problems that characterized the events during the next nine years. A centrally organized "summer-end sale" and various "special actions" (*Sonderaktionen*) began in 1954, costing the state about 170 million DM in discounts.[39] Starting on 1 November 1954 and lasting ten to fourteen days under the motto "clearance of all storage rooms" (*Räumung aller Läger*), special sales were supposed to be concentrated in the countryside and in special "cheap stores" (*billige Läden*).[40] In addition to reducing prices, organizers emphasized other methods of increasing sales such as moving surpluses to new stores in order to create a "novel view for the customer."[41] Building on these experiences, state trade officials significantly increased the scale of their operations for the inventory and winter-end sales scheduled to occur in early 1955.

Logistical problems and tensions among official institutions surfaced even before the sales started. As in the earlier sales, the first source of confusion was the complicated, subtle, and subjective definitions and distinctions between items to be included in the "winter-end sale" versus the "inventory sale."[42] Matters were made even more confusing by trade officials' decision to "link" and conduct both types of sales simultaneously because of an alleged dearth of items for an independent winter-end sale.[43] Proposals concerning discount rates revealed tensions both at the central level between leaders in trade and in finance and between these central authorities and local officials. While trade officials at all levels generally sought the largest price reductions possible in order to more easily fulfill their quotas and relieve their storage facilities, central finance officials were loath to allow any price reductions, which represented only economic losses in their eyes.[44] Indicative of this attitude was the almost comedic stipulation that the prices of unsold items be raised back to their original levels after the sale ended.[45] However, leaders in both the Ministry for Trade and Provisioning and the Ministry of Finances found that their thrifty, conservative guidelines were manipulated and undermined by trade officials at the grass roots who acted in their own interests and often sought to sell off goods at any price.

Given the mixture of confusing orders, conflicting interests, and suspicion of local officials, it is not surprising that audits ordered by central authorities once again discovered numerous "abuses" at the grass roots. Leading officials of the Central Commission for State Control (Zentrale Kommission für Staatliche Kontrolle) listed more than thirty examples to support their accusations that trade functionaries had acted in an "irresponsible" manner, resulting in the "squandering" (*Verschleuderung*) of state property and causing the state "great material damage."[46] The auditors rejected trade officials' arguments that the total clearance of all winter articles made economic sense because the costs of storing the goods until the next winter were nearly as much as the discounts. The desire to rid stores of all winter articles, the "unclear formulations" of the guidelines for the sales, and central trade officials' lack of control over grass roots operations combined to give stores "the greatest liberalness" and "clearly encouraged" the "squandering of valuable products, and especially scarce goods," the auditors concluded. Upper-level trade functionaries shared the blame through their "unreserved acceptance" of individual stores' suggestions for discounts and the absence of local audits, which resulted in the discounts exceeding the global cap of 15 million DM by 11.5 million DM.[47]

Many of these accusations were doubtless true. The managers and salespeople of individual stores had many reasons to sell as many items as possible and few incentives to sell them at the highest possible price. Their plans were based on volume rather than profit, and in any case, the state compensated them for any paper losses incurred during the sales. Most store managers probably welcomed the special sales as an opportunity to clear their overfilled storage spaces with virtually no risk. Many shared the attitude of a leading official in the Ministry for Trade and Provisioning, who allegedly declared, "this measure is the best and last occasion to get rid of the *Überplanbestände*."[48] Even if they had wanted to be thrifty, local trade officials lacked the resources to tackle the daunting task of painstakingly sorting through and classifying enormous stockpiles of poorly organized goods.

By the same token, the auditors and other officials were hypersensitive about "wasting the people's property" and refused to accept the fact that some "losses" were an inevitable part of retail sales. After all, the 26.5 million DM in sales during these special events was relatively insignificant compared with the estimated 1.2 billion DM in surpluses at the time. Such officials harbored unrealistic expectations of the increased turnover that modest discounts could bring. All too often, an item's marketability and price were judged purely according to economic and production criteria. The auditors in 1954 disapprovingly cited the example of a HO store in Frankfurt an der Oder that received shoes from state wholesalers that were made in 1953 and earlier and had been reduced in price by 40 to 50 percent. The fact that the shoes had spent at least one year in storage was immaterial to the auditors, who enclosed two shoes in their letter to prove that they were discounted without consideration of whether they were "marketable at normal prices."[49] Decisive was the fact that the shoes were made of valuable material and could not be "wasted." Such functionaries displayed little understanding of the contradictions of holding "seasonal" clearance sales in an economy where production output did not run according to schedule: the sales made little sense when seasonal items did not arrive in stores until the end of the season or even thereafter.[50]

Economic concerns may explain part of some officials' hypersensitivity about the (un)successful execution of clearance sales, but political and ideological concerns explain the lion's share. The chaotic, sometimes anarchic execution of the sales reflected poorly on the state and contradicted Marxist–Leninist notions about the relationship between value and price. The auditors worried that "this measure encountered misunderstanding among a large number of salespeople and did not help to solidify trust in measures of central government offices."[51] Many central officials and auditors believed that effective retail sales depended primarily on political willpower and that universal espousal of the correct ideology could overcome putatively superficial logistical problems. Reports of irresponsible functionaries provided scapegoats and supported the myth that the GDR's fundamentally sound economic system was being thwarted by relatively few people who simply needed a better ideological education.[52] This myth enabled party leaders to avoid blame for the planned economy's systemic problems, of which massive surpluses were but one symptom.

These problems became even more evident during the summer-end sale of 1955. In addition to the usual arguments between finance and trade officials over the size and legitimacy of discounts, the sales resulted in disappointing revenues and irritated shoppers.[53] Stores in Berlin sold only approximately 10 percent more goods than normal, leading local officials to remark that one could hardly call it a "clearance" sale.[54] The few bargains disappeared within the first days or even hours of the sale, after which purchases drastically decreased. Citizens engaged in "negative discussions" in which they expressed disappointment with the sale items' low quality and relatively high prices and called the event a "store leftovers sale" (*Ladenhüterverkauf*). Many were doubly disappointed to find that the 40 percent discounts promised in advertisements in the press applied only to the least desirable articles.[55] Perhaps most distressing to party functionaries were consumers' "hostile arguments," such as one addressed to trade officials in Gera: "Look at the summer-end sale in the West and you'll learn from it."[56]

Party and state officials pursued a variety of other methods for whittling down the GDR's excess stockpiles of textiles and garments, including exporting them, refashioning them, and reducing their production. Already in June 1954, leading trade officials had identified a group of surpluses, worth about 40 million DM, or 30 percent of all surpluses, that consisted of wares that could not be sold in the GDR even at a discount of 40 to 50 percent.[57] The officials warned that "one must guard against bringing these wares into our stores, since they too strongly differ from our current production. Today our population no longer goes for out-of-date production."[58] Minister for Trade and Provisioning Curt Wach decided that the state should try to export all of these goods by 3 July "and what remains of it will be given away or destroyed."[59] Exporting surpluses to other Soviet-bloc countries became a common method of eliminating surpluses by the mid-1950s.[60] Of the items that could not be exported, "zero wares' (*Nullwaren*) were those considered to be marketable only at a discount so high as to be "politically unjustifiable" – generally considered to be more than 80 percent. These items were written off and then either donated to the Volkssolidarität (People's Solidarity), a voluntary organization dedicated to helping disadvantaged (and mostly elderly) East Germans, or destroyed.[61] In fact, "large quantities of textiles" were shredded in 1955, according to trade officials.[62]

To avoid that fate, party functionaries ordered local trade officials to refashion wares into marketable forms. Leading trade officials ordered stores to have their stock of carded cellulose cloth made into "cheap work clothes."[63] In 1956 the regime tried to reduce surpluses by cutting back production, primarily in the smaller regionally-controlled state-owned and private factories.[64] But decreased production created concerns about underemployment and resulted in even larger shortages. The GDR's economy was not flexible and differentiated enough to allow officials to selectively stop the production of outdated production, eliminate the existing stock through clearance sales, and then start the production of new articles without creating shortages at some point.[65] Moreover, decreases in production stood in direct contradiction to the SED's promises of ever-increasing output, which many equated with growing affluence. A leading official in the State Planning Commission asked the functionaries who wanted to reduce textile production, "do you want to limit affluence [*Wohlstand*]? Do you not want to use economic principles for the satisfaction of the population's constantly rising needs?"[66] Party leaders tried to reduce production again in 1960 and 1963 in order to reduce surpluses but encountered essentially the same problems that they did in 1956.

Stores for "Cheap Goods": BIWA

In 1956 party and state leaders stepped up efforts to realize plans dating at least to 1954 to establish permanent stores dedicated solely to selling unsold surplus goods.[67] A lack of facilities and resources, especially in smaller cities and in the countryside, had obstructed the execution of long-standing orders to sell the items remaining after clearance sales only in "special price stores" (*Sonderpreisläden*).[68] But the Council of Ministers renewed this initiative in June 1956 by ordering the Ministry of Trade and Provisioning "to offer the population wares with a diminished use-value at prices reduced according to the diminution" in "special stores as well as in special sections of department stores" that were "to be developed into permanent institutions."[69] The stores were designed to address "the necessity of bringing the prices of wares that are fashionably or technically outdated into line with the corresponding use-values."[70] In addition to their main offerings of textiles, clothing, and shoes, the stores included various other surplus industrial goods and food products. In keeping with colloquial names for similar existing stores – such as "cheap stores" (*billige Läden*) or "junk stores" (*Ramschläden*) – the official name for this new chain of stores was BIWA, a shortening of *Billige Waren* (cheap wares).[71]

By establishing permanent, specialized stores for the sale of low-quality goods at reduced prices, many state officials hoped to overcome the chaos, costs, frustrations, and economic losses associated with orders for ad hoc special sales issued from above that made little sense at the grass roots.[72] Advocates of BIWA stores argued that "a far-reaching decentralization and strengthening of the responsibility of the local state organs and trade enterprises for carrying out the law of value" would ameliorate the regime's "stiff and inflexible" price policies that prevented stores from adjusting prices to fit demand.[73] All "normal" stores and even wholesalers and manufacturers now would be allowed to sell their "so-called non-sellers [*Ladenhüter*]" to the new stores at prices to be negotiated between them.[74] BIWA store managers were not required to report detailed inventories to central authorities, did not have to fulfill sales quotas, and were not constrained by preset limits on turnover. Rather than being bound by maximum reduction rates for individual items, store managers could set their own prices, provided that total sales did not represent an average reduction of more than 40 percent.[75] Store managers also could have their stock of cloth made into ready-to-wear or have garments refashioned and altered.[76] Trade officials even suggested giving store managers the right to raise the prices of certain items "according to supply and demand."[77]

Trade officials faced the same ambiguities in defining which items to place in BIWA stores as they had in selecting items to include in the special clearance sales. Inclusion and exclusion still depended on subjective judgements of individuals or committees about articles' use-value, quality, fashionableness, and potential marketability at a given price. Although the goods were supposed to be discontinued and to have been manufactured in 1955 or earlier, trade officials could make exceptions for "single pieces or smaller individual packages" of wares. Other types of wares to be sold in BIWA stores included goods whose prices already had been reduced in previous special sales; items that had been displayed in store windows, damaged goods, and cloth remainders.[78] These criteria were confusing and subjective enough on paper; in practice they proved much worse.

On 4 June 1957, 741 BIWA stores opened throughout the GDR. Sales initially were strong, but by the end of July, officials began to list numerous difficulties that prevented the chain's smooth functioning and resulted in disappointing revenues.[79] It was clear that the BIWA stores would not come close to achieving their goal of 300 million DM in sales by the end of the year: sales decreased during June, and despite an increase in the total number of stores to 808 in July, the average sales per store continued to decline.[80] In addition to struggling with inadequate facilities, insufficient space, and discontented sales personnel who earned less than their counterparts in normal stores, the BIWA stores experienced difficulties in obtaining a continuous supply of fresh stock from normal retailers and wholesalers.[81] This situation was due in part to familiar, chronic distribution problems, but a more decisive factor was inherent in the BIWA stores' regulations. To encourage sales, many managers reduced the prices of some items by 70 to 80 percent but had to limit the reduction of other pieces to only 20 to 30 percent in order to maintain the required overall average discount of 40 percent.[82] Not surprisingly, items with larger price reductions sold quickly while the others "remain[ed] lying in the store as dregs."[83] When searching for fresh stock for their BIWA stores, managers thus bought only goods from normal retailers and wholesalers that could be sold with less than a 40 percent discount.[84] But such items either did not match the criteria for inclusion in BIWA stores or could be sold in the normal season-end sales. As a result, the BIWA stores offered a stagnant and narrow assortment of low-quality items at only modest and unchanging discounts.[85]

An average discount of 40 percent clearly was not large enough to sell the items that ended up in BIWA stores, top officials in the Ministry for Trade and Provisioning argued. After initially recommending an increase in the limit to 60 percent, by September the state trade officials suggested eliminating the average reduction limit altogether and instead pricing the items "according to supply and demand."[86] Once again, state trade leaders encountered resistance from officials in the Ministry of Finances. Although they eventually agreed to raise the average reduction limit to 50 percent for most types of sale items, state finance officials and many other functionaries preferred to blame BIWA stores' problems on operational and ideological issues.[87] Audits discovered numerous examples of "irresponsible devaluations" and the conflation of goods from BIWA and normal stores.[88]

The BIWA stores received mixed reviews from consumers and the media, according to available official reports and articles in the press.[89] A local state trade official in Leipzig claimed in July 1957 that the stores had "a good resonance" among those that had purchased something in them but that others pejoratively called the offerings *Ladenhüter*.[90] When BIWA items occasionally were mixed together with "normal" goods in violation of regulations, officials noted that the rural populace had the impression "that one wants to offer shoddy wares and carries along only a few so-called 'goodies'."[91]

The BIWA stores themselves hardly represented the "retail culture" (*Verkaufskultur*) that the regime was constantly promoting. In March 1958 an article in *Die Bekleidung*, a magazine intended for both employees of the textile industry and regular consumers, noted "the crass difference" between "an unpleasant-looking" BIWA store in Berlin's recently renovated Schönhauser Allee and the streets' "many modern stores," which provided "a visible expression" of "the growing affluence of our state and our population." Most of the BIWA stores' wares were "irreproachable in design and quality but no longer totally match[ed] fashion." However, the author admitted that "one should soon pull a certain portion of the wares out of the offerings. They damage the reputation [*Ansehen*] of our state."[92]

But the stores needed more than just a facelift. The very existence of these "permanent institutions" not only contradicted the SED's consumerist promises but also symbolized and visualized dysfunctional aspects of the GDR's economy. Renate Holland-Moritz, who frequently wrote about fashion and clothing in the East German press, conveyed this message in a parable published in *Die Bekleidung* in February 1959.[93] In the year 1970, Eitel-Konrad Puschke, the director of BIWA store 2009, tries a novel method of ridding his overfilled store of enormous stockpiles of out-of-date shoes and apparel, some of which date back to 1949: he takes his best wares to the moon under the assumption that the inhabitants will gladly buy them. He finds the moon people, however, to be dressed immaculately in the most fashionable and chic apparel. They have no boutiques, for "every moon woman" can buy these items in normal stores. While touring the 25–story "moon fashion house," Eitel-Konrad felt as if he were "in the rooms of the German Fashion Institute in Berlin, only here the selection was decisively larger." The moon has no BIWA stores, the director of the moon fashion house explains, because "the factories always produce according to the newest methods. Otherwise the risk would be too great for them." Flabbergasted, Eitel-Konrad could only tell his hostess, "if you should come to us on the earth sometime, you will see how far we are behind the moon."[94] The story ends with moon children finding Eitel-Konrad's discarded suitcase full of BIWA wares, mistaking them for "odd carnival costumes," and dressing up in the "monstrosities decorated with little bows, sequins, and applications."

For Holland-Moritz and many other East Germans, a store stocked exclusively with "unmodern and value-diminished things" represented the antithesis of a socialist consumer utopia. The very limited amount of advertising for the stores suggests that party and state officials largely shared these sentiments.[95] BIWA stores doubtlessly contained some bargains, but officials knew better than to boast of selling low-quality clothes that were several years old and most likely had already been a year or two out-of-date when they came off the production line. During a time of rising standards and expectations, few consumers found such apparel attractive, regardless of how low the price was.

Consumers' objections and the poor image of the stores must have played some role in the eventual decision to dissolve the BIWA stores, although the available records do not provide evidence to directly support this. Although officials continued to claim that the stores were "welcomed by the populace," already in February 1958 the leadership of the Ministry for Trade and Provisioning ordered a reduction in the number of BIWA stores and in April suggested dissolving the chain by the end of the year.[96] The explicit reasons for dissolving the stores focused on the belief that other methods could achieve the same economic goals more efficiently. State trade leaders admitted that because the discounts were centrally subsidized by the state and did not affect individual stores' bottom line, BIWA stores had "violated our socialist principle of the strictest thriftiness."[97]

Looking beyond the problems with the BIWA stores themselves, most party and state leaders seemed to agree that measures were necessary to enable regular stores to perform the functions assigned to BIWA stores. State trade officials had argued from the beginning of the BIWA experiment that discounts of even 60 percent could not totally eliminate all surpluses as long as the normal stores could not also reduce their prices more quickly and drastically.[98] In addition, a middle ground had to be found between "zero wares" and goods that could be sold in BIWA stores. As a local state trade official in Leipzig explained, local trade officials often automatically classified as "zero wares" any item that could not be sent to BIWA stores because it required more than a 40 percent discount in order to be marketable. Trade officials needed to find a way to discount goods by more than 40 percent and yet avoid the impression of selling "junk" (*Ramsch* or *Plunder*).[99]

As an alternative to BIWA stores and a new cure-all for the problem of surpluses, state trade officials suggested allowing retailers and wholesalers to establish a special fund for "commercial risk" (*Handelsrisiko*) from which they could draw in order to discount certain goods at their own discretion.[100] This fund appears to have been an expansion of the modest "price reduction funds" (*Preissenkungsfonds*) that the Ministry of Finances grudgingly allowed enterprises in industry and trade to maintain starting in 1957.[101] In a resolution on 2 January 1959, the Council of Ministers ordered both the creation of the special fund for "commercial risk" and the dissolution of all BIWA stores.[102] The last stores were closed on 9 March 1959; officials simply removed the BIWA signs from the buildings and turned them into normal stores.[103]

Socialism on Sale: The Return, Rise, and Fall of Season-End Sales

The failure of the BIWA experiment to create permanent stores for the continuous purging of surpluses meant that trade officials had to return to ad hoc, short-term actions. Something had to be done quickly. The combination of stagnant or decreasing sales since 1957 and increasing production meant that a growing proportion of the surpluses at the end of the 1950s were goods fresh from the production line.[104] The situation only worsened over the next several years. As they simultaneously pursued a variety of methods to reduce stockpiles of unsold goods, party and state functionaries became enveloped in the familiar conflicts and confusion over the definition of surpluses, the size of discounts, and the point at which wares simply should be given away or destroyed.

As surpluses piled higher and political tensions mounted at the turn of the decade, the political stakes of eliminating surpluses increased proportionally. These years witnessed a chaotic, confusing, and contradictory mixture of liberal, decentralized, and radical initiatives to eliminate surpluses; attempts to retain centralized control and to resist the devaluation of goods and materials; and accusations of espousing "consumer ideology" and of "wasting the people's property." The task of identifying which officials held which positions is complicated by their often overlapping, ambiguous, and shifting arguments, but the basic conflicts occurred between two general groups. At the central level, more liberal party and state leaders, who tended to be in the Ministry for Trade and Provisioning and the State Planning Commission and advocated higher discount rates and decentralization, clashed with more conservative leaders, many of whom were in the Ministry of Finances and the Politburo and resisted any movement toward higher discount rates or a loosening of centralized control over the state's political and economic apparatus. Concerned by ever-increasing stockpiles of surpluses and disappointed with the results of previous efforts to eliminate them, more conservative leaders gradually but reluctantly allowed more aggressive measures. Due to a combination of factors inherent in the GDR's planned economy and the initiatives of more liberal officials, these actions became more radical and produced undesirable political results. In the intensified political context of the Berlin crisis around the turn of the decade, party leaders scrambled to regain stricter control of the GDR's political and economic apparatuses.

Some of these tensions manifested themselves in the use of the new funds for "commercial risk." Although potentially a powerful tool to quickly and significantly reduce prices to match demand, in practice the commercial risk funds disappointed those who advocated the decentralization of economic activities. An integral part of enterprises' plans, the funds theoretically gave store managers "their own responsibility" to execute "necessary price corrections to ensure the sale of fashionably and technically outdated wares." Among other possibilities, the funds could be used for "season-end sales" and for bonuses to be paid to salespeople for each discounted item that they sold.[105] But local trade functionaries complained that the central functionaries in the Ministry for Trade and Provisioning and the Ministry of Finances in Berlin were frugal and delinquent in freeing up the funds at the grass roots: stores received too little too late.[106] Despite the existence of at least 800 million DM worth of surplus textiles and garments, the regime allocated only 134 million DM for commercial risk funds to pay for discounts in 1959.[107]

Picking up where BIWA left off and hoping for a sort of great leap forward, the Council of Ministers ordered a nationwide, two-week-long "special sale" of textile surpluses starting on 23 February 1959. Trade officials discounted 817 million DM worth of the oldest and least marketable textiles and garments from retailers' and wholesalers' stock by an average of over 50 percent (416 million DM) and managed to sell 51 percent of it.[108] But after the sale, the dilemma remained of what to do with the still unsold discounted wares, now valued at 195 million DM. Part of the problem was solved, at least on paper, by simply increasing the prices of 56 million DM of leftovers to their original level under the pretense of correcting "price disparities," eliminating "exaggerations," and returning to normal stores items that had been "unjustifiably" included in the sale.[109] The remaining 139 million DM worth of goods were to be sold using the familiar special mobile sales and "consumer goods exchanges" (*Konsumgüteraustausch*) with other socialist countries.[110] Remaining stock was either to be donated to the Volkssolidarität or turned into pulp and recycled (*Altstoffverwertung*).[111] In order to prevent the future build-up of surpluses, trade officials were to hold "season-end sales," as they had done since 1954. Party and state leaders thought that their orders sufficiently differentiated the types of articles to be included in these various actions, but in practice, ambiguous instructions, organizational chaos, and differences in subjective judgments continued to dissolve distinctions among the categories.

Efforts during the next few years to salvage even a modicum of economic value from the remainders of special sales met with only limited success. The regime encountered increasing numbers of obstacles to its economic safety valve: the exporting of consumer goods. "Consumer goods exchanges" with other Soviet-bloc countries, especially Poland, Czechoslovakia, and the Soviet Union, "did not bring the expected results," largely due to the other countries' increasing unwillingness to accept such low-quality goods.[112] Top officials in the Ministry for Foreign and Intra-German Trade and the Ministry for Trade and Provisioning concluded in 1959 that "in the future it will be impossible to sell" *Überplanbestände* "through the organs of foreign trade."[113] That was also true for exports to capitalist countries. Despite initial failures and officials' warnings that it was "politically irresponsible" to export low-quality surpluses to capitalist countries at "throwaway prices" (*Schleuderpreisen*), the regime's increasingly urgent need for hard currency led it to explore possibilities of doing precisely that.[114] For the time being, however, foreign trade functionaries argued that these transactions were inadvisable "for reasons of political prestige" and recommended that the regime explore "whether an at least partial sale on the GDR's domestic market at possibly strongly reduced prices is not more economically correct after all."[115] In an effort to derive even a small amount of political capital from absolutely unmarketable clothing, the regime ordered trade officials to transfer a large proportion of the millions of marks worth of "zero wares" to the Volkssolidarität.[116] The organization then gave the items to the poorest East German citizens under mottoes like "A Gift of Our Government to Certain Retirees and Families with Children on the Occasion of the Tenth Anniversary of Our Republic."[117]

Also starting in mid-1959, party and state functionaries at both the central and local levels devoted increasing attention to occasional special sales and biannual season-end sales. The summer-end sale of 1959 fit the conservative pattern of previous sales, posting poor results, revealing conflicts of categorizations and prices, and prompting the investigation of "irresponsible" actions by trade officials, who allegedly "wasted" goods and sold them at "throwaway prices."[118] The complaints remained essentially the same because the underlying tensions and potential for political damage were unchanged. Central authorities remained painfully aware of their reliance on lower-level functionaries to practically and "responsibly" execute theoretical orders from above.[119]

At least as serious as the political and economic consequences of the sales' potential to facilitate "irresponsible price reductions" was the problem of the growing surpluses themselves. Despite the special sale in early 1959 that cost the state 400 million DM, the amount of *Überplanbestände* had grown from 450 million DM to 750 million DM during the year.[120] Given this growth and the difficulties in exporting the goods, conservative party leaders grudgingly and cautiously began to acquiesce to perennial pleas of officials at the local level as well as in the State Planning Commission to allow more aggressive measures. These party leaders discovered, however, that they had started a movement that quickly progressed beyond their original intentions. During the next three years, despite nearly constant criticism by more conservative functionaries, a large number of party and state functionaries at all levels adopted increasingly liberal attitudes and radical measures involving both seasonal sales and "zero wares."

Starting in 1960, many officials, especially within the Ministry for Trade and Provisioning and the State Planning Commission, adopted increasingly assertive and decentralized methods for clearing warehouses after each season, arguing that it was a "life-necessity of the garment industry."[121] Unlike most earlier justifications of special sales, officials' arguments relied less on references to the decreased "value" of surpluses and more on economics and a growing acknowledgment that "fashion" influenced the price of apparel.[122] Many officials intensified their arguments that the state could sell more surpluses only if it increased discount rates.[123] In part in response to orders from above, in part on their own initiative, local and central state trade officials invested an increasing amount of time and effort in preparing and executing the sales starting in early 1960, including intensifying advertisements in the press, showing film advertisements before movies, holding special fashion shows, and moving up the starting date before the season-end sale in West Berlin.[124] State Planning Commission officials even suggested a number of preemptory price reductions, including discounting certain winter clothing items already in September.[125] Trade and planning officials vowed to end the practice of including "excessively old" clothing and other generic surpluses in the "season-end sales," which now were to contain exclusively goods that had been produced during the previous season.[126] The Ministry for Trade and Provisioning apparently even enacted these and similar orders without the approval of the Politburo, which complained in April 1960 that a draft of suggestions for price reductions gave trade officials a "carte blanche" (*Blankovollmacht*) and reiterated the idea that ideological and organizational problems, rather than high prices and low quality, were the underlying causes of surpluses.[127] As they had done in 1954 and 1955, the more conservative leaders in the Politburo and Ministry of Finances dispatched ideologically reliable and highly motivated instructors (*Instrukteure*) and brigades (*Brigaden*) of special workers to audit and correct ideological and organizational problems at the grass roots.[128]

Central authorities had such brigades work in stores and warehouses and organize special sales to demonstrate that stores could increase sales and reduce surpluses without having to resort to high discounts. One of the most prominent events organized by the brigades was a modestly successful special sale at various locations in Berlin in November and December 1960 that party leaders hoped to make an example for future sales throughout the GDR.[129] The Central Committee followed up these intentions in early 1961 by announcing the "500-million-movement" (*500-Millionen-Bewegung*), a campaign to get retailers to sell 500 million DM worth of wares over and above industry's production during that time. Billed as one of the many attempts to tap the "reserves" of the GDR's economy, the campaign essentially aimed to increase sales through willpower and "ideological clarity."[130]

These special actions to increase turnover ironically may have encouraged trade officials to increase the volume and extent of discounts, which was precisely the behavior that party leaders were trying to eliminate. Given the subjectivity of the criteria for inclusion and the confusion resulting from central authorities' constantly changing guidelines, frequent "uncertainties" about exactly which items were to be included in sales are not surprising.[131] Chaos reigned as two opposite tendencies continued to exist side-by-side: while some officials refused to include selected seasonal items because they supposedly could be sold during the next year's season at the same price, other officials discounted goods that had never left industry's warehouses in order to reduce their prices to the level of the items in the season-end sales.[132]

Despite the regime's best efforts and local officials' liberal use of discounts, results of the season-end sales remained disappointing. The HO still did not sell more than 32 percent of the goods included in the winter-end and summer-end sales of 1960.[133] Both season-end sales in 1961 managed to sell just under half of the goods included, although these included older surpluses along with the "seasonal" wares.[134] Despite numerous resolutions to include only the newest seasonal items in the season-end sales, in the end, trade officials always included older surpluses and held concurrent but supposedly separate sales of the "discontinued stock" (*Abwicklungsbestände*).[135] Reports from the provinces expressed local officials' disillusionment with the "thirteenth or seventeenth textile action ... of which none was properly carried out to the end."[136]

Party and state leaders' concern about "irresponsible price reductions" were totally out of proportion to their modest frequency and economic impact. The limits set on discounts amounted to usually less than 3 and no more than 6 percent of total annual sales of textiles and garments, and stores never sold more than half of the total amount allowed.[137] During the five season-end sales from 1959 to 1961, state trade officials had reduced 795 million DM worth of goods by 249 million DM, an average discount of just over 30 percent.[138] Exact figures on how many of these goods were sold are not available, but it could not have been more than half. Any explanation of leading functionaries' hypersensitivity about "abuses" and "irresponsible discounts" during the sales must include their concern about the political impact of the actions, both within official institutions and in the eyes of ordinary citizens.

Officials had long noted "consumers' disappointment over the inadequate discount rates."[139] Many citizens resented being offered low-quality goods at minimal discounts and instead demanded higher quality and more fashionable items.[140] Central Committee functionaries noted "negative discussions" in which factory workers insisted that "one should sell regular wares in the factories and not things that one couldn't get rid of elsewhere."[141] Large discounts called the regime's entire system of price policies into question. As one party leader asserted, when discounts became too high, "the population asked, what's wrong, were the prices until now all totally false."[142]

Part of a speech given by Paul Verner, the influential first secretary of the Berlin district, in March 1961 during a Central Committee conference illustrates both the political sensitivities of many party leaders and the confusion and contradictions that resulted from dilemmas over surpluses and clearance sales.[143] Verner held up a wool dress to illustrate the interrelated problems posed by season-end sales and

East German industry's low-quality production. The price of the dress, which Erich Honecker had bought during that year's winter-end sale in Berlin's Schönhauser-Allee, had been reduced from 92.50 DM to 35 DM, according to Verner.[144] At the store, Honecker allegedly heard an older worker declare, "Either they swindled [*beschissen*] us before or they're swindling us now." In an internal memo to Verner, Honecker wrote that he had heard "the same discussion" in front of another store that displayed both the original and discounted prices of men's suits. Honecker privately admitted that the suits' quality may have justified the discounts of 61 percent and 47 percent, but he objected to the display of the old prices: "That arouses little trust in our arrangement of prices."[145] Verner echoed these sentiments in his speech for the Central Committee: "Through such measures we compromise the price policies of our republic." Verner, Honecker, and other party leaders considered the stability of prices to be a cornerstone of the regime's price policies and were extremely sensitive about the potential for East German citizens to view these fluctuations, whether upward or downward, as a violation of the "trust" between regime and people: in Verner's words, "One doesn't take us seriously. One says: what are those for prices, earlier that, today this."

This episode also reveals the confusing and contradictory messages that officials received during the execution of the sales. In an internal letter to Verner, local state trade officials from Berlin explained that the dress in question was made in the first half of 1959 and had been included in the special sale in Berlin during November and December 1960. According to the local officials, regulations for the winter-end sale of 1961 stipulated that old and new prices were to be displayed for most items but not for the leftovers from the special sale in 1960.[146] However, the available records indicate that the guidelines stated without qualification that old and new prices for all items should be displayed.[147] Even if these exceptions had been made, party officials could not have expected local officials, who were swamped with goods from all sorts of sources, to precisely execute such detailed orders, especially since earlier sales had specified that the price tags for all goods on sale display both the new and the old prices.[148]

Verner did not mention any of this in his speech, however, but instead concentrated on the quality and material of the dress. Even more outrageous to him than the steep discount was the fact that the garment's extremely poor quality meant that rare "pure, soft wool" had been "squandered." "No woman who has a little sense will wear that dress," Verner offered, "if a female comrade would like to wear it, we'll give it to her. But I'm not accepting it." Nevertheless, he argued that because the dress was made out of pure wool, it should not be discounted. In fact, regulations governing special sales generally prohibited the discounting of items made out of "valuable materials." But Verner offered no solution to the dilemma of what to do with such goods, which he underestimated to number in the "hundreds and hundreds."

Such goods were practically worthless, and yet Verner, like many others, objected to cutting the regime's losses by selling the goods for at least a fraction of their original prices. Instead, he used a common gendered trope: blame the male leaders of industry and claim that they would fix the situation if their own wives had to wear such apparel – in other words, if they were even indirectly affected by the poor quality of their factories' products. Verner suggested that the problem could be solved quickly by forcing the factory director's wife to "run around in this dress for half a year": "I don't want to go so far that he runs around in it. (Laughter) But the wife will make him get such a move on that it will be eliminated."

Political tensions further intensified starting in April 1961 in connection with a controversy over the disposal of "zero wares." As the result of audits, the Council of Ministers and the Politburo censured various trade organs for "the irresponsible destruction of stocks of wares" and other "shortcomings" that represented a break in the chain of command.[149] Although the absolute number and value of the violations were not great, the auditors argued that "under the given circumstances (devaluation to zero, giving away, destruction, etc.), even the smallest inadequacies in the preparation and execution of the necessary measures can cause great political damage, regardless of the volume of wares."[150] Although surpluses continued to mount, central authorities became increasingly suspicious of trade officials' claims that discounts were necessary.[151]

The construction of the Berlin Wall on 13 August 1961, one day after the end of the summer-end sale, soon prompted a reconsideration of the place of season-end sales in state socialism. In line with the general sentiment among party and state leaders of consolidation and starting anew, consensus for the elimination of the special sales quickly crystallized, although neither the Politburo nor the Council of Ministers seems to have passed an official resolution to this effect.[152] In both internal and public explanations of the cancellation of the winter-end sale of 1962, party leaders simply elaborated on the familiar objections to the "serious ideological and economic-organizational problems" that various officials had perennially listed during the past seven years.[153] Official explanations claimed that the proper functioning of production and distribution networks along with the use of the modest "commercial risk funds," as demonstrated in the 500-million-movement, made season-end sales "superfluous."[154] Although the available records do not provide any direct evidence, the new political and economic environment after the construction of the Wall undoubtedly contributed to the regime's decision to discontinue season-end sales. More important than the elimination of competition with stores in West Berlin was the strengthened position of more conservative leaders, who now pushed the *Produktionsaufgebot*, a campaign calling for workers to "produce more in the same amount of time for the same amount of pay," and called for increases in accumulation and decreases in consumption.[155]

The Persistence of "Consumer Ideology" and "Squandering of the People's Property"

Despite the ban on season-end sales, controversies over discounts continued. The wave of hoarding of textiles and other durables that followed the construction of the Wall temporarily slowed the growth of surpluses, but the problem regained urgency in the first half of 1962. Total surpluses of all industrial wares, of which textiles and garments comprised the lion's share, increased from 684 million DM at the beginning of the year to 1.16 billion DM by 31 May.[156] Although the regime had ended season-end sales, its support for initiatives like the 500-million-movement encouraged state trade officials at all levels to try other methods of increasing sales. Top officials at the Ministry for Trade and Provisioning had opened the door to the continued use of discounts already in January 1962 when they ordered utilization of the "commercial risk funds" for "broadened sales measures (for example special sales, itinerant sales, price changes for single pieces or small packages of remainders)."[157] While the Ministry explicitly stipulated that such special sales "may not take on the extent and character of regional clearance sales," it apparently did not ensure that local officials complied with these limitations.[158] By June, trade officials had launched a nationwide campaign to increase sales of textiles. Following the regime's entreaties to use "real initiative and inventiveness in advertising and offerings" to increase sales, local officials organized special fashion shows, car parades, advertising campaigns, and factory sales.[159] Among the initiatives to alter cloth and garments in order to increase their marketability were orders for managers of Konsum stores to dye "women's dresses in unfashionable colors and designs" black and sell them as "mourning apparel."[160]

Not all of these initiatives met with party leaders' approval. Local officials reported that although the "ideology" that surpluses "are only marketable at cheapened prices" was largely "overcome," the "tendency of 'cheap days' and even 'giving away' is still present."[161] The most controversial initiative to increase sales was a campaign in several cities under the motto *"Kleide Dich neu!"* (clothe yourself anew), which included giving away one of every thirty or 100 dresses and advertising slogans that encouraged women, "Get rid of the old, clothe yourselves anew!"[162] Party leaders immediately seized on this campaign and turned it into a catchphrase in the following months as an example of the type of "ideology" that they hoped to exterminate. Already on 28 June 1962, Walter Ulbricht sent Grete Wittkowski newspaper clippings about the *Kleide Dich neu* campaign and asked her to investigate, commenting, "obviously a psychosis is supposed to be created to buy quite a lot, since we allegedly have too many wares. That, however, stands in contradiction to the plan."[163]

Paul Fröhlich, the SED's First Secretary of the Leipzig district and a candidate of the Politburo, offered a more elaborate explanation of his objections to the campaign at a trade conference in Leipzig on 12 July, the same day the Council of Ministers discussed the campaign's "false orientation."[164] Fröhlich described some of the campaign's images, including an old-looking piece of clothing on fire on an ironing board with the caption "It doesn't matter – Buy yourself a new one!" Fröhlich argued that such images embodied an "ideology of squandering" (*Vergeudungsideologie*) or a "consumer ideology" (*Konsumentenideologie*) that encouraged East Germans to think that "we live in an era of squandering": "We create illusions about a condition that we *currently do not yet have*, about a *certainty* in provisioning with all food products and goods" (emphasis added).[165] In a speech at a Central Committee conference three months later, Politburo Candidate Edith Baumann seconded the idea that one of the most politically harmful aspects of *Kleide Dich neu* was that it "aroused needs that we cannot yet comprehensively satisfy at this time" and taught the population "squandering instead of thrift."[166] Günter Mittag, who also spoke at the conference, added, "some functionaries from trade and the consumer goods industry had the opinion that in the GDR, if at all possible, everything must be produced or procured that individual citizens demand, sometimes because of Western influences."[167]

The fallout from the *Kleide Dich neu* controversy only caused more confusion. Falling back on a familiar trope, the Politburo and the Council of Ministers ordered trade officials to exert "increased pressure" on industry in order to harmonize production with changing demands rather than concentrate "one-sidedly" on increasing sales.[168] But they failed to give trade functionaries the means to accomplish this. When trade officials began canceling production contracts, failing to fulfill their sales plans, and slashing their advertising budgets, party leaders scolded them for not understanding the true thrust of the objections to *Kleide Dich neu*.[169] At the same time, the regime ordered the Ministry for Trade and Provisioning to "stipulate differentiated measures to diminish the present excessive stock," including "strengthened efforts" to sell "excessively old stock."[170] Given such contradictory signals, it is not surprising that Central Committee officials found in October that an atmosphere of uncertainty and intimidation was preventing trade officials from organizing any sales initiatives for fear of possible comparisons to *Kleide dich neu*.[171]

Trade officials' paralysis came at a very inopportune moment. Surpluses were piling higher than ever with no end in sight.[172] Textiles comprised roughly half of the surpluses of all industrial goods, which climbed each year, from 1.048 billion DM at the end of 1961 to 2.012 billion DM at the end of 1962 to 2.183 billion DM as of 30 June 1963.[173] Despite the growing crisis, the regime limited trade officials to scattered, ad hoc "special sales" and refashioning old stock on a modest and local scale.[174]

In the mid-1960s, the regime began to return to exports as a major method of eliminating surpluses. This trend reflected the regime's shifting economic priorities and political sensitivities. "Consumer goods exchanges" were expanded by giving the GDR's fellow socialist countries long-term credits to pay for the goods, while the regime's increasingly urgent need for hard currency led it to export surpluses to capitalist countries "under special conditions," a euphemism for large discounts.[175] In 1964, for instance, state wholesalers were willing to sell 75 million DM worth of garments "by the kilogram" to capitalist countries at only 2 percent of the industrial price.[176] The regime now was exporting goods at prices that officials had considered politically untenable just a few years before.

But not all top party and state officials agreed. Already in August 1963, the Politburo's Office for Industry and Construction (Büro für Industrie und Bauwesen) complained, "the false conclusion was drawn from the mistakes of the action '*Kleide dich neu*' that well-prepared and economically thought-out seasonal clearance sales, flexible payment condition (installment payments) etc. are 'unsocialist' and encourage waste." This mistake "inevitably led to the opinion that it is better to sell difficult-to-market textile products and other wares at great losses in capitalist countries than to sell them in a timely manner through flexible prices and favorable payment conditions to citizens with low incomes and where the demand still is not satisfied by far."[177] In the context of continuously growing surpluses and the reforms of the New Economic System, the Office for Industry and Construction joined the Central Committee's Planning and Finances division in calling for the reintroduction of "season-end sales at strongly reduced prices," "flexible handling of prices according to supply and demand," the "discounted sale or free delivery to retirees, children's homes, social agencies, the Volkssolidarität, etc. as well as the industrial utilization of such wares that despite the above-mentioned measures remain unsold."[178]

Trade officials subsequently did hold "season-end sales" again, although they never matched the extent or regularity of those held between 1954 and 1961. But the same ideological tensions, organizational problems, and political concerns remained.[179] Until at least 1975, trade officials erratically held modest season-end and special sales, usually offering only a few hundred thousand marks worth of goods at minimal discounts.[180] The regime also continued to use the export of surpluses, especially to capitalist countries, as an "outlet" and as a way to obtain the hard currency required to pay for inexpensive, low-quality imports.[181]

Surpluses continued to plague the GDR's economy throughout the rest of the country's existence. Retail personnel surveyed in 1973 estimated that approximately half of the ready-to-wear articles currently in stores were "difficult to market."[182] Low-quality goods continued to pile up while high-quality goods made of certain materials – especially synthetics – continued to be snapped up.[183] More distressing than the economic losses that surpluses entailed was the political damage that they exacted. Officials were acutely aware of the inability of the GDR's economy to produce a variety of assortments at corresponding prices to match the differentiated needs of diverse consumers. Party functionaries worried that the visual and physical dominance of old, low-quality goods in East German stores reflected poorly on socialism, negatively influenced consumers' perceptions of their standard of living, and both visualized and embodied the regime's failure to fulfill its citizens' needs. Adding to the political damage was the regime's attempt to use the BIWA stores, special and season-end sales, and various other price reductions to exploit differences within the population in income and access to better goods while soaking up the buying power of lower-income groups. Instead of offering bargains for everyone and contributing to egalitarian consumer possibilities and social justice, such price reductions undermined the regime's consumer promises and strengthened hierarchies and social distinctions. The next chapter examines the regime's efforts to exploit these differences for economic gain by employing the opposite method: increasing prices for higher-quality and more fashionable apparel.

–6–

The Disillusionment of Dreams of Distinction: *Hochmodisch* Apparel, Fashion Boutiques, and Exquisit Stores

The counterpart of efforts to eliminate surpluses was the encouragement of the production of higher-quality, more fashionable apparel. While ridding stores of unsold goods aimed to minimize economic losses, assessing surcharges for exclusive garments was intended to maximize revenue for the state. The production of expensive, desirable clothing and its sale in special stores also represented a valuable political and cultural asset for a regime that promoted "clothing culture," promised to fulfill its citizens' increasing needs, and competed with the West on the basis of individual consumption. Inherent in these goals was the ambivalent legitimation of a certain amount of differentiation and distinction through consumption. But this differentiation conflicted with the SED's explicitly egalitarian principles and thus entailed significant political costs. Moreover, a variety of economic and organizational difficulties prevented the realization of dreams of distinctive fashion salons, exposed weaknesses in the SED's control over the GDR's state, industrial, and retail apparatuses, and aroused widespread consumer resentment.

Already in the early 1950s, fantasies began to circulate within the regime and in the media about not just fashionable, but "extravagant" apparel and special stores in which to sell it. In September 1952, while certain textiles and garments were still being rationed, the Ministry of Trade and Provisioning introduced plans to open "luxury shops" (*Luxusläden*) on East Berlin's historical showcase boulevard Unter den Linden.[1] The first burst of activity in this direction came in Berlin in late 1953 as part of the New Course's increased emphasis on consumption.[2] These initiatives for the production and sale of high-quality and extremely individual apparel received official sanction at the highest level in August 1954 when the Council of Ministers ordered the Ministry of Trade and Provisioning to establish several "studios for custom and made-to-measure clothing" and to "organize the sale of custom clothing of the best quality."[3]

These early plans for high-class stores stemmed from the regime's desire to create a *Verkaufskultur* (retail culture) that was crucial to realizing an ideal *Bekleidungskultur* and socialist consumer culture.[4] The stores were to serve as models for others, demonstrate the GDR's economic achievements, and visualize promises of future prosperity. But given the dominant model of trickle-down cultural dissemination and the existence of modest, yet nevertheless significant differences in income, these stores also embodied a certain elitism. Underlying the push for special stores was the common assumption that only a small number of fashion-conscious customers with high incomes would want to buy "highly fashionable" designs while the rest of the population preferred or at least was satisfied with more conventional or "standard" models. By spatially isolating certain customers from the masses, special salons would facilitate the fulfillment of their special wishes, tastes, and desires for distinction.[5]

Although the VEB Maßatelier, founded in Berlin in 1954 as one of the first studios for the production of "custom clothing in craftsman-like individual production," disappointed both officials and customers, expectations of future fashion salons continued to grow, encouraged by newspaper and magazine articles.[6] These visions emphasized the individual, "sophisticated" (*gehoben*) character of such stores – sometimes even claiming superiority to similar establishments in West Germany – and stressed that fashion salons could not attract the desired group of consumers with their offerings alone; the stores' atmosphere and service had to match the high quality and individuality of the goods for sale.[7] Authors often stressed that fashion salons would contribute toward official efforts to specialize and rationalize of trade as well as decrease the amount of labor that East German women themselves had to invest in clothing. Women could save enormous amounts of time and money by not having to make their own clothes and by not having to run from store to store in an almost always fruitless search for fashionable items.[8] Calls in the press for special boutiques inspired trade officials in cities across East Germany to ask central authorities for the resources to establish their own special stores.[9]

Justifying Differentiation

Not everyone enthusiastically endorsed such special stores, which embodied a fundamental ambivalence in official policies about the balance among the fulfillment of "basic needs," desires for differentiation, and the regime's economic exigencies. In establishing pricing policies, party leaders quickly achieved a consensus that all citizens had a right to "basic" or "standard" consumer goods. Functionaries disagreed, however, about the degree of choice and differentiation to which consumers should be entitled above and beyond this basic level and how much these other goods should cost. Actual practices that often contradicted these egalitarian principles further complicated matters. Already in 1948 with the founding of the state-owned Handelsorganisation (HO), the SED had displayed a willingness to forego its self-proclaimed egalitarian principles in order to combat the black market, to give favored (male) workers material incentives and rewards, and to make handsome profits for the state while soaking up excess buying power. The official purpose of the HO was to eliminate the postwar black market by offering otherwise rationed goods as well as "luxury" items for purchase at a price level between the ration coupons and the black market.[10] Katherine Pence and Mark Landsman have shown how the HO during its early years created and reinforced hierarchies and led to a two-class retailing system.[11]

That the HO did not have the sole purpose of combating the black market became apparent as clothing rationing was lifted gradually and many functionaries envisaged replacing the two-class system with a broad spectrum of differentiated goods at a variety of prices. Officials in the Ministry for Trade and Provisioning advocated imposing a "price differentiation" for the non-rationed goods "corresponding to the different qualities." This presupposed, the trade officials stressed, that "the population has the *choice* to obtain the standard quality at a somewhat normal price or to buy quality wares at a correspondingly higher surcharge-price" (emphasis added).[12] But as previous chapters have demonstrated, the SED's ideology and the GDR's economy were hardly geared toward producing fashionable, high-quality goods and selling them at higher prices in special stores. In addition to logistical and economic difficulties that resulted in a chaotic mish-mash of goods whose prices did not necessarily correspond to their value by any estimation, the proposition that articles of clothing should be differentiated in price solely because of subjective, aesthetic characteristics was highly controversial in the early 1950s when debates raged over the legitimacy of any dimension of consumer goods beyond "use-value."

Ironically, advocates of surcharges for "luxurious" and "fashionable" consumer goods often employed the concept of "use-value" to justify their position. One common argument posited that such items had no relation to "basic needs" and therefore represented superfluous societal work. The prices of such items could contain a higher profit to reflect their unnecessary nature.[13] Other officials argued that "fashionable" goods addressed "higher" needs, embodied "higher" use-values, and thus deserved higher prices.[14] By claiming that "luxury" and "fashionable" goods were simply supplemental to "standard" goods that fulfilled "basic needs," officials placed them outside the basic framework of the planned economy. This rhetorical positioning allowed advocates to overcome a socialist taboo and explicitly encourage responses to market mechanisms of supply and demand in the pricing of these special wares, which could serve as legitimate sources of accumulation.[15] Since the SED predicted gradual growth of higher-income groups, who presumably would prefer "luxury" and "fashionable" articles, production had to quickly and flexibly adapt to a developing market informed by "the changing need-wishes [*Bedarfswünschen*] that are created by changes in the income structure."[16]

Even more popular than ideological arguments for fashion surcharges were economic justifications based on the logic of production in the GDR's planned economy. Many officials argued that charging more for better quality could give manufacturers a necessary incentive for the production of the types of goods that the GDR needed most.[17] Advocates of charging higher prices for "better" goods benefited from many broad political and economic developments of the 1950s, including the growing official acceptance and even promotion of haute couture and distinction through consumption and consumers' rejection of low-quality, out-of-date apparel. Fashionable clothing produced in small series could "immediately and directly execute the fashion ideas of the haute couture collection of the Institute for Clothing Culture," functionaries argued, adding that improvements in quality and fashionableness were essential to preventing the further growth of surpluses.[18] Consumers were willing to pay extra for better quality, officials repeatedly noted.

For all these reasons, bureaucratic price regulations that did not account for aesthetic considerations increasingly came under attack by the late 1950s. At the Trade Conference in July 1959, Walter Ulbricht delivered the most prominent attack on the failure of industry and trade to charge higher prices for fashionable models compared with "standard" ones. His speech succinctly combined ideological and economic arguments and illustrates well how the SED's top functionaries used gender to justify price policies:

> It must not be that these fashionable shoes have the same price or are cheaper than standard shoes! Those who want to have such fashionable shoes [should] pay a higher price, like it is in every country! But some of our experts take the same price for these "highly fashionable" shoes – I always use that word in quotation marks – whereby the black marketers from West Berlin rake in quite high profits. We are in favor of everyone being able to dress as one wants. One can order shoes as one wants. One can wear sack fashion as one wants. One has full freedom! But, dear comrades, if a woman wants to wear a sack dress, she should pay a higher price! Please! The others wear dresses that correspond to the people's sensibilities [*Volksempfinden*], which as a rule are prettier – and that works just as well! We're footing the bill, and the others are getting their pleasure from it.[19]

Ulbricht inverted earlier debates about charging more for "good taste" to argue – contrary to all accounts, even within the party and state – that standard assortments were in fact the tasteful and popular ones. Although few East Germans would have agreed with this statement, Ulbricht's use of gendered discourses on Frau Mode and needs probably resonated in his audience. He argued that unproductive and luxurious feminine desires for sack dresses and other "highly fashionable" frivolities naturally should have a bigger price tag than sensible and practical standard assortments that fulfilled basic needs and embodied the moderation of Herr Geschmack. Rather than condemning the supposedly feminine desire for distinction, Ulbricht employed the regime's democratic rhetoric and insisted that the East German consumer enjoyed the freedom – almost the right – to choose.

The party leadership's proposed solution to the dilemma of differentiation seemed simple: consumers could choose to pay extra for the satisfaction of superfluous desires. Since the party expected no objections from women and certainly none from men, this position was considered politically justifiable. "Price differentiation" (*Preisdifferenzierung*), however, often became a euphemism and an excuse for charging more for certain items with little justification. Perhaps the most powerful argument for higher prices for "luxury" and "fashionable" items was their ability to serve as "bearers of accumulation" (*Akkumulationsträger*) and as an ideal means of correcting the imbalance between supply and demand by soaking up the chronic "surplus buying power" (*Kaufkraftüberhang*) that resulted from the tendency of wages to outpace prices and the supply of goods.[20]

Encouraging Differentiation

One of the most common proposals to improve the quality of textiles and garments called for manufacturers to produce various "genres" in order to more closely match consumers' heterogeneous tastes and pocket books. The question was how to achieve the right balance among "highly fashionable products, fashionable retail genre [*Verkaufsgenre*], and large-series production."[21] The proposed proportions of these genres reflected contrasting values and visions of the future development of socialist consumer culture. It boiled down to a choice between two simplified techniques of convincing the population (and the West) of socialism's merits: expensive, highly fashionable models that could be purchased only by a select few, or inexpensive, "solid," "normal," and standardized apparel for everyone.

Advocates of a more differentiated consumer culture called for production to shift from standard items to more fashionable ones. In January 1959 Paul Sonnenberg, head of the Central Committee's Department for Light Industry, Food Processing, and Local Industry, suggested that by 1961 the GDR should increase the proportion of "highly fashionable" shoes from 5 percent to 20 percent and of "fashionable" shoes from 10 to 50 percent of total offerings, while "standard" shoes should decrease from 85 to only 30 percent.[22] Such statements accompanied bureaucratic initiatives to encourage the production of *Modellkonfektion*, fashionable ready-to-wear models produced in very small series.[23] In early 1959 *Neues Deutschland* and other publications touted "models of which at the most 300 pieces are made for the entire GDR," while the garment manufacturer VEB Kunst und Mode in Berlin sent experts to Paris in order to produce only 1,000 pieces of *Modellkonfektion* each month "according to the newest international fashion guidelines."[24] But once again, reality failed to measure up to hopes and expectations, and sharp criticism of the new *Modellkonfektion* abounded within official institutions and in the press.[25] These highly publicized efforts soon created a backlash as other functionaries insisted that the production of "fashionable" goods not come at the expense of "standard" ones. At the Trade Conference in July 1959, the party leadership launched an offensive against what it claimed was the overproduction of Western-influenced, fashionable goods and the neglect of "the better provisioning of the working population with pretty, useful, and cheap standard products, as the party demands it."[26]

Despite such ideological diatribes, party and state officials, along with leaders of the state-owned textile and garment industries, increased the intensity of their long-standing calls to stimulate the production of "fashionable" apparel by adjusting production regulations and price calculations to account for the extra costs allegedly associated with such goods.[27] These early suggestions sounded remarkably market-oriented and decentralized. Since the GDR's planned economy was not at all suited to encourage the flexibility needed to react to changes in wishes and fashions, officials insisted that prices facilitate these functions. This meant that prices for "fashionable products" had to change to cover costs and to realize the "average planned profit." This could be achieved by allowing factories to add a "price surcharge" in order to create a fund that would cover the additional costs and serve as the "material incentive" to manufacture new and fashionable products.[28] Officials also stressed practical reasons to establish special stores in which to display and sell these high-quality and fashionable articles: they would help to simplify channels of distribution and achieve the largest possible visual and political effect. If the extremely small number of high-quality items were not pooled together, they would be practically invisible when scattered among the offerings of countless normal stores. Concentrating highly fashionable consumer goods in a few selected stores helped to ensure that at least some stores could carry "a full assortment" and achieve "an elevated level of *Verkaufskultur* in terms of furnishings and service."[29]

The Sibylle Boutique

The first major attempt at a full-fledged fashion boutique started in late 1957 and was named after the GDR's leading fashion magazine, *Sibylle*, which at the time was edited by the German Fashion Institute. At least 80 percent of the store's goods were to be "top-quality products" (*Spitzenerzeugnisse*) of the GDR's industry. Affiliated with the HO stores of Berlin's Mitte precinct, Sibylle received privileged access to "especially interesting wares" and had the right to make purchases before the normal buying negotiations in order to ensure that the boutique would become "tone-setting for our further development in the area of fashion."[30] However, a variety of problems with personnel, suppliers, and quality control forced officials to delay the original opening date of 1 May 1958 by several months.[31] When the store finally opened in August, it was supplied with ready-to-wear apparel by a small number of the GDR's leading garment factories and fashion institutes.[32] The demand on opening day was so great that the "female customers" had to be admitted "in batches" and administrative personnel had to assist the eight HO saleswomen.[33]

Located at the corner of Unter den Linden and Friedrichstraße, one of the most prominent sites in the heart of East Berlin's historical showcase district, the store's modernist architecture, generous use of interior space, and expensive, highly fashionable dresses created a dramatic visual contrast to the neighboring buildings and the offerings in normal stores (Figure 6.1). The media's reactions to the store reflected the familiar ambivalence about the promotion of haute couture and exclusive, expensive apparel. Enthusiastic endorsements of the store's realization of long-held wishes clashed with mockery of the "ridiculous," expensive models that embodied "fashion follies." *Neues Deutschland*'s fashion correspondent, Inge Kertzscher, was ecstatic: "A paradise is all around me – a ladies' paradise. [...]

Figure 6.1 Interior of the Sibylle boutique. S.G. "'sibylle' besuchte sibylle," *Sibylle* 3 (1958) 5: 59. (Photo: Helmut Fieweger, Courtesy Angela Heinrich-Fieweger)

Nothing is a mass-produced ware, nothing is unfashionable. Originality is trump."[34] A certain Steineckert echoed these sentiments and added a critical note in *Handelswoche*, the weekly newspaper for trade organizations:

> We hope that it doesn't become just any old ready-to-wear store but rather a treasure trove for good and very personal taste. That here within certain limits unusual wishes can be satisfied, and the petty-bourgeois charmeuse night shirts disappear from the shelves. Every woman should find here the little dot on the "i" in order to dress oneself fashionably and chicly. However, and this is not an insubstantial factor, her wallet may not thereby be affected all too detrimentally.

Sibylle was "not yet totally a real boutique," Steineckert lamented, for the "magical" dresses and models had "quite high" prices while "other affordable and very handsome dresses" already wore "sold" signs.[35] Others were even more critical and sarcastic: "We freely admit that one can buy very handsome things in our stores, especially if one has won the lottery jackpot and consequently is able to pay a visit to the 'Sibylle' boutique."[36]

Familiar battles concerning "good taste" also were fought over Sibylle's offerings. An article in *Frau von heute* facetiously attacked Sibylle's "high-fashion" models, including a "stunningly obscene" sack dress called "Rose cyclamen" that stepped "beyond the international level (*Weltniveau*) into the realm of the demimonde." The article also sarcastically praised Sibylle's "Lamé" model, which "was intended primarily for those female workers and housewives who once or twice a week participate in king's coronations, receptions by Rainier III of Monaco, or parties with the former empress Soraya. At 326 DM, this clothing article, which due to its metal padding will last for more than 50 years, should also be interesting for the cleaning lady." The article proceeded to quote women who criticized the boutique's offerings as being out of touch with the tastes and true wishes of the GDR's working women.[37]

Exquisit Stores and the "Hochmodisch" Label

Building on the experience of the VEB Maßatelier, the Sibylle boutique, and numerous aborted attempts to create incentives for high-quality apparel and establish fashion salons, central and local officials in Berlin began to plan a chain of special stores for high-quality apparel around October 1960. The German Fashion Institute and the VVB Konfektion, perhaps at the behest of the State Planning Commission, called for the creation of eleven specialized stores in major cities that would offer exclusively the Institute's "original models" in smaller series.[38] These "fashion houses" were intended to satisfy the "high standards" of "various parts of the GDR's population, especially the intelligentsia" and those with "higher incomes," whose buying power would be "more strongly siphoned off" by the items' high prices.[39] Independent of these efforts, by February 1961 SED officials in Berlin at the district level outlined plans to transform three existing stores on the city's historical showcase boulevard Unter den Linden into "special stores for valuable textiles." The new stores were to offer "only the most valuable articles predominantly from imports and outspoken top-quality products of GDR-production with special pricing" and were to open by 3 March 1961 so that the project could be discussed at the Central Committee's next plenary session on 10 March.[40] Based on the example of these three stores, party leaders planned to open two separate networks of special stores by the end of the third quarter of 1961. "Special" stores in the district and county capitals would offer "predominantly highly fashionable products, novelties, and developments of the textile industry" while even more exclusive "representative" stores in the district capitals ("of the type of 'Sibylle' in Berlin and 'Chic' in Leipzig") would sell "high-quality and highly fashionable products" that would be made by their own workshops and small collectives of tailors and shoemakers.[41] Although the exact origins of the name are unclear, these "representative" shops soon became known as "Exquisit" stores.[42]

Like the Sibylle boutique, Exquisit stores were to fulfill women's individual wishes for distinctive apparel. The stores' names – such as "Yvonne," "Jeanette," "Chic," "Pinguin," "Kavalier," "Picolo," "Charmant," or "Madeleine" – were intended to indicate French influence and the desired "international level" (*Weltniveau*).[43] Berlin's best multilingual saleswomen and salesmen were to staff the stores.[44] In an interview designated to be published in April 1962, Fritz Rechnagel, the deputy minister for trade and provisioning, claimed that "during the last years the wish was voiced in broad parts of the population to open special stores or fashion salons in which extraordinary [...] needs for extravagant, exquisite, or select clothing can be satisfied." Exquisit stores would give "our women" the possibility of being able to "dress themselves exquisitely" from "head to toe" for "special occasions." The Exquisit stores' direct connections to workshops and production factories would "ensure that the execution of individual customer wishes is possible at short notice."[45] The first Exquisit stores in Berlin, a local party official explained, were explicitly geared toward the "not small number of citizens, above all members of the intelligentsia, who earn high incomes and who want to spend their money for very specific high-quality and fashionable products. We have to, as one is in the habit of saying, siphon off [*abschöpfen*] their money quite quickly."[46]

A Politburo resolution on 10 March 1961 established what would become the nationwide network of Exquisit stores and at the same time introduced "material incentives" for the production and sale of "*hochmodisch*" (highly fashionable) items. From the start, the unpublished resolution created a great deal of confusion and ideological uncertainty among officials at all levels.[47] The reaction to and execution of the resolution augured the same type of problems that doomed the regime's efforts to rid stores of surpluses: the inability to objectively and bureaucratically classify items, problems with production and logistics, the tendency for officials at the grass roots to act according to their own interests rather than those of the party leadership, and political fallout from consumers' perceptions of unfair prices.

The resolution ordered a 10 to 20 percent increase in the prices of "novelties, highly fashionable [*hochmodisch*] products, and developments," which were to represent no more than 15 percent of the total volume of textiles.[48] For the items that soon were to fill Exquisit stores – "single models," "models that are manufactured in small numbers," and "extravagant productions" – the Politburo stipulated that prices and surcharges be set "corresponding to the prime costs." Despite the significance of the Politburo's resolution, the Council of Ministers did not approve the measures until 15 June and did not pass a resolution detailing their execution until 24 August, only days after the erection of the Berlin wall.[49] This new resolution increased the quantity and prices of *hochmodisch* items: "in exceptional cases," up to 25 percent of the total volume of any given group of wares could receive the surcharge, which could be up to 30 percent, "if the character of the products justifies it."[50]

Despite the fundamental commandment of the SED's price policies to ensure standard, inexpensive articles, these resolutions evinced the regime's tendency to allow the exclusive and expensive *hochmodisch* and Exquisit items to encompass an ever greater proportion of domestically produced apparel. The Council of Ministers defined Exquisit products as "model clothing (individually made and the smallest of series); clothing with pronounced luxury-character; valuable imported products; [and ...] shoes and leather goods with luxury-character."[51] Regardless of whether these "wares for extraordinary demands" were in fact "extraordinary," party and state leaders intended them to be extremely rare and highly individual.[52] The Council of Ministers' resolution contained examples of comparisons between new and old prices for both *hochmodisch* and Exquisit articles. The seven examples of price increases for *hochmodisch* garments ranged between 9.4 and 22 percent, with absolute prices ranging from 16.50 DM for a 100-percent cotton blouse (increased from 14.20 DM) to 160 DM for a men's 50-percent wool coat (increased from 143 DM).[53] The examples of Exquisit products were all imported from the West, were significantly more expensive (up to 550 DM for a mohair women's coat from Belgium), and received much higher price increases, ranging from 21 to over 100 percent.[54]

It is important to note that *hochmodisch* and Exquisit products were defined explicitly as supplements to the "standard" assortments. The Politburo limited these items to 15 percent of the total volume in order to ensure that "the current price level remains constant for at least 85 percent of this group of wares" and "that larger quantities of standard products in attractive finishing are offered to the population at the current prices."[55] Several voices within the party and state apparatus voiced concern that price increases could "lead to the limitation of the production of the so-called basic assortment" and thus hurt those with lower incomes.[56] Already by June 1961, Central Committee members organized meetings to correct the common attitude within the party that the price changes were the sole solution to the GDR's chronic problem of purchasing power outstripping the supply of goods. Many party members feared that the previous absolute ban on price increases would be replaced by a string of global price increases dictated solely by financial considerations. The Central Committee's Ernst Lange explained that these comrades needed to be taught that "supply and demand" and "market conditions" "objectively influenced the prices" of only these special items and not the "standard" ones.[57]

Officials still stood before the tricky task of defining exactly which articles should receive the surcharge. Many party and state functionaries viewed the *hochmodisch* category in purely economic terms, removed from any considerations of aesthetics or the politics of consumption. Minister of Finances Willy Rumpf, for instance, demanded that all textile products that appeared in a new form, color, or finishing – approximately 20 percent of total turnover – receive a 15-percent surcharge regardless of other considerations.[58] But other officials envisioned the special clothes as true role models, as visible, palpable evidence of the potential achievements of socialist industry.[59] Due to a combination of ambivalence about distinction, unwillingness to acknowledge the initiative's economic rationale, and inability to objectively define something as subjective as *hochmodisch*, the category remained undefined for the time being, a fateful mistake for the SED.

Little is known about the numbers and locations of the first group of Exquisit stores that were established gradually in larger cities across the GDR beginning in mid-1961, before the erection of the Berlin Wall in August, but officials seem to have been satisfied with initial revenues.[60] The Wall caused panic buying and hoarding that dramatically boosted sales for several months and encouraged the consumer cooperatives to successfully apply for permission to establish their own fashion salons. Due to the flood of customers and the potential for even higher volume and profits, many state officials, especially those involved with trade, pushed for a substantial expansion of the Exquisit network. The stores needed to increase in size and number so that "no jostling [*Gedränge*] develops and an individual consultation with the customers is possible."[61] But other functionaries, in cautioning against an enlargement, revealed a mixture of elitist impulses, a desire to soak up as much surplus buying power as possible, and a remarkably prescient foreboding of the consequences of expansion. Finance Minister Rumpf realized that given the GDR's productive capabilities, significant growth could be achieved only through falling back on goods that did not fulfill Exquisit's high standards. He insisted that "even the only partial inclusion of categories of wares that until now were classified as *hochmodisch* would have to lead to a sinking of the Exquisit stores' retail level." The prices for *hochmodisch* products also could "in no case fulfill the Exquisit standards." This in turn would mean that "completely different strata of customers" would be "steered into the Exquisit stores," preventing the stores from maintaining "their current level that satisfies the highest demands" and condemning them to have "at best the character of preferentially supplied stores for relatively broad sections of consumers."[62]

Officials in fact had noticed after the erection of the Wall that "the circle of customers had expanded considerably."[63] By late summer 1962 the Central Committee remarked that in addition to the "population groups with especially high incomes (some intelligentsia professions, craftsmen, and farmers)," Exquisit's customers included, "as was to be predicted," "young girls with low incomes" and "in relatively high amounts" "citizens with average incomes" who "want to afford themselves something special once in a while."[64] Such developments made at least the Central Committee's Ernst Lange wonder "whether and to what extent the Exquisit stores today are still correct."[65]

Such ambivalence among the party leadership, along with logistical problems and negative reactions from consumers, limited the Exquisit stores' growth during the first half of the 1960s. By January 1962 there were only thirty-one Exquisit stores throughout the GDR, with each district generally having one for women's and one for men's apparel.[66] By September the number of Exquisit stores had increased by only one.[67] The Exquisit network remained static until 1966, when it comprised only thirty-four stores.[68]

The Exquisit stores' stagnation was also due to the familiar mixture of logistical and bureaucratic difficulties. Despite their special access to resources and privileged status at the buying negotiations with industry, Exquisit stores had difficulties finding enough goods that met their high standards, just as Sibylle and other fashion boutiques had earlier.[69] Unable to rely on just a few manufacturers to provide sufficient and satisfactory products, the Exquisit stores, like normal stores, signed contracts with dozens of manufacturers, which directly contradicted the official intention of exclusive, specialized production.[70] Special price regulations and surcharges offered factories only modest incentives to produce Exquisit articles.[71] The stores' main offerings "developed not on the basis of long-term planning and designing of assortments," but rather were composed of the "accidental offerings" of "primarily smaller and the smallest manufacturers" as well as out of imports from capitalist countries.[72]

Another factor behind the stores' disappointing sales and macroeconomic losses was the chronic lack of differentiation between many of their expensive offerings and the assortments of normal stores. Officials often noted that the "relatively high price differences between Exquisit products and comparable products of the basic assortment" were "unfounded" and "are not understood by the population."[73] The stores also suffered from the familiar "creeping inflation."[74] The combination of these problems caused the stores' stock to pile up, which in turn caused another host of problems.[75]

At the same time, the *hochmodisch* classification was languishing. Party leaders estimated that price increases of textile "novelties" and "luxury articles" would account for at least 145 to 150 million marks of the planned increase in turnover of some 180 million marks from 7.2 to 7.38 billion marks.[76] But by June 1961 officials had been able to find only 50 million DM worth of "highly fashionable and interesting wares" to sell in the second half of the year, an amount that fell far short of the allowed limit of 15 percent of total production.[77] Sales of the items in "special stores" were scheduled to start on 1 July but were delayed for a variety of reasons.[78] The new prices for *hochmodisch* apparel finally went into effect on 1 September 1961 at the beginning of the fall/winter season, less than three weeks after the construction of the Wall.[79] By October central party and state officials once again were bemoaning the fact that significantly fewer articles received the surcharge than planned: the annual effect of the price increases amounted to only about 36 million marks. Only 5 percent of all garments included the surcharge, which was only 15 percent higher than normal prices rather than the allowed limit of 20 percent.[80]

Not long after this slow start, however, the quantity and prices of items that received surcharges began to spiral out of the regime's control in much the same way as official attempts to eliminate supluses. Party and state leaders worried about the political consequences of seemingly unjustified price increases for *hochmodisch* and Exquisit articles just as they complained of unjustified price reductions of *Überplanbestände*. The *hochmodisch* classification not only entailed complicated bureaucratic machinations that overwhelmed the party and state apparatuses, but the lack of clear and objective definitions invited inconsistent and arbitrary decisions about the appropriateness and size of surcharges.[81] By late 1961, reports from local officials and audits by the Central Commission for State Control revealed that some factories and officials were totally uninformed or reluctant to assess the new surcharge, while others recognized its lucrative potential and were surpassing all intended regulatory limits.[82] Trade officials in the Karl-Marx-Stadt district estimated that only approximately 30 percent of the outerwear cloth and 20 percent of the men's outerwear that received the surcharge actually deserved it.[83] Prices were rising even for assortments that were explicitly excluded from the classification, such as children's clothing.[84] The combination of bureaucracy and subjectivity produced classifications based on the logic of production rather than aesthetics or demand.[85]

Party and state officials who advocated increased rates of accumulation pushed to increase the prices and quantity of any and all possible items. At the forefront was Rumpf, who argued that all "novelties and [new] developments" and not just *hochmodisch* products should automatically receive higher prices.[86] For Gerhard Pfütze of the Central Committee's Division of Planning and Finances, the "basic idea" of the initiative was "to siphon off through 'fashion peculiarities' the buying power of groups of the population that spend freely [*zahlungsfreudig*]."[87] Such considerations found expression in the dramatic expansion of the network of stores that sold *hochmodisch* items starting in February 1962. The Ministry for Trade and Provisioning stipulated that the articles were "to be offered next to the usual assortment" in normal stores but warned that they should not be sold in Exquisit stores.[88] On the production side, the Ministry for Trade and Provisioning recommended that rather than just a few selected factories, all manufacturers should be given the opportunity to produce *hochmodisch* garments.[89]

The *hochmodisch* classification not only became a farce, it did nothing to encourage the production of "high-quality and desirable goods." In reality, manufacturers received no portion of any surcharges because officials simply established the new, higher prices as fixed prices.[90] The fact that the *hochmodisch* classification was not anchored in the GDR's economic system of plans and contracts led to additional misinformation, confusion, and lack of coordination and uniformity.[91] This bureaucratic chaos resulted in unintended random concentrations of the more expensive articles in normal stores that were not supposed to sell them.[92] This unequal distribution caused two main problems. First, in the context of the GDR's shortage economy, resources concentrated in one location necessarily were missing from one or more other locations.[93] Second, as the party leadership had feared, the widespread distribution of these more expensive items caused the "impression of a general price increase."[94]

Despite repeated attempts to reform the *hochmodisch* initiative during the next three decades, the same problems remained, while the classification's potential to serve as an incentive for manufacturers was reduced even further in December 1964 when the regime decreased the surcharge to only 4 percent of the factory price.[95] During the course of the 1960s, efforts to reform the *hochmodisch* classification were gradually eclipsed by the growing emphasis on Exquisit products. Polarization of the various "genres" into "standard" and "Exquisit" was the result of both the realities of the GDR's consumer goods industries and the desire of party leaders for increased accumulation.

Political Consequences and "Negative Discussions"

Party and state leaders were extremely sensitive to the political consequences, both within the party and state apparatuses and among the population, of the bungled attempts to introduce increased prices for *hochmodisch* articles. It was clear, trade officials in the Karl-Marx-Stadt district noted, that the "not-according-to-plan" classifications were being made "under the obvious primacy of commercial considerations." The fact that the Politburo had neither published nor explained the rationale of its resolution from 10 March 1961 represented "a dangerous policy of secretiveness," which undermined "the trust in the party leadership" and its consumer and price policies.[96] The concerns of these local trade officials soon proved valid.

In fall 1961 planned increases in consumer prices for sundries (*Kurzwaren*) contributed to the impression of a general price increase and incited strong disapproval among sales personnel and customers. According to a department store director in Berlin, saleswomen were "extremely dissatisfied" with the price increase "from their standpoint as consumers" and did not understand why final consumer prices had to reflect the raised retail profit margins ordered by the Politburo.[97] Customers said "quite openly that these are creeping price increases about which they were completely insufficiently informed in the press." A common opinion was that these price increases for "the small things" certainly would be followed with ones for "the big things." Many customers sarcastically complained about the media's hypocritical practice of trumpeting price decreases and ignoring increases in East Germany while never failing to report on price increases in West Germany. Others argued that customers of Exquisit stores could afford higher prices for luxury goods, "but in no case may there be such price increases for things of daily need." The increases, as one store director concluded, were "a blow to the trust in the stability of our prices."[98]

Perhaps most distressing to party leaders were reports of opinions within the populace that the price increases for textiles were "consequences" of the construction of the Berlin Wall. Many now claimed that "the same line of price development as in West Germany is to be expected in the GDR." Customers made comments like "after [13 August 1961] one can of course do such stuff with us" and "the wall must now be paid for."[99] The Central Commission for State Control asserted that "with such discussions the policies of the party and government are being discredited" and admitted that such conversations "are being led not only by people who are under the influence of the class enemy, but rather there is in general a certain insecurity among the broad masses" and trade personnel.[100] Store managers complained about surcharges "that we cannot justify [*vertreten*] to the customers."[101] One common impression among trade personnel and consumers was that factories used the surcharge to simply collect more money without improving the appearance or quality of goods.[102] Exacerbating the infuriation caused by seemingly unjustified price increases was the unavailability of less expensive items – one often had no choice but to buy a *hochmodisch* item and pay extra for no noticeable improvement in quality or fashionableness.

Consumers' reactions to the first Exquisit stores in Berlin were mixed. An anonymous SED functionary in Berlin quoted entries in the store's "customer books" (*Kundenbücher*) to show that "the opening of these stores was welcomed from the beginning by the population, especially the intelligentsia and other circles of the population with a high income."[103] But the official also admitted that "naturally there also were and are voices that are not yet in agreement with these types of stores."[104] In August 1962 the Central Committee's Planning and Finances division asserted that "it is in general understood that wares that are of especially high quality in terms of use-value must also have a higher price." But these leading functionaries also noted that even the stores' "regular customers who have accepted the high price level" also made "critical remarks about certain 'price jumps,' especially for imports."[105] Despite official attempts to educate and persuade the population, resentment and "negative discussions" abounded, as reflected in the popular name for the stores: "*Uwubus*," a shortening of the German for "Ulbricht's profiteering huts" (*Ulbrichts Wucherbuden*).[106]

In mid-1962 the party had to dispel rumors that the state was planning Exquisit stores that would offer consumers, in exchange for higher prices, the opportunity to immediately obtain consumer durables and even basic food items like meat, butter and sausage that were in short supply.[107] Paul Fröhlich was particularly upset that even salespeople were painting the Exquisit stores as "Requisite" shops that sold essential equipment and the normal broad assortment of wares.[108] Fröhlich's insistence that "such things were never intended," however, was not entirely true. Party officials had made internal plans in late 1961 for the "continuation and new establishment of Exquisit stores," including delicatessen stores and "restaurants with a very specific character."[109]

From Haute Couture to Mass Consumer Articles

Rumors about the expansion of the scale and scope of the Exquisit stores were remarkably prescient, for they drifted further and further away from their original grandiose goals over the next three decades. As their offerings worsened in quality and shifted from haute couture models to mass consumer articles, the stores' customer base expanded in number and variety. Increasing numbers of people visited the stores in search of items that they considered normal but could not find elsewhere.

Until 1962/1963, 90 percent of Exquisit stores' offerings were imports while only 10 percent were made in the GDR.[110] But already in late 1961 in the context of the *Störfreimachung* campaign, which aimed to "free" the GDR from the "disturbances" caused by dependence on imports from capitalist countries, some party officials began to call for a shift in the Exquisit stores' offerings from capitalist imports to domestically produced goods.[111] This shift occurred rather quickly, in part due to the haphazard methods of acquiring imports and in part due to the growing shortage of Western currency.[112] By 1969 Exquisit stores' offerings consisted of approximately 30 percent imports and 70 percent East German goods, which, however, were made mostly of imported materials.[113] The declining volume of imports along with the scarcity of domestically produced high-quality articles led to growing difficulties in securing enough goods to fulfill the state's demands for extraordinary increases in the Exquisit stores' sales. The stores' response starting in the early 1960s was to include more and more "scarce wares" (*Mangelwaren*) in their offerings, to search for additional domestic manufacturers, and to abandon their original plans to sell exclusively items produced in the smallest of series.[114] Central trade officials recognized that the constant increase of the production of Exquisit goods raised a whole complex of problems. Manufacturers that previously produced for normal stores – especially smaller, private or half-state-owned firms that could manufacture "top-quality products" – now delivered "a considerable portion" or even all of their production to Exquisit stores, causing significant shortages in regular stores.[115]

The Exquisit stores' inclusion of "normal" but scarce mass-produced goods in their offerings led increasing numbers of consumers to shop in the stores, which destroyed any pretensions of exclusivity and sophistication. For example, with 113,000 sales transactions during 1965 and a "stream of customers" that was far more numerous, the Exquisit store in Leipzig could hardly have provided the "individual consultations" that officials and consumers had originally envisioned. An estimated 15 percent of those who made purchases were "regular customers," another 25 percent were consumers "who in principle prefer qualitatively valuable standard wares and only sometimes buy luxury articles," while the remaining 60 percent represented "occasional customers from all groups of the population who make only a one-time purchase of certain fashion articles (mostly with mass-character, nyltest blouses, Silastic pants, nylon coats)."[116]

Although more than 70 percent of their initial offerings were women's apparel, the Exquisit stores further expanded their customer base during the 1960s by offering more men's apparel.[117] By 1973 market researchers found that the stores had "a certain circle of regular customers whose absolute numbers have hardly changed in the last years" but whose relative proportion "constantly receded through the generally growing stream of customers." The researchers estimated that regular customers accounted for 25 to 30 percent of total turnover for the men's assortments and only 10 to 15 percent for the women's. These regular customers were mainly "doctors, technical intelligentsia, actors, certain groups of craftsmen, working women for example teachers, middle and leading white collar workers, whereby in general the age groups *above 30-years-old* dominate" (original emphasis). But the market researchers noted that "currently all social strata (with the exception of retirees) are appearing as buyers." The researchers concluded that the stores' clientele would change only if the Exquisit stores dropped "normal" assortments and returned to the ideal of offering only "the most fashionable, up-to-date, and attractive products" and "qualitatively valuable articles of the highest price group."[118]

Siphoning Off Buying Power and Clinging to Dreams of Distinction

By the end of 1965, at a time when the SED was swinging back toward authoritarian centralization, any remaining impulses among party leaders to promote the *hochmodisch* classification and Exquisit stores as a means of cultivating *Bekleidungskultur* or displaying the achievements of socialism appear to have given way to the purely economic motivations of "siphoning off" excess buying power and making profits for the state.[119] In a resolution from 25 November 1965, the Council of Ministers asserted that the "unplanned" increase in incomes during the past few years had led to higher demand for valuable and durable consumer goods. The extra buying power, however, remained unused because limited industrial capacities and the high proportion of exports prevented the domestic supply of these goods from keeping pace with demand.[120]

Rather than relying on the *hochmodisch* and Exquisit surcharges to stimulate production of high-quality goods, the Council of Ministers hoped to raise consumer prices by a total of 388 million MDN by tapping industry's and trade's "inner reserves" and by increasing sales of certain imports from capitalist countries. Proposed measures ranged from changing the composition of materials in products to introducing new and more expensive goods into stores' offerings. The Exquisit stores' were to increase their revenues a staggering 61 percent, from 130 million marks in 1965 to 210 million marks in 1966.[121] The Council of Ministers planned to raise an additional 50 million marks by producing 700,000 wrinkle-free, synthetic men's shirts. By using imported synthetic yarn instead of worsted wool to make 380,000 pieces of knitted outerwear, the price for the final products would increase by 29 million marks. The resolution also foresaw large profits from the importation of a wide range of goods from capitalist countries, including televisions and radios from Japan, and Fiat automobiles from Italy. Other measures included producing an additional 38 million marks of whipping cream and high-quality curd cheese, and importing 60 million marks of "specialties" such as eggs, sugar, delicacies, "exquisite" wines, spirits, and champagne. The resolution also called for the "stepwise" establishment of "delicacies stores" (*Feinkost-Läden*), which essentially represented the equivalent of Exquisit stores for food products and materialized as "Delikat" stores in 1966.[122] Taking its cue from the Council of Minister's resolution, the Ministry for Trade and Provisioning began working out plans to increase the Exquisit stores' sales to 400 million marks by 1970, which was triple the actual sales in 1965 and double the sales planned for 1966. During these four years, the network of thirty-four stores in 1966 was to grow to fifty "predominantly large-scale stores."[123]

As party and state leaders strove in the second half of the 1960s to increase revenues and centralize management of the Exquisit stores, other officials, especially district and local functionaries, sought to return the stores to their original mission of offering only the most extravagant goods to a very select group of consumers. These officials feared that the regime's emphasis on the financial bottom line would exacerbate the already alarming tendency of the stores to lose all exclusive airs and become simply distribution centers for mass-produced goods that were in particularly short supply. In a memo dated 11 February 1966, a certain Höpfner, the head of the Department for Light Industry and Food Processing/Trade of the SED's district leadership in Leipzig, formulated these fears in unusually clear and frank language.[124] The Exquisit stores had long since drifted away from their original "specific task" of satisfying "the special luxury needs [*Luxusbedürfnisse*] or the special demand [*Bedarf*] for selected top-quality products for those citizens" who "on the basis of their social position or achievement have access to large funds." According to Höpfner, there were several reasons for this failure, all of which were related to the idea that the Exquisit stores were being overrun by the general public and thus had lost almost all distinction from normal stores.

In the case of Leipzig, the store's location and floor plan attracted "a high influx of occasional customers" and onlookers [*Schaulustige*] who "hinder the absolutely necessary individual service and customer consultation." For instance, "it is not pleasant for the customers and salesmen when, during the purchase of shoes, up to ten onlookers watch and make comments on the price and quality." This meant that "instead of the desired character of an efficient fashion house for the highest standards, the store currently still resembles a garment department in a busy department store. The difference exists essentially in the higher price level." In response, the Exquisit store's management had removed "wares with mass character," such as blouses and shirts made of nyltest and Silastic pants, from its primary offerings in 1965 and now carried them "only in small quantities as accessories to the big pieces." Other measures included holding "customer consultations in connection with Exquisit fashion shows" and offering custom tailoring. "Not every top-quality article may be an Exquisit article," Höpfner insisted, for the presence of "top-quality articles that satisfy a mass need [*Massenbedarf*] and underlie a broad demand" was "the cause for the widespread mood of the population against the Exquisit stores." In Höpfner's opinion, the only "final solution" to this dilemma was to discourage the general public from visiting by moving the store to an upper floor in a building outside the city center and simultaneously increase normal stores' offerings of "top-quality products of mass need."

Höpfner feared that the recently-issued central orders to increase the Exquisit stores' sales would further encourage the leveling tendencies that he and his colleagues hoped to reverse. In language carefully formulated to express disappointment but not insubordination, he warned that "it would be damaging if it is planned to achieve" the increased turnover "through the sale of high-quality mass-demand articles" rather than "real Exquisit articles that satisfy extreme, individual luxury needs." To Höpfner, realizing dreams of extravagance and fulfilling the desires of a small segment of the population were more important than the centrally issued order to raise money for the state by crudely siphoning off buying power.

Höpfner was not the only East German official in the second half of the 1960s who still hoped to realize dreams of distinction. Only a few months after his memo, officials in the central divisions of the Ministry for Trade and Provisioning called for the development of the Exquisit stores into "modern specialty trade establishments that take all demands into account and carry the character of cultured fashion salons."[125] The Ministry's trade policies department recommended "the reorganization of the assortments in the existing Exquisit stores" in order to "achieve a differentiation of the stream of customers for the products of the so-called mass demand (for example Silastic pants) and the other products."[126] In October 1966 district officials in Leipzig planned the establishment of a brand new fashion salon downtown that would sell primarily garments produced by the semi-private firm Lucie Kaiser KG in Altenburg, a firm known for its high quality and fashionableness.[127] The fashion salon's prices were to match the exclusivity of its offerings: officials estimated that each of the 3,000 individually tailored model dresses with matching accessories produced each year would cost an average of 1,000 marks. But Leipzig was to wait in vain for its exclusive fashion salon. The project was destined to be downgraded and absorbed into the network of Exquisit stores.[128]

Exquisit store managers also did their best to improve the quality of their stores' offerings by using the only weapon available to them: their right during the central purchasing negotiations (*Kaufhandlung*) to refuse to buy items that did not meet their standards. In late 1966 at the purchasing negotiations for the first half of 1967, Exquisit store managers instructed their wholesale buyers to accept production contracts only for items that met "a really extremely strict standard," one that was fitting for true Exquisit articles. The result was disheartening. Inspectors from the German Office for Measures and Inspection of Goods (Deutsches Amt für Meßwesen und Warenprüfung or DAMW) used its quality classifications to reject all articles that "did not correspond to the wishes of our special customers." As a result, only one-quarter of the men's shoes and two-thirds of the women's shoes planned for the first quarter of 1967 actually received contracts. The director of the HO's Exquisit working group estimated that only 6,000 women's and men's shoes would receive contracts at the second round of purchasing negotiations.[129]

While these efforts by Exquisit store managers were admirable, they point to the stores' ultimately weak position. The stores could refuse to buy garments and cloth that did not match their expectations and tell the manufacturers to try again, but sooner or later they had to buy something if they wanted to be able to sell anything. The factors that determined the quality of goods lay almost exclusively on the production side, and manufacturers had little reason to care about whether consumers actually bought their products. If Exquisit stores did not buy them, then the regular network of stores would or the state eventually would dispose of them somehow.

The Expansion and Dilution of Exquisit in the 1970s and 1980s

Exquisit's problems continued to worsen. Officials admitted internally in the early 1970s that the stores' offerings had deteriorated to simply "articles that were missing in the basic assortment of textile stores and in principle carried mass character." Exquisit's buyers desperately and chaotically used their privileged purchasing position to acquire whatever happened to be "scarce wares" (*Mangelwaren*) at the moment without reference to any plans or long-term goals.[130] The situation reached critical proportions by mid-1970 when the stores had signed future production contracts totaling only half of the necessary supply for that year. Among the reasons for this crisis were the state's own price regulations, which once again worked counter to official intentions. The "material incentive" for producing goods with the *hochmodisch* label allegedly was stronger than that for Exquisit production simply because of the larger volume of *hochmodisch* articles.[131] There was little incentive for a factory to limit itself to elaborate models in small numbers when it could mass-produce simpler models, perhaps using expensive material, and receive nearly the same surcharge per item. The stores' infrastructure also had stagnated: by mid-1971, the network had expanded to only forty-three stores. Revenues also were not meeting expectations. It was becoming clear to officials that Exquisit products had to be better integrated into the planned domestic production if the stores were to have a chance of acquiring the goods they needed.[132]

It also was becoming clear that demand – or better said, consumers' ability to pay – for high-quality goods was increasing with no end in sight. In the early 1970s, an anonymously authored official memo predicted that "the number of consumers interested in high-quality, highly fashionable products" would increase due to the 4-percent average annual increase in consumers' incomes and the entrance of even more women into the workforce.[133] These trends were only exacerbated by the well-known shift in policy after the SED's Eighth Party Congress to the "unity of social and economic policies," which allowed income and consumption to drastically outpace productivity.

In addition to organizational and financial difficulties, the Exquisit stores continued to encounter public criticism. Many voices objected that the stores' horrendously high prices officially sanctioned unequal access to the GDR's most desirable goods and represented a blatant injustice, especially given socialism's claims of equality. Many functionaries were at a loss to justify such inequalities even to themselves, let alone to their colleagues and the general public. "What am I supposed to answer," asked one retail store manager, "when they say to me: why may one [person] afford these things and the others, who also work industriously, cannot. I have simply no argument for that."[134] Other voices pointed to Exquisit stores as an example of state socialism's adoption of capitalist principles. As one ordinary woman worker commented in 1967, "earlier we paid [an exchange rate of] one to four in West Berlin, how is that today one must pay the same in the Exquisit stores?"[135] With or without the Wall, whether in the West or in the East, it seemed to many East Germans that they always had to pay exorbitant prices for Western-quality goods.

Researchers at the Institute for Market Research in the early 1970s asserted that consumers viewed Exquisit "often as the last possibility for the satisfaction of a specific purchase wish" that the normal stores could not fulfill. Otherwise the assortments of the two types of stores were often identical.[136] Any temporary absence of "negative comments" about the prices, market researchers asserted, "should not hide the fact that there is only an apparent contentedness among the population with the Exquisit offerings." This seeming satisfaction was actually more the result of dissatisfaction with the offerings of normal stores.[137]

Both internal party correspondence and broadly disseminated propaganda always had stressed that special fashion salons' more expensive offerings only supplemented regular assortments. But consumers had progressively less choice as Exquisit stores offered more and more normal items simply because they were in such short supply. During the course of the 1970s and 1980s, it became increasingly difficult to deny that rather than offering luxury articles to satisfy special, individual needs, Exquisit offered an unstable assortment of outrageously priced articles, most of which were known to be commonplace in the West.[138] Rather than attracting only a select group of discriminating, high-income connoisseurs, the Exquisit stores counted virtually all groups of East German consumers among its customers. The prices, however, were far from democratic. Although the forty-three Exquisit stores in 1970/71 represented only 1.2 percent of the total square feet of retail space for textile products, they accounted for about 3 percent of total sales.[139] Their share of the total sales of textile, garment, shoes, and leather goods was still relatively balanced in terms of value and quantity at the beginning of the 1970s.[140] But Exquisit's planned sales continued to rise, with 420.6 million marks planned for 1971.[141] Parallel to the growth in turnover was an increase in the dimensions of production series, which now ranged between 300 and 2,500, a far cry from the planned series of 12 to 15 in the early 1960s.[142]

For a whole complex of political and economic reasons, party and state leaders in early 1970 began to shift Exquisit production from smaller private and semi-private factories to larger state-owned enterprises.[143] In the midst of the forced build-up of enormous combines that had started in the late 1960s, it was not surprising that the large state-owned factories were given the task of increasing production in order to absorb as much buying power as possible. Rather than allowing a proliferation of smaller production units to satisfy "individual needs," officials proposed to specialize certain sections of the huge combines, supposedly combining the best of both worlds. Gone were the dreams of individually hand-measured and tailored garments – *hochmodisch* and even Exquisit garments now were to be produced in large series.[144]

Despite intensive efforts, however, the Exquisit stores were able to sign production contracts with state-owned enterprises for only 10 percent of the total volume of ready-to-wear outerwear and for none of the knitted outerwear that they needed for 1972. Instead, Exquisit still had to rely on the politically less desirable, smaller factories that were either only half-state-owned or completely private.[145] Only the elimination of all private enterprises in 1972 changed this balance. For the most part, these firms simply were absorbed into large combines and lost any remaining room to maneuver. All available sources indicate that almost no articles were industrially produced in tiny quantities (*Kleinstmengen*), while the sizes of production series at the combines continued to grow until the end of the GDR.

The expansion of Exquisit exacerbated the familiar contradictions and difficulties concerning social differentiation. On the one hand, Exquisit's goal remained "the satisfaction of personal needs for fashionable, up-to-date offerings, differentiated according to the age and social structure of different circles of consumers."[146] This was to be accomplished "under consideration of the differentiated development of buying power," that is, consumers' different incomes. On the other hand, the SED promised that wage and salary differentials would become increasingly small, and the current "consumption level" (*Verbrauchsniveau*) of better earning social groups, such as craftsmen and other self-employed people, would become less significant. The homogenization of income levels and the large-scale expansion of the Exquisit stores theoretically would result in "a stronger leveling [*Nivellierung*] of customers." Since "the demand of the population will be concentrated predominantly on high-quality, modern, and easy-care clothing," Exquisit faced the difficult task of producing increasing amounts of clothing to meet the multiplying, diversifying needs of an ever-expanding circle of consumers with high standards.[147] To assist in this task, party and state officials once again called for differentiating offerings and suggested three types of stores in which different kinds of Exquisit products would be sold: "modern," "boutique," and "salon," in order of exclusiveness.[148]

At the very least, Exquisit's offerings were supposed to be clearly distinguishable from normal, standard ones. But officials admitted that "the clear delimitation" of Exquisit assortments from "the normal supply" continued to prove exceedingly difficult to accomplish.[149] Nevertheless, Exquisit did offer items that could serve as means of social distinction. The network's exorbitant prices and the cursive lowercase "e" that appeared on its labels starting in 1969 helped to establish a certain brand-name character for its products, even if they were not always truly extraordinary. But the qualified and limited amount of prestige attached to Exquisit goods did not mean that consumers who purchased them felt that they had paid a fair price.

Such tensions and contradictions led leading functionaries to demand that Exquisit's goals "must be newly thought out. Fundamentally every ware must be an Exquisit ware in terms of quality."[150] Many consumers apparently shared these sentiments. Market researchers found in 1975 that women made Exquisit's offerings "the standard for their demands on the design of the general clothing offerings."[151] Far from considering Exquisit products to be extraordinary, unusual, or particularly high quality, consumers and many officials viewed them as normal and the items in normal stores as substandard. The official shift away from Exquisit's original purpose of serving as a highly visible instrument for shaping and directing a whole regime of tastes and desires can also be inferred from the Ministry for Trade and Provisioning's ban in 1972 of advertisements for products sold in Exquisit stores and the fashion salon "Boutique 70" in Berlin.[152] Prices and consumers' incomes became increasingly less important in determining Exquisit's revenues. Market researchers asserted that the Exquisit stores' "sales rhythm" was "determined singly and solely *by the supply of wares*" (original emphasis).[153]

The rapid increase of Exquisit sales starting in the early 1970s without a corresponding increase in the number of stores or sales personnel had predictable results. All of the Exquisit employees interviewed by market researchers in 1973 agreed "that the salespeople are overburdened and there can be no talk of an 'exquisite' *Verkaufskultur*." Most stores had reached their full spatial capacity and could no longer increase turnover. Market researchers in the early 1970s recommended expanding the network of Exquisit stores in order to allow further increases in turnover and to ensure "the absolutely necessary enhancement of the *Verkaufskultur*, the customer service, etc."[154]

At the same time, the regime explored other methods of making money for the state's coffers. While the previous expansion of Exquisit had aimed primarily at soaking up the population's excess buying power in East German marks, starting in the mid-1970s the regime began to expand the even more lucrative practice of absorbing the growing quantity of West German marks floating around the country. To these ends, the regime enlarged the network of Intershops, which had been established soon after the construction of the Berlin Wall as duty-free shops designed to absorb the hard currency in the pockets of Western visitors. East German citizens initially were forbidden from shopping in the stores, but in 1973 the regime legalized the possession of Western currency and even encouraged East Germans to spend it in the Intershops.[155]

While the same old problems with the poor quality and insufficient quantity of Exquisit products continued into the 1970s and 1980s, the party leadership continued to force the network's expansion.[156] By 1975 the Exquisit stores had increased their share to 6 percent of all sales in terms of quantity and even more in terms of value.[157] Politburo resolutions in 1977 and 1983 significantly enlarged the Exquisit as well as the Delikat networks.[158] By 1977 the number of Exquisit stores had increased to 109. While production figures either remained steady or increased only slightly, Exquisit's increasing prices enabled it to capture a larger and larger portion of the total turnover of textile and clothing products: the stores represented 8.8 percent of total sales of textiles and clothing in 1980, 10.4 percent in 1981, and 10.8 percent in 1982. The proportion was even higher in Berlin, where Exquisit accounted for 21.3 percent of total sales in 1982. By 1985 the number of stores had ballooned to 442, encompassing a network that reached into small towns and generated 13.6 percent of total sales of textiles, clothing, and shoes and 40.8 percent of the total growth in annual turnover. While revenues had totaled 12.3 billion marks during the nine years between 1977 and 1985, the state planned to increase Exquisit sales, "according to demand," by over 41 percent between 1986 and 1990, from 2.585 billion to 3.65 billion marks.[159]

Looking back in July 1989 on Exquisit's development since 1970, researchers at the Institute for Market Research told a story of an initiative that had unevenly but relentlessly spun out of control. The Exquisit stores had drifted far from their "originally intended profile": many of their offerings "should have been in normal stores," the number that "corresponds internationally to the middle genre" was "too high," and "top qualities" were "too rare." During the previous two decades, the original core offerings of outerwear had been supplemented by shoes, underwear, cosmetics, costume jewelry, and accessories. By 1989 Exquisit's share had grown to between 17 and 18 percent of women's outerwear sales and between 14 and 15 percent of men's outerwear sales. Officials predicted that Exquisit sales would be thirteen to fifteen times more in 1990 than they were in 1970, which represented an increase in their share of the total retail sales of textiles, clothing, and shoes from 2 to about 15 percent. The average Exquisit sales per capita had grown from 15 marks in 1970 to an estimated 250 marks in 1990. Whereas one of every fifty marks spent on textiles, clothes, and shoes went to Exquisit in 1970, by 1990 it was one of every six or seven marks. By the end of the GDR, normal stores accounted for only about half of the total volume of textile and garment sales measured in units and significantly less than that measured in marks.[160] The growth in Exquisit's turnover and market share resulted not from increased production and improved quality but rather from creeping inflation and the inclusion of ever more scarce "mass-need" assortments. From the perspective of consumers, Exquisit's expansion reflected the bankruptcy of the regime's consumer policies and industry's failure to fulfill basic needs.

–7–

Shopping, Sewing, Networking, Complaining: Consumer Practices and the Relationship between State and Society

Just as *hochmodisch* apparel and Exquisit stores diverged from the visions of distinction and extravagance that had inspired them, East Germans' actual consumption practices differed drastically from the officially promoted "socialist consumer habits" that were supposed to mark the new "socialist personality." Quotidian practices of consumption and expressions of dissatisfaction formed constitutive elements of the GDR's consumer culture, demonstrated consumers' agency, and created highly political meanings within the pseudo "public sphere" of consumption. Both the social construction of demand and the everyday practices that East Germans used to fulfill their sartorial needs and desires demonstrate some of the ways in which state and society – and domination and agency – overlapped, intersected, and shaped each other.

The SED based a crucial part of its legitimacy on the claim to "satisfy the needs of the population" and strove to cultivate and regulate these objectively defined needs and wishes. However, the regime's efforts achieved mixed results over the course of four decades, not only due to the GDR's own economic shortcomings, but also because the party was unable to control needs, desires, expectations, and perceptions of scarcity and affluence even within official institutions, let alone among ordinary citizens. The SED's view of consumption as a manipulable process of "need-fulfillment" failed to grasp the creation of demand and value through social practices. By the same token, individuals' agency had its own boundaries. Consumers could use numerous means to ameliorate their material circumstances and to voice discontent, but their actions were limited to the level of tactics and proved incapable of overcoming fundamental constraints of the system.[1] While the SED's domination and consumers' agency influenced and mutually limited each other, consumers clearly did not have the upper hand. The limitations of this agency, along with the regime's ability to diffuse popular

144

criticism, help to explain the regime's remarkable stability over four decades. But ultimately, consumers' dissatisfaction and disillusionment and the regime's loss of legitimacy even within its own ranks influenced the nature and rapidity of the GDR's collapse and unification with West Germany in 1989/1990.

In a landscape of images of individualistic opulence and stores full of drab, mass-produced garments, consumers used a wide variety of techniques to fulfill their needs and desires, whether they were for utilitarian products to cover so-called basic needs or for apparel that fulfilled desires for social distinction, individual expression, or non-conformity to official or social norms. These consumer techniques can be grouped roughly into the categories of shopping, sewing, networking, and complaining, although many techniques fit none or several of these categories.[2] While some of these practices conformed at least superficially to officially endorsed norms, others transgressed official boundaries. Although men increasingly participated in the labors of consumption, women remained the primary actors in this sphere.

Shopping

Starting already in the late 1940s, East Germans embarked on shopping trips with very specific desires and went from store to store and even from city to city in efforts to satisfy them.[3] During the first major stage in the elimination of rationing for clothing and shoes in February 1951, a state trade official remarked that "the streets offered an almost peacetime-like picture, that is, women are beginning to select very carefully and to look around in several stores, and no longer is every available ware immediately bought."[4] Officials noted that consumers made only "supplementary purchases" (*Ergänzungskäufe*): they bought "not simply clothing" but rather very specific assortments, styles, and materials.[5]

Even if a consumer found a sought-after garment that was made of the desired material and matched her or his individual tastes, it was often the wrong size. Until the end of the 1950s, only about one-third of women and girls and 60 percent of boys could find ready-to-wear apparel that fit them.[6] After measuring over 17,000 women of various ages throughout the GDR, officials claimed in 1959 that thirty-three new sizes would replace twenty-seven old ones and increase the proportion of women who could wear mass-produced apparel to two-thirds. Their goal was 88 percent by 1965.[7]

The specificity of consumers' demands and the limitations of stores' offerings combined to make shopping an extensive "running around" (*Herumlauferei*) which all too often met with the proverbial response of sales personnel: "*Hamwanich*" (don't have it).[8] The author of a Berlin newspaper article in 1956 provided an account of typical shopping frustrations:

In Treptow a young girl recently bought a nylon blouse. It was as if she had found a needle in a haystack; for during the last quarter there were only 2 (two) nylon blouses in stock in the HO stores in the Treptow district.

An expectant mother who wanted to buy herself a tasteful maternity dress had to run through all of Berlin. She was offered a bilious green silk dress and some still more tasteless models.

The young women [...] who in the HO voice the wish to become owners of shoes with the newly popular stiletto heel (9 cm high), get only a sympathetic look from the shoe saleswomen.

For the tea-dance, for the theater one prefers the little evening dress. To inquire about that in the HO borders on frivolity. Certainly, there are silk dresses available – but, oh, only little innocent dresses (*Kleidchen*). And the Berlin woman was once known for dressing in smart and chic ways.

Despite the progress over the previous year one can say of Berlin: There is certainly clothing available, but no dresses.[9]

To improve their chances, many shoppers visited stores every week or two, or tried to find out when shipments arrived in order to be among the first to peruse the new goods.[10]

Many consumers considered the time, effort, and frustration spent in searching for specific items far more costly than the goods' price in marks. A cartoon in the satirical magazine *Eulenspiegel* captured these sentiments: a woman asks a man, presumably her husband or boyfriend, "what did the seamless stockings cost, Peter?" to which he replies, "above all else perseverance."[11] Prices, however, did influence consumers' purchasing decisions. Shoppers searched not only for desired articles but also for a price which stood in proper relation to perceived value. Market researchers and other state and party officials noted that price was one of the prime reasons for consumers' dissatisfaction with and reluctance to buy most of the apparel in East German stores.[12]

Shopping was significantly more difficult in small towns and the countryside. Since goods generally were concentrated in stores in larger cities, rural inhabitants had to travel to the nearest district capital or even to Berlin to improve their chances of finding the objects of their desires. Trade officials experienced only limited success in their efforts to improve this situation by occasionally travelling through the countryside selling wares out of trailers or holding special sales at market places.[13] The media often joined consumers in demanding that rural areas receive their fair share of the goods, both in terms of quantity and quality.[14]

The regime tried to address this problem through the introduction of a mail-order catalogue in 1956. Despite claims that this more efficient and rational retailing technique would lead to improved provisioning, it suffered from the same problems that beset the rest of the GDR's economy. In addition to chronic problems of supply, the mail-order service failed to limit and specialize itself for its target audience. In 1961 the consumer cooperatives established their own mail-order catalogue, *konsument*, which was intended for the rural population, while the *centrum* catalogue of the state-owned HO featured more modern and chic models targeted to urban customers. But this differentiation existed only in the pages of the catalogues. Both rural and urban consumers placed orders for the same or similar items with both mail-order services in the hope of increasing their chances of receiving anything at all.[15]

The satisfaction of consumer demand was indeed "mostly a matter of pure chance," as top party officials noted in 1960.[16] An author in *Frau von heute* exclaimed in 1953, "if one could for once buy in the HO with a set shopping plan! Mostly one gets the long-sought-after sweater precisely when one went out to buy dress material or something similar."[17] Despite the tendency for grass-roots reports on consumption to become rosier as they percolated up, even Central Committee officials knew that "the population is indignant about the fact that it is obliged [*genötigt*] to 'scour' [*Abgrasen*] stores in order to satisfy their wishes to some degree. Many or even most sales occur only because customers give up [*resigniert*], they buy because they do not believe that they will come upon the ware that they actually would like to have."[18]

The centrality of serendipity to shopping encouraged impulse buying, which ran counter to the SED's ideal of rational, planned consumption.[19] A fashion designer explained this phenomenon in 1958: stores' incomplete offerings "force a rash purchase in many cases. One suddenly discovers some pretty fashionable object, which one, at that moment, actually is not at all searching for. In order to not miss this one-time opportunity, instead of the originally desired object one buys something that does not at all match the rest of one's wardrobe."[20] Impulse buying did not apply only to fashionable items. Claiming to share normal consumers' shopping frustrations, Bruno Leuschner, chairman of the State Planning Commission, joked at the Textile Conference in 1960 that "one wants to get underwear in a store and must leave with a tie because the right size is not there. I experience the same thing: I'm a size five, and only sizes four and six are there. What should I do there? I buy myself a tie!"[21] Sporadic and random deliveries of seasonal items also contributed to shoppers' impulsiveness.[22] Market researchers estimated that at least 40 percent of East Germans were "impulse buyers" when confronted with "interesting articles" and worried that they might miss the opportunity to obtain a certain article "if they don't immediately grab it and buy."[23] Most prone to buy impulsively, according to market researchers, were shoppers with higher incomes, who had more disposable income, and certain groups – such as women who worked full-time, youth, and white-collar workers – who had "higher standards" and were dissatisfied with normal offerings.[24]

Many of the motivations to buy impulsively also underlay the tendencies of hoarding and panic buying, which flared up particularly during times of political uncertainty – most notably after the construction of the Berlin Wall.[25] But also under normal circumstances, even false rumors of a shipment of particularly desirable or imported goods could create huge crowds at stores in a matter of hours.[26] So-called irrational consumption could take the less dramatic form of buying two or three pairs of nylon stockings, for instance, just because one happened to find several of a certain style or color, even though one planned to wear them one at a time until they wore out.[27] Another reason to hoard was the fear of "creeping inflation" or rumors of a price increase.[28] A different form of hoarding consisted of keeping an article of clothing for years after it was no longer worn: one never knew whether one might need it again or could use the fabric to make another piece of clothing.

Consumers' searches for apparel were not limited to the territory of the GDR before the construction of the Berlin Wall. West Berlin offered East Germans additional and generally more fertile hunting grounds. Surveys of GDR citizens caught illegally bringing Western goods into East Berlin revealed a mixture of motivations, including price, fashion, quality, and variety of available goods.[29] Despite an exchange rate of at least four East German marks to one West German mark, West German shoes and clothing still cost on average only about 40 to 60 percent as much as similar articles in East Germany. East German officials were also well aware of the fact that consumers' desires to keep up with the latest fashions were as important as price considerations.[30] But East German customs agents could hope to catch only a fraction of the illegally imported goods, and there are indications that enforcement was sometimes lax.[31] Alongside those who shopped in West Berlin for themselves were many others, both East and West Germans, who smuggled large quantities of goods into the GDR and sold them on the black market. Everything from shoes to fashionable zippers to cheap West German copies of Italian designs flowed into East Germany in significant quantities.[32] Smuggling of everything from nylon jackets to fashion magazines continued, although greatly diminished, even after the construction of the Berlin Wall.[33]

A purchase, however, did not necessarily mean the complete satisfaction of a wish or need. This fact found expression in the large percentage of women who modified their store-bought clothing in some way, whether adjusting length or width, dyeing, or bleaching. Market researchers estimated in 1971 that approximately two-thirds of women's industrially manufactured garments were altered in width or length before being worn.[34] Consumers altered clothes both to make them fit and to conform to fashions.[35]

Sewing

Given stores' unsatisfactory and poorly fitting offerings, it is not surprising that store-bought clothing accounted for a relatively modest portion of East Germans' wardrobes. Although market researchers lacked data for the 1950s and early 1960s, they noted in 1963 that the GDR lagged behind other countries in the relation between production of ready-to-wear versus cloth sold by the meter: the GDR's ratio of 80 to 20 compared unfavorably with the FRG's 90 to 10 and the USA's 93 to 7.[36] Not until 1966, however, did market researchers abandon "the generally prevailing opinion" that 60 to 70 percent of the demand for outerwear was satisfied by industrially produced garments.[37] The percentage was in fact much lower. In 1967 researchers conservatively estimated that the 40 million pieces of industrially manufactured ready-to-wear that stores sold each year were complemented by at least 30 million pieces of outerwear that stemmed from "other sources."[38] In some assortments, particularly of women's outerwear, East German store-bought clothing accounted for as little as one-third of total consumption.[39] The relatively modest proportion of store-bought apparel in East Germans' wardrobes reflected the prevalence of alternatives, including having garments made by tailors, acquaintances, or friends; sewing or knitting oneself; buying or receiving used clothes; and receiving apparel in packages from the West.[40]

During the 1950s and into the 1960s, a still common and relatively affordable alternative to buying ready-to-wear clothing in a store was to hire a tailor to personally fit and make one's apparel by hand. Using cloth either sold by the tailor or obtained by some other means, this option offered the most individual and best-fitting solutions to sartorial desires.[41] By 1956 the regime reconsidered its initial encouragement of this practice after realizing that the relatively insignificant price difference between ready-to-wear and hand-tailored apparel shifted demand in favor of the latter.[42] While still common, hiring a tailor became increasingly difficult during the 1960s as the regime raised the prices of custom-made clothing and forced tailors, along with many other craftspeople, out of business.[43]

Much more common than hiring a tailor was sewing or knitting clothes oneself or having relatives, friends, or acquaintances make them. Home dressmaking illustrates well how borders between acts of production and consumption blurred in everyday life in the GDR.[44] Throughout the history of the GDR, consumers continued practices, common in times of emergency or scarcity, of "making new out of old" and of using a variety of ingenious techniques to improvise solutions to their sartorial problems, needs, and wishes. These practices included repeatedly refashioning a garment to give it a new appearance; designing "changeable dresses" that transformed shapes and functions by the subtraction, addition, or moving of parts; and lengthening or shortening hems of old garments to fit new fashions.[45] Just as women had fashioned apparel out of military uniforms, linens, or curtains during the immediate postwar period, at the end of the 1960s women improvised solutions appropriate to that time, for instance by making outerwear out of otherwise scarce and expensive Silastic that was sometimes used to cover cheap pillows and cushions.[46]

At least one-third of women's and girls' outerwear articles were individually made. The share could reach as high as three-fourths for assortments that were easy to make or that were particularly scarce in stores.[47] A study in 1971 found that 56 percent of East German women owned at least one individually made dress; the percentages were 49 for skirts and 33 for blouses.[48] Individually made clothing generally constituted a very large proportion of the wardrobes of women who owned at least one such article.[49] Self-made items were less common in men's and boy's wardrobes, market researchers claimed, due to the higher degree of skill required to make such articles (like suits), the greater expense to have them made by a tailor, the relative ease with which men and boys found clothing that fit them, and men's and boys' lesser concern with dressing fashionably.[50]

Although reliable data were scarce and difficult to compare, market researchers estimated in 1973 that the absolute volume of individually made clothing had remained constant or increased since 1959. Despite a slight decline in their relative share of all clothes worn due to the increased volume of industrially made clothing, one-fifth of all outerwear and one-third of all knitted outerwear still were made individually. The figure was almost 60 percent for women's outerwear and children's knitted outerwear.[51] Contrary to the SED's promises and hopes, both the absolute volume and the relative share of individually made clothing only increased during the 1970s and 1980s, right up to the end of the GDR.[52]

Since virtually all home-made garments, regardless of the wearer's gender, were made by women, home sewing was an important issue in the regime's policies regarding women. From the beginning, official propaganda promised to help lighten women's task of producing clothes for themselves and others in the home. Numerous consumer magazines published paper patterns for everything from aprons to evening gowns.[53] Although many officials admitted in the late 1940s and 1950s that home sewing generally represented an involuntary practice that was necessary to compensate for the supposedly temporary shortcomings of the GDR's textile and garment industries, much of the official discourse either claimed that the practice was totally voluntary or tried to make a virtue out of this necessity. Texts that accompanied paper patterns in consumer magazines often boasted that they were enabling women to realize their "dreams" or were providing those who preferred to give their clothing "a personal touch" with "inspirations" for unique and fashionable models.[54] Official discourses alluded to stereotypically Protestant values by praising home sewing and knitting as a "meaningful free-time occupation" (*sinnvolle Freizeitbeschäftigung*). Such claims certainly contained some truth, and early fashion shows of self-made and self-displayed models evidenced much pride and enthusiasm.[55] But implicit in such statements was the admission that women had to compensate for the shortcomings of East German industry.

By the end of the 1960s, market researchers and others increasingly attacked myths about home-made clothing and argued that it caused economic waste and contradicted many of the SED's ideological and social welfare goals.[56] They argued that home sewing was "not primarily a gladly practiced hobby, but rather a not always avoidable solution [*Ausweg*] when one does not find the right item in the offerings of ready-to-wear."[57] The regional chair of the SED's mass organization for women, the DFD (Demokratischer Frauenbund Deutschlands), in Berlin asserted in 1968 that the reason for the increasing number of women enrolled in the DFD's tailoring courses was "not because they view it as their hobby! We also don't see it as the solution for trade and economic functionaries' absent feelings of responsibility."[58] A survey of the readers of the women's magazine *Für Dich* in 1968 revealed that although 64 percent of all women sewed "a large portion of their wardrobes" themselves, only 4 percent listed tailoring as a "hobby."[59] Market researchers also confirmed the common knowledge that stores' extremely poor offerings of larger sizes practically forced many "stronger women" to either make their own clothes or have them made.[60]

Far from being a "useful free-time activity," home sewing and knitting robbed women of much of their precious free time and represented an economically inefficient use of their labor. Market researchers estimated that the GDR's households spent 210 to 300 million hours per year on hand-knitting outerwear alone, which was equivalent to either 80,000 to 125,000 laborers working forty-eight hours per week or almost one hour per week for every household.[61] Market researchers also demonstrated that, contrary to common assumptions before the late 1960s, home sewing was actually more prevalent among working women and those with higher incomes than among housewives and those with lower incomes.[62] Researchers asserted that these unexpected and undesirable findings demonstrated that the GDR's industrially produced apparel was not meeting the "higher standards" and "demands" of women who worked and had higher incomes.[63] Unless stores' offerings improved, officials warned, the situation would worsen as incomes continued to rise. At the beginning of the 1970s, the regime seemed to be as distant as ever from the fulfillment of its implicit and explicit promises to eliminate the need for home sewing for all women by providing plentiful, inexpensive, and attractive industrially produced apparel.

Since stores' offerings did not significantly improve, consumers often complemented the active techniques of shopping and sewing with more passive practices, including abstaining from purchasing apparel in stores, waiting for something better, or substituting something else for the article that they originally desired. These practices also required a significant amount of work. In the early 1960s market researchers concluded that many if not most consumers repeatedly patched or refashioned articles of clothing and wore them to the point of almost complete physical deterioration.[64] Even after they were no longer worn, garments were seldom discarded but instead kept for years either untouched at the back of wardrobes or transformed into cleaning or polishing rags.[65] Despite claims that variables like the weather significantly affected sales, researchers concluded that consumers had little freedom and that a purchase often represented less a positive choice for an article of clothing than the result of a "no longer postponable utilitarian necessity."[66]

Networking

Informal networks complemented the above techniques of obtaining or making desired goods.[67] Most of the evidence on the social practices associated with these networks is indirect: recorded discussions of "connections" or "relationships" (*Beziehungen*) came primarily from those without them who resented those with them.[68] While almost everyone used some kind of informal relationship to procure scarce goods at some point, an individual might have more or fewer connections – for example, access to spare auto parts but no direct channel to fashionable dresses. Frustration or resentment over a lack of connections was a common theme in consumers' complaints:

In the Konsum store no aunt	*Beim Konsum keine Tante*
In the H.O. store no relatives	*Beim H.O. keine Verwandte*
From the West no package	*Aus dem Westen kein Paket*
And you still ask me how I'm doing.	*Und da fragen Sie mir noch wie es mir geht.*[69]

The type of "relationship" that appears most frequently in official documents, published articles, and citizens' petitions is the one between salesperson and customer. In what seems to have been its most common form, salespeople held desired products "under the table" for certain customers when a shipment arrived and allowed them to try on apparel in the back room. These connections could stem from family relations, repeated encounters and friendly conversations, small tips or bribes, or past *quid pro quo*.[70] Officials and the media periodically criticized these practices. The newspaper *Neue Zeit* complained that one could obtain the Institute for Clothing Culture's chic models only through "relative-like relationships to the corresponding HO-managers," while Paul Fröhlich, First Secretary of the District of Leipzig and a member of the Politburo, joked that "like the old Germanic tribes," there also was barter under the store counters of the GDR.[71]

The "black" and "gray" markets of the immediate postwar years comprised another type of informal network, one that continued in a modified form after the establishment of the HO and the lifting of formal rationing.[72] The unofficial economy consisted primarily of goods smuggled from the West or hoarded East German goods, and participants could either use money or barter. Women with tailoring skills often worked on the side, either as a favor or for pay. The packages from West Germany that already had flowed eastward in the 1950s became even more important after the building of the Wall and represented another significant method of obtaining scarce wares.[73] Western apparel could enter circulation in the GDR through a number of other channels: retirees who had traveled to the West often returned with goods, relatives and friends brought gifts during visits, and other Westerners sold items on the GDR's unofficial used clothing market.[74] Market researchers estimated that in the mid-1960s as much as 20 to 30 percent of all clothing in circulation in the GDR came from the West; for some assortments the proportion was even higher.[75]

Western clothing served as both a valuable source of desperately needed goods and as a highly prized means of social distinction, although evidence of this seldom appears in written sources.[76] The importance of West German apparel in dressing East Germans remained high during the 1970s and dramatically increased during the 1980s. The estimated value of the clothing that arrived in packages alone represented at least 20 percent of the GDR's retail sales and increased from 2.2 billion marks in 1978 to 3.9 billion marks in 1988.[77]

Informal networks and relationships – whether with sales personnel or relatives in the West – did not necessarily correspond to income, social group, profession, place of residence, or party membership. These networks thus added a certain element of randomness to privilege and access to scarce commodities.[78] A woman with a higher income was able to afford a greater quantity and quality of clothing made in the GDR, but she still may have been envious of someone with less income who wore Western apparel received from relations in the FRG. The dress bought in the Exquisit store for hundreds of marks did not necessarily bring more social distinction than the jeans received in a package from the West. Party functionaries were privileged in many ways, but they lacked one of the most distinctive and prestigious sources of consumer goods because they were expected to sever all personal connections with the West.[79]

Complaining

When other methods of acquiring or making apparel proved too ineffective or frustrating, consumers wrote letters of complaint to party and state institutions, manufacturers, trade organizations, the editorial boards of magazines and newspapers, and, starting in the 1960s, the television show *Prisma*. In February 1953 the regime established the first laws governing the treatment of both oral and written petitions (*Eingaben*) to official institutions, including required response times.[80] Often with much humor, sarcasm, and wit, consumers used petitions as a vent for anger and frustration, and more importantly as yet another technique of obtaining needed goods. As sources that offer insights into both consumers' quotidian practices of consumption and discourses about the respective responsibilities and rights of consumers and the regime, petitions reveal much about the relationship between state and society in the GDR.[81]

A letter dated 25 April 1967 from Magda G. to *Prisma* offers a good example of how petitions often contained thick descriptions of consumers' practices, frustrations, and expectations. Since January, Magda had been running around in vain in search of three items that she desired for her wedding scheduled for Whitsun: a white nylon petticoat, size 40, a nylon shirt, and a pair of white heels, size 37. "To the first two articles," Magda reported, "for weeks I was told only one word, 'export-obligations.' I understand that and resolved to be more simple in my wishes." She said she even would have been willing to give up her wish for white heels if her dress were not already finished, but no amount of "understanding" could bring her "to wear black, green, or red shoes with a white dress." For weeks she had searched for white heels in her size in every shoe store in her hometown of Fürstenwalde (including the Exquisit store), in the nearby cities of Frankfurt and Erkner, in the "many small towns of [her] work area," and even in Berlin. As a "working woman," she wrote, "you will understand that I unfortunately lack the time to travel every week to our capital," especially because she had an irregular work schedule and was unwilling to sacrifice her annual vacation time. "Is my wish unusual or has the fashion suddenly changed?" she added sarcastically.[82]

Magda's story featured one of the most common themes of petitions and complaints in the media: futilely "running around" in search of "simple" or "basic" items. Like Magda, many complainants noted that this enormous waste of "valuable time" contradicted the SED's emphasis on economic rationality and its promise to lighten the burdens of working mothers while ensuring that all workers gained more leisure time.[83] "My wife and I have been searching for weeks for a woman's suit in black in size g 94," wrote Ernst S. from the small town of Lohmen in 1967. "I don't want to count the cities of Mecklenburg, let alone the stores, that we visited in vain. If I calculate the travel and the time, I could definitely already pay for a suit with the resulting expenses! Is that economical?"[84] After abandoning their searches, many consumers resented having to waste additional time, money, and energy on improvising their own solutions. In a letter to *Prisma*, Margarete L. from Eisenach described having to balance her responsibilities as a mother of four with searching for children's clothing in stores "at least once a week" for several months. Margarete ended up having to tailor a pair of boy's pants and refashion girl's ski pants into boy's ski pants herself, "which was really only an emergency solution." Some of the items for which she was searching were available in stores, but at prices that Margarete considered too high, especially compared with prices "a few years ago" for the same items.[85]

The regime's own propaganda exacerbated consumers' anger about the gap between official promises and everyday reality. The "object of the misery" of Gertraude L.'s months-long search, she wrote, was "not some exaggerated demands, but rather very simply *plain, dark gray bouclé* [fabric] that one repeatedly presents to us as exhibition pieces in convention centers, exhibition halls, and

store windows" (original emphasis).[86] After receiving an unsatisfactory form letter
from the manufacturer of a women's dress featured in *Für Dich* in 1965, Ilse G.
asked *Prisma*, "why doesn't one forbid the magazines to publish such fashionable
dresses?"[87] Even published paper patterns caused tensions. In addition to errors in
the patterns themselves that rendered them useless, women often lacked the appropriate material: "what use to us are the wonderful models when we lack the material for the most beautiful ones?"[88] The effect of such displays was – to quote a
local party leader – "that our working people are being led by the nose" (*an der
Nase herumgeführt werden*) (Figure 7.1).[89] Typical of such criticisms was an
article in the satirical magazine *Eulenspiegel* by a woman who described the
resentment and disillusionment that she felt while viewing an "Exclusive Pre-
Premiere" at the Friedrichstadt-Palast in Berlin in 1967. Judging from the items on
display, she wrote,

„Gestalten, Deutsches Modeinstitut!" – „Gestalten, Einzelhandel!"

Figure 7.1 Cartoon of a fashion show with a man introducing a dress from the "German
Fashion Institute" (left) and another from "retail trade" (right). Peter Dittrich, *Eulenspiegel* 6 (1959) 30: 12. (Courtesy Peter Dittrich)

I had to conclude that the female portion of our population consists of 16- to at the most 20-year-old featherweight beings, whose primary occupation is being a wife and whose side-job is supervising a cleaning lady, a cook, a nanny, and a chauffeur for the Wartburg 1000 [the more expensive of the GDR's two makes of cars]. For only such lady-colleagues have the time and the opportunity to wear turquoise satin suits or bright red pants complemented with wildly frilled lace blouses in the morning, [...] only they have the necessary petty cash at their disposal, [...] only they have connections to certain stores [...] Perhaps I've once again unnecessarily gotten all worked up. The items from "Exclusive Pre-Premieres" mostly aren't available in stores, anyway.[90]

Consumers also complained to official institutions that fashion propaganda and stores' offerings did not reflect socialism's claims to fulfill the needs of individuals of all different ages and body types. The infamous uniformity of East German clothing was a favorite subject of sardonic articles and cartoons in the media (Figure 7.2).[91] "If only we didn't encounter each dress model and each cloth pattern at least three to four times a day on the street!" was an all-too-common exclamation already in 1953, according to an author in *Frau von heute*.[92] Heinz M. from Wilthen, who said he was forced to wear women's sweaters due to stores' poor offerings of men's knitted garments, lamented to the East German television station in 1971: "I still haven't seen a fashion show where one shows [...] something for those of us who

Figure 7.2 Cartoon about the uniformity of East German stores' offerings of clothing. Helmut Heidrich, "Das Margeritenmuster," *Konsum-Verkaufsstelle* 13 (1954): 5. (Courtesy Konsumverband e.G.)

are older. Fashion for young people dominates (which certainly is also correct), but we are also still around (for your information: I am 46). Could someone tell that to Bormann, Luci Kaiser, and the rest of the fashion designers?"[93] "I am all for every-thing fashionable, including short skirts, but at age 69 one doesn't wear them oneself anymore," W. Effmert, who had searched in vain for a petticoat "in normal length," wrote in a letter published in the newspaper *Handelswoche* in 1968, adding that "stronger women" certainly shared her concern.[94]

If consumers finally found a desired article, they often were dissatisfied with its quality or price. The poor quality of goods and the occasional necessity of exchanging defective items several times contributed to many consumers' sense of moral outrage over a situation that they felt powerless to influence. "You can't at all imagine how one feels when one gets bad wares each time," Evelin L. wrote to *Prisma* in 1966.[95] Petitioners echoed complaints and parodic cartoons in the press about substandard goods, including socks that developed holes after the first wearing, sweaters that shrank three sizes after the first washing, or shirts with one sleeve longer than the other.[96]

Petitioners often reproduced official rhetoric on the responsibilities and rights of worker-consumers in order to lend weight to their demands for a steady supply of reasonably priced, quality goods. In a petition addressed to Walter Ulbricht in December 1961, the widow E. Falk alluded to her status as a worker and the current official campaign to improve the quality of production before describing several shoddy products that she had bought for her three children. She continued, "after all, one earns one's money not so easily that one can throw it out the window. The prices are high enough already as it is, so that one can demand proper quality for one's money." By invoking official propaganda, Falk, like many other worker-consumers, claimed a right to the fulfillment of the regime's promises: "Now Mr. State Councilor, do I have reason to be angry or not?"[97]

Similarly, consumers invoked socialism's egalitarian principles in protesting the everyday realities of unequal distribution and access to goods. Many complainants claimed that stores were full of items that were appropriate for and would fit all kinds of people except themselves. In 1969, shortly after the launching of the GDR's Youth Fashion Program, Elsa F. complained in a petition that most of the garments in department stores were in "mini-style" and suited only youth. The few other models were appropriate only for particularly "chubby" women or "older grandmothers." Faced with these extremes, Elsa asked, "Where does one find the offerings for the working woman between 40 and 60 who is absolutely not fat and old-fashioned but is rather often slender and would also like to dress modernly?"[98] At the same time, however, most complaints about the sizes of clothing in stores appear to have come from women looking for the larger ones.

The highly publicized but unsuccessful campaign to produce special models for "stronger women" made larger women feel all the more justified in complaining about the regime's inability to fulfill their sartorial needs and desires. Women complained that if they found articles that fit, they often were not tasteful or appropriate to their ages. "Many dresses in [size] m 94 were very womanly and therefore did not at all match my taste," Gerlinde H. explained. "I'm 26 years old and would like to appear somewhat youthful in [my clothes] and not already look like 35 to 40."[99] Although most women at least superficially accepted officially propagated definitions of "stronger women" and their special status, some larger women refused to be placed in this category and insisted that their bodies were just as "normal" as the ideal, slender one. Unable for years to find a bright summer dress in size 94 large (an "oversize"), Christine S. from Döbeln wrote, "I am employed in the theater, have a normal figure (chest and hips 112 cm, waist 79 cm), am 1.69 m tall, and 32 years old." Her mother was a "normal" size 82 and could find "a large selection during every season." But since the models and colors were generally very youthful, "judging from the clothing, one could take me for the mother and my mother for my daughter!"[100]

Other groups of consumers also complained that they were disadvantaged when it came to access to scarce, high-quality, and fashionable apparel. Those from the countryside and small towns felt as if they were being treated as second-class citizens because they received both quantitatively and qualitatively inferior apparel compared with urban dwellers. Many agreed with Manfred S. and Erich H., who proclaimed, "We as the rural population don't want to stand behind the city, for we are modern people and also would like to dress modernly and advantageously."[101] Similarly, those without "connections" in retail stores or relatives in the West resented these inequalities and the fact that such methods were necessary to obtain even basic goods. Christine S. wrote that saleswomen told her that the summer dresses in her extra-large size were sold "in a flash" as soon as the shipment arrived. "Unfortunately I don't know these saleswomen so well that I could have one of these dresses put aside under the store counter for me when it arrives." She said that such behavior was "repugnant."[102]

But asking relatives or friends in the West for consumer goods also could be problematic. Although cartoons that appeared in *Eulenspiegel* in 1961 can be interpreted as supporting the regime's attempt to persuade East Germans to voluntarily reject West German gifts, they also conveyed the feelings of shame and inferiority expressed by many petitioners.[103] More than simply reproducing official propaganda that deprecated Western products, petitioners' reluctance to write what many called "begging letters" (*Bettelbriefe*) to Western relatives and friends reflected the reluctance and even shame often associated with having to rely on West Germans' noblesse oblige rather than being able to buy even the most basic consumers goods in the GDR.[104] "I could get myself a bra from West Germany," Siegrun J. wrote to the editors of *Sibylle* in 1965, "but that would be the wrong way. For I believe that we don't yet have to resort to that and thereby make fools of ourselves."[105] After describing her futile efforts to find women's Silastic stock-

ings, men's long socks, and warm children's underwear, Gerlinde M. asked the
Ministry for Trade and Provisioning, "does one need to wonder if 'begging letters'
are sent to the West? I ask you, are such things necessary? Must we expose
[*bloßstellen*] ourselves in this way?"[106]

Frustration and Disillusionment between Stability and Delegitimation

The connections that complainants made between their specific problems and the
performance of the GDR's entire political and economic system demonstrate the
potential of consumers' critiques to undermine the regime's legitimacy. In order to
understand this potential, petitions first must be placed within the larger context of
the GDR's ersatz public sphere in the realm of consumption.[107] Consumers certainly articulated demands and voiced discontent in public, whether verbally
grumbling and griping with sales personnel in stores or commiserating with fellow
citizens on the street, in factories, or in meetings of various state-sponsored organizations. But these public sites generally involved no more than a few dozen participants at any one time. The East German media also included a variety of often
conflicting and critical voices that central authorities failed to completely control.
In keeping with the rhetoric and superficial trappings of democracy that were an
element of all East German political and social institutions, the media created the
appearance of an open public sphere by not only publishing its authors' and
readers' criticisms but also encouraging readers to submit their opinions and suggestions and to "vote" on which models they liked most and least.[108]

That does not mean that GDR citizens enjoyed freedom of the press. More
common than explicit censorship, the media's quotidian self-censorship drew the
boundaries of mass-propagated discourses. Unpublished petitions to official institutions generally followed these boundaries and conventions. Like the media's
publication and even solicitation of criticism concerning consumption, petitions
allowed the regime to register, address, isolate, control, and thus ultimately ener-
vate consumer dissatisfaction and disillusionment under the guise of an apparently
open, democratic, and responsive forum.[109] Many petitioners' explicit claims to be
speaking on behalf of other consumers indicate both the lack of an open public
sphere and the widespread willingness to participate in the forum that the regime
offered as an ersatz. Statements like "I am certain that this not only affects me but
rather many women would rejoice with me ..." or "I know I address a problem that
has long interested our population" suggest a lack of faith in the East German
media's portrayal of real conditions and their representation of consumers' true
concerns.[110]

Given the dominant position of official discourse in the GDR's ersatz public
sphere, it is not surprising that most complaints used its language. This could work

to the complainants' advantage. By voicing their myriad criticisms in officially acceptable terms and language, East Germans could highlight the system's inconsistencies and hypocrisy. Most letter writers simply asked for the realization of the SED's own tirelessly propagated ideological, social, and economic goals. Whether published in the press or limited to an exchange of letters between individual consumers and functionaries, complainants almost never demanded something that had not already been officially promised either explicitly or implicitly. Most consumers insisted that their demands were reasonable and modest, that they already had made voluntary compromises and sacrifices, but that the situation had exceeded what might be reasonably expected of them.

But complaints also helped to stabilize the GDR's political system. By adopting the regime's language in order to ask the state to fulfill official promises and to respect worker-consumers' "rights," East Germans reproduced official discourses while practicing a form of self-regulation. Criticisms that remained within the boundaries of the official discursive framework implied that the GDR's entire political and economic system, despite its highly visible and dramatic flaws, was fundamentally sound and legitimate and could be reformed through relatively localized, cosmetic measures.

Petitions also undergirded the regime by enacting and reinforcing a paternalistic relationship between state and citizen. The individual consumer generally presented very specific, concrete problems or circumstances which officials attempted to alleviate or at least to justify and explain. The press often published both consumers' complaints and officials' responses; some common complaints could even serve as the basis for public relations campaigns to improve offerings of specific assortments like children's clothes, clothes for "stronger women," or women's work clothes in a specific town or factory.[111] Unpublished exchanges of letters between petitioners and functionaries followed the same pattern but could become much more personalized and concrete. State officials ordered manufacturers or retailers to provide complainants with specific articles, met with consumers in their homes to discuss provisioning problems, and even accompanied individuals to stores in search of specific items.[112] Of course the majority of complainants simply received form letters, especially as the number of petitions began to increase dramatically starting in the 1960s. But even form letters displayed extensive efforts to justify the situation by educating consumers and explaining the causes of problems, often with a plethora of "objective" reasons and technical details.[113]

Paternalism also was reflected in the common trope in complaints that provisioning problems would not exist if party and state leaders were aware of them. One common explanation for leaders' ignorance of problems at the grass roots was the observation that many reports became increasingly rosy as they moved upward through the bureaucratic hierarchy.[114] Apart from those who sincerely believed the myth of leaders' unawareness, petitioners had various reasons to reproduce it.

Petitioners could have reasonably assumed that thinly disguising their complaint as an attempt to alert central authorities to problems at the grass roots would increase their chances of success, for official propaganda often entreated East German citizens to actively contribute to the improvement of economic conditions and promised them material rewards in return. Another motivation for reproducing the myth was the opportunity to sharply criticize the regime without risking prosecution: by claiming that the GDR's benevolent leaders knew nothing of the country's true problems, petitioners could attack the regime without questioning its viability and legitimacy and without impugning individual leaders, tactics that could lead to sanctions, imprisonment, or expulsion.

Other petitioners used the distance between rulers and ruled to highlight their resentment of inequalities and of the immunity of party and state leaders to the provisioning problems faced by normal citizens. Such complainants sarcastically argued that certain problems would not exist if those responsible for them also had to suffer. In a petition that criticized the lack of various assortments of children's clothing in 1964, Rudi G. asked, "Did one forget while planning that children also live in the GDR, or do the responsible employees of the Ministry [for Trade and Provisioning] have no children?"[115] Feelings of neglect, frustration, and resentment could lead to cynicism about the gap between the government and industry on one side and ordinary citizens on the other.[116] Consumers' alienation and underlying currents of paternalism also found expression in the claims of many petitioners that specific incidences had damaged or destroyed their "trust" in official institutions.[117]

Petitioners could underscore their disillusionment and lack of trust in the regime by suggesting that their needs and wishes could be satisfied only by abandoning the GDR's system altogether and turning to West German sources. Although petitioners insisted that they would use Western sources only as a last resort, this veiled threat implicitly questioned the regime's legitimacy by suggesting that the East German state had failed to fulfill its citizens' basic needs. Margarete H., who like Gerlinde M. searched in vain for Silastic stockings in late 1970, asked, "should we now write begging letters to relatives in West Germany because of every little thing. [...] No, I don't want that, it would go decidedly too far to issue our honorable state such a certificate of poverty [*Armutszeugnis*] only because of faulty planning in the stocking industry's production." Margarete could not have been too concerned about the GDR's reputation, for she had her husband ask his sister in West Germany for the stockings. In fact, she might have never written her complaint to *Prisma* if the stockings had not been confiscated because the package was addressed to her husband.[118]

Of even greater concern to the East German regime than its citizens' reliance on Western goods was the fact that most East Germans, regardless of whether they had direct connections to the West, used Western products as yardsticks of quality, price, and modernity and complained that the GDR's offerings did not measure up. As local officials in Berlin noted in 1967,

> especially members of the intelligentsia and youth measure the conditions in both German states and West Berlin only by certain superficial appearances like the number and prices of cars, the quality and prices of textiles and other consumer goods, and therefore do not understand that we in the GDR possess the better societal system in Germany and that socialism is superior to capitalism.[119]

In their very specific and unfavorable comparisons between East and West German goods, many petitioners expressed the hope that East Germans would someday catch up to their cousins in the West.[120] After listing the merits of a pair of children's knee stockings "that an aunt in a city 300 kilometers west of here sent," M. Fischer wrote, "may our production reach this level as soon as possible (at stable or sinking prices)!"[121] She added, "twenty years after the war we must finally come to the point where our German neighboring country arrived already two years after the war, namely to be in the position to deliver perfect quality!"[122] Here, too, many petitioners held the regime to its own promises and its often overly rosy propaganda. In 1968 Renate M. asked,

> why are Silastic sweaters and nylon dresses and aprons here in the GDR very expensive in comparison with West Germany? Certainly a substantial part has to do with the fact that food is more expensive in West Germany and thus creates roughly a balancing out. But somehow this must be reflected in the light industry's production of textiles. After all, we have already advanced far with the development of technology and have suggestions for innovations and constantly increasing productivity. That must somehow have an effect on the final consumer price.[123]

By the end of the 1960s, petitioners increasingly made overt, fundamental criticisms of the regime by noting that official promises of progress still remained largely unrealized after two decades of "actually existing socialism." Günter N., the part-owner of a half-state-owned textile retail store, spoke for many when he wrote to party leader Günter Mittag in 1968 that

> I myself am sometimes unsettled [*erschüttert*] when I see how on the one hand gigantic industrial plants are built overnight from scratch and how on the other hand we fail and founder exactly on the small things of life, which however are the "alpha and omega" for our people. One sometimes gets complexes [*Komplexe*] about how and why this can be possible. And yet it is so! And unfortunately not only in the textile sector.[124]

Ernst S., a self-described proud member of the SED since 1954, considered it "simply ridiculous that a comrade in the year 1967, after the successful completion of our Seventh Party Congress, still must make a proposal for such a simple problem" as producing sufficient quantities of oversized women's apparel. "Or are my ideas and demands regarding this too illusionary and too high?"[125]

In 1968, as the regime struggled with yet another of its chronic textile provisioning crises, Ministry for Trade and Provisioning officials at the central level noted that high-quality industrial goods and textiles no longer stood in the foreground of petitions, but that "citizens are increasingly and more decisively opposing the condition that often the simplest articles of daily need are not sufficient or are available only temporarily or in bad quality."[126] But East Germans' conceptions of "basic needs" also had changed during the previous two decades. Goods like nylon stockings that had been luxury items were now articles for everyday use. The flames of discontent about the scarcity and high prices of these items were fanned by the regime's tireless promotion of synthetic materials, the low prices for the goods in West Germany, and the common knowledge that the overwhelming majority of these items were being exported.[127]

Such disillusionment and impatience with official promises to improve consumption were common not only among ordinary citizens but also among members of the SED and employees of state institutions. Magda G., the woman who searched in vain for white heels for her wedding in 1967, was a member of the SED and as a full-time employee of her county's agricultural council often explained provisioning problems to female farmers. "I explained to the women that only so much can be distributed as we ourselves produce, and the better we cover and use all reserves, the better we will live. That is not always so easily believed, but I flatter myself that I accomplished it." She did not tell her female farmers, however, that she privately thought that "white heels were no problem one to two years ago and that we must have produced" enough by now so that "they are not scarce wares."[128] Local officials in and around Leipzig in 1965 received a blunt response when they asked sales personnel why they rarely attempted to argue with customers who made disparaging remarks about East German textiles:

> What are we supposed to say to that? The people are right. The situation here was supposed to change now for years, but until now one can say that not much has changed regarding offerings and prices. We get wares that are more expensive than before because the quality allegedly has improved. Many customers are interested less in the quality than the prices. They then conclude that everything is becoming more expensive. What are we supposed to then answer as salespeople?[129]

There was little that salespeople could say, especially since they were more inclined to agree.

Through the everyday improvisations of shopping, sewing, networking, and complaining, consumers compensated for many of the shortcomings of the GDR's economy while simultaneously disrupting and distorting the regime's attempts to achieve complete control over production and consumption. But regardless of their creativity and industriousness, consumers still depended to a large extent on the formal system of the GDR's economy. The SED's leadership not only tolerated but even encouraged consumers' informal, unplanned actions because the regime relied on these individual actions at the grass roots to soften the impact of the official system's worst failures and to maintain the economy's ability to function. But consumers' spontaneous actions, which often seemed irrational to state planners, also contributed to the chaos and unpredictability of the official system. This in turn led to the need for further unplanned compensatory actions. The official and unofficial systems thus overlapped, shaping and limiting each other.

The strong connection between the satisfaction of consumers' needs and the regime's legitimacy combined with the meaninglessness of citizen's votes at the ballot box to make the consumption of East German products a highly politicized act: the decision to buy or not to buy, to sew one's own clothes, to go shopping in West Berlin, or to receive goods from Western relatives through the mail formed an indirect plebiscite on the GDR's political and economic system. The official discourse that linked achievement in the sphere of production with rights in the sphere of consumption further politicized consumption and strengthened the feeling of justified disgust when needs remained unfulfilled or the relationship between price and value seemed unfair.

No one consumer engaged in all the practices of shopping, sewing, networking, and complaining. Nor did any one consumer experience all the frustrations that accompanied these activities. Certainly a significant portion of the millions of purchases made each year resulted in some degree of satisfaction. These successes could result from luck, concerted campaigns to provide certain goods, or lowered consumer expectations. The structure and inconsistencies of the GDR's economy, however, ensured that these successes occurred randomly and were mixed with disappointment and frustration. A woman could be satisfied with her dresses but dissatisfied with her shoes, be one of the lucky customers present when a new shipment arrived on one day but run from store to store looking for a particular item on the next.

Unwilling and often unable to rely solely on the state to fulfill their needs and wishes, East Germans shaped at least part of their fate in the realm of consumption. This mixture of fortune and misfortune, along with the ability of individuals to muddle through, help to explain the GDR's relative stability over four decades: socialist consumer culture provided fertile grounds for discontent but seldom brought individuals to the point of utter despair. In the long term, however, the disillusionment, frustration, and resentment inherent in this precarious balance, along with the GDR's economic losses and the SED's loss of political control, ultimately contributed to the regime's delegitimation and destabilization. In addition to helping to explain both the GDR's precarious long-term stability and its sudden and peaceful collapse, the paradox of the co-dependent and overlapping relationship between state and society illuminates many of the contradictions, inconsistencies, and moments of conflict and consensus that characterized the politics, practices, and culture of consumption in the GDR.

Epilogue

In retrospect, it is tempting to view the early 1970s as the beginning of the end of the GDR. After more than two decades of consumer frustration and disillusionment, the announcement of the "unity of social and economic policies" in 1971 signaled that the regime no longer asked its citizens to make sacrifices and to defer consumerist dreams until they could be achieved through increases in production. Instead, party leaders hoped to pacify consumers and to encourage higher productivity by increasing actual consumption in the here and now. This shift seems to have had limited success for at least a few years: increased supplies of domestic goods and imports from the West contributed to the common retrospective impression of the early to mid-1970s as the heyday of consumption in the GDR.

But contradictions remained. On the one hand, officials acknowledged that the population's needs, desires, and tastes were becoming increasingly diverse and demanding. Yet the regime's push for the rationalization and standardization of production, as realized through the creation of ever larger units of production and the elimination of private industry in 1972, resulted in increasingly uniform and homogeneous products. Shortages and poor quality remained hallmarks of the GDR's consumer goods industries. Dissatisfied men and especially women continued to invest additional labor in informal activities in order to compensate for the shortcomings of the GDR's formal economy, which proceeded on an accelerating downward spiral caused by internal and external pressures. While the GDR suffered losses from its own inefficient economy, its insecure position in the increasingly competitive international market was weakened further by the worldwide energy crisis of the mid-1970s, which resulted in higher prices for crude oil and other raw materials imported from the Soviet Union. Although the GDR's development was neither linear nor teleological, the regime never managed to overcome the economic losses and foreign debt caused by domestic consumption on credit and international competition.

Just as fateful for East Germany's future was the regime's inability to create a coherent and desirable socialist alternative to Western, capitalist consumer culture.

Since at least the mid-1950s, East German fashion shows and displays had reinforced a modern semiotics of affluence and positioned "socialist" fashion as deriv-
ative of Western styles. Ideals of beauty and symbols of modernity and prosperity
remained virtually identical on both sides of the iron curtain. From the 1960s until
the end of the GDR, official attempts to create a distinctive socialist consumer
culture gradually faded as its inherent contradictions and weaknesses remained
unresolved, and as officials turned their attention to the standardization and rationalization of production as well as growing economic crises. Despite the regime's
attempts at economic and industrial reform, quality stagnated, clothing became
more uniform, and apparel drifted further and further from consumers' diversifying and increasing needs and desires. Party leaders backed themselves into a
self-constructed ideological and political trap and proved either unwilling or
unable to fundamentally reform an ideologically inconsistent and economically
unsound system.

Fashion propaganda and displays of commodities visualized a Western reality
that was unobtainable for East German consumers, despite their hard work and the
regime's promises. The crass contrast between these promises and propagated
images on the one hand and the bleak reality of East German consumers' everyday
experiences on the other both contributed to disillusionment with the entire system
of state socialism and encouraged enchantment with the West. As Michael
Ignatieff remarked in 1985, "by a perverse irony, the actually existing abundance
of Western capitalist society has become the utopia for many inhabitants of actually existing socialism."[1] The regime exacerbated this predicament when it
resorted to selling Western goods to its captive citizens for Western currency. Even
the GDR's best offerings in Exquisit and Delikat stores paled in comparison with
the imported goods in Intershops and in packages from West German relatives,
contributing to the impression that socialism's materialist promises were realized
just across the Wall. Continuing a pattern established in Western Europe already
before World War II, the individual consumption of goods in the GDR proved a
more visible and persuasive measure of affluence than the social consumption of
public resources and services such as housing, health care, child care, cultural programs, education, and public transportation.

In part because socialism shared with capitalism the goal of a modern consumer
paradise and many of the symbols used to visualize it, the SED proved incapable of
creating a desirable alternative consumer culture based on distinctly socialist values
and aesthetics. Instead, the unique consumer culture that had become established in
the GDR by the early 1970s was a contradictory and tension-filled amalgam of
"capitalist" and "socialist" images, promises, values, and practices. The regime's
futile competition with the West on capitalism's own terms and the inability of the
GDR's industry to fulfill the SED's promises help explain why East German
citizens judged their standard of living using the capitalist criteria of individual

consumption while taking for granted subsidized social consumption. Fashion in the GDR embodied the ambiguities and contradictions that arose on the seam between socialism and capitalism, between images of abundance and experiences of scarcity.

In keeping with official discourses that connected consumption to production, East Germans' disillusionment with socialist consumer culture was intertwined with alienation from the products of their labor. Frustrated with the realities of the GDR's planned economy that prevented them from continuing traditions of "German quality work," many East German workers seemed to take little pride in the consumer goods that they produced – and evinced even less enthusiasm about purchasing them. Many women may have resented the time spent making their own clothes, but they still registered a level of satisfaction in consumer surveys, a satisfaction that stemmed in part from their identification with their self-made apparel and from the large measure of control that they exercised over this act of both production and consumption.

Although the political and economic consequences of the GDR's consumer culture can be linked to the country's demise, this consumer culture paradoxically became the subject of nostalgia, indeed one of the focal points of attempts to reconstruct a distinct East German identity starting a few years after unification in 1990. During the months after the collapse of the Wall in November 1989, East Germans poured into West Berlin and West Germany, eager to enjoy objects of their long-held desires. This enthusiasm for Western consumer goods and the partial or total collapse of many East German industries were the source of much self-congratulation in the West and inspired many observers to proclaim the ultimate triumph of capitalism over socialism in the Cold War.[2] But political and cultural developments during the years following unification suggest a more complicated story. As West German political institutions and capital quickly supplanted East German ones, many East Germans began to develop drastically different and more positive attitudes about their former country.

There were several causes for what became known as *Ostalgie*, a neologism composed of the words for East (*Ost*) and nostalgia (*Nostalgie*), but the phenomenon found its most compelling form in material culture, complicating the narratives of pre-unification consumer dissatisfaction. Beginning a few years after the so-called *Wende* (literally "turning point," referring to the changes associated with the unification), former citizens of the GDR sought to reconstruct and maintain distinctly East German identities by rejecting Western products in favor of familiar East German brands and by establishing museums to memorialize everyday life in the GDR.[3] As this book went to press, nostalgia about the GDR's material and consumer culture was continuing with no end in sight, as evidenced by numerous enormously popular books, films, and exhibitions.[4]

Another major subject of *Ostalgie* was the working woman (*berufstätige Frau*).[5]

Many East Germans took pride in the high percentage – among the highest in the world – of women who had worked both inside and outside the home in the GDR. For those who indulged in *Ostalgie*, East German women's active roles in the spheres of consumption and especially production served as the basis for claims that East German women were more "emancipated" than their West German counterparts. While glossing over the tensions and contradictions that had been inherent in consumer goods and women's marginalized status in the GDR, *Ostalgie* used memories and artifacts of East German consumer culture to embody perceived differences between East and West and to express dissatisfaction and disillusionment with the political and economic system of the new Germany.

Only after the *Wende*, when prices for items of social consumption skyrocketed, did East Germans appreciate the subsidies and other familiar socialist elements of their former consumer culture. The new consumption regime of the united Germany conflicted sharply with previous rhetoric of the harmonization of individual and social needs as well as the guarantee of low prices for basic needs. These principles had been central to the politics of consumption in the GDR and represented a major point of consensus between the regime and its citizens throughout the four decades of the state's existence. The experiences of many East Germans with the realities of capitalism in the united Germany resulted in new disillusionment with visions of yet another apparent utopia.

Notes

Introduction

1. Martin Broszat, Klaus-Dietmar Henke, and Hans Woller, eds, *Von Stalingrad zur Währungsreform. Zur Sozialgeschichte des Umbruchs in Deutschland* (Munich, 1990); Haus der Geschichte der Bundesrepublik Deutschland, ed., *Markt oder Plan. Wirtschaftsordnungen in Deutschland 1945–1961* (Frankfurt/Main, 1997). Due to space limitations, references to primary and secondary sources have been kept to the bare minimum throughout the book. For additional references and details, see Judd Stitziel, "Fashioning Socialism: Clothing, Politics, and Consumer Culture in East Germany, 1948–1971," Ph.D. Dissertation, The Johns Hopkins University, 2001.
2. Ludwig Erhard, *Wohlstand für alle* (Düsseldorf, 1956).
3. I use the term "consumer culture" to refer to a broad set of social practices and attitudes through which individuals and groups create and share meanings. This includes not only the acquisition, possession, use, and disposal of material objects, but also the symbolic meanings and values that are created through their representation and exchange. These practices thus encompass the politics of consumption, both at the level of economic policy and in the material culture of everyday life.
4. Arjun Appadurai, "Introduction: Commodities and the Politics of Value," in *The Social Life of Things: Commodities in Cultural Perspective*, ed. Arjun Appadurai (Cambridge, 1986), 3–63.
5. I use "the party" to refer to the SED and "the regime" to refer collectively to all SED and state institutions, including state-owned enterprises and the SED's mass organizations.
6. Georg Simmel, "Fashion," *International Quarterly* 10 (1904): 130–55.
7. Alan Hunt, *Governance of the Consuming Passions: A History of Sumptuary Law* (New York, 1996); Leora Auslander, *Taste and Power: Furnishing Modern France* (Berkeley, 1996); Sheila Fitzpatrick, *The Cultural Front:*

Power and Culture in Revolutionary Russia (Ithaca, 1992); Victoria de Grazia, *How Fascism Ruled Women: Italy, 1922–1945* (Berkeley, 1992), 221–6.

8. Irene Guenther, *Nazi Chic? Fashioning Women in the Third Reich* (Oxford, 2004).

9. Klaus Schroeder, *Der SED-Staat. Partei, Staat und Gesellschaft 1949–1990* (Munich, 1998); Sigrid Meuschel, *Legitimation und Parteiherrschaft. Zum Paradox von Stabilität und Revolution in der DDR 1945–1990* (Frankfurt/ Main, 1992); Ina Merkel, *Utopie und Bedürfnis. Die Geschichte der Konsumkultur in der DDR* (Cologne, 1999). For recent overviews of the burgeoning literature on East Germany, see Corey Ross, *The East German Dictatorship: Problems and Perspectives in the Interpretation of the GDR* (Oxford, 2002); Rainer Eppelmann Bernd Faulenbach, and Ulrich Mählert eds, *Bilanz und Perspektiven der DDR-Forschung* (Paderborn, 2003).

10. Mary Fulbrook, "Retheorizing 'state' and 'society' in the German Democratic Republic," in *The Workers' and Peasants' State: Communism and Society in East Germany under Ulbricht 1945–71*, ed. Patrick Major and Jonathan Osmond (Manchester, 2002), 280–98; Corey Ross, *Constructing Socialism at the Grass-Roots. The Transformation of East Germany, 1945–65* (New York, 2000); Thomas Lindenberger, ed., *Herrschaft und Eigen-Sinn in der Diktatur. Studien zur Gesellschaftsgeschichte der DDR* (Cologne, 1999).

11. Ralph Jessen, "Die Gesellschaft im Staatssozialismus. Probleme einer Sozialgeschichte der DDR," *Geschichte und Gesellschaft* 21 (1995): 109.

12. Detlef Pollack, "Die konstitutive Widersprüchlichkeit der DDR. Oder: War die DDR-Gesellschaft homogen?" *Geschichte und Gesellschaft* 24 (1998): 110–31; Heiner Ganßmann, "Die nichtbeabsichtigten Folgen einer Wirtschaftsplanung. DDR-Zusammenbruch, Planungsparadox und Demokratie," in *Der Zusammenbruch der DDR. Soziologische Analysen*, ed. Hans Joas and Martin Kohli (Frankfurt/Main, 1993), 172–93.

13. Jessen, "Die Gesellschaft im Staatssozialismus," 108.

14. Katherine Pence, "From Rations to Fashions: The Gendered Politics of East and West German Consumption, 1945–1961," Ph.D. Dissertation, The University of Michigan, 1999; Mark Landsman, "Dictatorship and Demand: East Germany Between Productivism and Consumerism, 1948–1961," Ph.D. Dissertation, Columbia University, 2000; Axel Schildt and Arnold Sywottek, "'Reconstruction' and 'Modernization': West German Social History during the 1950s," in *West Germany under Construction: Politics, Society, and Culture in the Adenauer Era*, ed. Robert Moeller (Ann Arbor, 1997), 413–43. For a brief outline of consumption politics related to income, supply, and prices in the 1950s and 1960s, see Philipp Heldmann, "Negotiating Consumption in a Dictatorship: Consumption Politics in the GDR in the

1950s and 1960s," in Martin Daunton and Matthew Hilton, eds, *The Politics of Consumption: Material Culture and Citizenship in Europe and America* (Oxford, 2001), 185–202.

15. For example, Major and Osmond, eds, *The Workers' and Peasants' State*.

16. Monika Kaiser, *Machtwechsel von Ulbricht zu Honecker: Funktionsmechanismen der SED-Diktatur in Konfliktsituationen 1962 bis 1972* (Berlin, 1997); Gerhard Naumann and Eckhard Trümpler, *Von Ulbricht zu Honecker: 1970 Krisenjahr* (Berlin, 1990).

17. Jeffrey Kopstein, *The Politics of Economic Decline in East Germany, 1945–1989* (Chapel Hill, 1997); Charles Maier, *Dissolution: The Crisis of Communism and the End of East Germany* (Princeton, 1997).

18. For recent efforts to integrate consumption in Germany into these larger narratives, see Alon Confino and Rudy Koshar, "Régimes of Consumer Culture: New Narratives in Twentieth-Century German History," *German History* 19 (2001): 135–61; Paul Betts and Katherine Pence, eds, *Socialist Modern: East German Politics, Society and Culture* (Ann Arbor, forthcoming).

19. David Crew, ed., *Consuming Germany in the Cold War* (Oxford, 2003); Uta Poiger, *Jazz, Rock, and Rebels: Cold War Politics and American Culture in a Divided Germany* (Berkeley, 2000); Erica Carter, *How German Is She? Post-War West German Reconstruction and the Consuming Woman, 1945–1960* (Ann Arbor, 1997).

20. Arnold Sywottek, "Zwei Wege in die 'Konsumgesellschaft'," in *Modernisierung im Wiederaufbau. Die westdeutsche Gesellschaft der 50er Jahre*, ed. Axel Schildt and Arnold Sywottek (Bonn, 1993), 269–74; Michael Wildt, *Am Beginn der "Konsumgesellschaft". Mangelerfahrung, Lebenshaltung, Wohlstandshoffnung in Westdeutschland in den fünfziger Jahren* (Hamburg, 1994); Axel Schildt et al., eds, *Dynamische Zeiten. Die 60er Jahre in den beiden deutschen Gesellschaften* (Hamburg, 2000).

21. Charles Maier, "Consigning the Twentieth Century to History: Alternative Narratives for the Modern Era," *American Historical Review* 105 (2000): 807–31.

22. Heide Fehrenbach and Uta Poiger, "Introduction: Americanization Reconsidered," in *Transactions, Transgressions, Transformations: American Culture in Western Europe and Japan*, ed. Heide Fehrenbach and Uta Poiger (New York, 2000), xiii–xl; Michael Lemke, ed., *Sowjetisierung und Eigenständigkeit in der SBZ/DDR (1945–1953)* (Cologne, 1999); Konrad Jarausch and Hannes Siegrist, eds, *Amerikanisierung und Sowjetisierung in Deutschland 1945–1970* (Frankfurt/Main, 1997).

23. The few scholarly studies of fashion in socialist countries published after 1989 have consisted of only articles or book chapters. Anna-Sabine Ernst, "Von der Bekleidungskultur zur Mode: Mode und soziale Differenzierung in

der DDR," in *Politische Kultur in der DDR*, ed. Hans-Georg Wehling (Stuttgart, 1989), 158–79; Anna-Sabine Ernst, "Mode im Sozialismus. Zur Etablierung eines 'sozialistischen Stils' in der frühen DDR," in *Lebensstile und Kulturmuster in sozialistischen Gesellschaften*, ed. Krisztina Mänicke-Gyöngyösi and Ralf Rytlewski (Cologne, 1990), 73–94; René König, *Menschheit auf dem Laufsteg. Die Mode im Zivilisationsprozeß* (Munich, 1985), 354–67; Djurdja Bartlett, "Let Them Wear Beige: The Petit-bourgeois World of Official Socialist Dress," *Fashion Theory* 8 (2004): 127–64; Mary Neuburger, "Veils, *Shalvari*, and Matters of Dress: Unraveling the Fabric of Women's Lives in Communist Bulgaria," in *Style and Socialism. Modernity and Material Culture in Post-War Eastern Europe*, ed. Susan Reid and David Crowley (New York, 2000), 169–87; Olga Vainshtein, "Female Fashion, Soviet Style: Bodies of Ideology," in *Russia – Women – Culture*, ed. Helena Goscilo and Beth Holmgren (Bloomington, 1996), 64–93.

24. Sheryl Kroen, "A Political History of the Consumer," *The Historical Journal* 47 (2004): 709–36; Daunton and Hilton, eds, *The Politics of Consumption*; Belinda Davis, *Home Fires Burning. Food, Politics, and Everyday Life in World War I Berlin* (Chapel Hill, 2000); Victoria de Grazia, ed., *The Sex of Things: Gender and Consumption in Historical Perspective* (Berkeley, 1996).

Chapter 1 – Ideologies and Politics of Consumption

1. For the long and complex history of the concept of need, see Michael Ignatieff, *The Needs of Strangers* (New York, 1985); Margit Szöllösi-Janze, "Notdurft – Bedürfnis. Historische Dimensionen eines Begriffswandels." *Geschichte in Wissenschaft und Unterricht* 48 (1997): 653–73. For discussions of need in Marxist theory, see Edmond Preteceille and Jean-Pierre Terrail, *Capitalism, Consumption and Needs*, trans. Sarah Matthews (Oxford, 1985); Agnes Heller, *The Theory of Need in Marx* (London, 1974).

2. Jean Baudrillard, *The Consumer Society. Myths and Structures* (London, 1998); Daniel Miller, *Material Culture and Mass Consumption* (Oxford, 1994), 47, 206.

3. Werner Sombart, *Luxury and Capitalism*, trans. W.R. Dittmar (Ann Arbor, 1967); Warren Breckman, "Disciplining Consumption: The Debate About Luxury in Wilhelmine Germany, 1890–1914," *The Journal of Social History* 24 (1991): 484–505.

4. SSB-MA, SM10-9, p. 7.

5. BA-BL, DE1/11968, Bl. 17. Thoughout this book, all translations from the German are my own.

6. BA-BL, DC20/I/4-186, Bl. 9.

7. SSB-MA, SM9-6, p. 4 and SM3-7, pp. 10–11.

8. BA-BL, DE1/11968, Bl. 3.

9. SAPMO-BA, DY30/IVA2/2.021/46, Bl. 143.

10. "Programm der Sozialistischen Einheitspartei Deutschlands," in *Dokumente der Sozialistischen Einheitspartei Deutschlands. Beschlüsse und Erklärungen des Parteivorstandes des Zentralkomitees sowie seines Politbüros und seines Sekretariats* [hereafter *Dokumente der SED*], Vol. 9 (Berlin, 1965), 269.

11. See also Ina Merkel, "Luxus im realexistierenden Sozialismus," in *Luxus und Konsum. Eine historische Annäherung*, ed. Torsten Meyer and Reinhold Reith (Münster, 2003).

12. SäStAL, SED-BL Leipzig, IV/2/2/127, Bl. 74.

13. "Programm der SED ...," in *Dokumente der SED*, Vol. 9, 268.

14. Ibid., 269; Ignatieff, *The Needs of Strangers*, 18.

15. Erica Carter, *How German Is She? Post-War West German Reconstruction and the Consuming Woman, 1945–1960* (Ann Arbor, 1997), 96–7.

16. Annelies Albrecht et al., *Organisation und Methoden der Bedarfsforschung* (Berlin, 1960); Mark Landsman, "Dictatorship and Demand: East Germany Between Productivism and Consumerism, 1948–1961," Ph.D. Dissertation, Columbia University, 2000, 251–93. Officials did not mention, however, that such distinctions formed striking similarities to Nazi discourses, which contrasted "Jewish *Reklame*" with "German *Werbung*." Hartmut Berghoff, "Von der 'Reklame' zur Verbrauchslenkung. Werbung im nationalsozialistischen Deutschland," in *Konsumpolitik: Die Regulierung des privaten Verbrauchs im 20. Jahrhundert*, ed. Hartmut Berghoff (Göttingen, 1999), 92–7.

17. For West German discourses on rational consumption, see Carter, *How German Is She?*

18. Katherine Pence, "Labours of Consumption: Gendered Consumers in Post-War East and West German Reconstruction," in *Gender Relations in German History: Power, Agency, and Experience from the Sixteenth to the Twentieth Century*, ed. Lynn Abrams and Elizabeth Harvey (London, 1996), 211–38.

19. *Protokoll der Verhandlungen des 2. Parteitages der Sozialistischen Einheitspartei Deutschlands, 20. bis 24. September 1947* (Berlin, 1947), 306; SAPMO-BA, NY4215/63, Bl. 323; BA-BL, DE1/25687, untitled [Ref. Kahl 13 May 1958 Ind.–Zweigkonferenz] Berlin, 5 May 1958, pp. 10–11; BA-BL, DE1/26032, Bl. 48. On the regime's portrayal of shortages in the 1950s as a transitionary phase between the war's deprivations and socialism's future abundance, see Katherine Pence, "The Myth of a Suspended Present: Prosperity's Painful Shadow in 1950s East Germany," in *Pain and Prosperity: Reconsidering Twentieth-Century German History*, ed. Paul Betts and Greg Eghigian (Stanford, 2003), 137–59.

20. Horst Petzholdt, "Arbeitsmoral – das Herzstück der sozialistischen Moral," *Die Arbeit. Zeitschrift für den Gewerkschaftsfunktionär* 2 (1958) 9: 20–3.

21. Ina Merkel, *Utopie und Bedürfnis. Die Geschichte der Konsumkultur in der DDR* (Cologne, 1999), 120–2.
22. "Kommuniqué des Politbüros über die tausend kleinen Dinge des täglichen Bedarfs, der Dienstleistungen und Reparaturen," in *Dokumente der SED*, Vol. 8, 19.
23. On the regime's paternalism, see Konrad Jarausch, "Realer Sozialismus als Fürsorgediktatur. Zur begrifflichen Einordnung der DDR," *Aus Politik und Zeitgeschichte* B20/98 (1998): 33–46.
24. BA-BL, DC20/I/3/233, Bl. 58.
25. BA-BL, DE1/26173, Arbeitskreis "Bedarfsermittlung," n.d. [1960], p. 1.
26. SAPMO-BA, DY30/IV2/6.10/92, Bl. 246–7; Paul Sonnenberg, "Der Bevölkerung mehr und schöneres Schuhwerk," *Deutsche Schuh und Leder Zeitschrift*, Sonderbeilage zu Heft 3 (1959): 5.
27. Elizabeth Tobin and Jennifer Gibson, "The Meanings of Labor. East German Women's Work in the Transition from Nazism to Communism," *Central European History* 28 (1995): 301–42.
28. Lewis Siegelbaum, *Stakhanovism and the Politics of Productivity in the USSR 1935–1941* (Cambridge, 1988); Katherine Pence, "From Rations to Fashions: The Gendered Politics of East and West German Consumption, 1945–1961," Ph.D. Dissertation, University of Michigan, 1999, 235–42.
29. Alf Lüdtke, "'Helden der Arbeit' – Mühen beim Arbeiten. Zur mißmutigen Loyalität von Industriearbeitern in der DDR," in *Sozialgeschichte der DDR*, ed. Hartmut Kaelble, Jürgen Kocka, and Harmut Zwahr (Stuttgart, 1994), 191–2.
30. SAPMO-BA, NY4215/63, Bl. 81.
31. M.K., "Textil-Punkte," *Frau von heute*, 2. Novemberheft, 22/1948: 30.
32. SAPMO-BA, NY4215/63, Bl. 324.
33. SäStAL, SED-BL Leipzig, IV2/2/127, Bl. 72.
34. SäStAC, ZWK TuK, Nr. 200, Wagner, Stoffhaus Erwa, Auerbach, to Minister für HuV, Berlin, 2 December 1969, p. 2.
35. BA-BL, DL1/3764/1, Bl. 25.
36. The official added that the capitalist and socialist economic presses were "in full agreement" on this point. BA-BL, DE1/24418, Durchsicht des Materials des MfL über die Untersuchungen in der Textilindustrie nach Qualität, Preisen und technischen Problemen, Behrendt, HA-Leiter, HA Planung der LI, Berlin, 29 December 1956, p. 12.
37. SSB-MA, SM3-4, p. 2.
38. BA-BL, DE1/25687, untitled [Ref. Kahl, Berlin, 5 May 1958, pp. 7–8].
39. Ina Merkel has expounded on Rainer Land's claim that the communist movement attempted to construct an "alternate modernity" (*Gegenmoderne*), but she tends to understate the extent to which East Germans were enamored with

certain aspects of Western capitalist modernity and were unable to separate form from content. Rainer Land, "Unvereinbar: Avantgardismus und Modernismus, Diskussion: Waren die Reformsozialisten verhinderte Sozialdemokraten? Teil 1," *Neues Deutschland*, 23/24 April 1994: 10, quoted in Merkel, *Utopie und Bedürfnis*, 12–13. For a more complex and persuasive interpretation of East Germany's version of modernity, see Paul Betts and Katherine Pence, eds, *Socialist Modern: East German Politics, Society and Culture* (Ann Arbor, forthcoming).

40. BA-BL, DE1/26014, Einführungsreferat zur ersten Sitzung des Modisch-ökonomischen Beirates des DMI am 19.2.1959, p. 2.

41. SAPMO-BA, NY4215/63, Bl. 324.

42. SSB-MA, SM4-2, p. 2.

43. Michael Lemke, *Die Berlinkrise 1958 bis 1963. Interessen und Handlungsspielräume der SED im Ost-West-Konflikt* (Berlin, 1995), 46–7.

44. Walter Ulbricht, "Über den kampf um den Frieden, für den Sieg des Sozialismus, für die nationale Wiedergeburt Deutschlands als friedliebender, demokratischer Staat," in *Dokumente der SED*, Vol. 7, 259.

45. Landsman, "Dictatorship and Demand," 294–349.

46. Walter Hixson, *Parting the Curtain: Propaganda, Culture and the Cold War, 1945–1961* (New York, 1997), Chapter 6; Karal Ann Marling, *As Seen on TV: The Visual Culture of Everyday Life in the 1950s* (Cambridge, 1994), Chapter 7.

47. SAPMO-BA, DY30/IV2/6.02/42, Bl. 146.

48. "Maßnahmen zur Erhöhung der Arbeitsproduktivität und zur Verbesserung der Lebenslage der Bevölkerung," in *Dokumente der SED*, Vol. 2, 256.

49. For a recent overview of the voluminous scholarship on the uprising, see Ulrich Mählert, ed., *Der 17. Juni 1953. Ein Aufstand für Einheit, Recht und Freiheit* (Bonn, 2003).

50. Christoph Kleßmann, *Die doppelte Staatsgründung. Deutsche Geschichte 1945–1955* (Bonn, 1991), 277–82.

51. SäStAL, BT und RdB, Abt. HuV, Nr. 1864, Bl. 2; LAB, C Rep. 106-01, Nr. 544, Vorlage, Abt. ÖIH, Ref. LI, Berlin, 5 October 1953, p. 1.

52. On the New Course in the context of consumer politics, see Landsman, "Dictatorship and Demand," 192–250.

53. Jeffrey Kopstein, *The Politics of Economic Decline in East Germany, 1945–1989* (Chapel Hill, 1997), 11.

54. BA-BL, DE1/24191, Liste der wichtigsten von Bewohnern des DM-DN-Währungsbereiches in West-Berlin gekauften Waren, 19 January 1955, p. 1.

55. BA-BL, DE1/24204.

56. LAB, C Rep. 900, IVB2/6/822, Sekretär, BL der SED Gross-Berlin, to Lange, Abt. HuV – LI, ZK der SED, 24 August 1954, unpag.; LAB, C Rep. 106-01-

01, Vorläufige Signatur Nr. T/175, Volkseigene Konfektionsindustrie in Berlin, Schmidt, Stellvertreter des Oberbürgermeisters, 15 November 1955; SSB-MA, RB1956, Nr. 22, pp. 12–3.

57. BA-BL, DE1/24589, Bl. 35–6.

58. LAB, C Rep. 900, IV/7/128–8, Diskussionsbeitrag zur Kreisparteiaktivtagung, 18 November 1953, p. 1.

59. Uwe Westphal, *Berliner Konfektion und Mode. Die Zerstörung einer Tradition 1836–1939* (Berlin, 1992); Brunhilde Dähn, *Berlin Hausvogteiplatz. Über 100 Jahre am Laufsteg der Mode* (Göttingen, 1968); Werner Dopp, *125 Jahre Berliner Konfektion* (Berlin, 1962).

60. LAB, C Rep. 106-01-01, Vorläufige Signatur Nr. T/175, Nickel, IZL Konfektion Berlin, to Magistrat von Groß-Berlin, stellv. OB Zimmermann, 10 April 1956, p. 1.

61. Irene Guenther, *Nazi Chic? Fashioning Women in the Third Reich* (Oxford, 2004), Chapter 5.

62. LAB, C Rep. 106-01, Nr. 544, Engal, stellvertr. Abteilungsleiter, Abt. ÖIH, to Harry Krebs, stellvertr. Oberbürgermeister, Berlin, 26 November 1953, p. 1.

63. LAB, C Rep. 106-01, Nr. 544, Engal to Krebs, 26 November 1953, p. 2.

64. LAB, C Rep. 900, IVB2/6/822, Bericht des Genossen Gloth, Kommission für Staatliche Kontrolle Gross-Berlin, über die Lage in der Berliner Bekleidungsindustrie, Gomolla, Abt. HuV, LI, Berlin, 13 June 1955, p. 3.

65. Ibid., pp. 3–4.

66. "Modezentrum Berlin," *Berliner Zeitung*, 21 March 1956.

67. LAB, C Rep. 625, Nr. 113, Maßnahmen zur Realisierung des Beschlusses der BL der SED von Groß-Berlin "Berlin zum Modezentrum zu gestalten," VVB Konfektion, Berlin, 30 May 1958.

68. Manuel Schramm, *Konsum und regionale Identität in Sachsen 1880–2000. Die Regionalisierung von Konsumgütern im Spannungsfeld von Nationalisierung und Globalisierung* (Stuttgart, 2002), 29–30, 171–88, 210–38.

69. BA-BL, DE1/24418, Durchsicht des Materials des MfL …, p. 12; BA-BL, DE1/30278, Industriezweigökonomik der VVB Konfektion, n.d. [1960], p. 1.212.

70. The textile industry had accounted for 17.7 percent of total industrial production in 1936; the figure was 15.7 percent in 1950 and continued to gradually decline thereafter. By 1965 the textile industry's share of the GDR's total gross industrial production was only 8.2 percent. BA-BL, DE1/24268, Bl. 7; SäStAC, VVB T&S, Nr. 303, Bericht zur Entwicklung in der Textilindustrie der DDR unter Berücksichtigung internationaler Entwicklungstendenzen, SZS, Abt. Industrie, n.d. [1966], p. 1.

71. Shoes accounted for 5–6 percent of retail sales of industrial goods, or 2–3 percent of overall retail sales. BA-BL, DE1/11968, Bl. 49; SAPMO-BA,

DY30/IV2/6.09/70, Zu Fragen Sortiment – Qualität – Mode, n.p., 10 April 1959; BA-BL, DE1/30278, Industriezweigökonomik ..., p. 1.2152; BA-BL, DE1/24268, Bl. 4; BA-BL, DE1/619, Vorlage "Neue Textilpreise," Beschluß-entwurf, 2 June 1959, p. 13.

72. BA-BL, DE1/30278, Industriezweigökonomik ..., p. 1.211.
73. SAPMO-BA, NY4215/63, Bl. 384–5.
74. Gunilla-Friederike Budde, ed., *Frauen arbeiten. Weibliche Erwerbstätigkeit in Ost- und Westdeutschland nach 1945* (Göttingen, 1997).
75. BA-BL, DE1/24268, Bl. 8. With a time lag behind international trends, the number of jobs in the textile industry in the GDR began to decrease in 1960. SäStAC, VVB T&S, Nr. 303, Bericht zur Entwicklung in der Textilindustrie ..., p. 3.
76. BA-BL, DE1/24268, Bl. 8; BA-BL, DE1/30278, Industriezweigökonomik ..., p. 1.2145.
77. BA-CA, DL102/73, p. 3.
78. SAPMO-BA, DY30/IV2/6.09/56, Bl. 104.
79. BA-CA, DL102/73, p. 3.
80. SAPMO-BA, DY30/IV2/6.09/56, Bl. 104; BA-BL, DL1/3764/1, Bl. 21.
81. Jörg Börjesson and Hans-Peter Seliger, "Zur Einzelfertigung von Ober-bekleidung," *MIfM* 10 (1971) 4: 28.

Chapter 2 – The Logic and Contingencies of Planning, Producing, and Distributing

1. Arjun Appadurai, "Introduction: Commodities and the Politics of Value," in *The Social Life of Things: Commodities in Cultural Perspective*, ed. Arjun Appadurai (Cambridge, 1986), 3–63.
2. Christian Heimann, *Systembedingte Ursachen des Niedergangs der DDR-Wirtschaft. Das Beispiel der Textil- und Bekleidungsindustrie 1945–1989* (Frankfurt/Main, 1997), 101–5; Irene Guenther, *Nazi Chic? Fashioning Women in the Third Reich* (Oxford, 2004), chapters 5 and 7.
3. BA-BL, DE1/30278, Industriezweigökonomik der VVB Konfektion, n.d. [1960], p. 1.2.
4. SAPMO-BA, DY30/IV2/6.02/42, Bl. 148.
5. Bruno Gleitze, *Sowjetzonenwirtschaft in der Krise* (Cologne, 1962), 81–90.
6. Heimann, *Systembedingte Ursachen*, 104–5; BA-BL, DE1/30278, Industrie-zweigökonomik ..., p. 1.12/3; BA-BL, DE1/3749, Bl. 17.
7. Rainer Karlsch and Jochen Laufer, eds, *Sowjetische Demontagen in Deutschland 1944–1949. Hintergründe, Ziele und Wirkungen* (Berlin, 2002).
8. SAPMO-BA, DY30/IV2/1.01/36, Bl. 45–6, 49, 60.
9. BA-BL, DE1/30278, Industriezweigökonomik ..., pp. 1.12/3, 1.122/1.

10. BA-BL, DE1/24268, Bl. 11.

11. BA-DH, DL1/3074, Auswirkungen und Maßnahmen der Produktionsein-stellung von nicht vertragsgebundenen und nicht abssetztbaren Erzeugnissen der Textil- und Bekleidungsindustrie im 1./1960, n.d. [1960], p. 9.

12. Wolfgang Stolper, *The Structure of the East German Economy* (Cambridge, 1960), 201–19.

13. BA-BL, DE1/24586, Bl. 3.

14. BA-BL, DE1/26232, 1. Entwurf des Referats für die ökonomische Konferenz der Textilindustrie am 22. und 23.4. in KMSt, n.d. [1960], p. 56.

15. BA-BL, DE1/11562, Bl. 8; BA-BL, DE1/24586, Bl. 3; BA-CA, DL102/192, p. x.

16. SäStAC, RdB, Bezirksverwaltung der HO-Kreisbetriebe KMSt, Nr. 2894, Bericht Submission Konfektion in Leipzig, n.d. [1953], p. 2; SAPMO-BA, DY30/IV2/6.10/29, Bl. 7.

17. SAPMO-BA, DY30/IV2/1/255, Bl. 150; BA-BL, DE1/26096, Beispiele für HuV auf Grund Nichtausnutzung des Materials und der Kapazität für die Herstellung von Konsumgütern, SPK, Abt. LI, Sektor TeBeLe, Gr. Material-bilanzierg./Absatz, Berlin, 24 July 1959, p. 1.

18. LAB, C Rep. 900, IV-2/6/822, Letter from Sekretär, BL der SED Gross-Berlin, to Lange, Abt. HuV – LI, ZK, 24 August 1954.

19. BA-BL, DE1/25708, Bericht über die Durchführung der Ziffer 1 des Beschlusses des Präsidiums des MR von 15.11.1960 ..., Kommission zur Durchführung des Beschlusses des Präsidiums des Ministerrates vom 15.11.1960, Berlin, 7 January 1961, p. 6.

20. BA-BL, DE1/24495; LAB, C Rep. 106-01, Nr. 544, Vorlage, Abt. ÖIH, Ref. LI, Berlin, 5 October 1953, p. 1; BA-BL, DE1/30278, Industrie-zweigökonomik ..., p. 1.21452.

21. Andreas Herbst, Winfried Ranke, and Jürgen Winkler, *So funktionierte die DDR. Lexikon der Organisationen und Institutionen*, 3 vols. (Reinbek bei Hamburg, 1994), Vol. 1, 191–5.

22. The parliament (Volkskammer), nominally the highest authority in the GDR, formally elected or appointed the members of the Council of Ministers and the State Council.

23. The names and responsibilities of many of these institutions changed over the life of the GDR due to numerous restructurings.

24. There were also factories owned by the Association of German Consumer Cooperatives (Verband deutscher Konsumgenossenschaften or VdK) and by groups of craftsmen (*Produktionsgenossenschaften des Handwerks* or PGH).

25. Large industrial combines (*Kombinate*) began to replace the VVBs in 1968.

26. Although this institute had no direct connection with the Nazi regime's *Deutsches Mode-Institut*, there are many interesting points of comparison

between the two organizations' missions, operations, and ultimate failures. Guenther, *Nazi Chic?*, Chapter 6.

27. This chapter focuses on state-owned enterprises because of their exemplary nature and political importance. While small, privately owned factories differed in important ways from large, state-owned enterprises, they operated within the same general framework of material shortages and bureaucratic regulations.

28. SAPMO-BA, DY30/IV2/6.10/92, Bl. 175; BA-BL, DE1/26232, 1. Entwurf des Referats ..., p. 9.

29. Peter Caldwell, *Dictatorship, State Planning, and Social Theory in the German Democratic Republic* (Cambridge, 2003); Oskar Schwarzer, *Sozialistische Zentralplanwirtschaft in der SBZ/DDR. Ergebnisse eines ordnungspolitischen Experiments (1945–1989)* (Stuttgart, 1999).

30. SAPMO-BA, DY30/IV2/6.02/42, Bl. 147.

31. LAB, C Rep. 900, IV-2/6/822, Bericht des Genossen Gloth, Kommission für Staatliche Kontrolle Gross-Berlin, über die Lage in der Berliner Bekleidungsindustrie, Gomolla, Abt. HuV, LI, Berlin, 13 June 1955, p. 4; BA-BL, DE1/24700, Letter from Feldmann to Wittkowski, Abt. Versorgung der Bevölkerung, Neuregelung von Festpreisen für zugerichtete Felle und Pelzkonfektion ..., 16 November 1959, p. 1.

32. LAB, C Rep. 106-01, Nr. 544, Vorlage ..., p. 1; SäStAC, SED-KL, KMSt/Land, Nr. IV/4/10/158, Situation in der Textilindustrie 1955/56 Kreis KMSt/Land, KMSt, 25 October 1955, p. 4; BA-BL, DC20/I/4-186, Bl. 41.

33. SAPMO-BA, DY30/IV2/2.029/80, Lage in der Te- und Be-ind., from Posselt and Lehmann to Heinrich Rau, 14 April 1960, p. 1.

34. BA-CA, DL102/313, pp. 38–9.

35. János Kornai, *The Socialist System. The Political Economy of Communism* (Princeton, 1992), 233–45.

36. SAPMO-BA, DY30/IV2/2.101/1, Bl. 81–3.

37. André Steiner, *Die DDR-Wirtschaftsreform der sechziger Jahre. Konflikt zwischen Effizienz- und Machtkalkül* (Berlin, 1999), 32–4.

38. BA-BL, DE1/7061, Bl. 74, 131.

39. SAPMO-BA, DY30/IV2/2.029/12, Bl. 131.

40. SAPMO-BA, DY30/IV2/1.01/341, Bl. 72; BA-BL, DE1/24268, Bl. 45; BA-BL, DC20/I/4-577, Bl. 61.

41. SäStAC, ZWK TuK, Nr. 309, Welche Wirkungen ergeben sich aus der Durchschnittspreisentwicklung, 9 September 1970, unpag; Helmut Weiss, *Verbraucherpreise in der DDR: wie stabil waren sie?* (Schkeuditz, 1998).

42. SAPMO-BA, NY4215/63, Bl. 372–3; SAPMO-BA, DY30/IVA2/6.09/62, Information, Abt. LLI, Berlin, 20 May 1964, p. 2; SSB-MA, SM14-61, pp. 2–3.

43. LAB, C Rep. 900, IV/7/128-15, Protokoll der Parteileitungssitzung am 3.2.60., Betriebsparteiorganisation Treff-Modelle, Berlin, 9 February 1960, p. 2.

44. SAPMO-BA, DY30/IV2/2.101/21, Bl. 109.

45. SäStAL, SED-BL Leipzig, IVB-2/4/1/233, Information Nr. 6/70, Komitee der ABI Bezirksinspektion Leipzig, 9 February 1970, p. 1.

46. LAB, C Rep. 106, Nr. 138, Aktenvermerk, Berlin, 10 February 1949, p. 1; LAB, C Rep. 106, Nr. 142, Aktenvermerk, Köhler, Planök. Abt., Berlin, 19 March 1949.

47. BA-BL, DC20/I/3-233, Bl. 58; LAB, C Rep. 106-01, Nr. 544, Vorlage ..., p. 3. Officials also called trade "demand bearers" (*Bedarfsträger*), "allocation bearers" (*Kontingentträger*), or "mediator between production and the population." DC20/I/3-171, Bl. 93; SäStAL, SED-BL Leipzig, IV/2/2/127, Bl. 72.

48. Georg Bergler, *Die Entwicklung der Verbrauchsforschung in Deutschland und die Gesellschaft für Konsumforschung bis zum Jahre 1945* (Kallmünz/ Oberpfalz, 1959/1960).

49. Erica Carter, *How German Is She? Post-War West German Reconstruction and the Consuming Woman, 1945–1960* (Ann Arbor, 1997), 96–7.

50. Mark Landsman, "Dictatorship and Demand: East Germany Between Productivism and Consumerism, 1948–1961," Ph.D. Dissertation, Columbia University, 2000, 251–93; Annette Kaminsky, "'Warenproduktion und Bedürfnisse in Übereinstimmung bringen'. Markt- und Bedarfsforschung als Quelle der DDR-Sozialgeschichte," *Deutschland Archiv* 31 (1998): 579–93; Dorothea Hilgenberg, *Bedarfs- und Marktforschung in der DDR: Anspruch und Wirklichkeit* (Cologne, 1979).

51. LAB, C Rep. 106, Nr. 142, Aktenvermerk, Köhler ....

52. BA-BL, DE1/30278, Industriezweigökonomik ..., p. 2/4221/2.

53. BA-CA, DL102/171, p. 2; BA-CA, DL102/148, pp. 86–7.

54. LAB, C Rep. 900, IV/4/06/318, Durchführung neuer Kurs, Abtl. Wirtschaft, Erna F., Instrukteur, Berlin, 10 November 1953, pp. 1–2.

55. LAB, C Rep. 900, IV/7/128-6, Entwurf für die Entschließung der Partei-aktivtaung am 18.11.53: Berlin voran im neuen Kurs, p. 4.

56. BA-BL, DE1/27357, Bericht über die Bedarfsermittlung Textilwaren Oktober 1954, VdK, Handel/Textil, Berlin, 23 November 1954, p. 1; SäStAL, BT und RdB Leipzig, Abt. HuV, Nr. 1917, Bl. 2.

57. BA-BL, DE1/26175, Ausarbeitung des Arbeitskreises Handel anläßlich der ökonomischen Konferenz der Textilindustrie im Januar 1960, p. 8.

58. SAPMO-BA, DY30/IV2/1.01/328, Bl. 44; BA-BL, DE1/7073, Bl. 28.

59. SAPMO-BA, DY30/IV2/6.10/92, Bl. 98–108; SäStAL, BT und RdB Leipzig, Abt. HuV, Nr. 1864, Bl. 7–8.

60. SAPMO-BA, DY30/1VA2/2.021/704, Bl. 44–5.

61. BA-CA, DE1/34725, Vorschläge des Arbeitskreises Produktionsplanung zur Verbesserung der Produktionsplanung bei der Lösung der ökonomischen Hauptaufgabe, 12 February 1959, pp. 4–5.

62. BA-DH, DL1/16142, Probleme zu Selbstkosten und Preisen für technisch weiterentwickelte und modische Konsumgüter, Berlin, 5 May 1958, p. 9.

63. BA-BL, DE1/26014, Textilkonferenz. Arbeitskreis "Textilindustrie – Binnenhandel", p. 4; BA-BL, DE1/26096, Stellungnahme des Staatlichen Textilkontors zur Ordnung für den Einkauf von Textilwaren einschließlich Konfektions- und Näherzeugnisse, KMSt, 6 October 1959, p. 1.

64. SAPMO-BA, DY30/JIV2/2/753, Bl. 253–4.

65. *MIfM*, Vol. 6, Sonderheft (1967): 2.

66. Hannelore Fabiunke et al., *Handbuch der Konsumentenbefragung* (Berlin, 1972).

67. BA-BL, DE1/5446, Bl. 8; SäStAL, BT und RdB Leipzig, Abt. HuV, Nr. 1864, Bl. 8–9.

68. BA-BL, DE1/26096, Transcript of speech by Dümde, Hauptverwaltungsleiter Hauptverwaltung I Textilwaren KMSt at the Trade Conference, 6 August 1959, p. 1; SAPMO-BA, DY30/IV2/6.10/92, Bl. 244.

69. SAPMO-BA, DY30/IV2/1.01/36, Bl. 79–80.

70. BA-BL, DE1/26175, Ausarbeitung des Arbeitskreises Handel …, p. 36.

71. SAPMO-BA, DY30/IV2/6.10/28, Bl. 218.

72. LAB, C Rep. 106, Nr. 138, Aktenvermerk …, p. 3; LAB, C Rep. 106-01, Nr. 544, Vorlage …, p. 2.

73. LAB, C Rep. 106-01, Nr. 544, Letter from Dies to Radelt, Berlin, 8 January 1953, p. 1.

74. SAPMO-BA, DY30/IV2/1/115, Bl. 157.

75. LAB, C Rep. 106, Nr. 333, Wie lösen wir die Probleme in der Bekleidungsindustrie?, VEB Bekleidungswerk "Fortschritt" Werk II, Berlin-Lichtenberg, 28 February 1954, p. 1; BA-BL, DE1/25716, Auszug aus dem Gütebericht des DAMW – FA Textil – für das 1. Halbjahr 1959, p. 4; BA-BL, DE1/24495, Situationsbericht – Konfektionsindustrie, Berlin, 24 June 1958, p. 4.

76. SAPMO-BA, DY30/IVA2/6.09/85, Notiz über eine Aussprache mit dem Genossen Woitceck, Kaufhausleiter vom Modehaus "Elite" Guben, Ursula P., 3 June 1964, pp. 1–2.

77. Ibid.

78. SäStAC, RdB KMSt, Wirtschaftsrat, Abt. TeBeLe, Nr. 17997, Protokoll über die Untersuchungen und die Beratung des Arbeitskreises zur Verbesserung der Planung und Leitung der örtlichen Konfektionsindustrie, Möbius, Leiter des Arbeitskreises, KMSt, 21 June 1962, pp. 4–5; LAB, C Rep. 900, IV-2/6/822, Beschluss-Nr. 29/55, Ziff. 1, der Sitzung des Büros der BL vom 28.7.1955, Gomolla, Abt. HuV, LI, Berlin, 5 August 1955, pp. 3–4.

79. BA-BL, DE1/26450, Auszugsweise Abschrift eines Berichtes der Arbeiter-kontrolleure aus Leipzig vom 30.10.1959, p. 2.

80. BA-BL, DC20/I/4-148, Bl. 25; LAB, C Rep. 900, IV-2/6/822, Beschluss-Nr. 29/55, Ziff. 1 …, p. 4; BA-CA, DE4/10289.

81. BA-BL, DE1/27458, Protokoll der 6. Sitzung der Ständigen Kommission beim MHV – Überplanbestände, Rose, MHV, Stellv. des Ministers, Berlin, 25 April 1955, p. 2.

82. SäStAC, ZWK TuK KMSt, Nr. 5, Letter from Walter Grunewald KG Der Herrenausstatter, Erfurt-Anger, to MHV, Minister Lucht, Berlin, 23 April 1964.

83. SAPMO-BA, DY30/IVA2/6.09/139, Petition from Günter N., Modehaus Güni-Tuche, to Günther Mittag, Berlin, Glauchau, 21 June 1968.

84. BA-BL, DC20/I/4-184, Bl. 26.

85. SSB-MA, SM5-32, p. 1; SAPMO-BA, DY30/IV2/6.10/92, Bl. 105; BA-BL, DE1/26175, Ausarbeitung des Arbeitskreises Handel …, p. 27.

86. SAPMO-BA, DY30/IV2/6.09/72, Entwurf des Referates von Grete Witt-kowski für die Textilkonferenz, 13 April 1960, unpag.; SSB-MA, SM5-32, p. 1.

87. BA-BL, DC20/I/3-171, Bl. 92; SAPMO-BA, DY30/IV2/2.029/29, Bl. 236–7.

88. LAB, C Rep. 900, IV-2/6/822, Beschluss-Nr. 29/55, Ziff. 1 …, p. 1.

89. BA-BL, DE1/7013, Bl. 52; SAPMO-BA, DY30/IV2/2.029/79, Bl. 28.

90. SAPMO-BA, DY30/IV2/2.029/79, Bl. 248.

91. SäStAC, RdB KMSt, Wirtschaftsrat, Abt. TeBeLe, Nr. 17904, Haubold & Co. KG to RdK KMSt, Abt. Industrie und Handwerk, 9 May 1963.

92. LAB, C Rep. 470-01, Nr. 90, Bl. 2; Helmut Bergmann and Wilfried Lange, *Die Vorbereitung der Produktion in der Textilindustrie* (Berlin, 1960), 40–1.

93. SAPMO-BA, DY30/IVA2/6.09/62, Information, Abt. LLI …, p. 1; SAPMO-BA, NY4215/63, Bl. 360.

94. SAPMO-BA, DY30/JIV2/2A/914, Vorlage für das PB des ZK der SED, Wittkowski, Stellvertreter des Vorsitzenden des MR für HuV und Konsum-güterproduktion, Berlin, 27 July 1962, p. 4.

95. BA-CA, DE1/34725, Vorschläge des Arbeitskreises Produktionsplanung …, p. 4.

96. Ibid.

97. BA-BL, DC20/I/3-169; Autorenkollektiv, *Theorie und Praxis der neuen Planmethodik in Textil- und Bekleidungsbetrieben* (Leipzig, 1962).

98. Elfriede Philipp, "Bekleidung – aber keine Kleider. Ein geheimnisvolles Gremium bestimmt, was die Berlinerin tragen soll," *Die Wirtschaft*, n.d. [1955/1956], unpag., found in LAB, C Rep. 106-01-01, Vorläufige Signatur Nr. T/176; SAPMO-BA, DY30/IV2/6.10/28, Bl. 217–8.

99. BA-BL, DC20/I/4-577, Bl. 52; SAPMO-BA, NY4182/991, Bl. 318; SAPMO-BA, DY30/IV2/1.01/341, Bl. 178-9.

100. SAPMO-BA, DY30/IVA2/6.09/85, Einige Probleme zur Verbesserung der Versorgung der Bevölkerung mit Erzeugnissen der Textil-, Bekleidungs- und Lederindustrie, Abt. LLI, Berlin, 24 January 1964, pp. 1–5, quote: 4.

101. LAB, C Rep. 106-01, Nr. 544, Vorlage ..., p. 2; BA-BL, DE1/26173, Letter from Woida, Hauptdirektor, VVB Schuhe Weißenfels/Saale to Bethe, Sektor Leder-Schuhe-Rauchwaren, Abt. TeBeLe, SPK, 18 January 1961, p. 6.

102. BA-CA, DL102/73, p. 81.

103. LAB, C Rep. 113, Nr. 479, Maßnahmen zur Verminderung von Abwertungs- verlusten im sozialistischen Handel, MdF, Abt. Handel, Berlin, 9 May 1960, p. 5.

104. SAPMO-BA, DY30/IVA2/6.09/139, Petition from Günter N. to Mittag ..., unpag.

105. SAPMO-BA, DY30/IV2/1.01/36, Bl. 48.

106. BA-BL, DE1/24268, Bl. 6.

107. BA-BL, DE1/25687, Direktive zur Ausarbeitung der Planvorschläge zum Volkswirtschaftsplan 1959 für die Betriebe der VVB(Z) Konfektion, VVB Konfektion, Hauptdirektor, Berlin, 2 June 1958, p. 8.

108. SäStAC, VVB T&S, Nr. 303, Bericht zur Entwicklung in der Textilindustrie der DDR unter Berücksichtigung internationaler Entwicklungstendenzen, SZS, Abt. Industrie, n.d. [1966], p. 5.

109. Ibid., p. 6.

110. Frank Ebbinghaus, *Ausnutzung und Verdrängung. Steuerungsprobleme der SED-Mittelstandspolitik 1955–1972* (Berlin, 2003).

111. LAB, C Rep. 625, Nr. 8 (BEHALA), Grundlinie der Entwicklung der Bekleidungsindustrie im Rahmen der Konzeption bis 1975/1980, Klinger, Werkdirektor, Dresden, 10 June 1960, p. 2.

112. BA-BL, DE1/1821, Vorschlag über die Reorganisation der Vertragskontore und der Handelszentralen zur Durchsetzung der politökonomischen Ziele ..., Krämer, Fachgebietsleiter, FG Textil/Leder, 19 February 1953, p. 1.

113. LAB, C Rep. 900, IV-2/6/822, Aussprache über Massnahmen zur Überwin- dung der Schwierigkeiten der Konfektionsindustrie, 8 July 1955.

114. LAB, C Rep. 900, IV-2/6/822, Beschluss-Nr. 29/55, Ziff. 1 ..., p. 4.

115. BA-BL, DE1/1821, Vorschlag über die Reorganisation ...; BA-BL, DE1/24261; BA-CA, DE4/10289, Letter from Leiter, Sektor Planung u. Ökonomie, Abt. TeBeLe, to Wittik, Berlin, 3 April 1962, p. 1.

116. BA-BL, DE1/24641, Submissionen von Laube, Stellvertr. d. Abt.-Leiters, Wirtschaftsrat, Industrie und Handwerk Bezirk Erfurt an die Verkaufs- organisation Bekleidung, Leipzig, 17 November 1958.

117. *30 Jahre Modeinstitut der DDR 1952–1982*, n.p., n.d., unpag.

118. The following analysis of the garment industry represents a synthesis of figures from multiple sources, including BA-BL, DE1/30278, Industrie-

zweigökonomik ..., pp. 1.122/2–4, 1.214; BA-BL, DE1/25687, Rekon-struktionsplan der VVB Konfektion für die Jahre 1959–1965, VVB Konfektion, Kahl, Hauptdirektor, Berlin, 13 December 1958, pp. 2–3; BA-CA, DL102/196, pp. 52–3; BA-BL, DE1/7054, Bl. 258; SAPMO-BA, DY30/IVA2/2.021/705, Bl. 159; LAB, C Rep. 470-02, Nr. 12, Bl. 8.

119. BA-BL, DE1/30278, Industriezweigökonomik ..., p. 1.122/3.

120. LAB, C Rep. 625, Nr. 8 (BEHALA), Grundlinie der Entwicklung ..., p. 2; BA-BL, DE1/30278, Industriezweigökonomik ..., p. 1.122/3.

121. The following analysis of the textile industry represents a synthesis of figures from multiple sources, including BA-BL, DE1/3713, Bl. 4; BA-BL, DE1/3722, Bl. 98; BA-CA, DF5/82, Führungskonzeption der FA Textil. DAMW der DDR, n.d. [1968], p. 26.

122. BA-CA, DE4/29248, Information über Beschwerden der Komplementäre, Unternehmer, Handwerker zur Arbeit der Gutachterausschüsse des DAMW, Kahl, Generaldirektor, VVB Konfektion, Berlin, 18 August 1964, p. 1.

123. BA-DH, DL1/1419, Bl. 7; Werner Krackert, "Was die Arbeit der Konfektionsindustrie hemmt. Das Fortschrittwerk Friedrichshain im ersten Planmonat," *Berliner Zeitung*, 11 February 1953; SäStAC, RdB, Bezirks-verwaltung der HO-Kreisbetriebe KMSt, Nr. 2894, Bericht Submission Konfektion in Leipzig ..., p. 1.

124. BA-BL, DE1/30278, Industriezweigökonomik ..., p. 2/2.11.

125. BA-BL, DE1/348, Bl. 17–8.

126. BA-BL, DE1/26014, Textilkonferenz ..., pp. 30–1.

127. Ibid.

128. SAPMO-BA, DY30/IV2/1/303, Bl. 176.

129. BA-BL, DE1/7367, Bl. 58; SAPMO-BA, DY30/IV2/6.07/65, Bl. 333.

130. SäStAC, RdB KMSt, Wirtschaftsrat, Abt. TeBeLe, Nr. 17904, Haubold & Co. KG to RdK KMSt ..., p. 1.

131. LAB, C Rep. 106-01-01, Vorläufige Signatur Nr. T/131, Letter from Franken-berger, Hpt. Abt. Leiter, HA Konfektion, Handelsniederlassung Textilwaren, Konsum-Genossenschaftsverband Gross-Berlin, to IZL Konfektion der Berliner Örtl. VEB, 27 December 1955.

132. LAB, C Rep. 625, Nr. 8 (BEHALA), Grundlinie der Entwicklung ..., p. 1.

133. LAB, C Rep. 900, IV-2/6/860, Vorschlag für die Spezialisierung des Handels mit Konfektion in Berlin, n.d. [April 1961]; SäStAC, RdB KMSt, Wirtschaftsrat, Nr. 20812, Textanalyse zur Spezialisierung des Verkaufs-stellennetzes für Textilwaren, KMSt, 6 February 1963.

134. Hellmut Schurig, *Die Entwicklung der Textilindustrie in Westdeutschland und in der Deutschen Demokratischen Republik* (Berlin, 1959), 117. In the early 1950s larger garment factories commonly worked with over 100 suppliers. Krackert, "Was die Arbeit der Konfektionsindustrie hemmt."

135. BA-BL, DE1/26096, Transcript of speech of Dümde, Hauptverwaltungs-leiter Hauptverwaltung I Textilwaren KMSt, at the Handelskonferenz, 6 August 1959, pp. 4–5.

136. LAB, C Rep. 625, Nr. 59, Presseinformation der VVB Konfektion Berlin, "Aus dem Groschen die Mark: Bekleidungsindustrie spezialisiert."

137. LAB, C Rep. 900, IVA/7/001-5, Referat zur Parteiaktivtagung am 20.11.1964. Thema: Die Aufgaben der Parteiorganisation des Industrie-zweiges Konfektion bei der Erarbeitung des Perspektivplanes bis 1970, pp. 29–30.

138. LAB, C Rep. 106-2, Nr. 469, Vorlage für die Kommission für Fragen der Versorgung der Bevölkerung des Magistrats von Groß-Berlin, Schmidt, Direktor, Handelsgesellschaft Konfektion, Berlin, 17 May 1965, p. 3.

139. SAPMO-BA, DY30/IVA2/6.10/8, untitled, n.d. [1966].

140. SAPMO-BA, DY30/IVA2/2.021/722, Bl. 145.

141. SAPMO-BA, DY30/IVA2/6.09/66, Zusammenfassende Darstellung des Aufbaus eines Textil/Bekleidungs-Kombinates in Cottbus von 1968–1973 in 2 Aufbaustufen Polyesterversuchsprogramm, MfL, n.d. [1968], pp. 1–3.

142. SAPMO-BA, DY30/IVA2/6.09/111, Letter from Briksa, Abt. LLBI, to Mittag, 25 August 1969, pp. 1–2.

143. LAB, C Rep. 625, Nr. 8 (BEHALA), Grundlinie der Entwicklung …, p. 3.

144. SAPMO-BA, DY30/JIV2/2/711, Bl. 31.

145. BA-BL, DC20/I/4-2624, Bl. 45.

146. SAPMO-BA, DY30/IV2/2.029/79, Bl. 120, 135–6; BA-BL, DC20/I/4-2624, Bl. 45.

147. LAB, C Rep. 900, Nr. IVB-2/6/597.

148. SAPMO-BA, DY49/16/980/6846, Material für Genossein Posselt – IG Te/BeLe, für die Delegiertenkonferenz vom 18. bis 20. September 1959, p. 3.

149. SAPMO-BA, NY4215/63, Bl. 331; BA-CA, DL102/196, p. 56.

150. BA-CA, DE4/684, Interview für ADN anlässlich der Leipziger Früh-jahrsmesse 1961, p. 1; SäStAC, VVB T&S, Nr. 303, Bericht über einige Probleme des Exports und Imports in der Textil- und Konfektionsindustrie der DDR, SZS, Abt. Industrie, Vorbemerkung.

151. BA-CA, DL102/196, pp. 62, 64, 75–6; BA-CA, DL102/151, pp. 9, 11, 17.

152. LAB, C Rep. 470-02, Nr. 4, Bl. 27; LAB, C Rep. 470-02, Nr. 12, Bl. 39.

153. BA-BL, DC20/I/4-700, Bl. 59; BA-CA, DL102/151, pp. 8–9.

154. SAPMO-BA, DY30/IVA2/6.09/109, Information über dringende Probleme der bedarfsgerechten Produktion und der Vermeidung volkswirtschaftlicher Verluste 1963 in der Textil- und Bekleidungsindustrie, Abt. LLI, Berlin, 4 January 1963, p. 2.

155. BA-BL, DC20/I/4-342, Bl. 168–9; LAB, C Rep. 470–02, Nr. 4, Band 3, Bl. 27–8, 30.

156. SAPMO-BA, Vorläufige Signatur DY30/17018, Information über Probleme bei der Verbesserung der Versorgung der Bevölkerung mit Konfektionserzeugnissen, MR der DDR, Arbeitsgruppe für Organisation und Inspektion beim Vorsitzenden, Schenk, Behrend, Berlin, 15 February 1974, p. 7.

157. BA-CA, DL102/294, p. 84.

158. Herbst et al., *So funktionierte die DDR*, Vol. 1, 523–9; Jonathan Zatlin, "Consuming Ideology. Socialist Consumerism and the Intershops, 1970–1989," in *Arbeiter in der SBZ-DDR*, ed. Peter Hübner and Klaus Tenfelde (Essen, 1999), 555–72.

159. Guenther, *Nazi Chic?*, 232–5; SAPMO-BA, DY30/IV1/IV/1, Bl. 97, 104; SAPMO-BA, DY30/IVA2/2.021/891, Bl. 31.

160. Susannah Handley, *Nylon: The Story of a Fashion Revolution: A Celebration of Design from Art Silk to Nylon and Thinking Fibres* (Baltimore, 1999); Stiftung Haus der Geschichte der Bundesrepublik Deutschland, ed., *Künstliche Versuchung. Nylon – Perlon – Dederon* (Cologne, 1999). On economic and cultural dimensions of plastics and synthetics in East German consumer goods, see Eli Rubin, "The Order of Substitutes: Plastic Consumer Goods in the *Volkswirtschaft* and Everyday Domestic Life in the GDR," in *Consuming Germany in the Cold War*, ed. David Crew (Oxford, 2003), 87–119.

161. Stefan Paul, "Die Dederon-Kampagne 1959," in *Künstliche Versuchung*, ed. Stiftung Haus der Geschichte der BRD, 132–7.

162. BA-BL, DE1/11615, Bl. 8–15; BA-BL, DE1/24142, Bericht über die Entwicklung der Produktion und die Verarbeitung von synthetischen Fasern, SPK, Berlin, 10 March 1955; Zentralkomitee der SED, ed., *Chemie gibt Brot – Wohlstand – Schönheit. Chemiekonferenz […] in Leuna am 3. und 4. November 1958*, n.p., n.d.

163. SAPMO-BA, DY30/IVA2/6.10/237, Letter from DIA Textil to Leitung der Parteiorganisation Außenhandel, Schalck, n.p., 24 January 1964.

164. SAPMO-BA, DY30/IV2/1/283, Bl. 5.

165. SAPMO-BA, DY30/JIV2/2/1137, Bl. 1–6, 9–25.

166. Ibid., Bl. 4, 9, 11, 12, 15, 18, 22.

167. SAPMO-BA, DY30/IVA2/6.09/66, Zusammenfassende Darstellung …, p. 2.

168. Ibid., p. 3; SAPMO-BA, DY30/IVA2/6.09/111, Briksa to Mittag; SAPMO-BA, DY30/IVA2/2.021/722, Bl. 145; SAPMO-BA DY30/IVA2/6.09/89, Vorschläge zur Verbesserung der Versorgung der Bevölkerung in versorgungswichtigen Positionen und zur erhöhten Abschöpfung der Kaufkraft, MfL, Berlin, 5 January 1970, p. 2.

169. BA-CA, DL102/2124, p. 16.

170. SAPMO-BA, DY30/IVA2/6.09/66, Konzeption zur Neuprofilierung der Textil- und Bekleidungsindustrie der Bezirksstadt Cottbus …, n.p., n.d. [1968], p. 2.

171. SAPMO-BA, DY30/IVA2/6.10/237, Letter from DIA Textil to Schalck, pp. 1–2; BA-BL, DG4/2004, Komplex Konfektionsversorgung, p. 2; LAB, C Rep. 470-02, Nr. 132, Bl. 91–2.
172. BA-CA, DL102/2124, p. 16.

Chapter 3 – From "New Out of Old" to "Socialist Fashion": Patching Together an Alternative Consumer Culture

1. R. Kn., "Anarchie im Reich der Mode," *Die Frau von heute*, 3. Heft März 1946: 21.
2. Irene Guenther, *Nazi Chic? Fashioning Women in the Third Reich* (Oxford, 2004), 205–6, 259–64; Gloria Sultano, *Wie geistiges Kokain ...: Mode unterm Hakenkreuz* (Vienna, 1995), 30–9.
3. The phrase in German is *Aus Alt mach neu* or *Neues aus Altem*. Guenther, *Nazi Chic?*, 31, 219–20.
4. "Phönix" GmbH Chemnitz Berufliches Bildungs- und FörderCentrum, ed., *15 Milliarden Stunden im Jahr. Ein Blick auf Hausarbeit und Haushalttechnik in der DDR* (Chemnitz, 1997), 64–5; "Der letzte Schrei: Das Flickenkleid!" *Der Berliner*, 13 September 1945: 3, cited in Guenther, *Nazi Chic?*, 434, n. 570.
5. Drawings and photographs of women modeling paper pattern designs appeared in both general women's magazines such as *Frau von heute* or *Für Dich* and magazines devoted to displaying paper pattern models, including *Praktische Mode* (later *PRAMO*), *Flotte Kleidung*, *Die neue Mode*, *Modische Modelle*, *Saison*, and *Modische Maschen*.
6. I am suggesting a more complicated narrative than most retrospective accounts which claim that extreme shortages reduced Germans' desires for clothes, food, and shelter to a bare minimum, devoid of all aesthetic considerations. For example, in a speech in 1960 Elli Schmidt claimed that during World War II and the immediate postwar period "our women did not ask how the clothing that they wore looked. We were all very happy if there was enough to wear, when we got shoes on our feet." SSB-MA, SM6-7, p. 2.
7. Gertrud Berger, "Frau Mode – Entschleiert," *Frau von heute*, 1. Heft Feb. 1946: 23.
8. Elizabeth Heinemann, "The Hour of the Woman: Memories of Germany's 'Crisis Years' and West German National Identity," *American Historical Review* 101 (1996): 354–95; Ina Merkel, *... und Du, Frau an der Werkbank: Die DDR in den 50er Jahren* (Berlin, 1990), 31–47.
9. One example of an early unrealistic display of dress was the feature film *Modell Bianka*, released by the state-run film company DEFA in 1951, which climaxed in a fashion show of extravagant evening dresses at the Leipzig

Trade Fair. BA-FA, *Modell Bianka*, dir. Richard Groschopp, sw. Erich Conradi, DEFA, 1951.

10. Compare Anna-Sabine Ernst, "Mode im Sozialismus. Zur Etablierung eines 'sozialistischen Stils' in der frühen DDR," in *Lebensstile und Kulturmuster in sozialistischen Gesellschaften*, ed. Krisztina Mänicke-Gyöngyösi and Ralf Rytlewski (Cologne, 1990), 92.

11. Hellmut Schurig, *Die Entwicklung der Textilindustrie in Westdeutschland und in der Deutschen Demokratischen Republik* (Berlin, 1959), 64; SSB-MA, SM1-12, p. 4.

12. Guenther, *Nazi Chic?*, 35, 50–2, 83–4, chapter 5.

13. Erica Carter, *How German Is She? Postwar West German Reconstruction and the Consuming Woman, 1945–1960* (Ann Arbor, 1997), 16.

14. The personification of fashion as a woman is encouraged by the fact that the word itself, *die Mode*, is femininely gendered in the German language.

15. Elfriede Philipp, "Bekleidung – aber keine Kleider. Ein geheimnisvolles Gremium bestimmt, was die Berlinerin tragen soll," *Die Wirtschaft*, n.d. [1955/1956], unpag., found in LAB, C Rep. 106-01-01, Vorläufige Signatur Nr. T/176.

16. SSB-MA, SM3-15, p. 2.

17. SSB-MA, SM3-7, p. 14; Schurig, *Die Entwicklung der Textilindustrie*, 64.

18. BA-FA, DEFA-Wochenschauen *Der Augenzeuge*, 8/55; SSB-MA, G5, pp. 13–14. Anna-Sabine Ernst and Eric Weitz have outlined the uneasy coexistence of two broad "strands of nationalist claims" in the GDR, which can be categorized in simple terms as "proletarian" and "bourgeois." Anna-Sabine Ernst, "Vom 'Du' zum 'Sie'. Die Rezeption der bürgerlichen Anstandsregeln in der DDR der 1950er Jahre," *Mitteilungen aus der kulturwissenschaftlichen Forschung* 33 (1993): 190–209; Eric Weitz, *Creating German Communism: From Popular Protests to Socialist State, 1890–1990* (Princeton, 1997), 371–4.

19. SSB-MA, SM4-4, p. 3.

20. Guenther, *Nazi Chic?*, 109–19.

21. R. Kn., "Anarchie im Reich der Mode," 20.

22. SSB-MA, SM3-7, p. 19; Christoph Kleßmann, *Die doppelte Staatsgründung. Deutsche Geschichte 1945–1955* (Bonn, 1991), 333.

23. Alan Nothnagle, *Building the East German Myth: Historical Mythology and Youth Propaganda in the German Democratic Republic, 1945–1989* (Ann Arbor, 1999), chapter 2; Dietrich Mühlberg, "Die DDR als Gegenstand kulturhistorischer Forschung," *Mitteilungen aus der kulturwissenschaftlichen Forschung* 33 (1993): 36–50.

24. *SBZ-Archiv 1960*, 183ff., quoted in Christoph Kleßmann and Georg Wagner, eds, *Das gespaltene Land. Leben in Deutschland 1945–1990. Texte und*

Dokumente zur Sozialgeschichte (Munich, 1993), 33–4. On *Verkaufskultur* see Katherine Pence, "'You as a Woman Will Understand': Consumption, Gender, and the Relationship between State and Citizenry in the GDR's Crisis of June 17," *German History* 19 (2001): 218–52.

25. Julie Hessler, "Cultured Trade: The Stalinist Turn Towards Consumerism," in *Stalinism. New Directions*, ed. Sheila Fitzpatrick (London, 2000), 182–209.

26. "Anordnung über die Errichtung des Instituts für Bekleidungskultur. Vom 28. November 1952," *Ministerialblatt der Deutschen Demokratischen Republik*, 6 December 1952, Nr. 52, p. 198.

27. Holger Theuerkauf and Michael Reinicke, directors, *Flotter Osten*, Mit-Schnitt-Film, 1990.

28. Ernst, "Vom 'Du' zum 'Sie'"; "Beiderseits der Elbe: Küß die Hand," *Die Zeit* 9 April 1965, quoted in Kleßmann and Wagner, eds, *Das gespaltene Land*, 37–9; numerous books on good manners, many of which went through several editions during the following decades, including Karl Smolka, *Gutes Benehmen von A bis Z* (Berlin, 1957); Gertrud Oheim, *Einmaleins des guten Tons* (Gütersloh, 1955).

29. "Wenig Kleider – aber die richtigen," *Die Frau von heute*, August 1946, Nr. 12, 19.

30. "Herbst-Messe-Mode. Wohltemperiert ...," *Praktische Mode* 1 (1950): 1.

31. SSB-MA, SM3-7, pp. 18–19.

32. Inge Kertzscher, "Festliche Kleidung—aber wie?" *Neues Deutschland*, 6 December 1959, p. 2.

33. In German, the proverb *Kleider machen Leute* is gender-neutral. SAPMO-BA, DY30/IV2/6.09/72, Manuskript für eine Broschüre zur Auswertung der Ökonomischen Konferenz der Textil- und Bekleidungsindustrie am 22./23. April 1960 in KMSt, Russek, Berlin-Pankow, n.d. [Juni 1960], pp. 3–4.

34. LAB, C Rep. 106-01-01, Vorläufige Signatur Nr. T/176, Vorschlag für eine Veränderung der Arbeitsweise in der Berliner volkseigenen Bekleidungs-industrie ..., Maaß, Modeatelier Berlin, Berlin, 9 June 1955.

35. Leora Auslander, *Taste and Power: Furnishing Modern France* (Berkeley, 1996); Sheila Fitzpatrick, *The Cultural Front: Power and Culture in Revolutionary Russia* (Ithaca, 1992).

36. E.T., "Frauen wählen ihre Mode selbst! Modellschau des Demokratischen Frauenbundes Berlin," *Frau von heute* 4 (1949) 15: 29.

37. Eva Grabe, "So oder so?" *Steckenpferd. Beilage der Jungen Welt*, 1/2 November 1958. On similarities between East and West German concerns about the degenerative impact of American cultural influences in Germany during the 1950s, which echoed rhetoric during the Weimar Republic and Third Reich, see Uta Poiger, *Jazz, Rock, and Rebels: Cold War Politics and*

American Culture in a Divided Germany (Berkeley, 2000); Guenther, *Nazi Chic?*, chapters 3 and 4.

38. Grabe, "So oder so?," 1.

39. SAPMO-BA, DY30/IV2/1/283, Bl. 11–12.

40. East German officials never mentioned that this had been the name of Germany's central fashion institute during the Third Reich. Guenther, *Nazi Chic?*, Chapter 6; Kenneth McDonald, "Fascist Fashion: Dress, the State, and the Clothing Industry in the Third Reich," Ph.D. Dissertation, University of California, Riverside, 1998, 112–21.

41. Trickle-down explanations of fashion can be traced back to Thorstein Veblen's ideas about "conspicuous consumption" and Georg Simmel's socio-psychological theories. Thorstein Veblen, *The Theory of the Leisure Class* (New York, 1912 [orig. 1899]); Georg Simmel, "Fashion," *International Quarterly* 10 (1904): 130–55.

42. SSB-MA, SM1-13, p. 3.

43. SSB-MA, SM3-7, p. 27.

44. Susannah Handley, *Nylon: The Story of a Fashion Revolution: A Celebration of Design from Art Silk to Nylon and Thinking Fibres* (Baltimore, 1999), 77–115.

45. Helmut Gruber and Pamela Graves, eds, *Women and Socialism, Socialism and Women: Europe between the Two World Wars* (New York, 1998); Guenther, *Nazi Chic?*, Chapter 3.

46. SSB-MA, ML 1958, Modelinie der Nachmittags-, Fest- und Abendkleider ..., pp. 1, 3.

47. SAPMO-BA, DY30/IV2/17/62, Bl. 54–7. Thanks to Timothy Dowling for this reference. For the Institute's response see "Frankfurter Frauenausschüsse im Deutschen Modeinstitut," *Sibylle* 3 (1958): 77.

48. Inge Kertzscher, "Wir blättern in Modeheften," *Neues Deutschland*, 11 January 1958, Beilage.

49. "Das Modehaus ohne Kundschaft," *Neue Zeit*, 11 November 1956.

50. Inge Kertzscher, "Wir machen internationale Mode – für wen?" *Neues Deutschland*, 18 November 1956.

51. Inge Kertzscher, "Laufsteg-Mode oder schöne Kleider für alle?" *Neues Deutschland*, Beilage Kunst und Literatur, 7 April 1957.

52. Jo Schulz, *Messeschlager Gisela. Operette in einem Vorspiel und drei Akten (vier Bildern). Textbuch* (Berlin, 1961), 15.

53. BA-BL, DE1/26292, "Die Bekleidung für junge stärkere Frau", Referat der DDR, XII. Modekongreß Berlin, n.d. [1960/1961], p. 2; "Taille: 92 – Na und?" *Für Dich* 35 (1963): 43–7.

54. SSB-MA, SM3-7, p. 20.

55. "Wenn die Taille an Zentimetern zunimmt ...," *Konsum-Genossenschafter* 12 (1960) 40: 8.

56. BA-BL, DE1/26292, "Die Bekleidung für junge stärkere Frau" ..., p. 1.
57. SSB-MA, SM5-16, p. 5; BA-BL, DE1/26292, "Die Bekleidung für junge stärkere Frau" ..., p. 2.
58. SSB-MA, Modelinie 1954, Rundschreiben Nr. 1 ..., p. 3.
59. SSB-MA, SM5-16, p. 3.
60. "Taille: 92 – Na und?," 43.
61. SSB-MA, SM5-16, p. 5.
62. Inge Kertzscher, "Konfektion mit neuen Maßen," *Neues Deutschland*, 12 December 1959.
63. SSB-MA, SM5-16, p. 2; "Taille: 92 – Na und?," 43.
64. SSB-MA, SM5-16, p. 2.
65. [Mia Heim], "Modelinie berät Mollige," *Für Dich* 50 (1969): 43; [Mia Heim], "Modelinie berät Sie. Rund um die Hüften," *Für Dich* 48 (1969): 44.
66. SSB-MA, SM5-16, p. 1.
67. SäStAC, ZWK TuK, Nr. 157, Renate M. to Deutscher Fernsehfunk, "*Prisma*," Anklam, 16 August 1968.
68. *Eulenspiegel* 9 (1962) 21: 14.
69. Pál Pusztai, *Eulenspiegel* 9 (1962) 18: 5.
70. The paradoxical goal was to create "a peculiar fashion with international character." SSB-MA, 3–9, p. 4; SSB-MA, SM1-12, p. 4.
71. Traveling to haute couture shows in Paris was an longstanding German tradition that had continued during the Third Reich. Guenther, *Nazi Chic?*; Daniel Purdy, *The Tyranny of Elegance. Consumer Cosmopolitanism in the Era of Goethe* (Baltimore, 1998).
72. See the extensive collection of travel reports (*Reiseberichte*) in the Stiftung Stadtmuseum Berlin, Modeabteilung – Modearchiv. East German fashion officials also traveled to Soviet-bloc countries, but these trips superficially promoted "friendship" and technological exchange rather than lessons in aesthetics. Functionaries generally returned convinced of the GDR's superiority and the paucity of useful information to be gained from their East European colleagues. LAB, C Rep. 106-01-01, Vorläufige Signatur Nr. T/238, Tagung des MfL, HV Textil, Thema: Auswertung von Studienreisen ins Ausland IV/1955, Junghänel, n.d. [1955], unpag.; SSB-MA, RB1958, Nr. 12, unpag.
73. SSB-MA, RB1965, Nr. 12 and G18a; BA-CA, DE4/32826 and 32833.
74. SSB-MA, SM1-13, p. 2 and SM4-14, p. 9.
75. Ursula Paulini, "Hinken wir der Mode hinterher?" *Märkische Volksstimme*, 9 September 1956; BA-BL, DE1/5446, Bl. 6; SSB, SM3-9, p. 1.
76. Karl-Ernst Schubert and Georg Wittek, "Zur Aufgabenstellung des Modeschaffens in der Deutschen Demokratischen Republik," *MIfB* 2 (1963) 2: 55.
77. SAPMO-BA, DY30/IV2/6.09/75, Diskussionsbeitrag von Elli Schmidt, DMI, n.d. [Jan. 1959]; SSB-MA, SM4-14, p. 8.

78. BA-BL, DE1/26292, Kurzer Abriß der Geschichte der Internationalen Modekongresse und ihre Bedeutung, Arbeitsplan II 10./1960 – Modekongreß, 3 November 1960. The Institute for Clothing Culture was the youngest such fashion institute among the socialist countries. The Union House in Moscow, the Clothing Institute in Budapest, and the House of Models in Sofia all were founded in 1948, while the Central Laboratory in Lodz was created in 1946, the Institut Textilni Tvorba in Prague in 1949, and the Design Center in Bucharest in 1951. "Sieben Länder – sieben Modeinstitute – ein Ziel," *Sibylle* 3 (1958) 3: 4–5.

79. *25 Jahre Modeinstitut der DDR*, n.d., n.p., unpag. CMEA, or COMECON, was designed to facilitate trade and economic aid among its members, which included the Soviet Union, East Germany, Bulgaria, Czechoslovakia, Hungary, Poland, and Romania.

80. "Pariser Chic als Messegast," *Frau von heute* 11 (1959) 39: 6–7.

81. SSB-MA, SM3-11, pp. 11–12.

82. SSB-MA, SM1-13, p. 3.

83. BA-FA, DEFA-Wochenschauen *Der Augenzeuge* 45/58, 55/58, 32/59, 30/60, 46/60, and 9/62.

84. The state owned 69 percent Bormann's firm. LAB, C Rep. 470-02, Nr. 36, Bl. 1.

85. BA-BL, DE1/24938, Thesen zur Parteileitungssitzung am 20. Februar 1959 über die Probleme der Planerfüllung 1958 und den Plananlauf 1959, n.d., p. 2.

86. SAPMO-BA, DY30/IVA2/6.09/112, Information über die Durchführung von Modell-Modenschauen durch das Modehaus Bormann, Magdeburg, Briksa, Abt. LLI, und Steidl, Abt. Gewerkschaften und Sozialpolitik, Berlin, 18 March 1963.

87. Fritz Jahn, "Männer mit Millionen," *Freie Welt* 22 (1967): 10–15; SAPMO-BA, DY30/IVA2/2.021/706, Bl. 11–12.

88. SSB-MA, ML1958, Protokoll über die Absprache der Modelinie Frühjahr/ Sommer 1958 mit den Fachabteilungen, Abt. Modellentwurf, Berlin, 26 November 1957, p. 3.

89. SSB-MA, SM5-19, p. 6.

90. Walter Ulbricht, "Über Standardisierung und Mode," *Neues Deutschland* 13. August 1959, 4.

91. SAPMO-BA, DY30/IV2/6.09/72, Entwurf: Konzeption. Aufgabenstellung für die Tätigkeit der Arbeitskreise zur Vorbereitung der Textil-Konferenz 1960, Abt. Leichtindustrie, Sekt. Textil-Bekleidung-Leder, Berlin, 10 November 1959, unpag.

92. A small number of officials had long advocated this approach in vain. An official at the Ministry for Trade and Provisioning insisted in 1950 that state trade officials should not wait to see "which newest fashion cry comes from Paris

or London, but rather we should get to the point of determining and influencing fashion ourselves." SAPMO-BA, DY30/IV2/1.01/133, Bl. 79.

93. SSB-MA, SM7-25, p. 6.

94. SAPMO-BA, DY30/IV2/1/255, Bl. 161–2.

95. These initiatives form numerous interesting parallels with efforts to create "German fashion" during the Third Reich. Guenther, *Nazi Chic?*; McDonald, "Fascist Fashion," 93–112; Sultano, *Wie geistiges Kokain* ....

96. SSB-MA, SM7-17, pp. 13–14.

97. Schubert and Wittek, "Zur Aufgabenstellung des Modeschaffens," 55; BA-CA, DE4/19893, Die Konzeption für das Modeschaffen im Industriezweig Bekleidung in Auswertung des VI. Parteitages, VVB Konfektion, Berlin, 4 April 19[63], p. 2 of second section.

98. BA-CA, DE4/19893, Jahresarbeitsbericht 1962 des DMI, Fröbel, Berlin, 30 March 1963, p. 2; SSB-MA, G14, p. 8 and SM18-8, Band 6, pp. 1–2. On *Parteilichkeit*, see Nothnagle, *Building the East German Myth*, 17ff.

99. SSB-MA, SM12-26, p. 1.

100. SAPMO-BA, DY30/IV2/6.09/70, Zu Fragen Sortiment – Qualität – Mode, 10 April 1959, p. 4.

101. SSB-MA, SM7-25, p. 6 and SM9-6, p. 4; Schubert and Wittek, "Zur Aufgabenstellung des Modeschaffens," 54.

102. SSB-MA, SM18-8, Band 5, p. 20.

103. SSB-MA, SM13-3, unpag.

104. BA-CA, DL102/1260, p. 1.

105. SSB-MA, SM7-26, p. 1.

106. BA-FA, *Modell Bianka* ...

107. Critics both within and outside the party criticized the film for being too superficial and heavy-handed in its attempt to convey ideological messages. Joshua Feinstein, *The Triumph of the Ordinary: Depictions of Daily Life in the East German Cinema, 1949–1989* (Chapel Hill, 2002), 31–2.

108. SSB-MA, SM7-29, p. 1; SSB-MA, SM9-4, p. 4; SAPMO-BA, DY30/IV2/2. 029/195, Protokoll der ökonomischen Konferenz der Textil- und Bekleidungsindustrie am 22. und 23. April 1960 in KMSt, p. 16/5.

109. SAPMO-BA, DY30/IV2/2.029/195, Protokoll der ökonomischen Konferenz ..., p. 16/4.

110. SSB-MA, SM14-33.

111. SSB-MA, SM4-13, p. 13 and SM9-18, p. 2; SAPMO-BA, DY30/J IV2/2/841, Bl. 70.

112. SAPMO-BA, DY30/IV2/1/253, Bl. 142.

113. SSB-MA, SM4-2, pp. 3–5, 14.

114. SSB-MA, SM9-22, pp. 4–5; BA-BL, DE1/30278, Industriezweigökonomik der VVB Konfektion, n.d. [1960], p. 3/0/2.

115. Paul Nystrom, *The Economics of Fashion* (New York, 1928); Agnes Brooks Young, *Recurring Cycles of Fashion, 1760–1937* (New York, 1937); BA-BL, DE1/24608, Bl. 66; SSB-MA, SM12-23, pp. 18–9.

116. SSB-MA, SM7-14, pp. 6–7.

117. SSB-MA, SM4-13, pp. 2–3; BA-BL, DE1/11968, Bl. 13.

118. SAPMO-BA, DY30/IV2/2.029/195, Protokoll der ökonomischen Konferenz ..., p. 16/4; BA-BL, DE1/11968, Bl. 19.

119. SSB-MA, SM12-23, p. 15.

120. SäStAC, VVB T&S, Nr. 2190, Aufgabenstellung der Fachkommission "Mode und Werbung" ... beim DMI, Berlin, n.d. [19 March 1960].

121. BA-CA, DE4/19893, Jahresarbeitsbericht 1962 des DMI ..., p. 13.

122. BA-BL, DC 20/I/3-169, Bl. 184–6.

123. BA-BL, DE1/26014, Textilkonferenz. Arbeitskreis "Textilindustrie – Binnenhandel," n.d. [1959], p. 3.

124. SSB-MA, SM4-14, p. 10.

125. Ibid.; BA-BL, DE1/26014, Textilkonferenz ..., p. 32; "Aus 1 mach 4," *Sibylle* 5 (1960) 1: 35.

126. BA-BL, DE1/30278, Industriezweigökonomik ..., p. 2.151; Kurt Schille et al., *Probleme der Fertigungsart in der Textil- und Bekleidungsindustrie* (Leipzig, 1963).

127. SAPMO-BA, DY30/IV2/6.07/44 and 65; BA-BL, DE1/26233, Standardisierung, unpag.; SSB-MA, SM7-14, p. 2.

128. SSB-MA, SM7-29, p. 2.

129. SAPMO-BA, DY30/IV2/2.101/1, Bl. 88.

130. SAPMO-BA, DY30/IV2/1/283, Bl. 12.

131. Ibid., Bl. 135.

132. SAPMO-BA, DY30/IV2/6.07/44, Bl. 8; SM14-56, unpag.

133. BA-BL, DE1/30278, Industriezweigökonomik ..., p. 2.152; BA-BL, DE1/11968, Bl. 21–4; SAPMO-BA, DY30/IV2/6.07/65, Bl. 300.

134. BA-BL, DE1/30278, Industriezweigökonomik ..., p. 3/0/2, 2.152; SSB-MA, SM7-14, p. 11; SAPMO-BA, DY30/IVA2/6.09/56, Programm für die Entwicklung des Industriezweiges Konfektion in den Jahren von 1964 bis 1970, n.d. [1963], p. 25.

135. SSB-MA, SM7-29, p. 2; Schubert and Wittek, "Zur Aufgabenstellung des Modeschaffens," 54.

136. SäStAC, VVB T&S, Nr. 2190, Protokoll Betr.: Zusammenarbeit FK "Mode und Werbung"/MHV, Kohler, Abteilungsleiterin, Abt. Presse/Werbung, [DMI], Berlin, 28 December 1962, p. 2; BA-BL, DE1/25708, Bericht über die Durchführung der Ziffer 1 des Beschlusses des Präsidiums des MR von 15.11.1960 ..., Kommission zur Durchführung des Beschlusses des Präsidiums des Ministerrates vom 15.11.1960, Berlin, 7 January 1961, p. 4.

137. Judd Stitziel, "Fashioning Socialism: Clothing, Politics, and Consumer Culture in East Germany, 1948–1971," Ph.D. Dissertation, The Johns Hopkins University, 2001, 241–51.

138. BA-BL, DE1/25638, Bl. 384.

139. SSB-MA, SM15-13, pp. 11–13.

140. SäStAC, RdB, Abt. HuV, Nr. 8143; BA-DH, DL1/17741; Philipp Heldmann, "Konsumpolitik in der DDR. Jugendmode in den sechziger Jahren," in *Konsumpolitik: Die Regulierung des privaten Verbrauchs im 20. Jahrhundert*, ed. Hartmut Berghoff (Göttingen, 1999), 135–58.

141. SSB-MA, SM9-22, p. 19.

142. BA-BL, DE1/25708, Bericht über die Durchführung der Ziffer 1 ..., p. 4.

143. The Berlin garment industry sporadically held "fashion weeks" before World War I and during the Weimar Republic. Guenther, *Nazi Chic?*, 59.

144. LAB, C Rep. 900, IV/7/128-8, Diskussionsbeitrag zur Kreisparteiaktivtagung am 18.11.1953, p. 1; LAB, C Rep. 625, Nr. 113, Maßnahmen zur Realisierung des Beschlusses der Bezirksleitung der SED von Groß-Berlin "Berlin zum Modezentrum zu gestalten," VVB Konfektion, Berlin, 30 May 1958; BA-BL, DE1/25687, Letter from Berliner Modewoche, Organisationsbüro, to Güntzel, Plankommission, Berlin, 21 August 1958.

145. Inge Kertzscher, "Eine Schule des guten Geschmacks. Zur 2. Berliner Modewoche," *Neues Deutschland*, 14 February 1959, Beilage; LAB, C Rep. 113, Nr. 412, Entwurf der 4. Konzeption für die Berliner Modewoche September 1959, Berlin-Werbung Berolina, Berlin, 5 August 1959, p. 6.

146. LAB, C Rep. 113, Nr. 412, Entwurf der 4. Konzeption ..., p. 6.

147. BA-BL, DE1/25687, Nähere Programmerläuterung, n.d. [1958], p. 1.

148. LAB, C Rep. 113, Nr. 412, Entwurf der 4. Konzeption ..., pp. 8–10.

149. Ibid., pp. 14–15.

150. BA-BL, DE1/25687, Nähere Programmerläuterung ..., p. 2.

151. LAB, C Rep. 625, Nr. 2 (BEHALA), Vorlage für die "Berliner Modewoche" 1959, VVB Konfektion, Abt. Ökonomie, Henkel, Abteilungsleiter, Berlin, 27 July 1959, p. 3.

152. LAB, C Rep. 113, Nr. 412, Protokoll über die Beiratssitzung "Berliner Modewoche" am 12 August 1959, VVB Konfektion, Berlin, 13 August 1959, p. 2.

153. The following quotes are taken from LAB, C Rep. 625, Nr. 110, ausstellung der 2. berliner mode-woche 18.–25. Februar 1959, unpag.

154. Compare several *Augenzeuge* reports on fashion shows that expressed similar sentiments: BA-FA, DEFA-Wochenschauen *Augenzeuge* 45/58, 52/58, and 55/58.

155. LAB, C Rep. 625, Nr. 2 (BEHALA), Vorlage für die "Berliner Modewoche" 1959 ..., p. 1.

156. LAB, C Rep. 113, Nr. 412, Protokoll der 1. Beiratssitzung zur 3. Berliner Modewoche, VVB Konfektion, Zahl, Hauptdirektor, Berlin, 28 July 1959, p. 2 and Protokoll über die Beiratssitzung …, p. 4; BA-CA, DE4/679, Bl. 91, 94.

157. BA-CA, DE4/679, Bl. 93.

158. SAPMO-BA, DY30/IV2/6.10/72, Bl. 76–7.

159. BA-CA, DE4/679, Bl. 91–2.

160. Ibid., Bl. 95.

Chapter 4 – Economies of Value and Politics of Price

1. BA-BL, DC20/I/3-172, Bl. 69; *Gesetzblatt der Deutschen Demokratischen Republik*, 22 (1953): 313 ff.

2. BA-BL, DC20/I/3-172, Bl. 68.

3. SAPMO-BA, DY30/IV2/2.029/12, Bl. 124–5, 138.

4. BA-CA, DL102/196, p. 46.

5. BA-BL, DC20/I/4-186, Bl. 12.

6. BA-CA, DE4/29241, Konzeption zur Stabilisierung der Konsumgüterpreise im Bereich der Textil- und Bekleidungsindustrie, MR, VWR, Abt. TeBeLe, Reinhold, Berlin, 1 August 1964, pp. 2–3.

7. In 1964 state planners declared that while the quantity of textile and clothing articles would increase by 25 percent from 1963 to 1970, their total value would increase by 43 percent due to "the qualitative improvement of the products and the change of the structure of assortments." BA-CA, DE1/42051, Konzeption für die Entwicklung der Textil- und Bekleidungsindustrie im Perspektivplanzeitraum 1964 bis 1970, Leihkauf, Leiter der Abt. LI, Berlin, 17 June 1964, p. 2.

8. BA-BL, DE1/24268, Bl. 24; SAPMO-BA, DY30/IV2/2.029/12, Bl. 139; BA-BL, DE1/24586, Bl. 16–8.

9. BA-BL, DE1/24586, Bl. 16, 18; SAPMO-BA, DY30/IV2/2.029/12, Bl. 139–40.

10. BA-BL, DE1/24204.

11. SAPMO-BA, DY30/IV2/6.09/56, Bl. 100, 117.

12. BA-BL, DE1/24586, Bl. 17.

13. BA-BL, DE1/26175, Behandlung qualitätsgeminderter Waren und saisonbedingter Erzeugnisse, n.d., p. 1; LAB, C Rep. 625, Nr. 113, Zur Lage in der Konfektionsindustrie, Kahl, Hauptdirektor, VVB Konfektion, Berlin, 1 March 1960, p. 3; SAPMO-BA, DY30/IV2/6.09/56, Bl. 116.

14. SAPMO-BA, DY30/JIV2/2/753, Bl. 19–20.

15. SäStAC, RdB, Bezirksverwaltung der HO-Kreisbetriebe KMSt, Nr. 2894, Bericht Submission Konfektion in Leipzig, Müller, n.d. [1953].

16. BA-BL, DE1/24764, Partei-Kommission für Konsumgüter; Industrie-Fragen, Berlin, 17 August 1959.

17. BA-BL, DE1/26014, Exposé über die Ausgestaltung der Räume des Hauses "Auensee" Leipzig und die Gestaltung einer Ausstellung anläßlich der Textilkonferenz am 14. und 15. April 1959, SPK, Abt. LI, Sekt. TeBeLe, Berlin, 5 March 1959, p. 3.

18. "Wir stellen uns vor," *Neues Deutschland*, 14 January 1960: 3; "Es stellen sich vor: Ilse Güte und Otto Murks," *Konsumgenossenschafter* 4 (1960): 8.

19. "*Brauchst du eine neue Pelle, kauf dir niemals Treff-Modelle.*" "Trefflicher Murks," *Eulenspiegel* 7 (1960) 5: 12; BA-BL, DE1/26232, 1. Entwurf des Referats für die ökonomische Konferenz der Textilindustrie am 22. und 23.4. in KMSt, n.d. [1960], p. 10.

20. BA-BL, DE1/26233, Verzeichnis der Betriebe und Erzeugnisse, die zur Ausstellung "Schlußlichter der Qualität" vom 17.12.59 bis 19.12.59 in Leipzig, Technische Messe, Halle 15 gezeigt wurden, n.d.

21. BA-BL, DE1/24268, Bl. 11, 17; BA-BL, DE1/7054, Bl. 320.

22. BA-BL, DL1/2703 and 2707.

23. BA-BL, DE1/24268, Bl. 17; BA-BL, DE1/30278, Industriezweigökonomik der VVB Konfektion, n.d. [1960], p. 2/73.

24. BA-BL, DE1/9376; SAPMO-BA, DY30/IVA2/2.021/677, Bl. 137–41.

25. BA-BL, DE1/30278, Industriezweigökonomik …, p. 2/411/1; "Unsere aktuelle Umfrage: Mode und Ökonomie," *Die Bekleidungsindustrie* 2/1962: 4.

26. BA-BL, DE1/9376, Auszug aus der Analyse III. Quartal 1953 des Bezirkes Suhl, n.d.

27. BA-CA, DE4/685, Vorlage einer Konzeption, wie die Festpreisbildung entsprechend dem Beschluß des V. Parteitages, insbesondere auf dem Gebiet der Textil- und Bekleidungsindustrie zum Abschluß gebracht werden kann, n.d. [24 October 1961], p. 2; BA-DH, DL1/884, Information über Probleme, die im Zusammenhang mit der Industriepreisreform auf dem Gebiet der Textil-Einzelhandelspreise zu lösen sind, MHV, Berlin, 4 November 1964, pp. 3–4; BA-CA, DE4/10289, Letter from Leiter, Sektor Planung u. Ökonomie, Abt. TeBeLe, to Wittik, Berlin, 3 April 1962, p. 3; BA-DH, DL1/16488, Vorlage für die Dienstbesprechung des Ministers der Finanzen, Stellvertreter des Ministers Kirsten, 20 March 1965, p. 3.

28. BA-BL, DE1/24495; BA-BL, DE1/29773, Bl. 143; SAPMO-BA, DY30/IV2/6.10/37, Bl. 2–3; BA-BL, DC20/I/4-184, Bl. 29; BA-BL, DE1/27290. Beschluß 37/6 über die Sicherung der bedarfsgerechten Produktion von Massenkonsumgütern, 28 June 1956, p. 6; SAPMO-BA, DY30/JIV2/2A/717, Beschluss und Begründung für die Einführung fester Verbraucherpreise …, n.d. [15 September 1959], pp. 15–16.

29. BA-DH, DL1/16488, Vorlage für die Dienstbesprechung …, pp. 8–9;

SAPMO-BA, DY30/JIV2/2A/747, Beschluß vom ..., Begründung ..., n.d. [5 April 1960], p. 2; SAPMO-BA, DY30/IV2/6.10/13, Bl. 22; BA-BL, DE1/ 24765, Letter from Nagel Großhandelskontor f. Textilwaren Berlin et al. to SPK, Wittkowski, KMSt, 23 October 1958, p. 1.

30. BA-CA, DE4/29241, Ergänzung zur Vorlage: Stabilisierung der Einzel-handelsverkaufspreise und Umstellung der Preiserrechnung auf normierte Selbstkosten für Herrenhemden und Herrenschlafanzüge ..., 18 June 1964, Begründung, p. 2.

31. BA-DH, DL1/16488, Vorlage für die Dienstbesprechung ..., p. 3.

32. BA-CA, DE4/10289, Letter from [illegible] to Wittik, p. 2.

33. BA-CA, DE4/685, Vorlage einer Konzeption ..., p. 2; BA-CA, DE4/2436, Expertise über die Preisbildung in der Textil- und Bekleidungsindustrie, VWR, Abt. TeBeLe, Leiter, Bethe, Berlin, 31 March 1962, pp. 5–6.

34. BA-CA, DE4/10289, Letter from [illegible] to Wittik, p. 2; SAPMO-BA, DY30/JIV2/2/753, Bl. 282.

35. BA-CA, DE4/2436, Expertise über die Preisbildung ..., p. 6.

36. SAPMO-BA, DY30/IV2/2.029/12, Bl. 127–8, 130–1; SAPMO-BA, NY4215/63, Bl. 371.

37. BA-DH, DL1/12602, Gliederung zu den Thesen der Arbeitsgruppe Ökonomische Fragen des Handels in der Etappe des umfassenden Aufbaus des Sozialismus, n.d. [June 1963], unpag; BA-DH, DL1/24419, Neue Grundsätze der Preisbildung für Textilien dargelegt vom Minister Rumpf im Laufe einer Beratung am 8.1.1963, Bereich Preise, von Diemen, Sektoren-leiter, Sektor Grundsatz, Berlin, 10 January 1963, p. 3. See also Helmut Weiss, *Verbraucherpreise in der DDR: wie stabil waren sie?* (Schkeuditz, 1998).

38. BA-BL, DE1/25638, Bl. 384.

39. BA-DH, DL1/3995, Analyse zum Planablauf 1961 vom 1.1.-31.12.1961, ZWK für TuK, MHV, Naumann, KMSt, 23 January 1962, p. 7.

40. SAPMO-BA, DY30/IVA2/2.021/720, Bl. 62.

41. SAPMO-BA, DY30/IV2/2.029/12, Bl. 127.

42. SAPMO-BA, DY30/IVA2/2.021/705, Bl. 132; BA-DH, DL1/24419, Neue Grundsätze ..., p. 1.

43. BA-CA, DE4/29241, Konzeption zur Stabilisierung ..., p. 1.

44. SAPMO-BA, NY4215/63, Bl. 371.

45. SAPMO-BA, DY30/IV2/2.029/12, Bl. 125.

46. BA-DH, DL1/12602, Gliederung zu den Thesen ..., unpag.

47. BA-CA, DE4/29241, Konzeption zur Stabilisierung ..., pp. 8–9.

48. SAPMO-BA, DY30/IVA2/2.021/46, Bl. 143.

49. BA-DH, DL1/24419, Neue Grundsätze ..., pp. 1–2.

50. BA-BL, DC20/I/3-172, Bl. 69.

51. SAPMO-BA, DY30/JIV2/2A/717, Beschluss und Begründung ..., p. 6.
52. BA-CA, DE4/29241, Begründung für die Umstellung der Preisbildung in der Konfektionsindustrie, MfL, HV Bekleidung, Berlin, Günzel, HV-Leiter, 14 September 1956, p. 1. Price reform was complicated by the state's attempts to set three different types of prices: factory prices (*Betriebspreis* or BP), taxed industrial prices (*Industrieabgabepreis* or IAP), and final consumer prices (*Einzelhandelsverkaufspreis* or EVP). Since the state pocketed most of the differences between these prices, they did not necessarily correlate. For the sake of simplicity, the following discussion will refer to both factory prices and taxed industrial prices as "industrial prices."
53. SAPMO-BA, NY4182/991, Bl. 164–9; BA-BL, DL1/3819, Bl. 53.
54. BA-CA, DE4/29241, Referat für die konstituierende Sitzung der Arbeitskreise der HV Bekleidung im Rahmen des Regierungsarbeitsplanes für Preise 1958, n.d., p. 1.
55. SAPMO-BA, DY30/JIV2/2/753, Bl. 282; BA-BL, DE1/619, Vorschlag für die Einführung von Festpreisen in der Textilindustrie, n.d. [1959], p. 1.
56. SäStAC, ZWK TuK, Nr. 309, Welche Wirkungen ergeben sich aus der Durchschnittspreisentwicklung, n.d. [9 September 70], unpag.; BA-BL, DL1/1392, Bl. 4.
57. SAPMO-BA, DY30/IV2/2.029/79, Bl. 172–3; BA-BL, DE1/24268, Bl. 32–3.
58. BA-CA, DE4/29241, Ergänzung zur Begründung für die Umstellung der Preisbildung in der Konfektionsindustrie v. 14.9.56, MfL, HV Bekleidung, Günzel, HV-Leiter, Berlin, 16 October 1956, p. 3.
59. BA-BL, DE1/24418, Durchsicht des Material des MfL über die Untersuchungen in der Textilindustrie nach Qualität, Preisen und technischen Problemen, Behrendt, HA-Leiter, HA Planung der LI, Berlin, 29 December 1956, p. 5.
60. The state had established fixed production prices for 45 percent of all consumer goods by 1 January 1958; the "overwhelming portion" of these were set at the average of previous production prices. The regime hoped to set fixed prices for another 30 percent of all consumer goods by the end of the year. SAPMO-BA, DY30/IV2/2.029/12, Bl. 130.
61. BA-DH, DL1/16487, Bd. 2: Analyse der direkten und indirekten Preisstützungen, Büro der Regierungskommission für Preise, Bereich Preise, Sektor Op. Grundsatzfragen, Berlin, March 1962, p. 2.
62. SAPMO-BA, DY30/IV2/2.029/12, Bl. 139–40.
63. BA-BL, DE1/26450, Letter from Heese, Leiter, Gruppe Ökonomie, Sektor Te-Be, Abt. TeBeLe to Willy Maaß, Berlin-Köpenick, 5 February 1960.
64. BA-BL, DE1/24586, Bl. 20.
65. SAPMO-BA, DY30/IV2/2.029/79, Bl. 172; BA-DH, DL1/3974, Auswirkungen und Maßnahmen der Produktionseinstellung von nicht vertragsge-

bundenen und nicht absetztbaren Erzeugnissen der Textil- und Bekleidungs-industrie im 1./1960, n.d., p. 10; BA-BL, DE1/7054, Bl. 320.

66. BA-BL, DE1/7073, Bl. 26–7; SAPMO-BA, DY30/IV2/2.029/86, Information an die Mitglieder und Kandidaten des PB, Abt. HVuA, Berlin, 21 October 1958, pp. 1–2; SAPMO-BA, DY30/IV2/6.10/19, Bl. 8–17.

67. BA-DH, DL1/18400, Dienstbesprechung beim Gen. Jarowinsky am 19.10.1962, Bereich Preise, Lorenz, Berlin, 8 November 1962; SAPMO-BA, DY30/JIV2/2A/717, Beschluss und Begründung ..., p. 6.

68. BA-DH, DL1/16487, Bd. 2: Analyse ..., pp. 1ff.

69. BA-BL, DL1/1392, Bl. 4.

70. SAPMO-BA, DY30/JIV2/2A/717, Beschluss und Begründung ..., pp. 6–7; SAPMO-BA, DY30/IV2/6.09/56, Bl. 38.

71. BA-CA, DE4/685, Vorlage einer Konzeption ...; BA-CA, DE4/2436, Expertise über die Preisbildung in der Textil- und Bekleidungsindustrie, VWR. Abt. TeBeLe, Leiter, Bethe, Berlin, 31 March 1962. On price reforms during the 1960s, see André Steiner, *Die DDR-Wirtschaftsreform der sechziger Jahre. Konflikt zwischen Effizienz- und Machtkalkül* (Berlin, 1999), Chapter 2.

72. BA-DH, DL1/884, 2. Entwurf. Information über Probleme, die im Zusammenhang mit der Industriepreisreform auf dem Gebiet der Textil-Einzelhandelspreise zu lösen sind, MHV, Berlin, 4 November 1964, p. 2.

73. BA-CA, DE4/2436, Expertise über die Preisbildung ..., pp. 2–3.

74. BA-CA, DE4/10289, Letter from [illegible] to Wittik, p. 2.

75. On the debate over the East German economy's potential for reform, see Steiner, *Die DDR-Wirtschaftsreform der sechziger Jahre*; Jeffrey Kopstein, *The Politics of Economic Decline in East Germany, 1945–1989* (Chapel Hill, 1997), Chapter 2; Jörg Roesler, *Das Neue Ökonomische System – Dekorations- oder Paradigmenwechsel?* (Berlin, 1994).

76. BA-DH, DL1/884, 2. Entwurf. Information über Probleme ..., p. 2. In March 1965 a deputy minister of finance noted that until then, price reform had affected primarily industrial prices and only 3 percent of consumer products. BA-DH, DL1/16488, Vorlage für die Dienstbesprechung ..., p. 1.

77. BA-DH, DL1/884, 2. Entwurf. Information über Probleme ..., p. 5.

78. Ibid., pp. 5–8.

79. Officials stressed that "wares that are particularly important for lower income groups will thereby continue to remain on the market at low prices." BA-DH, DL1/884, 2. Entwurf. Information über Probleme ..., p. 11.

80. *Gesetzblatt der Deutschen Demokratischen Republik*, Teil II, Nr. 146, 16 December 1966.

81. SAPMO-BA, DY30/IVA2/6.09/58, Zuarbeit für die Ausarbeitung der Einschätzung der "Grundprobleme des Perspektivplanes 1970" der LLI, Abt. LLI, Berlin, 23 November 1965, pp. 2–3.

82. SAPMO-BA, DY30/IVA2/6.09/111, Maßnahmen zur Sicherung der Produktion und der Sortimente von Kinderbekleidung für die Versorgung der Bevölkerung, Sieber, Minister, MHV and Wittik, Minister, MfL, Berlin, 12 February 1970, p. 4; SSB-MA, SM17-135 and SM17-136.

83. SSB-MA, SM17-55, pp. 57–9, Anlage 16.

84. SAPMO-BA, DY30/IVA2/6.10/157, Zur Entwicklung des EVP-Niveaus (Durchschnittspreise), MHV, Bereich Preise, Berlin, 23 November 1970, pp. 5–6.

85. SäStAC, ZWK TuK, Nr. 309, Welche Wirkungen ..., unpag.

86. SästAC, VVB T&S, Nr. 2190, Bericht über die Tagung der FK "Mode und Werbung" am 26.5.1961, Schoope, Gruppenleiter Werbung, Kohle, Abteilungsleiterin, Berlin, 23 June 1961, p. 3; BA-DH, DL1/24419, Neue Grundsätze ..., pp. 1–4.

87. BA-DH, DL1/24419, Neue Grundsätze ..., p. 3.

88. SSB-MA, SM17–55, p. 57.

89. SAPMO-BA, DY30/IVA2/6.10/195, Aus dem Bericht der BL Dresden vom 21.12.1970, p. 8.

90. SAPMO-BA, DY30/JIV2/2A/383, Politbürositzung vom 9.11.1954, unpag., quoted in Ina Merkel, *Utopie und Bedürfnis. Die Geschichte der Konsumkultur in der DDR* (Cologne, 1999), 60.

91. BA-DH, DL1/16487, Bd. 2: Analyse, pp. 3, 20.

92. SAPMO-BA, DY30/IV2/2.101/1, Bl. 153.

93. SAPMO-BA, DY30/IV2/1/303, Bl. 178; SAPMO-BA, DY30/IVA2/2.021/705, Bl. 157; SAPMO-BA, DY30/IVA2/2.021/706, Bl. 244.

94. SAPMO-BA, DY30/IVA2/2.021/677, Bl. 75.

95. SAPMO-BA, DY30/IV2/6.10/130, Bl. 255; SAPMO-BA, DY30/IVA2/2.021/677, Bl. 74–5; SAPMO-BA, DY30/IVA2/6.10/200, Analyse über die Arbeit mit den Eingaben der Bevölkerung im Verantwortungsbereich des MHV für die Zeit vom 1.1.1967 bis 31.3.1968, MHV, Berlin, 17 April 1968, p. 15. See also Merkel, *Utopie und Bedürfnis*, 62.

96. BA-BL, DG4/2004, Zuarbeit zu einer Rechenschaftslegung des MHV in Zusammenarbeit mit den Industrieministern vor dem Präsidium des MR zu Schwerpunktproblemen der Versorgung der Bevölkerung, Werner, MfL, Sonderbevollmächtigter, Berlin, 9 February 1970, Anlage 4, pp. 1–3.

97. SAPMO-BA, DY30/IVA2/6.10/157, Information über Stand und Probleme bei der Vorbereitung von Preismaßnahmen auf dem Gebiet der Kinderbekleidung im Zusammenhang mit der Erhöhung des Kindergeldes, Berlin, 25 June 1970, pp. 1–7.

98. Ibid., p. 4.

99. André Steiner, "Zwischen Frustration und Verschwendung. Zu den wirtschaftlichen Determinanten der DDR-Konsumkultur," in *Wunderwirtschaft. DDR-*

Konsumkultur in den 60er Jahren, ed. Neue Gesellschaft für Bildende Kunst (Cologne, 1996), 33–5; Merkel, *Utopie und Bedürfnis*, 63–4.

100. LAB, C Rep. 900, IVA-2/9.01/490, 1. Entwurf zur Einschätzung des Bewußtseins der Berliner Bevölkerung, Berlin, 11 January 1967, p. 11.
101. BA-CA, DL102/580, p. 14.

Chapter 5 – The Embarrassment of Surpluses

1. Ina Merkel also has noted the simultaneous existence of shortages and surpluses of consumer goods in the GDR, but this chapter argues that her interpretation contains significant lacunae and inaccuracies and underestimates the organizational and political motivations behind official measures to eliminate surpluses. Ina Merkel, *Utopie und Bedürfnis. Die Geschichte der Konsumkultur in der DDR* (Cologne, 1999), 88–119.
2. BA-BL, DL1/3731, Letter from Ministerpräsident, Landesregierung Sachsen, to Heinrich Rau, Vorsitzenden der Deutschen Wirtschaftskommission, Dresden, 18 January 1949.
3. BA-BL, DL1/3741, Bl. 3.
4. LAB. C Rep. 106-01, Nr. 544, Vorlage, Abt. ÖIH, Ref. LI, Berlin, 5 October 1953.
5. Judd Stitziel, "Konsumpolitik zwischen 'Sortimentslücken' und 'Überplanbeständen' in der DDR der 1950er Jahre," in *Vor dem Mauerbau. Politik und Gesellschaft in der DDR der fünfziger Jahre*, ed. Dierk Hoffmann et al. (Munich, 2003), 191–204.
6. BA-BL, DE1/24586, Bl. 19; BA-BL, DE1/24589, Bl. 47.
7. LAB, C Rep. 900, IV-2/6/822, Bericht des Genossen Gloth, Kommission für Staatliche Kontrolle Gross-Berlin, über die Lage in der Berliner Bekleidungsindustrie, Abt. HuV, LI, Berlin, 13 June 1955, pp. 2–3.
8. SAPMO-BA, DY30/IV2/6.09/72, Entwurf des Referates von Grete Wittkowski für die Textilkonferenz, 13 April 1960, unpag.
9. BA-BL, DC20/I/4-186, Bl. 11.
10. SAPMO-BA, DY30/IV2/2.029/85, Bl. 148; LAB, C Rep. 900, IV-2/6/860, Bericht über die Durchführung der Ziffer 1 des Beschlusses des Präsidiums des Ministerrates vom 15.11.1960 ..., Kommission zur Durchführung des Beschlusses des Präsidiums des Ministerrates vom 15.11.1960, Berlin, 7 January 1961, p. 3.
11. LAB, C Rep. 113, Nr. 479, Maßnahmen zur Verminderung von Abwertungsverlusten im sozialistischen Handel, MdF, Abt. Handel, Berlin, 9 May 1960, pp. 1, 3.
12. SAPMO-BA, DY30/IV2/6.10/79, Bl. 78.
13. LAB, C Rep. 900, IV-2/6/860, Bericht über die Durchführung der Ziffer 1 ..., p. 1.

14. SäStAC, KL der SED, KMSt/Land, Nr. IV/4/10/158, Situation in der Textilindustrie 1955/56 Kreis KMSt/Land, KMSt, 25 October 1955, p. 2.

15. LAB, C Rep. 900, IV/4/06/297, RELAG Schieritzstr. 34 der HO-Industriewaren 9702, Erna F., 20 February 1953.

16. BA-BL, DC20/I/4-184, Bl. 24.

17. BA-BL, DE1/11562, Bl. 6.

18. SAPMO-BA, DY30/IV2/6.09/56, Bl. 88; BA-BL, DE1/7073, Bl. 25.

19. Herbert Fischer, "Zu einigen Problemen der operativen Bedarfsforschung im Textilgroßhandel," *MIfB* 3 (1964) 2: 43.

20. Elfriede Philipp, "Bekleidung – aber keine Kleider. Ein geheimnisvolles Gremium bestimmt, was die Berlinerin tragen soll," *Die Wirtschaft*, n.d. [1955/1956], unpag., found in LAB, C Rep. 106-01-01, Vorläufige Signatur Nr. T/176.

21. BA-BL, DL1/3739, Bl. 172.

22. BA-BL, DE1/24933, Letter from Arthur Grübler Reissspinnstoff-Fabrik to Wirtschaftsreferat beim ZK, Radeberg-Sa., 16 February 1959, p. 2.

23. BA-BL, DL1/3741, Bl. 26; LAB, C Rep. 900, IV/4/06/297, RELAG …

24. LAB, C Rep. 106-01, Nr. 544, Vorlage …, p. 1.

25. BA-BL, DC20/I/4-186, Bl. 12.

26. BA-BL, DL1/3731, Letter from Ministerpräsident to Rau; BA-CA, DE4/10290, Massnahmen zur Verringerung der Abwertungsbeträge für Textil- und Konfektionserzeugnisse, VWR, Abt. TeBeLe, Sektor Planung und Ökonomie, Berlin, 24 November 1961, pp. 1, 4; SäStAC, KL der SED, KMSt/Land, Nr. IV/4/10/158, Situation in der Textilindustrie …, pp. 1–2, 4; BA-BL, DC20/I/4-186, Bl. 8-12.

27. SäStAC, KL der SED, KMSt/Land, Nr. IV/4/10/158, Situation in der Textilindustrie, p. 1.

28. BA-BL, DL1/3739, Bl. 136.

29. BA-BL, DL1/3739 and 3742.

30. BA-BL, DL1/3741, Bl. 27, 1, 3.

31. Ibid., Bl. 1, 26.

32. Ibid., Bl. 3.

33. "'Sonder'-Verkauf mit allerlei Besonderheiten," *Der Handel* 1 (1951) 9: 289; Fridolin, untitled, *Der Handel* 2 (1952) 16: 394; LAB, C Rep. 900, IV/4/06/297, HO-Industriewaren 9702 Diesterwegstr., Abt. Wirtschaft, Instrukteur, Erna F., Berlin, 30 July 1953.

34. Walter Ulbricht, "Weg zu Frieden, Einheit und Wohlstand", 16. Tagung des ZK vom 17.-19.9.53, quoted in BA-BL, DE1/9388, Hausarbeit zum Staatsexamen des Kandidaten Walter B. …, Erfurt, 12 April 1954, p. 28.

35. BA-BL, DL1/1041, Bl. 18–21.

36. Ibid., Bl. 22–3.

37. Ibid., Bl. 21-2.
38. BA-BL, DE1/9388, Hausarbeit zum Staatsexamen ..., p. 28.
39. BA-BL, DE1/7436, Protokoll über die Arbeitsberatung der SPK vom 9.8.1954, p. 1; BA-BL, DE1/24268, Bl. 26.
40. SäStAC, RdB KMSt, Bezirksverwaltung der HO-Kreisbetriebe KMSt, Nr. 2917, Bericht über die Besprechung beim Minister Wach am 27.10.54, KMSt, 28 October 1954.
41. Ibid.
42. SäStAL, BT und RdB Leipzig, Abt. HuV, Nr. 1625, Bl. 56; BA-BL, DE1/27458, Protokoll über die 2. Sitzung der Ständigen Kommission beim MHV am 31.12.1954, Rose, MHV, 31 December 1954, p. 1.
43. SAPMO-BA, NY4090/373, Bl. 10–11; BA-BL, DE1/27458, Entwurf Beschluss über die Durchführung eines Inventur- und Winterschlussverkaufes im volkseigenen und genossenschaftlichen Einzelhandel, Präsidium des Ministerrates, Berlin, n.d. [December 1954].
44. SAPMO-BA, NY4090/373, Bl. 11–12; BA-BL, DE1/27458, Protokoll über die 2. Sitzung ..., p. 1; BA-BL, DE1/27458, Inventurverkauf, MHV, Berlin, 4 January 1955 and Winterschlußverkauf, MHV, Berlin, 4 January 1955.
45. SäStAL, BT und RdB Leipzig, Abt. HuV, Nr. 1625, Bl. 56.
46. SAPMO-BA, NY4090/373, Bl. 10–41, quotes: 12–13, 26. On the Central Commission for State Control, see Thomas Horstmann, *Logik der Willkür. Die Zentrale Kommission für Staatliche Kontrolle in der SBZ/DDR 1948–1958* (Cologne, 2002).
47. SAPMO-BA, NY4090/373, Bl. 12–4, 16, 20, 22, 39.
48. Ibid., Bl. 28.
49. Ibid., Bl. 23.
50. BA-BL, DE1/27458, Protokoll der Besprechung am 4.7.1955 im MHV betr. Sommerschlussverkauf 1955 ..., Oehme, Hauptabteilungsleiter, MHV, Berlin, 5 July 1955, p. 1.
51. SAPMO-BA, NY4090/373, Bl. 26.
52. Ibid., Bl. 24–5.
53. BA-BL, DE1/27458; LAB, C Rep. 106-01-01, Protokoll der Besprechung über die Regelung des Absatzes von Überplanbeständen an Konfektionserzeugnissen in der sozialistischen Industrie, MfL, HV Textil, Abt. Absatz, Schorsch, Leiter, Leipzig, 22 September 1955, p. 1.
54. BA-BL, DE1/27458, Sommerschlussverkauf in Berlin Aufgesucht alle Stadtbezirke Berlins, ausser Treptow am 17.8.1955.
55. BA-BL, DE1/27458, Sommerschlussverkauf in Leipzig Aufgesucht HO Warenhaus + Konsum Warenhaus am 18.8.55; Situationsbericht – Sommerschlußverkauf per 18.8.1955, Korb, Stellv. Abt. Leiter, Gera, 19 August 1955.
56. BA-BL, DE1/27458, Situationsbericht – Sommerschlußverkauf per

16.8.1955, Korb, Stellv. Abt. Leiter, 17 August 1955.

57. BA-BL, DL1/1055, Bl. 6–8.

58. Ibid., Bl. 6–7.

59. Ibid., Bl. 6–8; BA-BL, DL1/1590, Protokoll über die Dienstbesprechung mit den Hauptabteilungsleitern am 17.10.1955, MHV, Stellvertreter des Ministers, Lütgens, Berlin, 18 October 1955, p. 2.

60. BA-BL, DE1/27458, Protokoll der 5. Sitzung der Ständigen Kommission beim MHV – Überplanbestände – am 25.2.1955, Oehme, Hauptabteilungsleiter, MHV, Stellv. des Min. Industriewaren, p. 2; BA-BL, DE1/24764, Material für die Besprechung mit Handel und Versorgung – Warenfonds, SPK, Abt. LI, Sektor TeBeLe, Gruppe Materialbilanzierung, Berlin, 7 November 1958, p. 1.

61. On the Volkssolidarität, see Marcel Boldorf, *Sozialfürsorge in der SBZ/DDR 1945–1953. Ursachen, Ausmass und Bewältigung der Nachkriegsarmut* (Stuttgart, 1998), 173–86.

62. BA-BL, DL1/1322, Bl. 34.

63. BA-BL, DL1/1041, Bl. 20.

64. BA-BL, DC20/I/4-186, Bl. 40.

65. BA-DH, DL1/16142, Probleme zu Selbstkosten und Preisen für technisch weiterentwickelte und modische Konsumgüter, Berlin, 5 May 1958, p. 2.

66. BA-BL, DE1/24418, Durchsicht des Material des MfL über die Untersuchungen in der Textilindustrie …, Behrendt, HA-Leiter, HA Planung der LI, Berlin, 29 December 1956, p. 13.

67. BA-BL, DL1/1041, Bl. 21–2; SäStAC, RdB KMSt, Bezirksverwaltung der HO-Kreisbetriebe KMSt, Nr. 2917, Bericht über die Besprechung …

68. BA-BL, DE1/27458, Letter from Oehme, Hauptabteilungsleiter, HA Handel – Industriewaren to Gentsch, HA-Leiter, MdF, Inventur- und Winterschlußverkauf, 8 February 1955.

69. BA-BL, DC20/I/4-184, Bl. 29.

70. BA-BL, DL1/1322, Bl. 34.

71. BA-BL, DL1/3905, Bl. 33; BA-BL, DL1/1322, Bl. 21.

72. SäStAC, KL der SED, KMSt/Land, Nr. IV/4/10/158, Informationsbericht über "Sonderverkauf," Abt. Wirtschaftspolittik, KMSt, 17 November 1955, p. 2; BA-BL, DL1/1322, Bl. 34.

73. BA-DH, DL1/16142, Begründung für BIWA und Vorschläge zur Veränderung, HA Handel, Abt. Industriewaren, Berlin, 29 April 1958, p. 1.

74. BA-BL, DL1/3905, Bl. 33; BA-BL, DL1/1322, Bl. 22.

75. BA-BL, DL1/1322, Bl. 25, 34–5; BA-BL, DL1/1340, Bl. 50.

76. BA-BL, DL1/1322, Bl. 22.

77. Ibid., Bl. 17.

78. BA-BL, DL1/1322, Bl. 22; BA-BL, DL1/1340, Bl. 49–50.

79. BA-DH, DL1/16142, Begründung für BIWA ..., p. 1; SäStAL, BT und RdB Leipzig, Abt. HuV, Nr. 1834, Bl. 93.

80. BA-BL, DL1/1340, Bl. 39.

81. SäStAL, BT und RdB Leipzig, Abt. HuV, Nr. 1923, Bl. 65, 68; BA-BL, DL1/1340, Bl. 40, 42.

82. BA-BL, DL1/1340, Bl. 40, 44; "BIWA-Läden – eine neue Einkaufsquelle," 4.

83. BA-BL, DL1/1340, Bl. 40.

84. Ibid., Bl. 40, 44; BA-DH, DL1/16142, Begründung für BIWA ..., p. 2.

85. BA-BL, DL1/1340, Bl. 42.

86. Ibid., Bl. 3–4, 40; BA-BL, DL1/1347, Bl. 3.

87. LAB, C Rep. 113, Nr. 318, Bl. 17–22; BA-BL, DL1/1358, Bl. 3; SäStAL, BT und RdB Leipzig, Abt. HuV, Nr. 1923, Bl. 66, 68.

88. BA-BL, DL1/1340, Bl. 42–3; LAB, C Rep. 113, Nr. 318, Bl. 26.

89. In one of the few brief discussions to date of BIWA stores in secondary literature, Ina Merkel bases her claim that they had "good success among the population" solely on a handful of newspaper articles from summer 1957. Merkel, *Utopie und Bedürfnis*, 107–8.

90. SäStAL, BT und RdB Leipzig, Abt. HuV, Nr. 1923, Bl. 68.

91. Ibid., Bl. 66.

92. "Weshalb nicht auch Basar?" *Die Bekleidung* 5 (1958) 3: 3.

93. Renate Holland-Moritz, "Biwa auf dem Mond," *Die Bekleidung* 6 (1959) 2: 10.

94. This is a pun in German: *"hinter dem Mond sein"* means to be naively out-of-touch with reality and behind the times.

95. SäStAL, BT und RdB Leipzig, Abt. HuV, Nr. 1923, Bl. 68.

96. SAPMO-BA, DY30/IV2/2.029/12, Bl. 144; DL1/1350, Bl. 2; BA-DH, DL1/16142, Begründung für BIWA ..., p. 2.

97. BA-DH, DL1/16142, Begründung für BIWA ..., p. 1.

98. BA-BL, DL1/1340, Bl. 44.

99. SäStAL, BT und RdB Leipzig, Abt. HuV, Nr. 1834, Bl. 12–13.

100. BA-DH, DL1/16142, Begründung für BIWA ..., p. 2; SAPMO-BA, DY30/IV2/2.029/12, Bl. 143–4.

101. BA-BL, DL1/1322, Bl. 37.

102. BA-BL, DC20/I/4-312, Bl. 47.

103. LAB, C Rep. 113, Nr. 479, Memo from Jarowinsky, Stellv. Minister, MHV, to Magistrat von Groß-Berlin, Abt. HuV, Berlin, 5 March 1959.

104. SAPMO-BA, DY30/JIV2/2A/747, Begründung zu den Preissenkungsvorschlägen, p. 1.

105. BA-BL, DC20/I/4-312, Bl. 47.

106. BA-BL, DE1/26175, Bericht des Arbeitskreises Qualität zur Vorbereitung der Ökonomischen Konferenz der Textilindustrie, Berlin, 21 December

1959, p. 64; LAB, C Rep. 113, Nr. 479, Maßnahmen zur Verminderung ...,
pp. 5, 9.

107. BA-BL, DC20/I/4-339, Bl. 88.

108. BA-BL, DC20/I/4-325, Bl. 69–70.

109. BA-BL, DC20/I/4-324, Bl. 25–6; BA-BL, DC20/I/4-339, Bl. 95.

110. BA-BL, DC20/I/4-324, Bl. 25–6.

111. Ibid., Bl. 69.

112. BA-BL, DC20/I/4-339, Bl. 97–8.

113. BA-BL, DC20/I/4-342, Bl. 168–9; BA-BL, DC20/I/4-339, Bl. 97–8.

114. BA-BL, DC20/I/4-342, Bl. 169; BA-BL, DC20/I/4-339, Bl. 98; BA-BL,
DL1/1405, Bl. 22.

115. SAPMO-BA, DY30/IV2/6.10/13, Bl. 268, 286–7.

116. BA-BL, DC20/I/4-339, Bl. 97; SäStAC, RdB KMSt, Wirtschaftsrat, Abt.
HuV, Nr. 4814.

117. SäStAC, RdB KMSt, Wirtschaftsrat, Abt. HuV, Nr. 4814, Bericht betreffs
Übergabe von Waren aus der Sonderaktion Februar/März 1959 an die
Volkssolidarität, Dressel, KMSt, 5 October 1959.

118. BA-BL, DC20/I/4-338, Bl. 22; BA-BL, DE1/7061, Bl. 109; BA-BL,
DE1/26096, Anweisung Nr. 61/59 Qualitätsgeminderte Ware zu stark her-
abgesetzten Preisen, Merkel, Berlin, 15 December 1959.

119. BA-BL, DC20/I/4-339, Bl. 88.

120. LAB, C Rep. 113, Nr. 479, Letter from the Ministers of MHV and MdF to
the Oberbürgermeister des Magistrats von Groß-Berlin Ebert, Berlin, 16
June 1960, p. 1.

121. SAPMO-BA, DY30/IV2/6.09/56, Bl. 140.

122. BA-BL, DE1/26175, Bericht des Arbeitskreises Qualität ..., p. 64.

123. BA-BL, DL1/1405, Bl. 21.

124. SAPMO-BA, DY30/IV2/2.029/149, Bl. 108, 53–4.

125. BA-BL, DE1/7073, Bl. 27, 33.

126. SAPMO-BA, DY30/IV2/2.029/149, Bl. 54, 105; BA-BL, DL1/1465, Bl. 9.

127. SAPMO-BA, DY30/JIV2/2/696, Bl. 5.

128. LAB, C Rep. 113, Nr. 479, Maßnahmen zur Verminderung ..., pp. 3, 13.

129. SAPMO-BA, DY30/IV2/1.01/328, Bl. 50; LAB, C Rep. 900, IV-2/6/860,
Bericht über die Durchführung der Ziffer 1 ..., pp. 3, 15, Anlage 2; SAPMO-
BA, DY30/IV2/6.10/72, Bl. 3, 6–9.

130. SäStAL, BT und RdB Leipzig, Abt. HuV, Nr. 1690, Bl. 27–31, 32–5; BA-
BL, DL1/3995, Analyse 1961 – Industriewaren, Bereich Industriewaren,
Berlin, 16 February 1962, pp. 3, 15–6.

131. SAPMO-BA, DY30/IV2/6.10/130, Bl. 318–9.

132. LAB, C Rep. 113, Nr. 479, Einschätzung der Überplanbestände der GHG"en
Industriewaren ..., Ref. Industriewaren, Berlin, 9 November 1960, p. 1; BA-

BL, DE1/25697, Begründung zum Beschluß der Einbeziehung der Über-planbestände der volkseigenen Textil- und Bekleidungsindustrie in den Winterschlußverkauf 1961, n.d., p. 1.

133. SAPMO-BA, DY30/IV2/2.029/149, Bl. 54.

134. SAPMO-BA, DY30/IV2/6.10/130, Bl. 330; SAPMO-BA, DY30/IV2/6.10/129, Bl. 94, 86.

135. SAPMO-BA, DY30/IV2/2.029/149, Bl. 105; BA-BL, DL1/1467, Bl. 3–4.

136. BA-BL, DL1/1467, Bl. 4.

137. BA-CA, DL102/196, p. 39.

138. SAPMO-BA, DY30/IV2/6.10/129, Bl. 74.

139. LAB, C Rep. 900, IV-2/6/855, Wochenbericht, Magstrat von Groß-Berin, Bezirksdispatcher, Berlin, 31 August 1959, p. 6.

140. BA-BL, DC20/I/4-339, Bl. 97.

141. SAPMO-BA, DY30/IV2/2.029/86, Memo from Müller and Lange, Abt. HVuA, PuF, to Apel, 1 July 59, p. 3.

142. LAB, C Rep. 900, IV-2/6/868, untitled document, p. 3.

143. All of the following quotes from Verner's speech are contained in SAPMO-BA, DY30/IV2/1/254, Bl. 21–3.

144. According to an internal memo from Honecker to Verner, one of his assis-tants bought the dress, whose original price was actually 81.20 DM, along with a men's jacket, which had been discounted from 93 DM to 38 DM. LAB, C Rep. 113, Nr. 390, Note from Honecker to Verner, 3 February 1961.

145. Ibid.

146. LAB, C Rep. 113, Nr. 390, Letter from [illegible] Magistrat von Groß-Berlin, Abt. HuV and Stein, Sekretär der BL, to Verner, Textilien, Winterschluss-verkauf 1961, 6 February 1961.

147. LAB, C Rep. 900, IV4/01-205, Winterschlussverkauf, from BL der SED Gross-Berlin, Abt. Landwirtschaft/Handel to Sekretär für Wirtschaftspolitik, Berlin, 6 January 1961; BA-BL, DE1/25697, Gemeinsame Anweisung über die Durchführung von Abwertungen bei den Beständen …, MHV, Der Minister, MdF, Der Minister, Berlin, 29 December 1960, p. 4.

148. BA-BL, DE1/25697, [Entwurf] Direktive über die Durchführung eines Sommerschlußverkaufes von Textilwaren im volkseigenen und genossen-schaftlichen Handel, Der Minister, MHV, Berlin, n.d. [summer 1960], p. 6.

149. SAPMO-BA, DY30/IV2/6.10/129, Bl. 114–57, 160–1; BA-BL, DC20/I/4-443, Bl. 2; SAPMO-BA, DY30/JIV2/2A/816, Verschleuderung von Volksei-gentum durch Staats- und Handelsfunktionäre (Beschluß des Politbüros vom 11.4.1961), Ulbricht, Berlin, 22 April 1961.

150. SAPMO-BA, DY30/IV2/6.10/129, Bl. 136.

151. Ibid., Bl. 5, 22, 25, 57–64, 74, 82, 86, 93.

152. Ibid., Bl. 73–5, 77, 84–7.

153. Ibid., Bl. 73, 85, 93–4.

154. Ibid., Bl. 87, 93–5, 97–100; Erwin Otto, "Saisonschlußverkäufe werden durch bessere Zusammenarbeit überflüssig," *Der Handel* 12 (1962) 3: 103–6; "Zur Vorbereitung und Durchführung Delegiertenkonferenzen 1962," *Konsumgenossenschafter* 5 (1962): 3.

155. On the *Produktionsaufgebot*, see Corey Ross, *Constructing Socialism at the Grass-Roots: The Transformation of East Germany 1945–65* (New York, 2000), 165–74.

156. SAPMO-BA, DY30/IV2/6.10/28, Bl. 227.

157. SAPMO-BA, DY30/IV2/6.10/129, Bl. 99–100.

158. Ibid., Bl. 100.

159. SäStAC, RdB KMSt, Wirtschaftsrat, Abt. HuV, Nr. 6599, Einschätzung über die Entwicklung der Warenbestände und die Wirksamkeit der Maßnahmen zur Verringerung der Bestände ..., RdB KMSt, Stellvertreter des Vorsitzenden, Löffler, KMSt., 4 July 1962, pp. 4–5.

160. "4. Fortsetzung zum Beschluß vom 9.4.1962 über die obligatorische Durchführung von Maßnahmen zum Absatz bestimmter über die vorgegebenen Richttage lagernder Bestände im genossenschaftlichen Einzelhandel," *Beschlüsse-Anweisungen-Informationen des Verbandes Deutscher Konsumgenossenschaften* 6 (21 December 1962) 22: 187.

161. SäStAC, RdB KMSt, Wirtschaftsrat, Abt. HuV, Nr. 6599, Einschätzung über die Entwicklung ..., p. 5.

162. Ibid.; BA-BL, DC20/I/4-577, Bl. 64–5; SäStAL, SED-BL Leipzig, IV/2/2/127, Bl. 76.

163. SAPMO-BA, NY4182/991, Bl. 121–2.

164. SäStAL, SED-BL Leipzig, IV/2/2/127, Bl. 76–9; BA-BL, DC20/I/4-577, Bl. 41, 64–5.

165. SäStAL, SED-BL Leipzig, IV/2/2/127, Bl. 76–8.

166. SAPMO-BA, DY30/IV2/1/283, Bl. 10; SAPMO-BA, DY30/JIV2/2/841, Bl. 62; SAPMO-BA, DY30/IV2/1/281, Bl. 62.

167. SAPMO-BA, DY30/IV2/1/281, Bl. 62. Edith Baumann repeated these words almost verbatim in her speech. SAPMO-BA, DY30/IV2/1/283, Bl. 10.

168. BA-BL, DC20/I/4-577, Bl. 64–5.

169. SAPMO-BA, DY30/IV2/1/281, Bl. 63; SAPMO-BA, DY30/IV2/1/283, Bl. 4–5, 8–10; SAPMO-BA, DY30/IVA2/6.10/157, Anlage 1 zur Ausarbeitung der Pressestelle für den Gen. Minister Lucht vom 25.4.64, Sektor Werbung, Berlin, 24 April 1964, p. 2.

170. SAPMO-BA, DY30/JIV2/2/841, Bl. 70.

171. SAPMO-BA, DY30/IV2/6.10/33, Bl. 103–4; SäStAC, RdB KMSt, Abt. HuV, Nr. 17086, Analyse der Versorgung der Bevölkerung und der Planerfüllung des Binnenhandels im Jahre 1962, Löffler, Stellvertreter des Vorsitzenden,

RdB, KMSt, 25 January 63, pp. 4, 17.

172. SAPMO-BA, DY30/IV2/6.10/33, Bl. 104.

173. SAPMO-BA, DY30/IVA2/6.10/182, Grundorientierung für die weitere Arbeit des Büros für Industrie und Bauwesen beim Politbüro auf dem Gebiet der perspektivischen Entwicklung der Konsumgüterproduktion und der Versorgung der Bevölkerung, Büro für Industrie und Bauwesen beim Polibüro, Berlin, 28 August 1963, p. 1.

174. LAB, C Rep. 900, IV/4/07/166, 6. Informationsbericht zu Lenkungsmassnahmen, SED-KL Treptow, Abt. Org.-Kader, Berlin, 1 August 1962, p. 2; BA-BL, DC20/I/4-700, Bl. 63–4.

175. BA-BL, DC20/I/4-700, Bl. 65; SäStAC, ZWK TuK, Nr. 25, Die Ergebnisse der Arbeit mit der Sammellagerware, n.d. [23 October 1964].

176. SäStAC, ZWK TuK, Nr. 25, Abschlussbericht über die Durchführung und das Ergebnis des zentralen Warenabkaufes (Warenbörse) für Sammellagerware, ZWK für TuK, Arbeitsgruppe Warenbestände, Polzin, KMSt, 15 August 1964, p. 9.

177. SAPMO-BA, DY30/IVA2/6.10/182, Grundorientierung …, p. 12.

178. Ibid.; SAPMO-BA, DY30/IVA2/6.10/182, Konzeption für das Büro für Industrie und Bauwesen beim Politbüro auf dem Gebiet der Konsumgüterproduktion und des Absatzes, Abt. PuF, Berlin, 19 August 1963, pp. 10–11.

179. SäStAL, BT und RdB Leipzig, Abt. HuV, Nr. 31737, Ergebnisse der Aussprache im HOWA CENTRUM über Werbemaßnahmen zum Sommerausklang, RdB Leipzig, Abt. HuV, Leipzig, 24 August 1965; SAPMO-BA, DY30/IVA2/6.10/182, Letter from Sieber, Minister MHV, to Weiß, Leiter, Abt. HVuA, ZK, Berlin, July 1968.

180. SAPMO-BA, DY30/IVA2/2.021/722, Bl. 218–9; LAB, C Rep. 900, Nr. IVB-2/6/597; BA-CA, DL102/1026, pp. 1–6.

181. SAPMO-BA, DY30/IVA2/6.10/182, Memo from Eltze, Bereich Großhandel Industriewaren, to Sieber, 18 June 1968, p. 1; SAPMO-BA, Vorläufige SED Signatur DY30/17018, Information über Probleme bei der Verbesserung der Versorgung der Bevölkerung mit Konfektionserzeugnissen, MR der DDR, Arbeitsgruppe für Organisation und Inspektion beim Vorsitzenden, Berlin, 15 February 1974, pp. 1–7.

182. BA-CA, DL102/755, p. 34.

183. SAPMO-BA, DY30/IVA2/6.09/70, Mündliche Berichterstattung vor dem Sekretariat der SED-BL über die Neuprofilierung der Textilindustrie in der Bezirksstadt Cottbus, VVB Volltuch Cottbus, Generaldirektor, Bullan, Cottbus, 14 May 1968, p. 2.

Chapter 6 – The Disillusionment of Dreams of Distinction: Hochmodisch Apparel, Fashion Boutiques, and Exquisit Stores

1. BA-BL, DL1/1494, Bl. 3.
2. LAB, C Rep. 900, IV/4/06/318, Durchführung neuer Kurs, Abt. Wirtschaft, Franke, Instrukteur, Berlin, 10 November 1953, pp. 1–2.
3. BA-BL, DC20/I/3-233, Bl. 64.
4. On *Verkaufskultur* concerning textiles, see Otto Baier, *Umgang mit Textilwaren. Arbeitsanleitung für Einkäufer, Verkaufsstellenleiter und Verkaufskräfte im Textilhandel* (Leipzig, 1958), 91–109.
5. S.G., "Das Vertrauen der Kundschaft fehlt," *Die Bekleidung* 1 (1956): 17.
6. LAB, C Rep. 106-01, Nr. 544, Bericht über die Untersuchung des VEB Massatelier Berlin, Hoppe, Berlin, 5 November 1954.
7. S.G., "Das Vertrauen der Kundschaft fehlt," 17.
8. Helga Borchert and Annelise Döpke, "Flugblatt für die Mode," *Wochenpost* 15 (1957): 23.
9. LAB, C Rep. 106-01-01, Vorläufige Signatur Nr. T/176, Siebold, Vorstand Handel, Konsum Genossenschaft, Stadt Erfurt eGmbH, to Industrie- zweigleitung Konfektion, Berlin, Erfurt, 20 April 1956.
10. "Vom Schwarzmarkt zur HO," *Frau von heute* 6 (1951) 41: 8; Jörg Roesler, "The Black Market in Post-War Berlin and the Methods used to Counteract it," *German History* 7 (1989): 92–107.
11. Katherine Pence, "Building Socialist Worker-Consumers: The paradoxical construction of the Handelsorganisation – HO, 1948," in *Arbeiter in der SBZ-DDR*, ed. Peter Hübner and Klaus Tenfelde (Essen, 1999), 497–526; Mark Landsman, "Dictatorship and Demand: East Germany Between Productivism and Consumerism, 1948–1961," Ph.D. Dissertation, Columbia University, 2000, Chapter 2.
12. BA-BL, DL1/3764, Bl. 14–15.
13. SSB-MA, SM6-23, p. 17.
14. SAPMO-BA, DY30/JIV2/2/753, Bl. 280.
15. BA-BL, DE1/24700, Begründung zur Preisneureglung für Pelzbekleidung, Gorny, Leiter des Arbeitskreises, Leipzig, 14 July 1958, p. 2.
16. LAB, C Rep. 900, IV-2/6/861, Wie hat sich die Einrichtung von Exquisitläden für den Verkauf hochwertiger Industriewaren schon bewährt? –, n.d. [some-time in 1961 after 13 August], pp. 2–3, 7.
17. BA-BL, DE1/30278, Industriezweigökonomik der VVB Konfektion, p. 2/733; SSB-MA, SM6-23, p. 13.
18. SSB-MA, SM3-4, pp. 6–7.
19. Walter Ulbricht, "Über Standardisierung und Mode," *Neues Deutschland*, 13 August 1959, p. 4. A local official in Berlin later claimed that these remarks

were the justification for Exquisit stores: LAB, C Rep. 900, IV-2/6/861, Wie hat sich die Einrichtung ..., p. 3.

20. SAPMO-BA, DY30/IV2/1/115, Bl. 218; SAPMO-BA, DY30/JIV2/2A/875, Beschluss über Auswahl hochmodischer Erzeugnisse und die Festlegung ihrer Preise, MHV, n.d. [2 February 1962], pp. 2–3; SAPMO-BA, DY30/IVA2/ 2.021/891, Bl. 31.

21. LAB, C Rep. 470-01, Nr. 37, Bl. 24.

22. SAPMO-BA, DY30/IV2/6.09/75, Hauptreferat des Gen. Sonnenburg, p. 25.

23. SSB-MA, SM3-4, pp. 6–7; BA-BL, DE1/25687, Direktive zur Ausarbeitung der Planvorschläge zum Volkswirtschaftsplan 1959 für die Betriebe der VVB (Z) Konfektion, VVB Konfektion, Der Hauptdirektor, Berlin, 2 June 1958, p. 5.

24. "Da wird sich Ihre Frau freuen," *Neues Deutschland*, 8 January 1959, p. 6.

25. LAB, C Rep. 470-01, Nr. 37, Bl. 24; "Saumseligkeit brachte hinkende Mode-vorläufer," *Berliner Zeitung*, 30 July 1958, p. 5.

26. SAPMO-BA, DY30/IV2/6.10/92, Bl. 20; SAPMO-BA, DY30/IV2/6.10/34, Bl. 25.

27. BA-BL, DL1/3764, Bl. 14; BA-DH, DL1/16142, Probleme zu Selbstkosten und Preisen für technisch weiterentwickelte und modische Konsumgüter, Berlin, 5 May 1958, pp. 10–13.

28. The calculation regulations for these surcharges supposedly would allow enterprises to change their prices only "for a short time" for "as long as fashion allows," a determination that would be made "self-responsibly" by individual manufacturers. BA-DH, DL1/16142, Probleme zu Selbstkosten ..., pp. 10–3.

29. SäStAC, RdB KMSt, Wirtschaffsrat, Abt. HuV, Nr. 4544, Vorschlag für das Verfahren bei Erzeugnissen hochmodischen Charakters, KMSt, 18 November 1961, p. 1.

30. LAB, C Rep. 113, Nr. 622, Protokoll über die am 4.6. stattgefundene Besprechung betreffend Boutique Sibylle, HO Industriewaren Berlin-Mitte, Jakobi, Berlin, 12 June 1958.

31. LAB, C Rep. 113, Nr. 622, Kurzprotokoll über die am 13.2.1958 durchge-führte Aussprache betr. Warenbereitstellung für die Verkaufsstelle "Sibylle" (Boutique) ..., Magistrat von Groß-Berlin, Abt. HuV, Referatsleiter, Berlin, 14 February 1958 and Stellmacher, Handelsleiter, HO-Industriewaren Berlin-Mitte, to Magistrat von Groß-Berlin, Abt. HuV, 30 June 1958.

32. These included Heinz Bormann's firm in Magdeburg, VEB Elegant, VEB Fortschritt, the University for Applied Art (Hochschule für angewandte Kunst), the Engineering School for Clothing (Ingenieurschule für Bekleidung), and the German Fashion Institute.

33. Inge Kertzscher, "Berlin hat seine erste Boutique," *Neues Deutschland*, 16 August 1958, Beilage.

34. Ibid.

35. Steineckert, "Berlin hat seine Boutique," *Handelswoche*, 20 August 1958.

36. Renate Holland-Moritz, "Da liegt die Hose im Pfeffer oder Wem die Jacke paßt," *Eulenspiegel* 5 (1958) 51: 813.

37. "Neues und Altes von der sibylle," *Frau von heute* 13 (1958) 50: 17.

38. SSB-MA, SM6-15; BA-CA, DE4/682, Richtlinie zur Fertigung von Modellerzeugnissen des DMI ...im VEB Kunst und Mode ..., Berlin, 20 March 1961, pp. 2–4.

39. LAB, C Rep. 470-01, Nr. 29, Bl. 36, 38; BA-CA, DE4/682, Richtlinie zur Fertigung ..., pp. 1, 3–4; BA-CA, DE4/684, Information über Beratungen des MdF zur besseren Differenzierung der Endverbraucherpreise für Textilerzeugnisse, n.d. [1961], p. 1.

40. LAB, C Rep. 900, IV-2/6/860, Eröffnung von Spezialverkaufsstellen für hochwertige Textilien durch den HO-I-Kreisbetrieb Mitte in der Strasse Unter den Linden, Stranz, Leiter der Abt. HuV, Magistrat von Gross-Berlin, Berlin, 13 February 1961; LAB, C Rep. 900, IV-2/6/861, Wie hat sich die Einrichtung ..., pp. 2, 4.

41. SAPMO-BA, DY30/JIV2/2/753, Bl. 276, 282; BA-BL, DC20/I/4-461, Bl. 157.

42. SAPMO-BA, DY30/IV2/2.101/24, Bl. 230.

43. SAPMO-BA, DY30/IV2/6.10/130, Bl. 156.

44. LAB, C Rep. 900, IV-2/6/861, Wie hat sich die Einrichtung ..., pp. 6–7.

45. SAPMO-BA, DY30/IV2/6.10/130, Bl. 156–7.

46. LAB, C Rep. 900, IV-2/6/861, Wie hat sich die Einrichtung ..., p. 2.

47. SäStAC, RdB KMSt, Wirtschaftsrat, Abt. HuV, Nr. 4544, Vorschlag für das Verfahren ..., pp. 3, 7.

48. SAPMO-BA, DY30/JIV2/2/753, Bl. 282–3.

49. BA-BL, DC20/I/4-482, Bl. 26; BA-BL, DC20/I/4-483, Bl. 87. While some scholars have argued that the establishment of Exquisit stores was a direct response to the Wall, the extensive activities related to the precursors of these stores in the months and even years before 13 August 1961 suggest a more complicated evolution.

50. BA-BL, DC20/I/4-482, Bl. 27-8.

51. BA-BL, DC20/I/4-482, Bl. 31.

52. SäStAC, RdB KMSt, Wirtschaftsrat, Abt. HuV, Nr. 4544, Vorschlag für das Verfahren ..., p. 1.

53. BA-BL, DC20/I/4/482, Bl. 30.

54. Ibid., Bl. 32.

55. SAPMO-BA, DY30/JIV2/2/753, Bl. 283.

56. BA-BL, DC20/I/4-483, Bl. 100.

57. SAPMO-BA, DY30/IV2/2.101/24, Bl. 230-1.

58. BA-CA, DE4/684, Information über Beratungen des MdF zur besseren

Differenzierung der Endverbraucherpreise für Textilerzeugnisse, n.p., n.d.; SAPMO-BA, DY30/IV2/2.029/87, Beratung bei Genossen Rumpf am 17.2.1961, Knobloch, Sektorenleiter, Ender, APO-Sekretär, MHV, Berlin, 20 February 1961.

59. BA-BL, DE1/26033, Beantwortung der Fragen 1-8, Henkel, Ökonomischer Leiter, VVB Konfektion, Berlin, 8 March 1960, p. 2.

60. SAPMO-BA, DY30/IVA2/2.021/720, Bl. 26; LAB, C Rep. 470-01, Nr. 29, Bl. 48.

61. LAB, C Rep. 900, IV-2/6/861, Wie hat sich die Einrichtung ..., pp. 7–8.

62. SAPMO-BA, DY30/IV2/6.10/130, Bl. 102–3.

63. LAB, C Rep. 900, IV-2/6/861, Wie hat sich die Einrichtung ..., p. 4.

64. SAPMO-BA, DY30/IV2/6.10/130, Bl. 168, 304; SAPMO-BA, DY30/IVA2/2.021/720, Bl. 27.

65. SAPMO-BA, DY30/IVA2/2.021/720, Bl. 27.

66. SAPMO-BA, DY30/IV2/6.10/130, Bl. 140.

67. SAPMO-BA, DY30/IVA2/2.021/720, Bl. 26; SAPMO-BA, DY30/IV2/6.10/130, Bl. 167.

68. BA-DH, DL1/17947, Die perspektivische Entwicklung des Exquisithandels im NÖSPL, Cramer, Hauptdirektor, HO, Berlin, 10 July 1966, Anlage.

69. BA-DH, DL1/3995, Analyse über die Versorgung der Bevölkerung mit Schuhen und Lederwaren im Jahre 1961, Keller, ZWK für Schuhe und Lederwaren des MHV, Leipzig, 17 January 1962, p. 15.

70. LAB, C Rep. 900, IV-2/6/861, Wie hat sich die Einrichtung ..., pp. 8–9.

71. BA-BL, DC20/I/4-482, Bl. 31.

72. SAPMO-BA, Vorläufige SED Signatur DY30/17018, untitled report on Exquisit, n.d. [1972/1973], p. 3.

73. BA-DH, DL1/17947, Probleme der Sortimentsgestaltung in Exquisit-Verkaufsstellen, n.d. [1966], p. 1; SAPMO-BA, Vorläufige SED Signatur DY30/17018, untitled report on Exquisit ..., p. 13.

74. SAPMO-BA, DY30/IV2/6.10/130, Bl. 164, 168, 170–1, 185; SAPMO-BA, DY30/IVA2/2.021/720, Bl. 26–7.

75. SAPMO-BA, DY30/IV2/6.10/130, Bl. 164, 171–2, 184–7.

76. SAPMO-BA, DY30/JIV2/2/753, Bl. 70; SAPMO-BA, DY30/JIV2/2A/806, Maßnahmen zur Verbesserung der Leitung, Planung und Organisation auf dem Gebiet der Versorgung der Bevölkerung, Anlage Preise.

77. SAPMO-BA, DY30/IV2/2.101/24, Bl. 222–3, 231–2.

78. Ibid., Bl. 130, 228.

79. SAPMO-BA, DY30/IV2/6.10/130, Bl. 112.

80. SAPMO-BA, DY30/IV2/6.10/14, Bl. 74, 159.

81. SäStAC, RdB KMSt, Wirtschaftsrat, Abt. HuV, Nr. 4544, Vorschlag für das Verfahren ..., p. 2; SAPMO-BA, DY30/IV2/2.029/87, Bericht über durch-

geführte Maßnahmen und deren Auswirkungen zur Erreichung einer besseren Preisdifferenzierung bei hochmodischen Erzeugnissen, ZKK, Berlin, 6 November 1961, pp. 15–16.

82. SAPMO-BA, DY30/IV2/2.029/87, Lange to Baumann, Handel, Versorgung, und Außenhandel, Kandidat d. PB, Preiserhöhung bei hochmodischen Erzeugnissen, 1 November 1961, and Bericht über durchgeführte Maßnahmen …, p. 16.

83. SäStAC, RdB KMSt, Wirtschaftsrat, Abt. HuV, Nr. 4544, Information über den Verkauf von Industriewaren mit hochmodischen Charakter, n.d. [30 October 1961], p. 1.

84. SAPMO-BA, DY30/IV2/2.029/87, Lange to Baumann …

85. SäStAC, RdB KMSt, Wirtschaftsrat, Abt. HuV, Nr. 4544, Vorschlag für das Verfahren …, p. 2.

86. BA-CA, DE4/10290, Aktennotiz über Maßnahmen zur Durchsetzung des Beschlusses des Präsidiums des Ministerrates vom 24.8.1961 …, Höhne, VWR, Abt. TeBeLe, Sektor Planung und Ökonomie, Fachgebiet Finanzen und Preise, Berlin, 7 March 1962.

87. SAPMO-BA, DY30/IV2/6.10/130, Bl. 124–5.

88. Ibid., Bl. 116; SAPMO-BA, DY30/JIV2/2A/875, Beschluss über Auswahl …, pp. 2, 4.

89. SAPMO-BA, DY30/IV2/6.10/130, Bl. 130.

90. SäStAC, RdB KMSt, Wirtschaftsrat, Abt. HuV, Nr. 4544, Vorschlag für das Verfahren …, p. 3.

91. SAPMO-BA, DY30/IV2/2.029/87, Bericht über durchgeführte Maßnahmen …, pp. 13, 17–8; SAPMO-BA, DY30/IV2/2.101/24, Bl. 131.

92. SäStAC, RdB KMSt, Wirtschaftsrat, Abt. HuV, Nr. 4544, Vorschlag für das Verfahren …, p. 2; SAPMO-BA, DY30/IV2/6.10/14, Bl. 160.

93. SAPMO-BA, DY30/IV2/2.029/87, Bericht über durchgeführte Maßnahmen …, p. 18.

94. SAPMO-BA, DY30/IV2/2.029/87, Lange to Baumann …; SAPMO-BA, DY30/IV2/6.10/14, Bl. 160.

95. *Gesetzblatt der Deutschen Demokratischen Republik*, Teil II, Nr. 130, 30 December 1964, p. 1060.

96. SäStAC, RdB KMSt, Wirtschaftsrat, Abt. HuV, Nr. 4544, Vorschlag für das Verfahren …, pp. 3–4, 7.

97. Other sales personnel "enthusiastically welcomed" the price increases because they increased the volume of turnover, brought high sales bonuses, and facilitated a more rapid fulfillment of the plan. SAPMO-BA, DY30/IV2/6.10/130, Bl. 58–9.

98. Ibid., Bl. 58–60.

99. Ibid., Bl. 59–60.

100. SAPMO-BA, DY30/IV2/2.029/87, Bericht über durchgeführte Maßnahmen
    …, p. 1, 15–16.
101. Ibid., p. 16.
102. BA-BL, DY31/1048, Bl. 4.
103. LAB, C Rep. 900, IV-2/6/861, Wie hat sich die Einrichtung …, p. 4.
104. Ibid., pp. 4–5.
105. SAPMO-BA, DY30/IV2/6.10/130, Bl. 304.
106. Joachim Nawrocki, *Das geplante Wunder. Leben und Wirtschaften im anderen Deutschland* (Hamburg, 1967), 64.
107. SAPMO-BA, DY30/IV2/6.10/130, Bl. 158; SäStAL, SED-BL Leipzig,
    IV/2/2/127, Bl. 79; "Exquisiter Irrtum," *Neues Deutschland*, 19 April 1962,
    p. 3.
108. SäStAL, SED-BL Leipzig, IV/2/2/127, Bl. 79–80.
109. LAB, C Rep. 900, IV-2/6/861, Wie hat sich die Einrichtung …, p. 10.
110. SAPMO-BA, Vorläufige SED Signatur DY30/17018, untitled report on
    Exquisit …, pp. 2–3.
111. Ibid., p. 8.
112. SAPMO-BA, DY30/IVA2/2.021/720, Bl. 26.
113. SAPMO-BA, Vorläufige SED Signatur DY30/17018, untitled report on
    Exquisit …, p. 3.
114. Ibid., p. 3.
115. BA-DH, DL1/17947, Probleme der Sortimentsgestaltung in Exquisit-
    Verkaufsstellen …, p. 1.
116. SäStAL, SED-BL Leipzig, IVA-2/6/285, Exquisit-Verkaufsstelle Leipzig,
    Höpfner, Abt. Leiter, SED-BL Leipzig, Abt. LLI/Handel, Leipzig, 11
    February 1966, pp. 1–2.
117. SAPMO-BA, Vorläufige SED Signatur DY30/17018, untitled report on
    Exquisit …, p. 3.
118. BA-CA, DL102/713, pp. 8–9.
119. On the political context and consequences of this shift in the SED's policies,
    see Monika Kaiser, *Machtwechsel von Ulbricht zu Honecker: Funktions-
    mechanismen der SED-Diktatur in Konfliktsituationen 1962 bis 1972*
    (Berlin, 1997).
120. BA-BL, DC20/I/4-1226, Bl. 108–9.
121. Ibid., Bl. 112; BA-DH, DL1/17947, Die perspektivische Entwicklung …, p.
    1.
122. BA-BL, DC20/I/4-1226, Bl. 110–20. On Delikat, see Ina Merkel, *Utopie
    und Bedürfnis. Die Geschichte der Konsumkultur in der DDR* (Cologne,
    1999), 270–7.
123. BA-DH, DL1/17947, Vermerk für den Minister Sieber, n.d. [1966] and Die
    perspektivische Entwicklung …, p. 3.

124. SäStAL, SED-BL Leipzig, IVA-2/6/285, Exquisit-Verkaufsstelle ...

125. BA-DH, DL1/17947, Die perspektivische Entwicklung ..., p. 2.

126. BA-DH, DL1/17947, Vermerk für den Minister Sieber, Bereich Handelspolitik – Einzelhandel, Berlin, 17 August 1966, p. 2.

127. SäStAL, Lucie Kaiser, Nr. 3.

128. Ibid., Bl. 1–4.

129. BA-DH, DL1/17947, Hartwig, Direktor, Hauptdirektion des volkseigenen Einzelhandels HO – Arbeitsgruppe Exquisit – to Abteilungsleiter Ciechowski, Bereich Handelspolitik – Einzelhandel, MHV, Berlin, 9 December 1966.

130. SAPMO-BA, Vorläufige SED Signatur DY30/17018, untitled report on Exquisit ..., p. 4.

131. Ibid., p. 3–4, 15.

132. Ibid., p. 4, 9, 12.

133. Ibid., p. 6.

134. LAB, C Rep. 900, IVA-2/9.01/490, 1. Entwurf zur Einschätzung des Bewußt-seins der Berliner Bevölkerung, Berlin, 11 January 1967, Anhang 1, p. 6.

135. LAB, C Rep. 900, IVA-2/9.01/490, Kurzversammlung in der Dewag-Werbung II, Abt. Versand, am 5.1.1967, Buchler, Sektor Agitation, Berlin, 9 January 1967, p. 2.

136. BA-CA, DL102/713, p. 7.

137. Ibid.

138. My interpretation contrasts with the "success story" offered by Ina Merkel, who downplays consumers' complaints and measures the network's success primarily in terms of its rapidly growing turnover and its "brand-name character." Merkel, *Utopie und Bedürfnis*, 251–69.

139. SAPMO-BA, Vorläufige SED Signatur DY30/17018, untitled report on Exquisit ..., pp. 9, 16.

140. Ibid., p. 16.

141. SSB-MA, SM16-69, p. 1.

142. Ibid., Anlagen 1 and 2.

143. SAPMO-BA, Vorläufige SED Signatur DY30/17018, untitled report on Exquisit ..., p. 17, Anlage 13.

144. LAB, C Rep. 470–02, Nr. 132, Bl. 320–1.

145. SSB-MA, SM16-69, p. 1; SAPMO-BA, Vorläufige SED Signatur DY30/17018, untitled report on Exquisit ..., p. 16, Anlagen 10, 11.

146. SSB-MA, SM16-129, unpag.

147. Ibid.

148. SAPMO-BA, Vorläufige SED Signatur DY30/17018, untitled report on Exquisit ..., Anlage 6; SSB-MA, SM16-129, unpag.

149. SSB-MA, SM18-36, unpag.; SAPMO-BA, Vorläufige SED Signatur 38624/1, Versorgung der Bevölkerung mit Exquisiterzeugnissen, VE PHU Exquisit, Schneider, Generaldirektor, Leipzig, 6 September 1972.

150. LAB, C Rep. 900, Nr. IVB-2/6/597, Fiedler, Abt. Handel/ÖVW, SED-BL Berlin, to Haumann, 1. Sekretar der BL, Berlin, 11 August 1971, pp. 1–2.

151. BA-CA, DL102/973, p. 20.

152. BA-DH, DL1/20148, Anlage: Realisierung der Werbeaufgaben im Bereich des Konsumgüterbinnenhandels. Grundsätze, n.d. [1972].

153. BA-CA, DL102/713, pp. 9–10.

154. Ibid., pp. 10–11.

155. Intershops carried only a small quantity of clothing. For short histories of the Intershops and GENEX, a mail-order catalogue through which Westerners used Western currency to purchase East German goods for relatives and friends in the GDR, see Jonathan Zatlin, "Consuming Ideology. Socialist Consumerism and the Intershops, 1970–1989," in *Arbeiter in der SBZ-DDR*, ed. Peter Hübner and Klaus Tenfelde (Essen, 1999), 555–72; Franka Schneider, "'Jedem nach dem Wohnsitz seiner Tante'. Die GENEX Geschenkdienst GmbH," in *Wunderwirtschaft. DDR-Konsumkultur in den 60er Jahren*, ed. Neue Gesellschaft für Bildende Kunst (Cologne, 1996), 223–32.

156. SAPMO-BA, Vorläufige SED Signatur 31976/1 and 31976/2.

157. BA-CA, DL102/973, p. 20.

158. SAPMO-BA, Vorläufige SED Signatur 38624/1, Konzeption zur Entwicklung der Versorgung der Bevölkerung mit Exquisiterzeugnissen im Zeitraum 1986 bis 1990, n.d. [September 1986], p. 1.

159. BA-CA, DL102/1875, p. 11; SAPMO-BA, Vorläufige SED Signatur 38624/1, Konzeption zur Entwicklung der Versorgung ..., pp. 1, 9.

160. Normal stores' relatively modest portion of sales was also due to the growth of special stores for "youth fashion" (*Jugendmode*), which after their establishment in 1967 grew almost as dramatically as the Exquisit stores. Originally intended for the relatively small portion of the population between the ages of thirteen and twenty-five, by 1989 the stores accounted for 35 percent of the unit volume of men's outerwear and almost 30 percent of women's outerwear. Market researchers wryly noted that the stores did not offer "truly 'young fashion'" and over half of their customers "have exceeded the age of youth." BA-CA, DL102/2124, pp. 11–13. On the Youth Fashion Program, see Philipp Heldmann, "Konsumpolitik in der DDR. Jugendmode in den sechziger Jahren," in *Konsumpolitik: Die Regulierung des privaten Verbrauchs im 20. Jahrhundert*, ed. Hartmut Berghoff (Göttingen, 1999), 135–58.

Chapter 7 – Shopping, Sewing, Networking, Complaining: Consumer Practices and the Relationship between State and Society

1. For theoretical discussions of practices and tactics of consumption, see Michel de Certeau, *The Practice of Everyday Life*, trans. Steve F. Rendall (Berkeley, 1984); David Sabean, "Die Produktion von Sinn beim Konsum der Dinge," in *Fahrrad, Auto, Fernsehschrank. Zur Kulturgeschichte der Alltagsdinge*, ed. Wolfgang Ruppert (Frankfurt/Main, 1993), 37–51.

2. Relying heavily on oral interviews conducted in the 1990s, the ethnologist Ina Merkel has sketched many of these "individual strategies of acquisition" primarily in order to examine their "cultural consequences for the lifestyles of individuals" in the GDR. Ina Merkel, *Utopie und Bedürfnis. Die Geschichte der Konsumkultur in der DDR* (Cologne, 1999), 277–300.

3. LAB, C Rep. 106, Nr. 142, Aktenvermerk, Köhler, Planök. Abt., Berlin, 19 March 1949.

4. BA-BL, DL1/3764/1, Bl. 23.

5. LAB, C Rep. 106-01-01, Vorläufige Signatur Nr. T/175, Nickel, IZL Konfektion Berlin, to FR LI, Abt. ÖIH, Magistrat von Groß-Berlin, 4 February 1956, p. 2.

6. SSB-MA, SM5-18, p. 4; BA-BL, DE1/3710, Bl. 118.

7. Inge Kertzscher, "Konfektion mit neuen Maßen," *Neues Deutschland*, 12 December 1959; BA-BL, DE1/30278, Industriezweigökonomik der VVB Konfektion, p. 3/21/2.

8. "Das Modehaus ohne Kundschaft," *Neue Zeit*, 11 November 1956.

9. Elfriede Philipp, "Bekleidung – aber keine Kleider. Ein geheimnisvolles Gremium bestimmt, was die Berlinerin tragen soll," *Die Wirtschaft*, n.d. [1955/1956], unpag., found in LAB, C Rep. 106-01-01, Vorläufige Signatur, Nr. T/176.

10. SäStAC, ZWK TuK, Nr. 157, Frau L. Bieler, Sangerhausen, to *Für Dich*, 8 October 1968; SäStAC, ZWK TuK, Nr. 33, Manfred S. to Kanzlei des Staatsrates der DDR, Judenbach, 23 July 1965.

11. Back cover, *Eulenspiegel* 8 (1961) 7.

12. SAPMO-BA, DY30/IV2/6.09/56, Bl. 23–4; BA-CA, DL102/294, pp. 44–5.

13. "Industriewaren rollen aufs Land," *Der Handel* 6 (1956) 1: 6–7; "Konfektion im abulanten Handel," *Konsumgenossenschafter* 48 (1960): 1.

14. "Mit Barbara im Kaufhaus," *Bauern-Echo*, 25 October 1958.

15. The two mail-order catalogues closed their doors in 1974 and 1976, respectively. Annette Kaminsky, *Kaufrausch. Die Geschichte der ostdeutschen Versandhäuser* (Berlin, 1998).

16. SAMPO-BA, DY30/IV2/6.10/29, Bl. 8.

17. Madelon, "Farbenfroh und schön woll'n unsere Frauen gekleidet geh'n," *Frau*

von heute 8 (1953) 28: 11.

18. SAMPO-BA, DY30/IV2/6.10/29, Bl. 8.

19. Karl-Ernst Schubert and Georg Wittek, "Zur Aufgabenstellung des Mode-schaffens in der Deutschen Demokratischen Republik," *MIfB* 2 (1963) 2: 64; SSB-MA, SM9-2, p. 20.

20. "Unsere aktuelle Umfrage zum Jahreswechsel," *Die Bekleidung* 6 (1958): 26.

21. SAMPO-BA, DY30/IV2/2.029/195, Protokoll der ökonomischen Konferenz der Textil- und Bekleidungsindustrie am 22. und 23. April 1960 in Karl-Marx-Stadt, p. 33/2.

22. BA-CA, DL102/73, p. 49.

23. BA-CA, DL102/357, pp. 31–2.

24. Ibid.

25. LAB, C Rep. 900, IV-2/6/861, Bericht über die Lage im Handel im Stadtbezirk Treptow, SED-KL Treptow, 22 August 1961; BA-DH, DL1/3995, Analyse über die Versorgung der Bevölkerung mit Schuhen und Lederwaren im Jahre 1961, ZWK für Schuhe und Lederwaren des MHV, Leipzig, 17 January 1962, p. 11.

26. LAB, C Rep. 900, Nr. IVB-2/6/597, numerous memos from Schirmer, Abteilungsleiter, Abt. Handel/ÖVW, to Stein and Naumann, BL, Berlin in October 1971.

27. SäStAC, VVB T&S, Nr. 474, Evelin L. to Redaktion *Prisma*, Gersdorf, 17 January 1966.

28. SAPMO-BA, DY30/IVA2/6.10/195, Aus dem Bericht der BL Dresden vom 21.12.1970, p. 9.

29. BA-BL, DE1/24191, Liste der wichtigsten von Bewohnern des DM-DN-Währungsbereiches in West-Berlin gekauften Waren, 19 January 1955; BA-BL, DE1/5446, Bl. 3–4.

30. BA-BL, DE1/24191, Liste …, p. 1.

31. One of several "market observation reports" from 1959 noted that while some East Germans returning from West Berlin hid coffee and chocolates in their pockets, many others did nothing to hide bulging nylon net bags and large shopping bags from the West German department store C&A. BA-BL, DL1/3907, Bl. 9–10. Illegal clothing and shoe purchases in West Berlin were even easier to conceal since the articles could be simply worn while crossing back over the border.

32. BA-BL, DE1/24142, Vermerk über die Beratung der Schuhindustrie am 29.6.1955 in Weißenfels, Hieke, Berlin, 1 July 1955, p. 3; BA-BL, DE1/5446, Bl. 2; SSB-MA, RB1958, Nr. 24, p. 2.

33. SAPMO-BA, DY30/IV2/6.10/156, Bl. 38–40, 93, 100, 125–34.

34. BA-CA, DL102/509, p. 44; BA-CA, DL102/471, 21–2, Anlage 2, p. 2; BA-CA, DL102/516, p. 48. Market researchers found in 1970 that only 22 percent

of store-bought clothing for female youths and 45 percent of store-bought clothing for male youths did not need to be altered before being worn. BA-CA, DL102/475, pp. 24, 69.

35. BA-CA, DL102/471, pp. 21–2.

36. BA-CA, DL102/28, p. 117.

37. BA-CA, DL102/150, p. 46.

38. BA-CA, DL102/484, p. 16.

39. BA-CA, DL102/730, p. 8. A study in 1964 found that the per-capita production of industrially manufactured clothing from 1962 to 1964 accounted for only 20 to 30 percent of women's and 30 to 40 percent of men's average wardrobes. BA-CA, DL102/150, p. 8; Erhard Scholz, "Einige Probleme der Ausstattung mit Herren- und Damenoberbekleidung," *MIFB* 5 (1966) 3: 26.

40. BA-CA, DL102/150, p. 46; Scholz, "Einige Probleme der Ausstattung," 26.

41. BA-BL, DL1/3764/1, Bl. 21; "Eine Modenschau 'FÜR DICH'," *Für Dich* 4 (1949) 47: 7; Lothar Starke, "Gute Maßkonfektion bringt treue Kunden," *Der Handel* 6 (1956) 18: 10.

42. BA-BL, DC20/I/4-184, Bl. 29; SAPMO-BA, DY30/JIV2/2A/866, Bericht über die Durchführung des Beschlusses des Politbüros vom 10 March 1961 über Maßnahmen zur Verbesserung der Leitung, Planung und Organisation auf dem Gebiete der Versorgung der Bevölkerung – Teil Preise und Handelsspannen, n.d., pp. 26–7.

43. SAPMO-BA, DY30/IVA2/6.09/56, Programm für die Entwicklung des Industriezweiges Konfektion in den Jahren von 1964 bis 1970, n.d., p. 23.

44. Scholarship on home dressmaking has begun to complicate the relationship of these two categories but has focused largely on capitalist contexts in the US and Great Britain. See Barbara Burman, ed., *The Culture of Sewing. Gender, Consumption and Home Dressmaking* (Oxford, 1999).

45. A. L., "Mode – ?" *Frau von heute*, 1. Heft Feb. 1946: 23; numerous articles in *Junge Welt* in the 1950s with titles like "Drei Kleider – ein Schnitt" and "Aus eins mach fünf"; "Aus Omas Leinenlaken," *Konsum-Genossenschafter*, 24 August 1963: 6.

46. SäStAC, ZWK TuK, Nr. 157, Herbert H., Freiberg, to Radio DDR, Berlin, K.-Heinz Gärstner, Freiberg, 7 October 1968.

47. BA-CA, DL102/294, p. 38; BA-CA, DL102/357, pp. 6, 8; BA-CA, DL102/438, pp. 39, 54–5; Georg Wittek and Erhard Scholz, "Probleme der Erarbeitung und Umsetzung von Bedarfseinschätzungen," *MIfM* 10 (1971) 4: 15.

48. Jörg Börjesson and Hans-Peter Seliger, "Zur Einzelfertigung von Oberbekleidung," *MIfM* 10 (1971) 4: 27.

49. Ibid.

50. BA-CA, DL102/198, p. 40; BA-CA, DL102/302, p. 31; BA-CA, DL102/512, p. 8.

51. BA-CA, DL102/754, p. 10.

52. Ruth Weichsel, "Individuell geschneiderte Oberbekleidung – Luxus, Hobby oder 'Notlösung'?" *MIfM* 15 (1976) 1: 13–16; Ruth Weichsel, "Die Einzelanfertigung von Bekleidung – ein Maßstab des Versorgungseffekts," *MIfM* 23 (1984) 1: 26–8.

53. Among the magazines that published paper patterns were *Frau von heute*, *Für Dich*, *Praktische Mode* (later *PRAMO*), *Flotte Kleidung*, *Die neue Mode*, *Modische Modelle*, *Saison*, and *Modische Maschen*. The Publisher for Women (Verlag für die Frau) offered "a few million cuts from around 2,000 models" in 1958. Inge Kertzscher, "Wir blättern in Modeheften," *Neues Deutschland*, 11 January 1958, Beilage.

54. "Sie näht am liebsten alles selbst," *Frau von heute* 12 (1957) 5: 5–6; "Hübsche Kleider sind kein Wunschtraum mehr," *Frau von heute* 4 (1949) 22: 31; *Die Handarbeit* 1/1968 and 4/1968: 34; Börjesson and Seliger, "Zur Einzelfertigung von Oberbekleidung," 25.

55. "Wir schneidern selbst," *Frau von heute* 11 (1956) 20: 17; "Selbst Geschneidert Selbst Vorgeführt," *Frau von heute* 12 (1957) 48: 16–17.

56. SäStAC, ZWK TuK, Nr. 5, Abschrift eines Leserbriefes von Frau Karla R., Mitglied der ehrenamtlichen Frauenredaktion und stellvertretende Kreisvorsitzende des DFD in Halle, n.d [1964].

57. BA-CA, DL102/294, p. 46. Moreover, the fact that knitting was relatively unpopular among the elderly, researchers argued, suggested that it was not a "good old tradition" to the extent that many had assumed. BA-CA, DL102/357, p. 8.

58. Annelies Glaner, "Das Kleid dort auf der Stange ...," *BZ am Abend*, 15 May 1968.

59. Susanne Kluge, "Wie modern muss die Mode sein?" *Für Dich* 23 (1968) 29: 13.

60. One-third of "very strong women" had all their apparel professionally tailored. BA-CA, DL102/471, pp. 24–9.

61. BA-CA, DL102/578, pp. 45, 47.

62. BA-CA, DL102/171, p. 7; BA-CA, DL102/471, p. 29.

63. BA-CA, DL102/357, pp. 9, 13.

64. BA-CA, DL102/419, pp. 44, 46; BA-CA, DL102/471, pp. 61–3.

65. BA-CA, DL102/512, pp. 5, 6, Anlage 9.

66. BA-CA, DL102/196, p. 140; BA-CA, DL102/45, pp. 25, 27.

67. On networks in general, see Martin Diewald, "'Kollektiv', 'Vitamin B' oder 'Nische'? Persönliche Netzwerke in der DDR," in *Kollektiv und Eigensinn. Lebensverläufe in der DDR und danach*, ed. Johannes Huinink et al. (Berlin, 1995), 223–60.

68. For a suggestive but problematic use of oral history as a source on informal networks, see Merkel, *Utopie und Bedürfnis*, 293–6.

69. Gertrud Krause, "Oma Krauses Start ins Glück," *Frankfurter Rundschau*, 30 June 1990 [letter from 15 July 1962], quoted in *Das gespaltene Land*, 37.

70. Merkel, *Utopie und Bedürfnis*, 293–6.

71. "Das Modehaus ohne Kundschaft," *Neue Zeit*, 11 November 1956; SäStAL, BL Leipzig, IV/2/2/127, Bl. 27, 74.

72. The "gray market" resulted from the practice during the early postwar years of paying workers at least partly in kind from the products of the factory in which they worked.

73. Christian Härtel and Petra Kabus, eds, *Das Westpaket. Geschenksendung, keine Handelsware* (Berlin, 2000).

74. BA-CA, DL102/294, p. 47.

75. BA-CA, DL102/198, pp. 40–1; BA-CA, DL102/323, pp. 36–7, 49, 69.

76. BA-CA, DL102/294, pp. 47–9; BA-CA, DL102/198, p. 41.

77. Compiled from reports in BA-CA, DL102/Karton 244/VA247 and VA248.

78. Unfortunately the current underdeveloped state of empirical research does not provide much concrete evidence to support these hypotheses. Market researchers almost never asked direct questions about the acquisition or use of Western clothing because they anticipated incomplete or dishonest answers. BA-CA, DL102/198, pp. 16, 23; BA-CA, DL102/294, p. 47.

79. Top party leaders, however, enjoyed access to Western goods through other channels.

80. Jonathan Zatlin, "Ausgaben und Eingaben. Das Petitionsrecht und der Untergang der DDR," *Zeitschrift für Geschichtswissenschaft* 45 (1997): 902–17.

81. Katherine Pence has examined this relationship by analyzing letters written by women to Elli Schmidt, the only woman Politburo member before the June 1953 uprising. While the petitions examined below evince many of the same rhetorical strategies found by Pence, gender plays a more explicit role in her analysis, perhaps in part due her focus on Schmidt's role as both a woman and "a bridge" between state and populace. Katherine Pence, "'You as a Woman Will Understand': Consumption, Gender and the Relationship between State and Citizenry in the GDR's Crisis of 17 June 1953," *German History* 19 (2001): 218–52.

82. SäStAC, ZWK TuK, Nr. 124, Magda G. to *Prisma*, Fürstenwalde, 25 April 1967.

83. SAPMO-BA, DY34/24904, Präsidiumsinformation und Schlußfolgerungen zu Fragen der Versorgung der Bevölkerung entsprechend dem Präsidiums-beschluß vom 22.7.1966, Rösel, Mitgl. d. Präsidiums, Kupke, Stellv. d. Vors. des ZV Handel/Nahrung/Genuß, Abt. Arbeiterversorgung/Arbeiterkontrolle,

Berlin, 1 August 1966, p. 1; SäStAC, ZWK TuK, Nr. 199, Charlotte P. to Bundesvorstand des DFD, Antragskommission des 2. Frauenkongresses, Berlin, Strausberg, 7 May 1969.

84. SäStAC, ZWK TuK, Nr. 124, Ernst S. to Redaktion des *Neuen Deutschland*, Leserbriefredaktion, Lohmen, 24 April 1967.

85. BA-CA, DE4/29248, Margarete L. to Deutscher Fernsehfunk, Redaktion *Prisma*, Eisenach, 25 June 1964.

86. SäStAC, ZWK TuK, Nr. 156, Gertraude L. to MHV, KMSt, 25 April 1968.

87. SäStAC, ZWK TuK, Nr. 32, Ilse G. to Deutscher Fernsehfunk Berlin – *Prisma*, Brandis, 11 June 1965.

88. "Modische Stoffe in Sicht," *Sibylle* 5 (1957): 66.

89. SAPMO-BA, DY30/IV2/1.01/245, Bl. 92–3.

90. Katherina Schulze, "Ich kann mir nicht helfen," *Eulenspiegel* 14 (1967) 38: 1.

91. *Eulenspiegel* 6 (1959) 48: 9; *Konsum-Genossenschafter* 1 (1964): 8; *Handelswoche*, 20 October 1964: 5; *Eulenspiegel* 15 (1968) 46: 9.

92. Madelon, "Farbenfroh und schön," 11.

93. SäStAC, ZWK TuK, Nr. 292, Heinz M. to Karl-Heinz Gerstner, Deutscher Fernsehfunk, Wilthen, 30 July 1971.

94. W. Effmert, "Minimode für Omas," *Handelswoche*, 23 May 1968: 11.

95. SäStAC, VVB T&S, Nr. 474, Evelin L. to Redaktion *Prisma*, Gersdorf, 17 January 1966.

96. SäStAC, VVB T&S, Nr. 109, Ilse H. to MfL, VVB Textilindustrie, Berlin-Altglienicke, 12 April 1967; SäStAC, ZWK TuK, Nr. 124, Barth, Abt.-Leiter, Abt. Leserbriefe, Wochenpost, Berliner Verlag, to GHD TuK, Abt. Staatl. Güteinsprektion, KMSt, 2 June 1967.

97. BA-CA, DE4/3000, E. Falk to Walter Ulbricht, Auerbach, 17 December 1961.

98. SäStAC, ZWK TuK, Nr. 199, Elsa F., VEB Wäscherei-Färberei-Chem. Reinigung, Görlitz, n.d.

99. SäStAC, ZWK TuK, Nr. 124, Gerlinde Hantke to K.-Heinz Gerstner, Prisma, Geithain, 13 June 1967.

100. SäStAC, ZWK TuK, Nr. 32, Christine S., Döbeln, Döbeln, 23 June 1965.

101. SäStAC, ZWK TuK, Nr. 33, Manfred Streng to Kanzlei des Staatsrates der DDR, Berlin, Judenbach, 23 July 1965.

102. SäStAC, ZWK TuK, Nr. 32, Christine S., Döbeln, 23 June 1965.

103. John Stave, "Vorsicht: Liebesgaben!" *Eulenspiegel* 8 (1961) 51: 8–9; Ina Dietzsch, "Deutsch-deutscher Gabentausch," in *Wunderwirtschaft. DDR-Konsumkultur in den 60er Jahren*, ed. Neue Gesellschaft für Bildende Kunst e.V. (Cologne, 1996), 204–13.

104. This reluctance also may have resulted in part from the difficulty of finding

appropriate reciprocal gifts. Dietzsch, "Deutsch-deutscher Gabentisch," 211–13.

105. SäStAC, ZWK TuK, Nr. 32, Siegrun J. to Redaktion Sibylle, Saalfeld, 11 May 1965.

106. SäStAC, ZWK TuK, Nr. 250, Gerlinde M. to MHV, Kostebrau, 9 December 70.

107. Ina Merkel and Felix Mühlberg, "Eingaben und Öffentlichkeit," in *"Wir sind doch nicht die Meckerecke der Nation." Briefe an das DDR-Fernsehen*, ed. Ina Merkel (Cologne, 1998), 17.

108. "Modelle stehen zur Diskussion," *Konsum-Verkaufsstelle* 13 (1954): 5; "Sie hatten die Wahl," *Sibylle* 4 (1959) 5: 10.

109. My interpretation combines aspects of the perspectives of Ina Merkel, who enthusiastically but often uncritically celebrates East German consumers' agency and ingenuity, and Jonathan Zatlin, who stresses the regime's attempts to use petitions as an instrument of domination and suppression of discontent. Merkel, ed., *"Wir sind doch nicht die Meckerecke der Nation"*; Zatlin, "Ausgaben und Eingaben."

110. SäStAC, ZWK TuK, Nr. 124, Gerlinde H. to K.-Heinz Gerstner, *Prisma*, Geithain, 13 June 1967; SäStAC, VVB T&S, Nr. 2177, Barbara J. to VVB T&S, Limbach-Oberfrohna, Halle, 28 July 1964.

111. "Frau Frieda Uszakiewicz aus Zepernick fragt," *Die Bekleidung* 5 (1958) 1: 3; "Sibylle schlägt vor: Arbeitsschutzbekleidung für die Bitterfelder Frauen," *Sibylle* 12 (1967) 2: 61–9; SäStAC, VVB T&S, Nr. 109, various correspondence.

112. SäStAC, ZWK TuK, Nr. 5, Dressel, Hauptdirektor, to Gitschel, 23 December 1964; SäStAC, ZWK TuK, Nr. 33, Polzin, Fachdirektor, FD Meterware/Raumtextilien, to Sekretariat, Hauptdirektor, Eingabe der Bürgerin Marie F., KMSt, 22 November 1965.

113. SäStAC, VVB T&S, Nr. 2177, Hochmut, Abt. Absatz, to Zeitschrift "für dich", 10 December 1963; SäStAC, VVB T&S, Nr. 109, numerous letters from Teucher and Emmrich, general directors of the VVB Trikotagen und Strümpfe, in 1964 and 1967.

114. SäStAC, ZWK TuK, Nr. 249, Kurt A. to MHV, Frankfurt/Oder, 15 April 1970, p. 3.

115. SäStAC, ZWK TuK, Nr. 5, Rudi G. to MHV, Berlin, Merseburg-Süd, 3 December 1964.

116. SäStAC, ZWK TuK, Nr. 250, Fritz M. to Gerstner, Liebstadt, 5 November 1970.

117. SäStAC, RdB KMSt, Abt. HuV, Nr. 19423, Herbert D. to Löffler, Stellvertreter des Vorsitzenden des RdB für HuV, KMSt, 10 April 1963; SäStAC, ZWK TuK, Nr. 156, W. Eggert, Berlin-Oberschöneweide, to Hauptdirektor Dressel, GH Direktion TuK, KMSt, 5 February 1968.

118. SäStAC, ZWK TuK, Nr. 250, Margarete H. to Karl-Heinz Gerstner, *Prisma*, Cunewalde, 22 November 1970.

119. LAB, C Rep. 900, IVA-2/9.01/490, 1. Entwurf zur Einschätzung des Bewußtseins der Berliner Bevölkerung, Berlin, 11 January 1967, pp. 9–10.

120. SäStAC, VVB T&S, Nr. 109, Ilse H. to MfL, VVB Textilidnustrie, Berlin-Altglienicke, 12 April 1967.

121. SäStAC, ZWK TuK, Nr. 124, Barth to GHD TuK ...

122. SäStAC, ZWK TuK, Nr. 124, M. Fischer, Neustadt/Orla, to GDH TuK, Generaldirektor, KMSt, n.d.

123. SäStAC, ZWK TuK, Nr. 157, Renate M. to Deutscher Fernsehfunk, *Prisma*, Anklam, 16 August 1968.

124. SAPMO-BA, DY30/IVA2/6.09/139, Günter N., Modehaus Güni-Tuche to Günther Mittag, Berlin, Gauchau, 21 June 1968, unpag.

125. SäStAC, ZWK TuK, Nr. 124, Ernst S. to Redaktion des *Neuen Deutschland*

126. SAPMO-BA, DY30/IVA2/6.10/200, Analyse über die Arbeit mit den Eingaben im Verantwortungsbereich des MHV im 1. Halbjahr 1968, n.d. [9 September 1968], p. 2.

127. SäStAC, VVB T&S, Nr. 2177, Hensel, Abt. Leserbriefe, "für dich", to VVB T&S, 28 November 1963.

128. SäStAC, ZWK TuK, Nr. 124, Magda G., Fürtstenwalde/Spree, to *Prisma*, Fürstenwalde, 25 April 1967.

129. SäStAL, SED-BL Leipzig, IVA-2/6/285, Zusammenfassung der Informationsberichte der KL Döbeln, Borna und Wurzen und einiger Stadtbezirksleitungen Leipzig zur Versorgungslage per 30.7.1965, SED-BL Leipzig, Abt. LLI/Handel, Leipzig, 12 August 1965, p. 5.

Epilogue

1. Michael Ignatieff, *The Needs of Strangers* (New York, 1985), 127–8.

2. The extremely outdated technology and deteriorated physical capital of the East German textile and garment industries, which had received very little investment since the early 1970s, contributed to the branch's particularly harsh and virtually complete collapse after 1990. Christian Heimann, *Systembedingte Ursachen des Niedergangs der DDR-Wirtschaft. Das Beispiel der Textil- und Bekleidungsindustrie 1945–1989* (Frankfurt/Main, 1997), 1, 350–3.

3. Andreas Ludwig, "Objektkultur und DDR-Gesellschaft. Aspekte einer Wahrnehmung des Alltags," *Aus Politik und Zeitgeschichte* B 27/1999: 3–11; Charity Scribner, "Eastern Time: The Race to Curate the Communist Past in Germany," *Documents* 13 (Fall 1998): 8–25. Among the myriad nostalgic books about East German material culture are Rudolf Kurz, Tobias Strengel

and Fabian Tweder, *Vita-Cola und Timms Saurer. Getränkesaison in der DDR* (Berlin, 1999); Jörg Engelhardt, *Schwalbe, Duo, Kultmobil. Vom Acker auf den Boulevard* (Berlin, 1995).

4. For recent discussions of *Ostalgie*, see Paul Betts, "Remembrance of Things Past: Nostalgia in West and East Germany, 1980–2000," in *Pain and Prosperity: Reconsidering Twentieth-Century German History*, ed. Paul Betts and Greg Eghigian (Stanford, 2003), 178–208; several articles in *Deutschland Archiv* 36 (2003) 6; Rainer Gries, *Produkte als Medien. Kulturgeschichte der Produktkommunikation in der Bundesrepublik und der DDR* (Leipzig, 2003), 11–51.

5. Gunilla-Friederike Budde, ed., *Frauen arbeiten. Weibliche Erwerbstätigkeit in Ost- und Westdeutschland nach 1945* (Göttingen, 1997); Rachel Alsop, *A Reversal of Fortunes? Women, Work, and Change in East Germany* (New York, 2000).

Abbreviations

ABB	Arbeits- und Berufsbekleidung
ABI	Arbeiter-und-Bauern-Inspektion
Abt.	Abteilung
BA-BL	Bundesarchiv, Berlin-Lichterfelde
BA-CA	Bundesarchiv, Außenstelle Coswig/Anhalt
BA-DH	Bundesarchiv, Außenstelle Dahlwitz-Hoppegarten
BA-FA	Bundesarchiv, Filmarchiv
BL	Bezirksleitung
BStB	Betrieb mit staatlicher Beteiligung
BT	Bezirkstag
BWR	Bezirkswirtschaftsrat
DAMW	Deutsches Amt für Material- und Warenprüfung
	Deutsches Amt für Meßwesen und Warenprüfung
DDR	Deutsche Demokratische Republik
DEFA	Deutsche Film-Aktiengesellschaft
DEWAG	Deutsche Werbe- und Anzeigengesellschaft
DFD	Demokratischer Frauenbund Deutschlands
DFF	Deutscher Fernsehfunk
DIA Textil	Deutscher Innen- und Außenhandel Textil
DM	Deutsche Mark
DMI	Deutsches Modeinstitut
DOB	Damenoberbekleidung
DWK	Deutsche Wirtschaftskommission
EVP	Einzelhandelsverkaufspreis
FA	Fachabteilung
FDJ	Freie Deutsche Jugend
FG	Fachgruppe
FRG	Federal Republic of Germany
GDR	German Democratic Republic

GHD	Großhandelsdirektion
GO	Grundorganisation
HA	Hauptabteilung
HO	Handelsorganisation
HOB	Herrenoberbekleidung
HuV	Handel und Versorgung
HV	Hauptverwaltung
HVuA	Handel, Versorgung und Außenhandel
IBK	Institut für Bekleidungskultur
IfB	Institut für Bedarfsforschung
IfM	Institut für Marktforschung
IZL	Industriezweigleitung
KG	Konsumgenossenschaft
KL	Kreisleitung
KMSt	Karl-Marx-Stadt
KOB	Kinderoberbekleidung
KoKo	Bereich Kommerzielle Koordinierung im Ministerium für Außenhandel
LAB	Landesarchiv Berlin
LI	Leichtindustrie
LLBI	Leicht-, Lebensmittel- und bezirksgeleitete Industrie
LLI	Leicht- und Lebensmittelindustrie
LLÖI	Leicht-, Lebensmittel- und örtlichgeleitete Industrie
LPG	Landwirtschaftliche Produktionsgenossenschaft
MdF	Ministerium der Finanzen
MfL	Ministerium für Leichtindustrie
MIfB	*Mitteilungen des Instituts für Bedarfsforschung*
MIfM	*Mitteilungen des Instituts für Marktforschung*
MHV	Ministerium für Handel und Versorgung
MDN	Mark der Deutschen Notenbank
MR	Ministerrat der DDR
NÖS(PL)	Neues Ökonomisches System (der Planung und Leitung der Volkwirtschaft)
OB	Oberbürgermeister
ÖIH	Örtliche Industrie und Handwerk
ÖSS	Ökonomisches System des Sozialismus
OT	Obertrikotagen
ÖVW	Örtliche Versorgungswirtschaft
PB	Politbüro des Zentralkomitees der SED
PGH	Produktionsgenossenschaft des Handwerks
PuF	Planung und Finanzen

RdB	Rat des Bezirkes
RdK	Rat des Kreises
Ref.	Referat
RGW	Rat für gegenseitige Wirtschaftshilfe
SAG	Ständige Arbeitsgruppe
SAPMO-BA	Stiftung Archiv der Parteien und Massenorganisationen der DDR im Bundesarchiv
SäStAC	Sächsisches Staatsarchiv Chemnitz
SäStAL	Sächsisches Staatsarchiv Leipzig
SBZ	Sowjetische Besatzungszone
SED	Sozialistische Einheitspartei Deutschlands
SPK	Staatliche Plankommission
SSB-MA	Stiftung Stadtmuseum Berlin, Modeabteilung – Modearchiv
SZS	Staatliche Zentralverwaltung für Statistik
TeBeLe	Textil-Bekleidung-Leder
T&S	Trikotagen und Strümpfe
TuK	Textil- und Kurzwaren
UT	Untertrikotagen
VDK	Verband Deutscher Konsumgenossenschaften
VdK	Verband der Konsumgenossenschaften, e.G., Berlin
VEB	Volkseigener Betrieb
VVB	Vereinigung Volkseigener Betriebe
VWR	Volkswirtschaftsrat
ZK	Zentralkomitee der SED
ZKK	Zentrale Kommission für Staatliche Kontrolle beim Ministerrat
ZV	Zentralvorstand
ZWK	Zentrales Warenkontor

Select Bibliography

Archival Sources

Note: Although some of the following records have been transferred from the locations at which I originally consulted them (listed below) to other facilities within the same archive, their call numbers remain the same.

Bundesarchiv, Abteilungen Berlin, Berlin-Lichterfelde (BA-BL)
DC20-I/3 Sitzungen des Ministerrates
DC20-I/4 Sitzungen des Präsidiums des Ministerrates
DE1 Staatliche Plankommission
DG4 Ministerium für Leichtindustrie
DL1 Ministerium für Handel und Versorgung

Bundesarchiv, Abteilungen Berlin, Außenstelle Coswig/Anhalt (BA-CA)
DE4 Volkswirtschaftsrat
DE1 Staatliche Plankommission
DL102 Institut für Bedarfsforschung/Institut für Marktforschung

Bundesarchiv, Abteilungen Berlin, Außenstelle Dahlwitz-Hoppegarten (BA-DH)
DL1 Ministerium für Handel und Versorgung

Bundesarchiv, Filmarchiv, Berlin (BA-FA)
Modell Bianka. Richard Groschopp, dir. Erich Conradi, sw. DEFA, 1951.
DEFA-Wochenschauen *Der Augenzeuge*

Landesarchiv Berlin, Breitestraße (LAB)
C Rep. 106 Magistrat von Berlin, Abt. Wirtschaft
C Rep. 106-01 Magistrat von Berlin, Abt. Örtliche Industrie und Handwerk

C Rep. 106-01-01 Magistrat von Berlin, Abt. Industrieverwaltungen [unprocessed, provisional file numbers (vorläufige Signaturen)]
C Rep. 113 Magistrat von Berlin, Abt. Handel und Versorgung
C Rep. 470-01 VEB Damenoberbekleidung "Fortschritt"
C Rep. 470-02 VEB Herrenbekleidung "Fortschritt"
C Rep. 625 VVB Konfektion

Landesarchiv Berlin, Kalkreuthstraße (LAB)
C Rep. 900, IV-2/6 (including IVA-2/6 and IVB-2/6) and IV-2/9.01 SED-Bezirksleitung Berlin, Abt. Wirtschaftspolitik
C Rep. 900, IV/4/01, SED-Kreisleitung Friedrichshain
C Rep. 900, IV/4/04, SED-Kreisleitung Mitte
C Rep. 900, IV/4/06, SED-Kreisleitung Prenzlauer Berg
C Rep. 900, IV/4/07, SED-Kreisleitung Treptow
C Rep. 900, IV/4/14, SED-Kreisleitung SPK/VWR
C Rep. 900, IV/7/001 Grundorganisation VVB Konfektion
C Rep. 900, IV/7/128 Grundorganisation VE Kombinat Oberbekleidung, Betrieb "Treffmodelle"/Damenbekleidung
C Rep. 910 FDGB, Bezirksvorstand Berlin IG Textil-Bekleidung-Leder

Sächsisches Staatsarchiv Chemnitz (SäStAC)
Rat des Bezirkes Karl-Marx-Stadt, Bezirksverwaltung der HO-Kreisbetriebe Karl-Marx-Stadt
Rat des Bezirkes Karl-Marx-Stadt, Wirtschaftsrat
Rat des Bezirkes Karl-Marx-Stadt, Wirtschaftsrat, Abt. Handel und Versorgung
Rat des Bezirkes Karl-Marx-Stadt, Wirtschaftsrat, Abt. Textil-Bekleidung-Leder
SED-Bezirksleitung Karl-Marx-Stadt
SED-Kreisleitung Auerbach
SED-Kreisleitung Glauchau
SED-Kreisleitung Karl-Marx-Stadt/Land
VVB Trikotagen und Strümpfe, Karl-Marx-Stadt
Zentrales Warenkontor Textil- und Kurzwaren, Karl-Marx-Stadt

Sächsisches Staatsarchiv Leipzig (SäStAL)
Bezirkstag und Rat des Bezirkes Leipzig, Abt. Handel und Versorgung
Bezirkstag und Rat des Bezirkes Leipzig, Abt. Textil-Bekleidung-Leder
CENTRUM-Versandhaus Leipzig
Lucie Kaiser, Kleiderfabrik und Modeatelier, Altenburg
SED-Bezirksleitung Leipzig

Stiftung Archiv der Parteien und Massenorganisationen der DDR im Bundesarchiv (SAPMO-BA)
DY30/IV2/1 Tagungen des ZK
DY30/IV2/1.01 SED Konferenzen und Beratungen des Parteivorstandes
DY30/IV2/2 and DY30/JIV2/2 Protokolle der Sitzungen des Politbüros
DY30/JIV2/2A Arbeitsprotokolle der Sitzungen des Politbüros
DY30/JIV2/2.02 Büro Walter Ulbricht
DY30/IVA2/2.021 Büro Günter Mittag
DY30/IV2/2.029 Büro Erich Apel und Wirtschaftskommission beim Politbüro des ZK
DY30/IV2/2.101 Wirtschaftskommission beim Politbüro des ZK
DY30/IV2/6.02 Abt. Wirtschaftspolitik des ZK
DY30/IV2/6.07 Abt. Forschung und technische Entwicklung des ZK
DY30/IV2/6.09 Teilbestand Leicht- und Lebensmittel Industrie des ZK
DY30/IVA2/6.09 Teilbestand Leicht-, Lebensmittel- und bezirksgeleitete Industrie des ZK
DY30/IV2/6.10 and DY30/IVA2/6.10 Teilbestand Handel, Versorgung und Außenhandel des ZK
DY30/IV2/17 Teilbestand Frauen
DY31 Demokratischer Frauenbund Deutschlands
DY34 Freier Deutscher Gewerkschaftsbund, Abt. Sozialpolitik
DY49/16 Freier Deutscher Gewerkschaftsbund, Abt. Textil-Bekleidung-Leder
NY4090 Nachlaß Otto Grotewohl
NY4182 Nachlaß Walter Ulbricht
NY4215 Nachlaß Fred Oelßner
vorläufige SED Signaturen

Stiftung Stadtmuseum Berlin, Modeabteilung – Modearchiv (SSB-MA)
AD Diplomarbeiten und Hausarbeiten
G Geschäftsberichte
ML Modelinien
RB Reiseberichte
RGW Grundsatzausarbeitungen und Referate
SM Schriftensammlungen
Verträge und Vereinbargungen von 1961 bis 1968
Zeitungsausschnitte-Ordner
Zeitungsausschnitte 1953–1972
Zeitungsausschnitte und Broschüren: IBK, DMI, Modeinstitut der DDR, 1962, 1967, 1972, 1977, 1982

Archiv des Verbands der Konsumgenossenschaften, e.G., Berlin (VdK) (now Konsumverband e.G.)

Beschlußprotokolle und Beschlußvorlagen der Sitzungen des Vorstandes des VDK

Fotos von Konsum-Schaufenstern

Fotos von der Leipziger Messe

Periodicals and Newspapers

Bauern-Echo

Die Bekleidung

Bekleidung und Maschenware

Die Bekleidungsindustrie

Berliner Zeitung

Beschlüsse-Anweisungen-Informationen des Verbandes Deutscher Konsumgenossenschaften

BZ am Abend

Deutsche Schuh und Leder Zeitschrift

Deutsche Textiltechnik

Eulenspiegel

Flotte Kleidung

Gesetzblatt der Deutschen Demokratischen Republik

Die Frau von heute

Freie Welt

Für Dich

Guter Rat

Der Handel

Handelswoche

Junge Welt

Konsum-Genossenschafter

Konsum-Verkaufsstelle

Lausitzer Rundschau

Das Magazin

Ministerialblatt der Deutschen Demokratischen Republik

Mitteilungen des Instituts für Bedarfsforschung

Mitteilungen des Instituts für Marktforschung

Die Mode

Modenschau

Mode-Informationsdienst

National-Zeitung

Neue Berliner Illustrierte

Die neue Mode

Neues Deutschland
Neues Leben
Neue Zeit
Norddeutsche Neueste Nachrichten
Märkische Volksstimme
Praktische Mode (PRAMO)
Presse-Informationen
Sächsisches Tageblatt
Sächsische Zeitung
Saison
Sibylle
Sonntag
Das Volk
Die Wirtschaft

Published Primary Sources

80 Modelle für junge Mädchen. Jugendweihe Schule, Beruf, Sport, festliche Stunden. Leipzig; Berlin: Verlag für die Frau, 1959.
Adam, Eberhard and Horst Tzschoppe. *Stellung, Bedeutung und Entwicklung der Textilindustrie im Rahmen der Volkswirtschaft der DDR.* Leipzig: Fachbuchverlag, 1962.
Die aktuelle Mode. Berlin; Leipzig: Universalverlag, 1947.
Albrecht, Annelies, Hans Dietrich, and Esther Matterne. *Organisation und Methoden der Bedarfsforschung.* Berlin, 1960.
Albrecht, Annelies, Hans Dietrich, and Werner Schilling. *Werbung auf dem Konsumgüterbinnenmarkt.* Berlin: Die Wirtschaft, 1964.
Autorenkollektiv. *Theorie und Praxis der neuen Planmethodik in Textil- und Bekleidungsbetrieben.* Leipzig: Fachbuchverlag, 1962.
Baier, Otto. *Textilwarenkunde für den Verkäufer.* Leipzig: Fachbuchverlag, 1953.
_____. *Umgang mit Textilwaren. Arbeitsanleitung für Einkäufer, Verkaufsstellenleiter und Verkaufskräfte im Textilhandel.* Leipzig: Fachbuchverlag, 1958.
Bergmann, Helmut and Wilfried Lange. *Die Vorbereitung der Produktion in der Textilindustrie.* Berlin: Die Wirtschaft, 1960.
Beschluß der Textilkonferenz des Zentralkomitees der SED, Abteilung Leicht-, Lebensmittel- und örtliche Industrie und der Staatl. Plankommission, Abteilung Leichtindustrie, vom 15. April 1959 zur Lösung der ökonomischen Hauptaufgabe bis 1961 und der Aufgaben im Siebenjahrplan. n.p., n.d.
Bischoff, Bernd. "Die Herausbildung des sozialistischen Verbrauchsverhaltens der Menschen als Bestandteil der sozialistischen Lebensweise sowie auf der Grundlage sozialer Verhaltensnormen und der Beitrag des Konsum-

güterbinnenhandels zur Entwicklung des Verbrauchsverhaltens der Menschen." Dissertation, Handelshochschule Leipzig, 1973.

Borodin, W.A. and T.B. Poljak. *Organisation und Planung in Textilbetrieben.* Berlin: Die Wirtschaft, 1956.

Dänhardt, Reimar. *Fein oder nicht fein. Eine Plauderei über den guten Ton.* Berlin: Deutscher Militärverlag, 1968.

Döbler, Martin. *Triebkraft Bedürfnis. Zur Entwicklung der Bedürfnisse der sozialistischer Persönlichkeit.* Berlin: Dietz, 1969.

Döring, Manfred. "Das Konsumentenverhalten bei hochwertigen und langlebigen Konsumgütern in der Deutschen Demokratischen Republik und Schluß-folgerungen für die perspektivische Entwicklung des sozialistischen Konsumentenverhaltens." Dissertation, Wirtschaftswissenschaften, Hochschule für Ökonomie Berlin, 1971.

Dokumente der Sozialistischen Einheitspartei Deutschlands. Beschlüsse und Erklärungen des Parteivorstandes, des Zentralkomitees sowie seines Politbüros und seines Sekretariats. 12 vols. Berlin: Dietz, 1948–74.

Eilhauer, Hans-Dieter and Ursula Altenburg. *Mode zwischen Bedürfnis und Konsumtion. Komplexe Produktionsvorbereitung modeabhängiger Erzeugnisse der Schuhe- und Bekleidungsindustrie.* Leipzig: Fachbuchverlag, 1981.

Erhard, Ludwig. *Wohlstand für alle.* Düsseldorf: Econ-Verlag, 1956.

Fabiunke, Hannelore, Herbert Fischer, Joachim Jäger, and Willi Köppert. *Handbuch der Konsumentenbefragung.* Berlin: Die Wirtschaft, 1972.

Fehlig, Ursula. *Mode gestern und heute: ein kulturgeschichtlicher Abriß.* Leipzig: Fachbuchverlag, 1985.

Fischer, Herbert and Willi Köppert, *Konsumentenbefragung in der sozialistischen Marktforschung.* Berlin: Die Wirtschaft, 1967.

Friedrich, W. and G. Kolbe. *Otto, benimm dich!* Berlin, 1957.

Fröbel, Wolfgang and Karl-Ernst Schubert. "Mode und Gemeinschaftsarbeit." In *Presse-Informationen,* 23 November 1962: 8.

Giewald, Roger, Kurt Wolf, Klaus Meinhardt, and Kurt Schille. *Zu Fragen der Standardisierung in der Textilindustrie.* Leipzig: Fachbuchverlag, 1962.

Haustein, Heinz-Dieter, Günter Kuciak, Horst Model, and Helmut Richter. *Konsumgüterproduktion — grundlegende Ziele, aktuelle Aufgaben.* Berlin: Die Wirtschaft, 1974.

Heinitz, Günther. *Messung und Analyse der Arbeitsproduktivität in Textilbetrieben.* Leipzig: Fachbuchverlag, 1962.

Institut für Marktforschung, *Grundsätze über die Durchführung der Bedarfs-forschung im Wirtschaftszweig Binnenhandel.* Leipzig, 1971.

Institut für Ökonomie der Textilindustrie der Technischen Hochschule Dresden, ed. *Wege zur Steigerung der Arbeitsproduktivität in der Textilindustrie. Referate und Diskussionsbeiträge vom Internationalen Kolloquium des Instituts für*

Ökonomie der Textilindustrie der Technischen Hochschule, Dresden, am 24. und 25. September 1959. Berlin: Die Wirtschaft, 1960.

Institut für Werbemethodik, ed. *Grundzüge der sozialistischen Werbung in der DDR.* Berlin, 1960.

Junge Mode. Sibylle-Sonderheft. Leipzig; Berlin: Verlag für die Frau, n.d. [1973].

Kelm, Martin. *Produktgestaltung im Sozialismus.* Berlin: Dietz, 1971.

Der kleine Werbeberater. Berlin, 1965.

Kleinschmidt, Karl. *Keine Angst vor guten Sitten. Ein Buch über die Art miteinander umzugehen.* Berlin: Das Neue Berlin, 1957.

Manz, Gerhard. *Was darf es sein? Was Du vom Handel wissen solltest!* Berlin: Die Wirtschaft, 1959.

Ministerium für Arbeit und Berufsausbildung, ed. *Textil-Bekleidung-Leder Kleiderstoff- und Buntweber.* Berlin: Volk und Wissen, 1954.

Ministerium für Handel und Versorgung, ed. *Konsumgüterpreise in Industrie und Handel.* Berlin: Die Wirtschaft, 1966.

[Modeinstitut der DDR, ed.] *25 Jahre Modeinstitut der DDR.* n.p., n.d. [Berlin, 1977].

Model, Horst. *Der Absatz der sozialistischen Industriebetriebe – Aufgaben, Methoden, Organisation.* Berlin: Dietz, 1973.

Müller, Eugen. "Vom Schneiderhandwerk zur Bekleidungsindustrie." In *Maße und Formen. Vom Schneiderhandwerk zur Bekleidungsindustrie,* 22–32. Leipzig: Fachbuchverlag, 1955.

Müller, Kay and Hans-Werner Teige. *Die Rechte der Käufer. Qualitätsmängel, Reklamationsfristen, Nachbesserung oder Kaufpreiserstattung, Garantie und vieles mehr.* Berlin: Die Wirtschaft, 1967.

Naupert, Alfred. *Textile Faserstoffe.* Leipzig: Fachbuchverlag, 1963.

Oheim, Gertrud. *Einmaleins des guten Tons.* Gütersloh: C. Bertelsmann, 1955.

Ökonomische Konferenz der Textil- und Bekleidungsindustrie. Veranstalter: Abteilung Textil/Bekleidung/Leder der Staatlichen Plankommission am 22. und 23. April 1960 in Karl-Marx-Stadt. Protokoll. Berlin: Die Wirtschaft, 1960.

Paproth, Adelheid. "Bekleidungskultur in der entwickelten sozialistischen Gesellschaft. Beiträge zur Marxistisch-Leninistischen Theorie der Bekleidungskultur." Dissertation, Humboldt-Universität zu Berlin, Berlin, 1976.

Pfannstiel, Margot, ed. *Sibylles Modelexikon. ABC der Mode.* Leipzig, Berlin: Verlag für die Frau, 1968.

Pinkau, Karl. *Die Methode zur Ermittlung der Produktionskapazität in der Textlindustrie.* Leipzig: Fachbuchverlag, 1962.

_____. *Die sozialistische Planung und ihre Durchführung in der Textilindustrie.* Berlin: Volk und Wissen, 1962.

Redeker, Horst. *Chemie gibt Schönheit.* Berlin: Institut für angewandte Kunst, 1959.

Rößler, Hans, ed. *Beiträge zur sozialistischen Konsumtionsforschung der Institute für Politische Ökonomie und Planung und Leitung der Volkswirtschaft*. Halle: Martin-Luther-Universität Halle-Wittenberg, 1965 and 1974.

Rogowin, S.A. *Chemiefasern*. Leipzig: Fachbuchverlag, 1960.

Schille, Kurt. *Die operative Produktionsplanung in der Textilindustrie*. Berlin: Die Wirtschaft, 1960.

_____, Herbert Schlehahn, and Egon Hasler. *Probleme der Fertigungsart in der Textil- und Bekleidungsindustrie*. Leipzig: Fachbuchverlag, 1963.

Schulz, Jo. *Messeschlager Gisela. Operette in einem Vorspiel und drei Akten (vier Bildern). Textbuch*. Berlin: VEB Lied der Zeit, 1961.

Schurig, Hellmut. *Die Entwicklung der Textilindustrie in Westdeutschland und in der Deutschen Demokratischen Republik*. Berlin: Die Wirtschaft, 1959.

Schweickert, Walter Karl and Bert Hold. *Guten Tag Herr von Knigge. Ein heiteres Lesebuch für alle Jahrgänge über alles, was "anständig" ist*. Berlin: Henschelverlag, 1963 [14th ed.; 1st ed. 1959].

Selbmann, Karl-Heinz, Herbert Fischer, and Ruth Weichsel. *Bedarfsgerechter Einkauf des Einzelhandels – Bekleidung und andere Textilwaren – Dargestellt am Sortiment konfektionierte Oberbekleidung*. Berlin: Die Wirtschaft, 1964.

Siegel, Heinz. *Die Gütesicherung in der Textilindustrie*. Berlin: Die Wirtschaft, 1961.

Smolka, Karl. *Gutes Benehmen von A bis Z*. Berlin: Neues Leben, 1957.

_____. *Benehmen ist nicht nur Glückssache*. Berlin: Neues Leben, 1959.

_____. *Junger Mann von heute*. Berlin: Neues Leben, 1963 [1st ed. 1958].

Strecker, Helmut. "Zur Bedarfsforschung für Konsumwaren in der Übergangsperiode vom Kapitalismus zum Sozialismus." Dissertation, Humboldt-Universität zu Berlin, 1961.

Thiel, Erika. *Künstler und Mode. Vom Modeschöpfer zum Modegestalter*. Berlin, 1979.

_____. *Geschichte des Kostüms. Die europäische Mode von den Anfängen bis zur Gegenwart*. Berlin: Henschelverlag Kunst und Gesellschaft, 1982 [1st ed. 1960].

Tordy, Arthur. "Maße und Formen in der Bekleidung." In *Maße und Formen. Vom Schneiderhandwerk zur Bekleidungsindustrie*, 7–21. Leipzig: Fachbuchverlag, 1955.

Uhlmann, Irene. *Die Frau. Kleine Enzyklopädie*. Leipzig: Enzyklopädie, 1961.

Ulbricht, Walter. *Der Siebenjahrplan des Friedens, des Wohlstands und des Glücks des Volkes*. Berlin: Dietz, 1959.

Unser Handarbeitsbuch. Modelle für Stickereien. Leipzig: Verlag für die Frau, 1955.

Vorstand des Fachausschusses Bekleidung der Kammer der Technik, Berlin, Fachverband Leichtindustrie, ed. *Bekleidungsfertigung. Beiträge zu techni-*

schen, ökonomischen, modischen und anderen Fragen der Bekleidungsindustrie.
2 vols. Berlin: VEB Verlag Technik, 1959 and 1963.

Waltuch, K.K. *Entwicklungsproportionen und Befriedigung der Bedürfnisse.*
Berlin: Die Wirtschaft, 1972.

Warenzeichenverband für Kunststofferzeugnisse der DDR, ed. *Kleine
Chemiefaserstoffkunde.* Rudolstadt, 1982.

Wutge, Vera. *Mode für junge Leute.* Berlin: Neues Leben, 1970.

Secondary Sources

Appadurai, Arjun. "Introduction: Commodities and the Politics of Value." In *The
Social Life of Things: Commodities in Cultural Perspective*, edited by Arjun
Appadurai, 3–63. Cambridge: Cambridge University Press, 1986.

Backhaus, Jürgen. "Der Konsument im ökonomsichen System der DDR." Ph.D.
Dissertation, Universität Köln, 1971.

Barthel, Horst. *Die wirtschaftlichen Ausgangsbedingungen der DDR. Zur
Wirtschaftsentwicklung auf dem Gebiet der DDR 1945–1949/50.* Berlin:
Akademie-Verlag, 1979.

_____. "Die Einführung des doppelten Preissystems für Einzelhandels-
verkaufspreise in der DDR durch die Schaffung der HO-Läden von 1948 bis
1950/51 als komplexe Maßnahme der Wirtschaftspolitik." *Jahrbuch für
Geschichte* 31 (1984): 273–89.

Bartlett, Djurdja. "Let Them Wear Beige: The Petit-bourgeois World of Official
Socialist Dress." *Fashion Theory* 8 (2004): 127–64.

Berghoff, Hartmut, ed. *Konsumpolitik. Die Regulierung des privaten Verbrauchs
im 20. Jahrhundert.* Göttingen: Vandenhoeck & Ruprecht, 1999.

Bertsch, Georg C. and Ernst Hedler. *SED – Schönes Einheits-Design – Stunning
Eastern Design – Savoir eviter le design.* Cologne: Benedikt Taschen, 1990.

Bessel, Richard and Ralph Jessen, eds. *Die Grenzen der Diktatur. Staat und
Gesellschaft in der DDR.* Göttingen: Vandenhoeck & Ruprecht, 1996.

Betts, Paul and Katherine Pence, eds. *Socialist Modern: East German Politics,
Society and Culture.* Ann Arbor: University of Michigan Press, forthcoming.

Boldorf, Marcel. *Sozialfürsorge in der SBZ/DDR 1945–1953. Ursachen, Ausmass
und Bewältigung der Nachkriegsarmut.* Stuttgart: Franz Steiner, 1998.

Boyer, Christoph. "Die Sozial- und Konsumpolitik der DDR in den sechziger
Jahren in theoretischer Perspektive." In *Repression und Wohlstandsversprechen.
Zur Stabilisierung von Parteiherrschaft in der DDR und der CSSR*, edited by
Christoph Boyer and Peter Skyba, 37–48. Dresden: Hannah-Arendt-Institut für
Totalitarismusforschung, 1999.

Brückner, Katrin. "Die Kleidermode in der DDR in den 70er und 80 Jahren."
Diplomarbeit, Technische Universität Dresden, Fakultät Erziehungs-

wissenschaften, Dresden, 1994.

Bryson, Phillip J. *The Consumer under Socialist Planning. The East German Case*. New York: Praeger, 1984.

Budde, Gunilla-Friederike. "'Tüchtige Traktoristinnen' und 'schicke Stenotypistinnen'. Frauenbilder in den deutschen Nachkriegsgesellschaften – Tendenzen der 'Sowjetisierung' und 'Amerikanisierung'?" In *Amerikanisierung und Sowjetisierung in Deutschland 1945–1970*, edited by Konrad Jarausch and Hannes Siegrist, 243–73. Frankfurt/Main: Campus, 1997.

_____. "Der Körper der 'sozialistischen Frauenpersönlichkeit'. Weiblichkeits-Vorstellungen in der SBZ und frühen DDR." *Geschichte und Gesellschaft* 26 (2000): 602–28.

Buxbaum, Gerda. "Asymmetrie symbolisiert einen kritischen Geist! – Zum Stellenwert von Mode, Uniform und Tracht im Nationalsozialismus." In *Zeitgeist wider den Zeitgeist: eine Sequenz aus Österreichs Verirrung*, edited by Oswald Oberhuber, 181–8. Vienna: Hochschule für angewandte Kunst, 1987.

_____, ed. *Ausgeblendete Realität. Modefotos aus der DDR*. Vienna: Hochschule für angewandte Kunst, 1989.

Caldwell, Peter. *Dictatorship, State Planning, and Social Theory in the German Democratic Republic*. Cambridge: Cambridge University Press, 2003.

Carter, Erica. *How German Is She? Post-War West German Reconstruction and the Consuming Woman, 1945–1960*. Ann Arbor: University of Michigan Press, 1997.

Christmann, Marlis. "Von der Trümmerfrau zur Nylonbraut. Frauenrollen der 50er Jahre an Beispielen der Haute Couture (Frankreich), der Konfektionsmode (BRD) und der Bekleidungskultur (ehemalige DDR)." Diplomarbeit in Design-Theorie an der Fachhochschule für Design Bielefeld, Bielefeld, 1991.

Confino, Alon and Rudy Koshar. "Régimes of Consumer Culture: New Narratives in Twentieth-Century German History." *German History* 19 (2001): 135–61.

Crew, David, ed. *Consuming Germany in the Cold War*. Oxford: Berg, 2003.

Dähn, Brunhilde. *Berlin Hausvogteiplatz. Über 100 Jahre am Laufsteg der Mode*. Göttingen: Musterschmidt, 1968.

Delille, Angela and Andrea Grohn, eds. *Perlonzeit. Wie die Frauen ihr Wirtschaftswunder erlebten*. Berlin: Elefanten Press, 1985.

Diewald, Martin. "'Kollektiv', 'Vitamin B' oder 'Nische'? Persönliche Netzwerke in der DDR." In *Kollektiv und Eigensinn. Lebensverläufe in der DDR und danach*, edited by Johannes Huinink, Karl Ulrich Mayer, Martin Diewald, Heike Solga, Annemette Sørensen, and Heike Trappe, 223–60. Berlin: Akademie, 1995.

Dopp, Werner. *125 Jahre Berliner Konfektion*. Berlin: Ernst Staneck, 1962.

Döring, Friedrich-Wilhelm. *Vom Konfektionsgewerbe zur Bekleidungsindustrie: zur Geschichte von Technisierung und Organisation der Massenproduktion von*

Bekleidung. Frankfurt/Main: Lang, 1992.

Ernst, Anna-Sabine. "Von der Bekleidungskultur zur Mode: Mode und soziale Differenzierung in der DDR." In *Politische Kultur in der DDR*, edited by Hans-Georg Wehling, 158–79. Stuttgart: Kohlhammer, 1989.

_____. "Mode im Sozialismus. Zur Etablierung eines 'sozialistischen Stils' in der frühen DDR." In *Lebensstile und Kulturmuster in sozialistischen Gesellschaften*, edited by Krisztina Mänicke-Gyöngyösi and Ralf Rytlewski, 73–94. Cologne: Wissenschaft und Politik, 1990.

_____. "Erbe und Hypothek: (Alltags-)Kulturelle Leitbilder in der SBZ/DDR." In *Kultur und Kulturträger in der DDR: Analysen*, edited by Stiftung Mitteldeutscher Kulturrat, 9–72. Berlin: Akademie, 1993.

_____. "Vom 'Du' zum 'Sie'. Die Rezeption der bürgerlichen Anstandsregeln in der DDR der 1950er Jahre." *Mitteilungen aus der kulturwissenschaftlichen Forschung* 33 (1993): 190–209.

_____. "The Politics of Culture and the Culture of Daily Life in the DDR in the 1950s." In *Between Reform and Revolution. Studies in German Socialism and Communism from 1940 to 1990*, edited by David Barclay and Eric Weitz, 489–506. Providence: Berghahn, 1998.

Flotter Osten. dir. Holger Theuerkauf and Michael Reinicke. Mit-Schnitt-Film, 1990.

Fogelberg, Karianne. "Updating the Look of Socialism – Dressing Workers and Consumers in East Germany (1957–77)." M.A. Dissertation, Victoria and Albert Museum/Royal College of Art, 2002.

Gries, Rainer. *Die Rationen Gesellschaft. Versorgungskampf und Vergleichsmentalität. Leipzig, München und Köln nach dem Kriege*. Münster: Westfälisches Dampfboot, 1991.

_____. *Produkte als Medien. Kulturgeschichte der Produktkommunikation in der Bundesrepublik und der DDR*. Leipzig: Leipziger Universitätsverlag, 2003.

Guenther, Irene. "Nazi 'Chic'? German Politics and Women's Fashions, 1915–1945." *Fashion Theory: The Journal of Dress, Body and Culture* 1 (1997): 29–58.

_____. *Nazi Chic? Fashioning Women in the Third Reich*. Oxford: Berg, 2004.

Günther, Cordula. "1969–1979: Zehn Jahre 'Präsent 20' – zehn Jahre Polyesterseide 'systemverstrickt'." In *Wiedergeburten. Zur Geschichte der runden Jahrestage der DDR*, edited by Monika Gibas, Rainer Gries, Barabara Jakoby, and Doris Mueller, 98–102. Leipzig: Leipziger Universitätsverlag, 1999.

Harsch, Donna. "Approach/Avoidance: Communists and Women in East Germany, 1945–9." *Social History* 25 (2000): 156–82.

Härtel, Christian and Petra Kabus, eds. *Das Westpaket. Geschenksendung, keine Handelsware*. Berlin: Links, 2000.

Heimann, Christian. *Systembedingte Ursachen des Niedergangs der DDR-Wirtschaft. Das Beispiel der Textil- und Bekleidungsindustrie 1945–1989.* Frankfurt/Main: Lang, 1997.

Heldmann, Philipp. "Konsumpolitik in der DDR. Jugendmode in den sechziger Jahren." In *Konsumpolitik: Die Regulierung des privaten Verbrauchs im 20. Jahrhundert*, edited by Hartmut Berghoff, 135–58. Göttingen: Vandenhoeck & Ruprecht, 1999.

———. "Negotiating Consumption in a Dictatorship: Consumption Politics in the GDR in the 1950s and 1960s." In *The Politics of Consumption: Material Culture and Citizenship in Europe and America*, edited by Martin Daunton and Matthew Hilton, 185–202. Oxford: Berg, 2001.

Heller, Agnes. *The Theory of Need in Marx.* London: Allison & Busby, 1974.

Hessler, Julie. *A Social History of Soviet Trade: Trade Policy, Retail Practices, and Consumption, 1917–1953.* Princeton: Princeton University Press, 2004.

Hilgenberg, Dorothea. *Bedarfs- und Marktforschung in der DDR: Anspruch und Wirklichkeit.* Cologne: Wissenschaft und Politik Nottbeck, 1979.

Hirdina, Heinz. *Gestalten für die Serie. Design in der DDR 1959–1985.* Dresden: VEB Verlag der Kunst, 1988.

Höfig, Carolyn C. "'Organized Cheerfulness': A Regional Study of Popular Culture and Identity in the German Democratic Republic." Ph.D. Dissertation, University of California, Santa Cruz, 1997.

Holzweißig, Gunter. *Die schärfste Waffe der Partei. Eine Mediengeschichte der DDR.* Cologne: Böhlau, 2002.

Jarausch, Konrad H., ed. *Dictatorship as Experience: Towards a Socio-Cultural History of the GDR.* trans. Eve Duffy. New York: Berghahn, 1999.

——— and Hannes Siegrist, eds. *Amerikanisierung und Sowjetisierung in Deutschland 1945–1970.* Frankfurt/Main: Campus, 1997.

Jessen, Ralph. "Die Gesellschaft im Staatssozialismus. Probleme einer Sozialgeschichte der DDR." *Geschichte und Gesellschaft* 21 (1995): 96–110.

Kaiser, Monika. *Machtwechsel von Ulbricht zu Honecker: Funktionsmechanismen der SED-Diktatur in Konfliktsituationen 1962 bis 1972.* Berlin: Akademie, 1997.

Kaminsky, Annette. "'Adrett auf große Fahrt'. Die Erziehung des neuen Verbrauchers in der DDR." *Deutschland Archiv* 30 (1997): 231–42.

———. *Kaufrausch. Die Geschichte der ostdeutschen Versandhäuser.* Berlin: Links, 1998.

———. "'Warenproduktion und Bedürfnisse in Übereinstimmung bringen'. Markt- und Bedarfsforschung als Quelle der DDR-Sozialgeschichte." *Deutschland Archiv* 31 (1998): 579–93.

———. *Wohlstand, Schönheit, Glück. Kleine Konsumgeschichte der DDR.* Munich: Beck, 2001.

Karlsch, Rainer and Jochen Laufer, eds. *Sowjetische Demontagen in Deutschland 1944–1949. Hintergründe, Ziele und Wirkungen.* Berlin: Duncker & Humblot, 2002.

Kopstein, Jeffrey. *The Politics of Economic Decline in East Germany, 1945–1989.* Chapel Hill: University of North Carolina Press, 1997.

Kornai, János. *The Socialist System: The Political Economy of Communism,* Princeton: Princeton University Press, 1992.

Kosak, Eva. "Bekleidungskultur und schöpferisches Verhalten. Beobachtungen in der DDR." In *Kleidung zwischen Tracht + Mode. Aus der Geschichte des Museums 1889–1989,* edited by Museum für Volkskunde, 152–57. n.p., n.d. [1989].

Kuhn, Gerd and Andreas Ludwig. *Alltag und soziales Gedächtnis. Die DDR-Objektkultur und ihre Musealisierung.* Hamburg: Ergebnisse, 1997.

Landsman, Mark Evan. "Dictatorship and Demand: East Germany Between Productivism and Consumerism, 1948–1961." Ph.D. Dissertation, Columbia University, 2000.

Lindenberger, Thomas, ed. *Herrschaft und Eigen-Sinn in der Diktatur. Studien zur Gesellschaftsgeschichte der DDR.* Cologne: Böhlau, 1999.

Lüdtke, Alf and Peter Becker, eds. *Akten, Eingaben, Schaufenster. Die DDR und ihre Texte. Erkundungen zu Herrschaft und Alltag.* Berlin: Akademie, 1997.

Major, Patrick and Jonathan Osmond, eds. *The Workers' and Peasants' State: Communism and Society in East Germany under Ulbricht 1945–71.* Manchester: Manchester University Press, 2002.

McDonald, Kenneth. "Fascist Fashion: Dress, the State, and the Clothing Industry in the Third Reich," Ph.D. Dissertation, University of California, Riverside, 1998.

Melis, Dorothea, ed. *Sibylle. Modefotografie aus drei Jahrzehnten DDR.* Berlin: Schwarzkopf & Schwarzkopf, 1998.

Merkel, Ina. *... und Du, Frau an der Werkbank. Die DDR in den 50er Jahren.* Berlin: Elefanten Press, 1990.

————. "Consumer Culture in the GDR, or How the Struggle for Antimodernity Was Lost on the Battleground of Consumer Culture." In *Getting and Spending: European and American Consumer Societies in the Twentieth Century,* edited by Susan Strasser, Charles McGovern, and Matthias Judt, 281–99. Cambridge: Cambridge University Press, 1998.

————. ed. *"Wir sind doch nicht die Meckerecke der Nation." Briefe an das DDR-Fernsehen.* Cologne: Böhlau, 1998.

————, *Utopie und Bedürfnis. Die Geschichte der Konsumkultur in der DDR.* Cologne: Böhlau, 1999.

Merl, Stephan. "Sowjetisierung in der Welt des Konsums." In *Amerikanisierung und Sowjetisierung in Deutschland 1945–1970,* edited by Konrad Jarausch and

Hannes Siegrist, 167–94. Frankfurt/Main: Campus, 1997.

Meuschel, Sigrid. "Machtmonopol und homogenisierte Gesellschaft. Anmerkungen zu Detlef Pollack." *Geschichte und Gesellschaft* 26 (2000): 171–83.

Mittelbach, Hans and Jörg Roesler. "Entwicklung von Einkommen und Verbrauch der Bevölkerung der DDR in den vergangenen vierzig Jahren." *Jahrbuch für Soziologie und Sozialpolitik* 5 (1989): 172–201.

Mühlberg, Dietrich. "Haute Couture für alle? Über Mode und Kulturverständnis." In *Sibylle. Modefotografie aus drei Jahrzehnten DDR*, edited by Dorothea Melis, 8–18. Berlin: Schwarzkopf & Schwarzkopf, 1998.

_____. "Auf der Suche nach der 'sozialistischen Bekleidungskultur': Mode und ihre Leitbilder im Osten." In *Künstliche Verswuchung: Nylon – Perlon – Dederon*, edited by Stiftung Haus der Geschiche der Bundesrepublik Deutschland, 140–51. Cologne: Wienand, 1999.

Mühlberg, Felix. "Konformismus oder Eigensinn? Eingaben als Quelle zur Erforschung der Alltagsgeschichte der DDR." *Mitteilungen aus der kulturwissenschaftlichen Forschung* 19 (1996): 331–45.

Nawrocki, Joachim. *Das geplante Wunder. Leben und Wirtschaften im anderen Deutschland*. Hamburg: Christian Wegner, 1967.

Neue Gesellschaft für Bildende Kunst e.V., ed. *Wunderwirtschaft. DDR-Konsumkultur in den 60er Jahren*. Cologne: Böhlau, 1996.

Paul, Stefan. "1959: Die Geburt des 'Dederon' aus dem Geiste des Kapitalismus." In *Wiedergeburten. Zur Geschichte der runden Jahrestage der DDR*, edited by Monika Gibas, Rainer Gries, Barbara Jakoby, and Doris Mueller, 91–5. Leipzig: Leipziger Universitätsverlag, 1999.

Pence, Katherine. "Labours of Consumption: Gendered Consumers in Post-War East and West German Reconstruction." In *Gender Relations in German History: Power, Agency, and Experience from the Sixteenth to the Twentieth Century*, edited by Lynn Abrams and Elizabeth Harvey, 211–238. London: UCL Press, 1996.

_____. "Building Socialist Worker-Consumers: The paradoxical construction of the Handelsorganisation – HO, 1948." In *Arbeiter in der SBZ-DDR*, edited by Peter Hübner and Klaus Tenfelde, 497–526. Essen: Klartext, 1999.

_____. "From Rations to Fashions: The Gendered Politics of East and West German Consumption, 1945–1961." Ph.D. Dissertation, The University of Michigan, 1999.

_____. "'You as a Woman Will Understand': Consumption, Gender, and the Relationship between State and Citizenry in the GDR's Crisis of June 17." *German History* 19 (2001): 218–52.

_____. "The Myth of a Suspended Present: Prosperity's Painful Shadow in 1950s East Germany." In *Pain and Prosperity: Reconsidering Twentieth-Century German History*, edited by Paul Betts and Greg Eghigian, 137–59. Stanford:

Stanford University Press, 2003.

"Phönix" GmbH Chemnitz Berufliches Bildungs- und FörderCentrum, ed. *15 Milliarden Stunden im Jahr. Ein Blick auf Hausarbeit und Haushalttechnik in der DDR*. Chemnitz: PrintDesign, 1997.

Poiger, Uta. *Jazz, Rock, and Rebels: Cold War Politics and American Culture in a Divided Germany*. Berkeley: University of California Press, 2000.

Pollack, Detlef. "Die offene Gesellschaft und ihre Freunde." *Geschichte und Gesellschaft* 26 (2000): 184–96.

Poutrus, Patrice. *Die Erfindung des Goldbroilers. Über den Zusammenhang zwischen Herrschaftssicherung und Konsumentwicklung in der DDR*. Cologne: Böhlau, 2002.

Reid, Susan and David Crowley, eds. *Style and Socialism. Modernity and Material Culture in Post-War Eastern Europe*. Oxford: Berg, 2000.

Roesler, Jörg. "The Rise and Fall of the Planned Economy in the German Democratic Republic, 1945–1989." *German History* 9 (1991): 46–61.

____. *Das Neue Ökonomische System – Dekorations- oder Paradigmenwechsel?* Berlin: Helle Panke, 1994.

Ross, Corey. *Constructing Socialism at the Grass-Roots. The Transformation of East Germany, 1945–65*. New York: St. Martin's, 2000.

____. *The East German Dictatorship: Problems and Perspectives in the Interpretation of the GDR*. Oxford: Oxford University Press, 2002.

Sabean, David. "Die Produktion von Sinn beim Konsum der Dinge." In *Fahrrad, Auto, Fernsehschrank. Zur Kulturgeschichte der Alltagsdinge*, edited by Wolfgang Ruppert, 37–51. Frankfurt/Main: Fischer, 1993.

Schenk, Ingrid. "From Calories to Kidney-Shaped Tables: Consumerism and the Constitution of West German National Identity, 1945–1965." Ph.D. Dissertation, University of Pennsylvania, 1996.

Schildt, Axel, Detlef Siegfried, and Karl Christian Lammers, eds. *Dynamische Zeiten. Die 60er Jahre in den beiden deutschen Gesellschaften*. Hamburg: Hans Christians, 2000.

Schmidt, Hans-Walter. "Schaufenster des Ostens. Anmerkungen zur Konsumkultur der DDR." *Deutschland Archiv* 27 (1994): 364–72.

Schramm, Manuel. *Konsum und regionale Identität in Sachsen 1880–2000. Die Regionalisierung von Konsumgütern im Spannungsfeld von Nationalisierung und Globalisierung*. Stuttgart: Steiner, 2002.

Simmel, Georg. "Fashion." *International Quarterly* 10 (1904): 130–55.

____. *Philosophie der Mode*. Berlin: Pan, n.d. [1905].

Stade, Ronald. "Designs of Identity: Politics of Aesthetics in the GDR." *Ethnos* 3–4 (1993): 241–58.

Steiner, André. "Dissolution of the 'Dictatorship over Needs'? Consumer Behavior and Economic Reform in East Germany in the 1960s." In *Getting and Spending:*

European and American Consumer Societies in the Twentieth Century, edited by Susan Strasser, Charles McGovern, and Matthias Judt, 167–85. Cambridge: Cambridge University Press, 1998.

———. *Die DDR-Wirtschaftsreform der sechziger Jahre. Konflikt zwischen Effizienz- und Machtkalkül.* Berlin: Akademie, 1999.

Stiftung Haus der Geschiche der Bundesrepublik Deutschland, ed. *Künstliche Versuchung. Nylon – Perlon – Dederon.* Cologne: Wienand, 1999.

Stitziel, Judd. "Fashioning Socialism: Clothing, Politics, and Consumer Culture in East Germany, 1948–1971," Ph.D. Dissertation, The Johns Hopkins University, 2001.

———. "Konsumpolitik zwischen 'Sortimentslücken' und 'Überplanbeständen' in der DDR der 1950er Jahre." In *Vor dem Mauerbau. Politik und Gesellschaft in der DDR der fünfziger Jahre*, edited by Dierk Hoffmann, Michael Schwartz, and Hermann Wentker, 191–204. Munich: Oldenbourg, 2003.

———. "On the Seam between Socialism and Capitalism: East German Fashion Shows, 1945–1971." In *Consuming Germany in the Cold War*, edited by David Crew, 51–86. Oxford: Berg, 2003.

———. "Von 'Grundbedürfnissen' zu 'höheren Bedürfnissen'? Konsumpolitik als Sozialpolitik in der DDR." In *Sozialstaatlichkeit in der DDR. Sozialpolitische Entwicklungen im Spannungsfeld von Diktatur und Gesellschaft 1945/49–1989*, edited by Dierk Hoffmann and Michael Schwartz. Munich: Oldenbourg, forthcoming.

Sultano, Gloria. *Wie geistiges Kokain ... Mode unterm Hakenkreuz.* Vienna: Verlag für Gesellschaftskritik, 1995.

Sywottek, Arnold. "Zwei Wege in die 'Konsumgesellschaft'." In *Modernisierung im Wiederaufbau. Die westdeutsche Gesellschaft der 50er Jahre*, edited by Axel Schildt and Arnold Sywottek, 269–74. Bonn: Dietz, 1993.

Tippach-Schneider, Simone. *Messemännchen und Minol-Pirol. Werbung in der DDR.* Berlin: Schwarzkopf & Schwarzkopf, 1999.

Vainshtein, Olga. "Female Fashion, Soviet Style: Bodies of Ideology." In *Russia – Women – Culture*, edited by Helena Goscilo and Beth Holmgren, 64–93. Bloomington: Indiana University Press, 1996.

Veenis, Milena. "Consumption in East Germany. The Seduction and Betrayal of Things." *Journal of Material Culture* 4 (1999): 79–112.

Volze, Armin. "Die Devisengeschäfte der DDR. Genex und Intershop." *Deutschland Archiv* 24 (1991): 1145–59.

von der Lippe, Peter. "The Political Role of Official Statistics in the former GDR (East Germany)." *Historical Social Research* 24 (1999) 4: 3–28.

Weiss, Helmut. *Verbraucherpreise in der DDR: wie stabil waren sie?* Schkeuditz: GNN, 1998.

Weitz, Eric. *Creating German Communism: From Popular Protests to Socialist*

State, 1890–1990. Princeton: Princeton University Press, 1997.

Westphal, Uwe. *Berliner Konfektion und Mode. Die Zerstörung einer Tradition 1836–1939*. Berlin: Hentrich, 1992.

Wildt, Michael. *Am Beginn der "Konsumgesellschaft". Mangelerfahrung, Lebenshaltung, Wohlstandshoffnung in Westdeutschland in den fünfziger Jahren*. Hamburg: Ergebnisse, 1994.

_____. *Vom kleinen Wohlstand. Eine Konsumgeschichte der fünfziger Jahre*, Frankfurt/Main: Fischer Taschenbuch, 1996.

Wolf, Birgit. *Sprache in der DDR. Ein Wörterbuch*. Berlin: Walter de Gruyter, 2000.

Zatlin, Jonathan R. "Ausgaben und Eingaben. Das Petitionsrecht und der Untergang der DDR." *Zeitschrift für Geschichtswissenschaft* 45 (1997): 902–17.

_____. "Consuming Ideology. Socialist Consumerism and the Intershops, 1970–1989." In *Arbeiter in der SBZ-DDR*, edited by Peter Hübner and Klaus Tenfelde, 555–72. Essen: Klartext, 1999.

Index

accelerated construction of socialism, *see* SED, Second Party Congress

accumulation, 3, 23, 25, 80–1, 88, 92, 114, 121, 123, 132
  attempts to increase, 114, 123, 132
  industrial goods as source of, 23
  prices and, 80–1, 92, 121
  textiles and garments as source of, 3, 25, 92, 123

Activist campaigns, 19

advertising, 5, 17, 115, 142, 174n16

aesthetics, 15, 30, 33, 49, 61–8 passim
  as higher need, 15
  Marxist-Leninist, 65–8
  production and, 33
  socialist fashion and, 63–8
  stronger women and, 61

agency, 1, 7, 94, 96, 144

alienation, 168

Altstoffverwertung, *see* surpluses, recycling of

American cultural barbarism, 56, 190n37

Americanization, 9, 58, 190n37

anti-Semitism, 52

Appadurai, Arjun, 27

Arbeitsmoral, *see* work morals

Association of German Consumer Cooperatives, *see* Verband deutscher Konsumgenossenschaften

Association of State-Owned Factories, *see* VVB

Augenzeuge, 70, 196n154

autarky, 46

bargains, 100, 118

bargain tables, 99

barter, 152
  see also networking

basic assortments/garments, 70, 120

basic needs, 3–4, 14, 50, 79, 85, 91, 120–1, 123, 143, 145, 163, 169
  clothing as, 3, 14
  Marxist-Leninist theories of, 50
  prices and, 85, 121, 123, 169
  shifting perceptions of, 163
  socialism's promise to fulfill, 4, 14, 79, 85, 91
  subsidies and, 79, 91

basic silhouettes, 72

Baudrillard, Jean, 14

Baukastenprinzip, *see* building blocks principle

Baumann, Edith, 71, 116, 210n167

beauty, 15, 59, 61–3, 75, 167

Bedarfsanalysen, *see* demand analyses

Bedarfsforschung, *see* needs, research

Bedürfnis, *see* needs

begging letters, 158–9, 161
  see also West Germany, packages from

Bekleidung, Die 106

Bekleidungskultur, *see* clothing culture

Benimmbücher (good manners manuals), 55

Bergler, Georg, 34

Berlin, 24–5, 38, 44, 95, 102, 108, 111, 113, 119–20, 142–3, 145–6, 154–5
  crisis, 108
  garment industry, 24–5, 38, 44, 95
  sales in, 102, 111, 113
  shopping in, 145–6, 154
  special stores in, 119–20, 142
  see also Berlin Fashion Week
  see also Berlin Wall
  see also Modezentrum Berlin
  see also Sibylle boutique

Berlin Fashion Week, 74–7, 196n143

Berlin Wall, 8, 31, 67, 114–15, 128–31, 133, 140, 142, 147–8, 152, 168, 214n49
  as historical caesura, 8, 31
  collapse of, 168
  consumers complaints and, 133, 140
  Exquisit stores and, 128–31, 140, 214n49
  fashion and, 67
  hoarding and, 115, 147–8
  Intershops and, 142
  sales and, 114–15
  surcharges and, 128–9, 131

berufstätige Frau, *see* women, working

Betrieb mit staatlicher Beteiligung, *see* factories, half-state-owned

Bettelbriefe, *see* begging letters

BIWA stores, 103–7, 118

black market, 37, 121–2, 148, 152

body, 3, 60–3, 156, 158

Bormann, Heinz, 66, 157, 193n84, 213n32

bourgeois influences, 52, 54–5, 189n18

Boutique 70, 142

249

Lightning Source UK Ltd.
Milton Keynes UK
UKOW04f0509040914

238024UK00004B/67/P